Gloria Victis!

Gloria Victis!

edited by Flemming Friborg

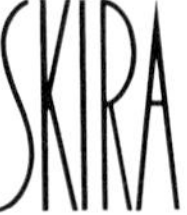

Cover
Pierre-Auguste Renoir
Boy with a Cat, 1868–69
Oil on canvas, 124 × 67 cm
Paris, Musée d'Orsay
(cat. no. 50, fig. 54)

Back Cover
Gustave Courbet
Three English Girls at a Window, 1865
Oil on canvas, 92.5 × 72.5 cm
Copenhagen, Ny Carlsberg Glyptotek
(cat. no. 20, fig. 13)

Design
Marcello Francone

Editing
Emanuela di Lallo

Catalogue, biographies and captions
Sidsel Maria Søndergaard
with the assistance of
Pernille Stockmarr
and Signe Westergaard-Nielsen

Layout
Sabina Brucoli

Translation from Danish
Neil Martin Stanford

First published in Italy in 2001
by Skira Editore S.p.A.
Palazzo Casati Stampa
via Torino 61
20123 Milano
Italy

Printed and bound in Italy.
First edition

ISBN 88-8118-701-9

Distributed in North America and Latin America by Abbeville Publishing Group, 22 Cortlandt Street, New York, NY 10007, USA.
Distributed elsewhere in the world by Thames and Hudson Ltd., 181a High Holborn, London WC1V 7QX, United Kingdom.

This book has been made possible through the generous support of

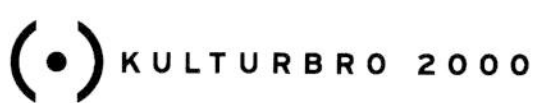

(•) KULTURBRO 2000

This book is published in conjunction with the special exhibition *Gloria Victis! Victors and Vanquished in French Art 1848–1910* at the Ny Carlsberg Glyptotek, Copenhagen, 29 May – 15 October, 2000

Note
The illustrations without catalogue numbers refer to works of art not featured in the exhibition

Foreword

The guiding principle of the Modern has always been revolution. One consequence of this is that "deviant" artistic expression tends to be ruthlessly dispatched from Parnassus by whatever "good taste" currently prevails. History frequently makes fleeting references to judgements of taste associated with a particular period, but just as often, these pronouncements long remain unchallenged, if only because they conform so readily to the notion of stylistic development entertained by the academic mandarins. Impressionism was initially anathematised, but it quickly became the most popular trend in twentieth-century art, while the painters and sculptors of the Salon were banished to an outer darkness from which they were not to emerge until the opening of the Musée d'Orsay in Paris in 1986.

The point of departure for the project Gloria Victis! *(Honour the Vanquished) is that fertile but turbulent period between 1848 and 1910. Paris inherited from Rome the mantle of European cultural capital, and French art began to manifest a whole series of crucial new directions. Against a background of ideas concerned with liberating figurative art from the leaden lockstep of the Academy, the second half of the nineteenth century witnessed the advent of the concept of avant-garde, whose self-awareness brought them into direct conflict with the taste and norms of the established order. Among the first devotees were the so-called Impressionists, who came to pave the way for the new. That, at least, is the accepted version of the story.*

Everything which was now regarded as hopelessly old-fashioned, was shunted onto the sidings of art history as "un-modern". The hardest fate was that suffered by the nationally-recognised, established French figurative art which was on show at every annual Salon — the exhibitions which had been favoured with the imprimatur of the Academy.

For much of the modern history of art, the Salon was no more than a background of hidebound, mendacious ideals, against which the avant-garde could project its own, clearly outlined shadows. Correspondingly, the established schools saw all this as extremely provocative; the Realism of Courbet and the Barbizon School, and the image of society presented by such artists as Daumier and Manet were singled out for massive destructive criticism by contemporary art critics. The battle lines were drawn. But the truth, as is so often the case, is multifaceted, and in the subsequent years the "matter of taste" has been subjected to far closer scrutiny than, quite understandably, in the hectic years of the conflict itself.

As far as developments in France itself are concerned, the Musée d'Orsay, ever since its opening in 1986, has done its best to give the forgotten Salon artists a historical place next to the popular Impressionists and Post-Impressionists. They are not to be regarded as misunderstood geniuses, but rather as part of the whole picture, active participants in the history of modern art.

Right from its foundation by Carl Jacobsen (1842–1914) the Ny Carlsberg Glyptotek has been dedicated to the "the most and the best" of

1
G. Le Gray
The Steamer, 1857
Albumen print from two wet-collodion glass plate negatives,
32 × 41.3 cm
Paris, Musée d'Orsay

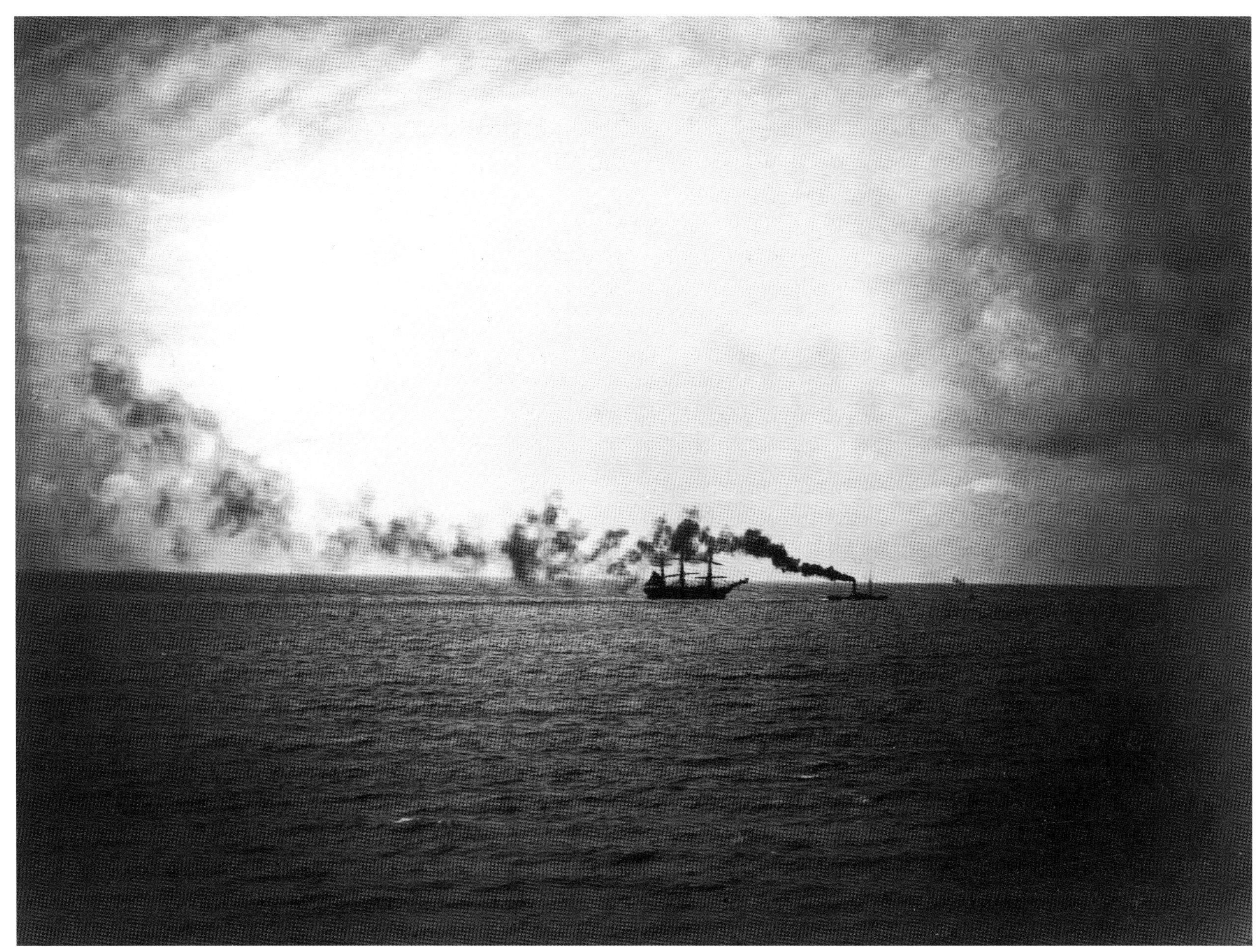

figurative art: and that included the work of contemporary artists. Jacobsen (who was two years younger than Monet) hated Impressionism and adored the Salon: he was a flamboyant collector of work by exponents of the academic-traditional style in sculpture and painting, because it was there that he found the Classical in a form he conceived to be directly inherited from the noble Greek ideals of antiquity. This taste however managed to include Rodin, who is regarded as one of the fathers of modern sculpture. Time and taste were quick to change — Jacobsen's son Helge continued his father's work at the museum, but proclaimed his own, markedly different predilections by large-scale purchases of Impressionist work.

The exhibition, which includes sixty works of painting and sculpture, juxtaposes exhibits from the modern collection of the Glyptotek with a series of works loaned from abroad. The majority of the latter are from the Musée d'Orsay, but a number come from other important museums from all over the world.

The Franco-Danish character of the project has led the Ny Carlsberg Glyptotek to hope that His Royal Highness, the Prince, might favour us by becoming the Official Patron of the exhibition. His Royal Highness has honoured us by graciously accepting our invitation.

Many institutions and public bodies have contributed to the realisation of the exhibition. In this context we would like to offer our special thanks to His Excellency, the French Ambassador to Denmark, Jean-Pierre Masset, and the Director of the Institut Français, Georges Zask, both of whom have lent their support and goodwill to the project.

Among those kind enough to lend works for Gloria Victis!*, thanks must go first and foremost to the Musée d'Orsay for their invaluable support in the form of 17 works from their collection: may I extend personal thanks to their Director, Henri Loyrette, and also to the Director of La Réunion des Musées Nationaux, Madame Françoise Cachin, for their exceptional kindness. Others who have been kind enough to assist us through loans of works for the exhibition include: the Musée des Beaux-Arts of Lille, Director, Patrick Ramade; the Nationalmuseum of Stockholm, Director, Olle Granath, and Head of Collections, Torsten Gunnarsson; the Rijksmuseum Vincent van Gogh, Amsterdam, Director, Dr. John Leighton; the Sterling and Francine Clark Art Institute, Massachusetts, Director, Dr. Michael Conforti, and the Kunsthaus Zürich, Director, Dr. Felix Baumann; our warmest thanks to them all.*

Gloria Victis! *is part of the comprehensive Danish-Swedish cultural collaboration Kulturbro 2000, which has set itself the task of celebrating the millennium with an "Øresundsbiennale".*

The Ny Carlsberg Glyptotek would like to thank the Kulturbro 2000 Foundation and DANISCO for their economic support in the realisation of this project.

Søren Dietz
Director of the Ny Carlsberg Glyptotek

2
Paul Cézanne
A Modern Olympia,
ca. 1873–74
Oil on canvas, 46 × 55.5 cm
Paris, Musée d'Orsay

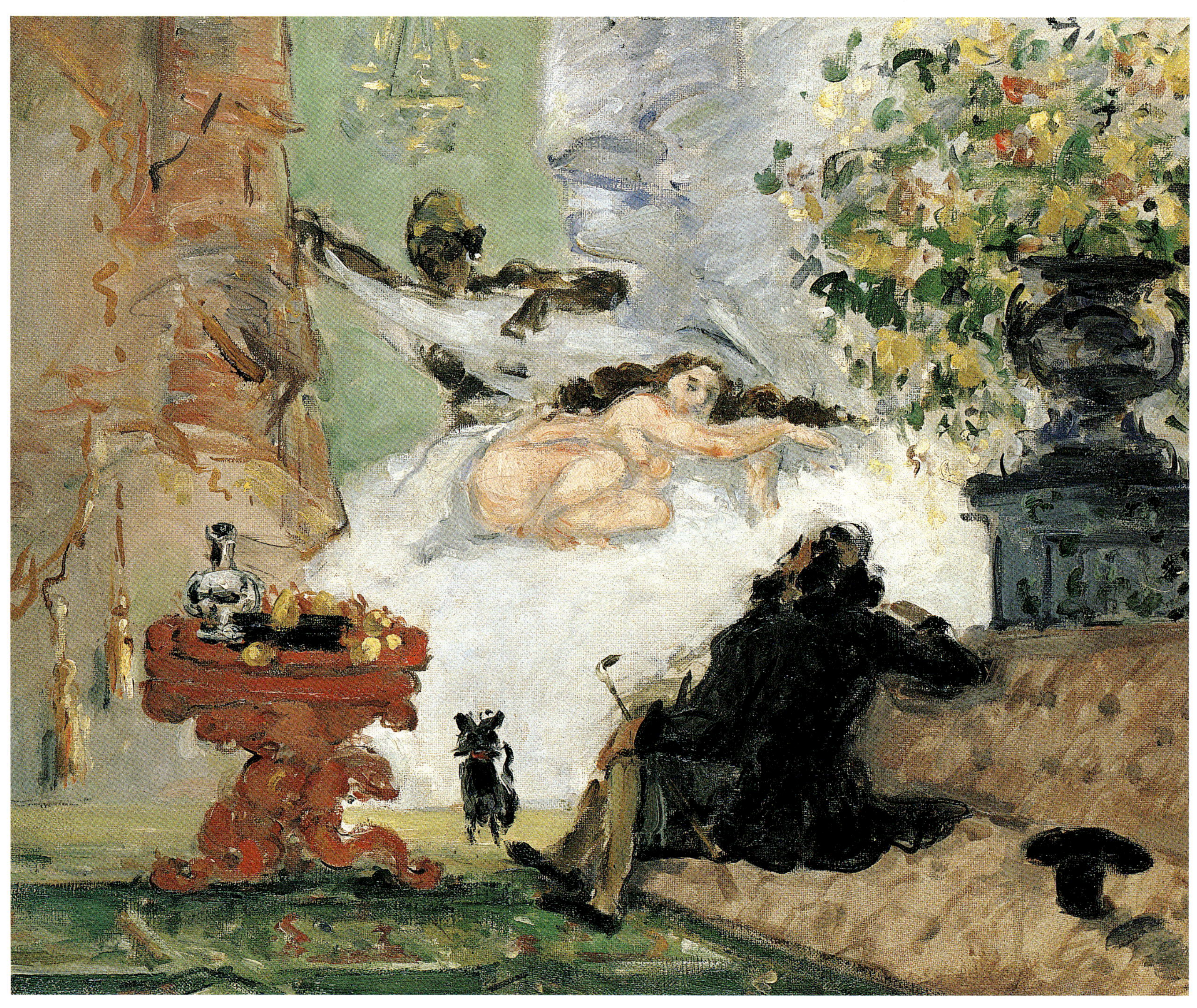

A mere twenty years ago the opportunities for art enthusiasts wanting to undertake research in Paris into art from the second half of the nineteenth century were extremely limited. There were Impressionist works in the Jeu de Paume — a charming, but overly unassuming building in the Tuileries Gardens — and a narrow selection of Post-Impressionist paintings in the Palais de Tokyo. In addition the most important works by Courbet and Millet, as well as by representatives of the Barbizon School, were on exhibition, along with a selection of foreign paintings, in the Louvre.

The sculpture of the period seemed even less worthy of attention, being represented, by and large, by a single artist, Carpeaux, who was given his own room at the Louvre. Sculpture by les academiciens *had not seen the light of day since the closure of the Luxembourg Museum in the 1930s and those of their works which had not been relegated to storage were now scattered among museums throughout the provinces.*

It was against this background of inadequate exhibition space, and the consequent neglect of the national collections from the second half of the nineteenth century, that the Gare d'Orsay (formerly a railway station) was converted into a museum. The national collections, which cover the artistic production of half a century, were taken out of storage, bringing about a genuine revolution in the history of taste; this put to flight the cultivated Manichaeism, which, for fifty years, had brutally divided the Good (Realists, Impressionists, and those favoured with the vague appellation of Post-Impressionists) from the Bad (the artists of the Academy, who continued to be regarded as over-blown and bombastic). It was now accepted that the dividing lines were not so clearly drawn, and artists such as Puvis de Chavannes and Gustave Moreau, were awarded a more just position enabling them to return to the light from their long exile in the shadows. At the same time, interest was growing in what Degas has called "the dubious kinship". How, otherwise, is one to evaluate Manet's full-blown revolutionary power, unless he can be confronted by his adversaries, Gérôme, Bouguereau or Baudry? How is one to understand the scandal surrounding Olympia *except by juxtaposing it with the contemporary success achieved by Cabanel's* Vénus*? The hanging arrangement at the Musée d'Orsay confirms something art historians had long suspected — that the early Degas was not far removed from his mentor, Gustave Moreau, nor from Delaunay, and that Tissot, Stevens and Carolus-Duran in the 1860s were not ignorant of the developments in the new painting. Other questions emerge from this fabric, and other avenues are opened to research: facts of which this exhibition is clear proof.*

Henri Loyrette
Director of the Musée d'Orsay, Paris

Contents

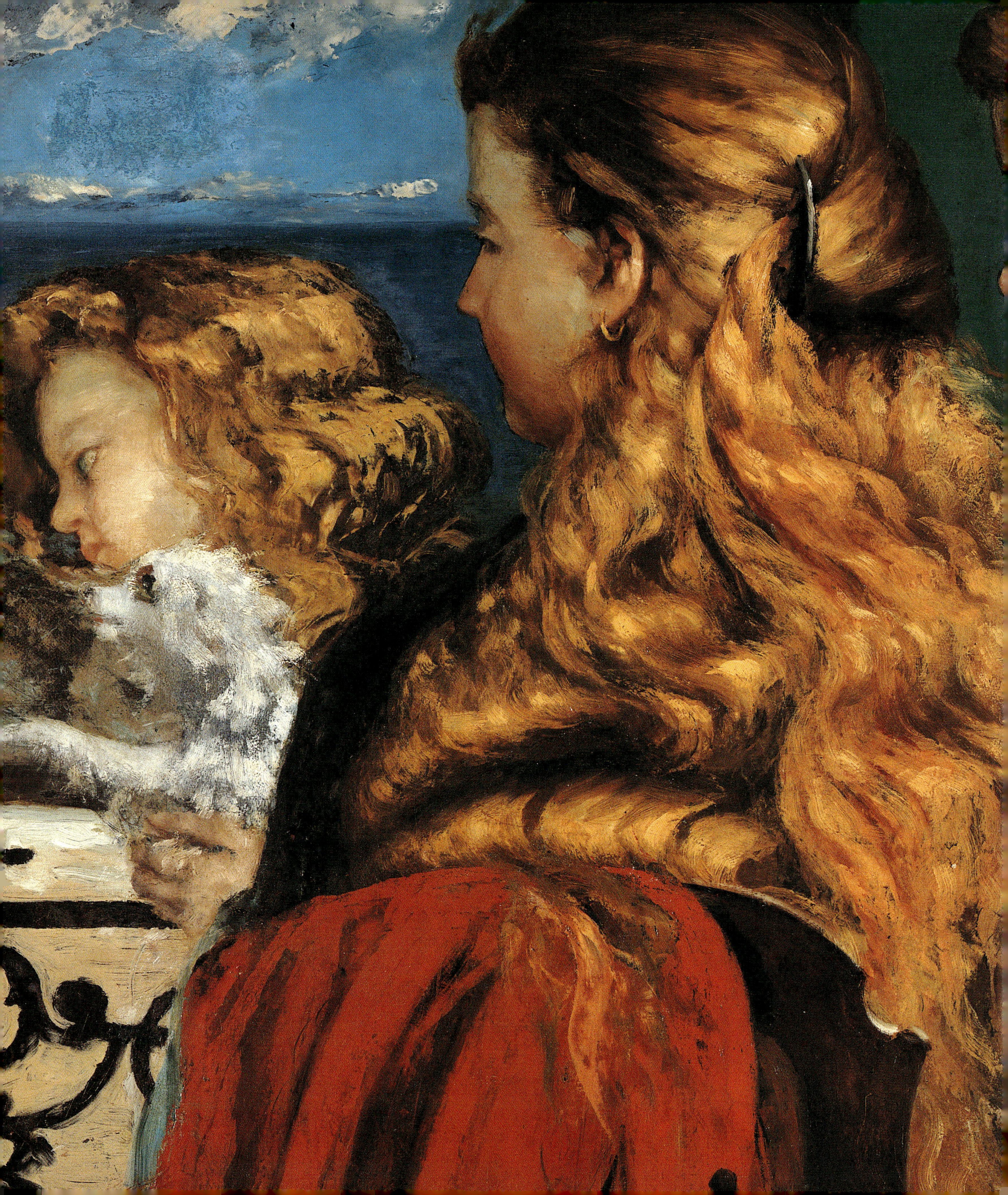

Flemming Friborg

The Battle over Taste. The Modern and the Un-Modern in French Art 1848–1910

Large areas of European figurative art between 1850 and 1900 have been consigned to oblivion. At first glance this need not be anything remarkable — art as much as anything else is at the mercy of changes in taste and style, and when something new arrives on the scene and seizes the attention, that which already exists is obliged to adapt or leave the stage. At times this can lead to violent conflict, and in our own century — which we have accustomed ourselves to regarding as the epoch which witnesses the zenith of Modernism — the idea of the development of art's movement as the consequence of a constant battle for supremacy with tradition and forerunners has become predominant. This thought, however, has such a firm grip on art history, that it has been able to make short work of a good 50 years of figurative art by putting it under its own microscope, which is the modern perspective. As far as the French Academic art of the second half of the nineteenth century is concerned, this has entailed surrender, banishment and oblivion.

The Salon was the French state's officially-approved exhibition, the self-proclaimed citadel of the academics. It was within these confines that taste was freshly defined, each year: the Salon took place annually, and functioned, at one and the same time, as a forum for those most firmly ensconced — masters of contemporary art, who had become venerable pillars of the establishment and who, most frequently, held teaching posts at the art schools under the control of the Academy — and their pupils or successors, who would make their own debut at the exhibition. Comparison, evaluation and competition for the favour of the powers that were, as well as the public, were the keywords in this attempt to impose controlling limits on artistic evolution. It was the duty of art, above all else, to present an edifying image of the nation, its merits in war and peace, an image which should serve as the exemplary model for every citizen. The history of the Salon, its triumph and its decline, has yet to be written — it emerges only tentatively and indirectly from the history of that Modernism which has excluded it; one might say that the significance of the Salon Exhibition as a cultural power factor was closely related to the absolutist principle of which it was a product, and when that slowly gave way, the stubborn attrition of the press and critics eventually brought about the system's collapse. The political dimension of culture is not insignificant in the story of the revolt in taste, which occurred in the period 1848–1910, but it is hardly the whole story of the rise of modern art. History is written by the victors, and the

3
Gustave Courbet
Three English Girls at a Window, 1865, detail
(full fig. 13)

artworks of any given period are witnesses — but the selection made by the survivors frequently hampers any future evaluation. Crucial elements of the artistic developments which contributed to the formation of the Modern are hard to identify, because they are most clearly in evidence in a number of artworks which are not "modern" to twenty-first century eyes, nor do they exhibit any such inclination. If one may borrow a term from psychoanalysis, whose breakthrough occurred around 1900, they have been "repressed", rather than forgotten. The question is, whether it is possible to trace the repressed matter, which is also a constituent of the Modern, by focusing on the losers in the battle over taste — Salon artists, academicians, the late successors to Neo-Classicism, as against the winners: Realism, Impressionism and the initial trends of Modernism. It is thus a matter of isolating some of the key themes, which figure in important roles, as much for Salon artists as for modernists.

This does not necessarily entail starting from scratch. The last twenty years have witnessed an intensified interest in the "Unmodern" in many parts of the world, both in the museum context and in the sphere of art theory. This has led to many exhibitions and other documentation of the period between "the European Revolt" in 1848 and the breakthrough of Cubism around 1908, proceeding from more subtle basic assumptions as to the currents in the culture. One consequence of the increased attention paid to the period as a whole is that a few years ago the Salon painters and sculptors returned to the exhibition halls of several major European museums — a development in which the initiative was taken by the Musée d'Orsay in Paris. However, despite a certain curiosity value, there is little to suggest any genuine renaissance on the art-historical or general public interest level for this group of works. In the Musée d'Orsay, works by the Salon artists can be seen side by side with a wealth of Impressionist and Post-Impressionist masterpieces — which, however, still manage to steal the show. Exactly the same thing happens in the Glyptotek's French Collection, which, on a smaller scale, covers the same spectrum of taste; Modernism has, once and for all, changed our perception of figurative art and it has become very difficult to take on trust — or even sufficiently seriously — a generation of artists both forgotten and relegated to obscurity. There is still a paucity of literature concerned with these artists and in the standard works of reference they are disposed of in a few, caustic words. The greatest attendant problem is possibly a certain "stylistic indecision" in the works of these neglected artists; most of the period's principal trends are present here — but frequently there is insufficient differentiation between them, they are mixed up within a single work. This is a further reason why, for the observer of today, the works themselves are at a disadvantage when competing for attention against what appears as decent, full-blooded Modernism.

The exhibition *Gloria Victis! Victors and Vanquished in French Art 1848–1910* is an attempt to follow a series of "turning points" which determined the development from the academic idealisation to the avant-garde's "merciless" and ostensibly, historically-imperative triumph in French art. It is an attempt to problematise particular explanatory models for the development of modern art, outline other ways of looking at the art of a period, and postulate the existence of some clear kinship between the good and the garish. The Ny Carlsberg Glyptotek is a natural setting for such a project; the museum with its collection of French painting and sculpture from Gérôme and Delaplanche up to Manet and Gauguin, is the ideal laboratory for such an examination of the evolution of taste and the attitude of art history's to the good and the beautiful.

It is useful to see the breakthrough of the new against a background of some definite historical and cultural events in France in the years 1860–74. In 1863 Napoléon III yielded to considerable pressure and granted an exhibition of their own to the many artists who had been denied a place at that year's Salon. This exhibition, the Salon des Refusés, was a modest success, but despite promises to the contrary, was not repeated the following year: in fact it did not reappear until 1873. But the critical verdict of the Ecole des Beaux-Arts, and by extension the arts-administrative establishment in the Second Empire and its Salons had endured for many years. As early as the 1840s Théophile Thoré had made the provocative assertion that French art had gone into reverse, Maxime du Camp and Ernest Chesneau followed in the same strain and bewailed the general downhill trend in art, Baudelaire's lone voice was beginning to make itself heard, and the number of critics of the system was growing — both among the artists themselves and those who wrote about art — at both ends of the political spectrum. Even the arbiters of taste, who enjoyed the approval of the state, broke their silence by proclaiming an increasing decline in art — a decline which, at least initially, had nothing to do with any Manet-like, sketchy, unacademic, new style.[1] The criticism came from within, and it was, to a considerable extent, linked to the country's political situation. This hostile climate became impossible to ignore on the advent of the World Exhibition in Paris in 1867. This exhibition coincided with the beginning of the end for historical painting, that genre which, in political and aesthetic terms, had been the most significant in a long tradition of French art.

A World Exhibition should always bring honour to the host country and there was a substantial element of competition among even the rival exhibition concepts. Every nation contributed their best and medals of various classes were awarded. It was, therefore, a serious blow for French self-respect, the master of all masters, the historical painter, Jean-Auguste-Dominique Ingres, died shortly before the exhibition opened; he had been an example to many successive generations of artists and art teachers, but also a paradigm of the more rigid. Thoré wrote thus: "What has died with M. Ingres, according to one of his eulogists, M. de Ronchaud, is the last *authority*, which has maintained a remnant of rule [...] it is the glorious *past*. The past being dead, let us try to console ourselves with the present, and let us hope in the future".[2] So much for the purely artistic consequences of this death: the political ramifications were enormous, since historical painting was the noble artistic genre in which French supremacy could best be displayed.[3] Ingres was, besides, the last in a long line of the nation's great historical painters who all died within a relatively short space of time — i.e. since the previous World Exhibition in the French capital, held twelve years before, in 1855. Patricia Mainardi has pointed out how vital it was for the shakily constructed political power of Napoléon III to acquire a legitimacy in art, internally as in relation to other European countries; every suggestion of "decadence" in French art was seen as a thinly veiled attack on the throne. Therefore the political-cultural establishment hung on for dear life to Ingres after his death; a gigantic retrospective exhibition was immediately organised which ran concurrently with the World Exhibition.[4]

In that same year of 1867, Manet painted two pictures, each of considerable significance, and both of which exemplified a new approach to historical painting. Between April and August he executed his first and only view of Paris, *View of the World Exhibition in Paris 1867* (Nasjonalgalleriet, Oslo, fig. 4), a picture whose most prominent element is a hot-air balloon hovering like a landmark over a new era and its exhibition. The balloon has been interpreted as an optimistic and highly French symbol of progress (the hot-air balloon was a French invention) and this applies equally in Manet's painting. The view becomes the modern historical painting

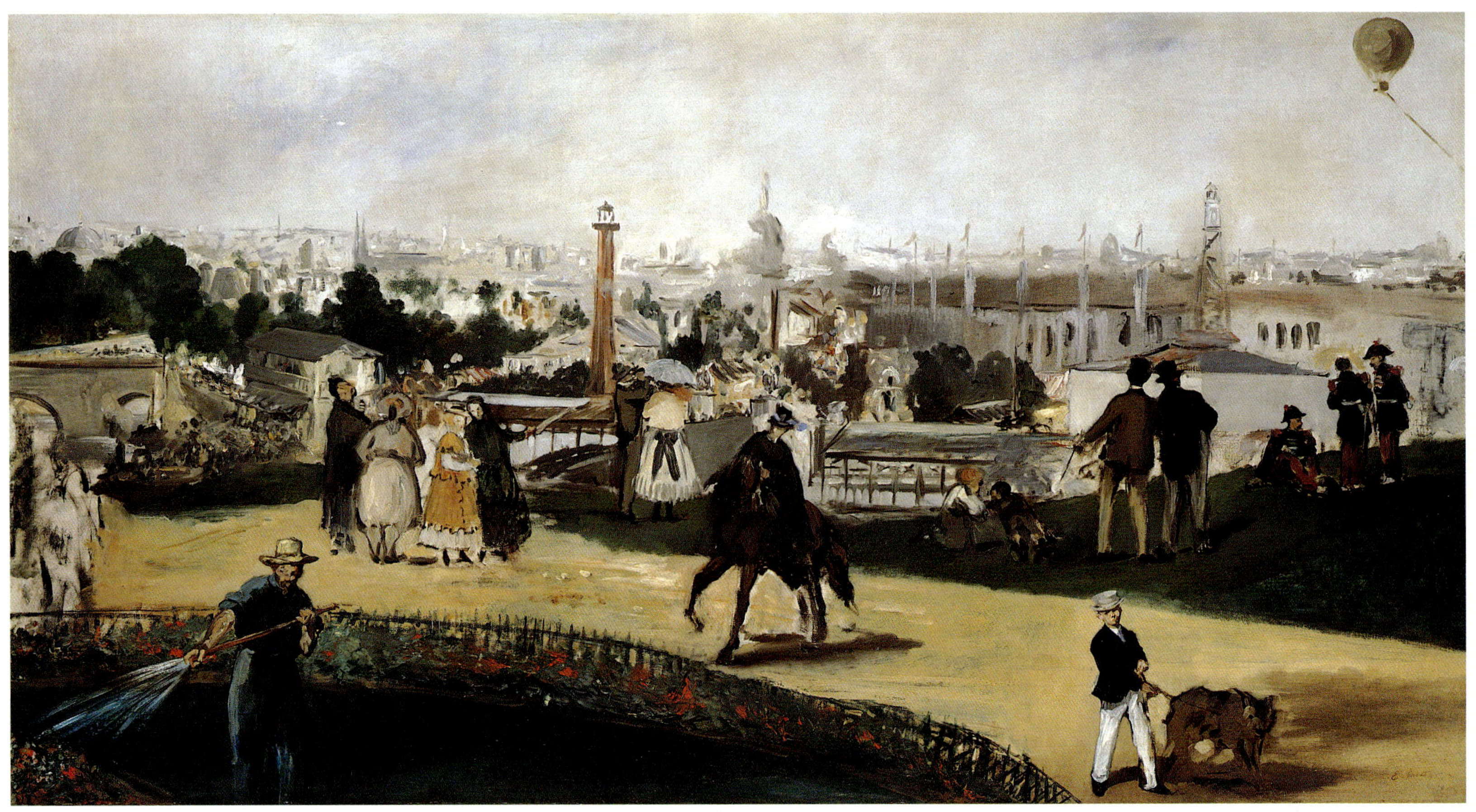

4
Edouard Manet
View of the World Exhibition in Paris 1867, 1867
Oil on canvas, 108 × 196.5 cm
Oslo, Nasjonalgalleriet

through its immediacy, its enthusiasm about an event and its desire simply to be present, part of something grand. The painting's size and peculiarly sketchy character is of a piece with an artistic declaration of war, and neither it nor any of the other works submitted by Manet were shown at the great exhibition. Instead Manet exhibited it in his alternative pavilion next to Courbet's own autonomous exhibition on the Place de l'Alma.

The second historical work by Manet from 1867 is the large composition dealing with the execution of Emperor Maximilian I of Mexico. On 19 June of that year the puppet emperor, who had otherwise received French support was executed by the Mexican rebel army. Napoléon had done nothing to hinder the killing and Manet managed to twist the knife in the political wound by painting the event of the execution in the format of a monumental historical picture. The small sketch in the Glyptotek is one of many leading to the large work (cat. no. 42, fig. 51). Manet has given the firing squad French uniforms to emphasise the infamy of the episode and the government prevented the publication of the subject in popular lithography. Set against *View of the World Exhibition in Paris 1867* the Maximilian picture bears especially powerful witness to Manet's involvement in the history of his time and his attempt to bring about a new concept of the historical work of art and its role.

The Franco-Prussian War of 1870–71 was, however of far greater significance for the next crucial development in French art; the ignominious defeat by the Prussians and the loss of the important industrial area of Alsace-Lorraine was a devastating blow, and the Siege of Paris, with its miniature civil war, known thereafter as the Paris Commune drew the horrors of war into the capital and split the inhabitants into two armed camps. Many of the artists joined the people (i.e. the insurgents) on the barricades; among them was Edouard Manet — despite the subsequent dry assertion of his daughter-in-law and fellow artist Berthe Morisot that he spent the war in front of a mirror changing uniforms.[5]

Courbet had been, without doubt, directly involved in the disturbances and later appeared in court for his part in having toppled the Vendôme Column. Despite considerable political rhetoric about "the Socialist Message" in his letters and reminiscences, Courbet seems to have been somewhat naive politically; his participation in the Commune turned out to cost him his career, and he spent the last ten years of his life in exile in Switzerland.[6] Others — such as Monet, but also the system's own champion Gérôme — spent the entire war in exile, not least out of fear of being incriminated as sympathisers. Very gradually, artists were beginning to be regarded as a class of their own, a class with their own sympathies and antipathies. That art could be an area of life with its own potential political powers was clear. This might in itself be evidence of a new concept of "avant-garde artist" who would henceforth be eagerly seen as a born rebel, capable of anything. This kind of avant-garde thinking begins with Manet.

Painting. A Matter of Morals

When, a year after his death in 1883, the decision was taken to honour Edouard Manet as one of the giants of the new painting with an exhibition at the Ecole des Beaux-Arts in Paris it provoked a strong reaction from one of the most traditionally-minded of contemporary masters, the painter and sculptor, Jean-Léon Gérôme; Manet had never studied nor taught at the Ecole, and an artist who was out of step with the academic tradition to such a degree was, according to Gérôme, unworthy of a place in the citadel of Academia. His response was perhaps only natural given the respective standpoints of the two artists: what is significant is the academician's definition of what crucially sets him apart from Manet: "I am certain that Manet was capable of painting good pictures. He chose to be the apostle of decadent fashion, *l'art du morceau* ["the art of the fragment" — the italics are mine]. I, for my part, was chosen by the state to teach the grammar of art to young students. Once I have accomplished that I will tell them to look around themselves, to study nature, to be sincere, to be naïve, and to work. Consequently I do not think it right to offer them as a model the extremely arbitrary and sensational work of a man, who although gifted with rare qualities, did not develop them".[7] The wording goes right to the heart for this painter and his Academy. A true artist is permitted to choose his form of expression, and develop it according to one model or the other; Gérôme will accept Manet as far as his natural talent is concerned, but calls him to account for his morality. In the same way that an artist heeds the call of "nature", one can obey the summons of the state in the service of art, or one can refuse, and it is here, according to Gérôme, that Manet is at fault. Morality and painting are two intangibles in close proximity, but there must be no departure from the order of precedence, *first things first*: the principles of painting must be soundly established before the senses are allowed free rein — and freedom of expression which the Salon master, albeit in his own way, was prepared to support, but only when a young painter or sculptor's character has reached moral maturity.

Gérôme's deep-rooted "hatred" of Manet is glaringly obvious from another exchange of words over the Manet exhibition; Gérôme is supposed to have said to a colleague that it would be altogether more appropriate if the venue for the event had been the Folies Bergères rather than the hallowed halls of the Ecole[8] — that vulgarly plebeian bar would have been far better suited to the painter's works, of which at least one of the later ones had supplied Gérôme with his ammunition by its title and subject-matter: *A Bar at the Folies Bergères* (1881–82, Courtauld Galleries, London).

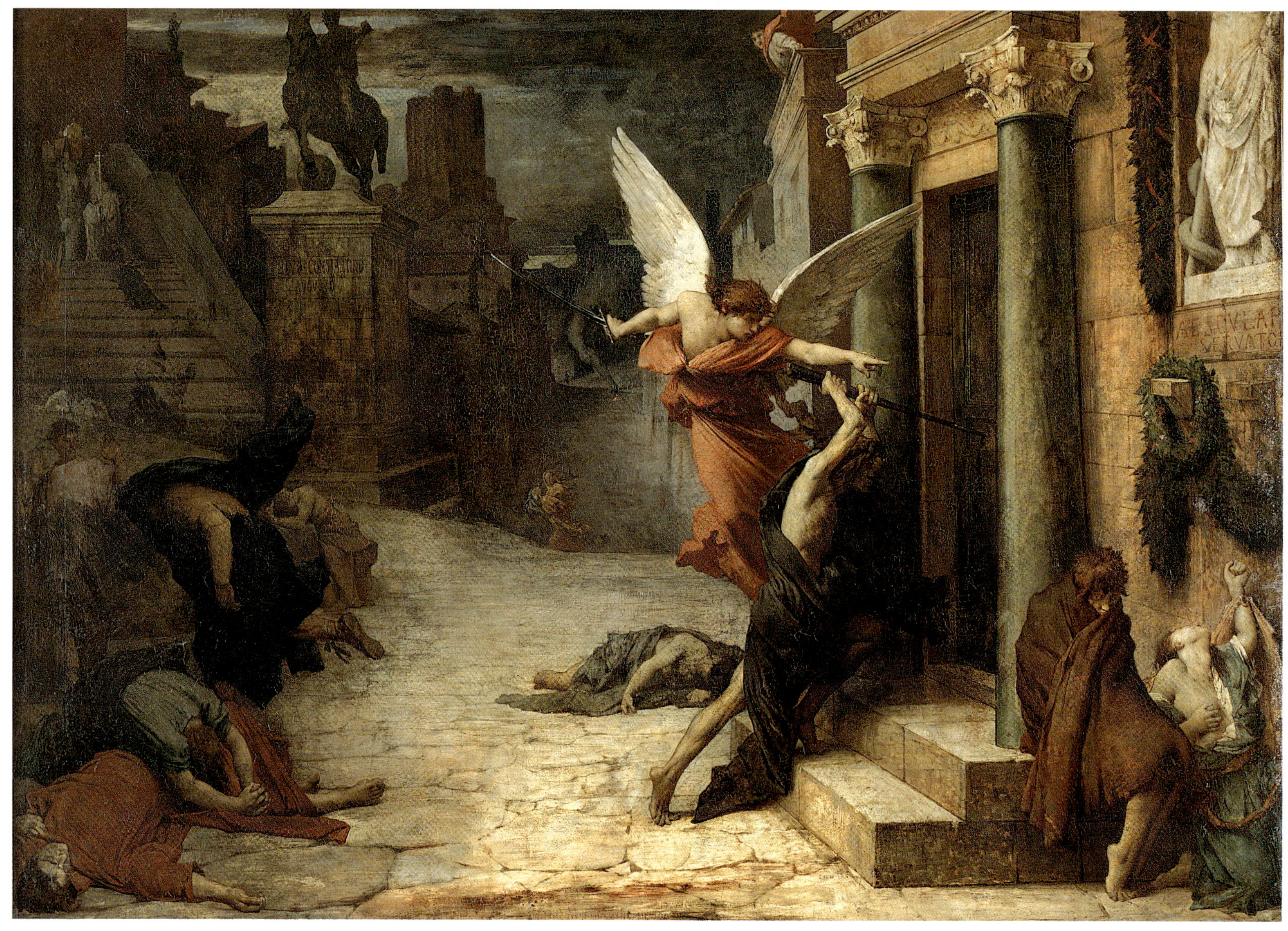

But these clear pronouncements on Manet's lack of morals did not mean that Gérôme's own painting was without sensuality (cat. no. 32, fig. 46, *The Cock-Fight*). His concept of sensuality is simply of a fundamentally different character to that of Manet and the Impressionists. Sensualism and morality can be found either side of the rift dividing tradition from the avant-garde, but expressed through various different elements in each individual work of art. According to the traditions of the Academy the subordination of sensuality to the stylistic framework was absolutely crucial. That gushing sentimental-romantic sensuality which distinguishes so much Salon art, has proved unacceptable in modernist eyes, but it rests alone on two factors: on one side the artist's building-up of the narrative content (that which Gauguin very tellingly groups under the category "Literature"); on the other his use of line. The retina of Gérôme — and those of a whole generation of artists — retained the paradigms of Neo-Classicism: outlines were of paramount importance and in this respect Ingres was God. It should be possible to express the substance of a work of art through drawing alone; for many the use of paint was merely a matter of filling in, "colouring", unless one's point of departure for a composition was Frans Hals, Van Dyck, Fragonard, or some corresponding Rococo

5
Jules-Elie Delaunay
The Plague in Rome, 1869
Oil on canvas, 131 × 176.5 cm
Paris, Musée d'Orsay
(cat. no. 25)

According to legend, Rome was visited by the plague about AD 590. So the Pope prayed for mercy, after which in a heavenly vision he saw an angel with a drawn sword hovering above his head. The angel then sheathed its sword, which the Pope saw as a good omen. The plague ceased that same day. The epidemic was subsequently seen as God's punishment for the wanton debauchery of the Romans. In his painting, Delaunay pays homage to the healing power of Christianity, which in the shape of the Archangel Michael drives away the disease. With its dramatic style inspired by Renaissance art, the painting became a popular example of morally-uplifting Salon paintings.

master as his chosen, stylistic forerunner; the fundamentally eclectic pantheon permitted a certain local latitude in draughtsmanship, but this was conditional on the observance of that still-prevailing legal code, forbidding the sketchy to ever have the upper hand. That was the road to perdition, both in terms of painting and morality.

An important aspect of the break-through of a new and different mode of thought in painting is the moral position in the aesthetic which the Modern forces its opponents to adopt. Posterity would reckon the opening of the First Impressionist Exhibition in April 1874 as heralding the rout of the bogus ideals of an effete period, a victory with which Modernism became so synonymous. The idea of a new beginning, an uprising and the eternal revolution as the core of Modernism drew much of its substance from the history of bursts of public outrage, razor-sharp criticism and broken heads at the infamous exhibition in the Boulevard des Capucines. The reality, as has been cogently demonstrated in the last twenty years, was rather different[9]; for the most part the resulting criticism was indifferent rather than indignant — out of the fourteen reviews which actually appeared, only four were decidedly negative, six were positive, three mixed, but predominantly favourable, and one mixed but predominantly negative.[10] By the same token it has been shown that the new movement in painting was by no means some freak of nature which had sprung up overnight, as myth would dearly have it. *Société Anonyme des Artistes peintres, sculpteurs, graveurs, etc.* as they called themselves before the derogatory term "impressionism" stuck and was accepted as an umbrella term by the artists themselves from 1877 onwards,[11] was, from the beginning, a forum acutely conscious both of itself and the media, and the leading figures behind the exhibition and its new fellowship of critical artists had planned the event meticulously. Thus, in January 1874, Monet, Pissarro and Degas had arranged for journalists favourable to their cause to release news of the formation of a new group of artists, and the decision had been taken to start fourteen days before the opening of the Salon's censured exhibition to maximise public awareness of the rebels' own exhibition. What has been conveniently passed over in silence is that the group had invited a number of far more traditionally-minded painters and sculptors, thereby lending the exhibition a veneer of academic "respectability" while at the same time creating the best background against which to make their entrance as a new wave in painting which was decidedly anti-academic[12]; a good half of the thirty participating artists were people outside the self-constituted group and included such names as Beliard, Colin and Meyer. They contributed a series of works of quite conventional stamp (i.e. non-Impressionist) and today are completely forgotten, but that was precisely why they were there.

By freely accepting this expression, the Impressionists made common cause of their struggle in painting, and as a consequence of the way their expression differed from the way the existing art world communicated — their new style — they were brought together under a definite concept of radical freshness and spontaneity in painting. They had a predilection for painting in the open air, directly from the subject, as Corot had done for a long time, and their so-called *plein-air* painting finally triumphed in the history of art via Impressionism. It was precisely Corot who could be incorporated into the traditionally historicising picture of the "development" of the style; by granting him the role of a painter who early on had worked in the open air with a — if only relatively — "free", sketchy brushwork, it was possible for art history unscrupulously to reckon Corot as an important forerunner of Impressionism. For a long time their status as innovators rested purely on the freshness in the painting, a concept which, since Romanticism, has been regarded as synonymous with spontaneity. The idea of Impressionism as the spontaneous — i.e. unmitigated, direct and, by definition, triumphantly truthful — went unchallenged for a long time in the history of Western art, not least because a certain diametrically-opposed school of thought had become widespread. The development lines of the history of art would like to have seen themselves summarised in the following brief formula: a style of painting based on its predecessors, which by the appropriation of its painterly means and characteristics attempts to continue the development and steady refinement. A mode of painting or "style" (the most difficult word in art history) must continue the struggle to transform what has survived, so that it can become part of the new artistic context — in a synthesis of experience previously acquired — and "something new", which is added to Art in a development and improvement which can continue *ad infinitum*.[13]

In the years from 1860 to around 1900 the epoch's own art history added certain radical elements to this model, so that it was now popular to talk of a *conflict* between expressions or schools. The battle metaphor indicates that there is always a victor and a vanquished: every style has its day, after which it stagnates, decays and must vacate the stage for another (or in the case of Modernism, several other) expression, to which it bears the least possible resemblance. The new winner emerges from the chaos as an inherently naturally-born, but always unrecognised child of its time, who must first undergo cruel rites of passage before that fame, which the style demands, comes about. It is not Courbet's self-styled Realism, but the idea of the Impressionists' *plein-air* painting, which breaks through as the crucially new ingredient in the new painting. In relation to Courbet's work, the Impressionists' "tache" painting is far more oriented towards the sensory impression itself: as one of the time's leading critics, Jules Castagnary (who was one of the first to use the word "Impressionist") could maintain: "They are *Impressionists* in the sense that they render not the landscape but the sensation produced by the experience of the landscape..."[14] It was the immediacy in the apprehension of the sensory impression, which became one of criticism's most reiterated catch-phrases concerning Impressionism.

The relation between tradition and the new received its crucial literary form in 1876, when a supporter of the Impressionists' work published an essay as a direct spin-off of the group's second exhibition. The critic, Louis-Emile Duranty (1833–80) grouped all the avant-garde movements in art under the single term "La Nouvelle Peinture", and his article so-entitled became the focus of considerable attention. Duranty took his polemical point of departure in a text from February of the same year by the academic painter Eugène Fromentin (1820–76), who lamented the decline of painting in melancholy terms; Fromentin attacked the new directions in painting, all of which he bracketed together under the term "Realism" — a term which recalled Courbet's scandalous exhibition of twenty years before, when the word was first consciously used in connection with painting which Fromentin now extended to additionally include the latest movement in art, Impressionism. He complained about the craving of these provocateurs for sensation and their need to throw overboard all acquired wisdom, together with every idealisation to the advantage of "striking and direct pictures [...] purged of every artifice" — i.e. a painting which would carefully recreate the feeling (*la sensation*) of what one can see on the street.[15] For Fromentin it was clear evidence of a crisis that the atelier was opening its doors to the surrounding world, and that a great tradition, more inwardly speculative and learning-oriented, must submit to being forced into the shade. But Duranty put his finger on the circumstances that the evocation of "modern life" was the work of art's

6
Alfred Sisley
The Flood, 1872
Oil on canvas, 45 × 60 cm
Copenhagen, Ny Carlsberg Glyptotek
(cat. no. 55)

Here Sisley depicts the consequences of the Seine bursting its banks. His rendering of the catastrophe is, however, in the manner of a sober observer. The light brush strokes occasionally leave the canvas visible, giving the painting a suggestion of the unfinished. This makes it a typical example of Impressionist painting, traditionally associated with a sketch-like, spontaneous record of a real situation. However, the composition is in fact carefully constructed: the tree and the telegraph pole divide the picture into sections, and the spectator's gaze is drawn into the picture by the telegraph wire. Japanese woodcuts probably influenced the composition of this painting, which was hailed as one of the best landscapes of the First Impressionist Exhibition of 1874.

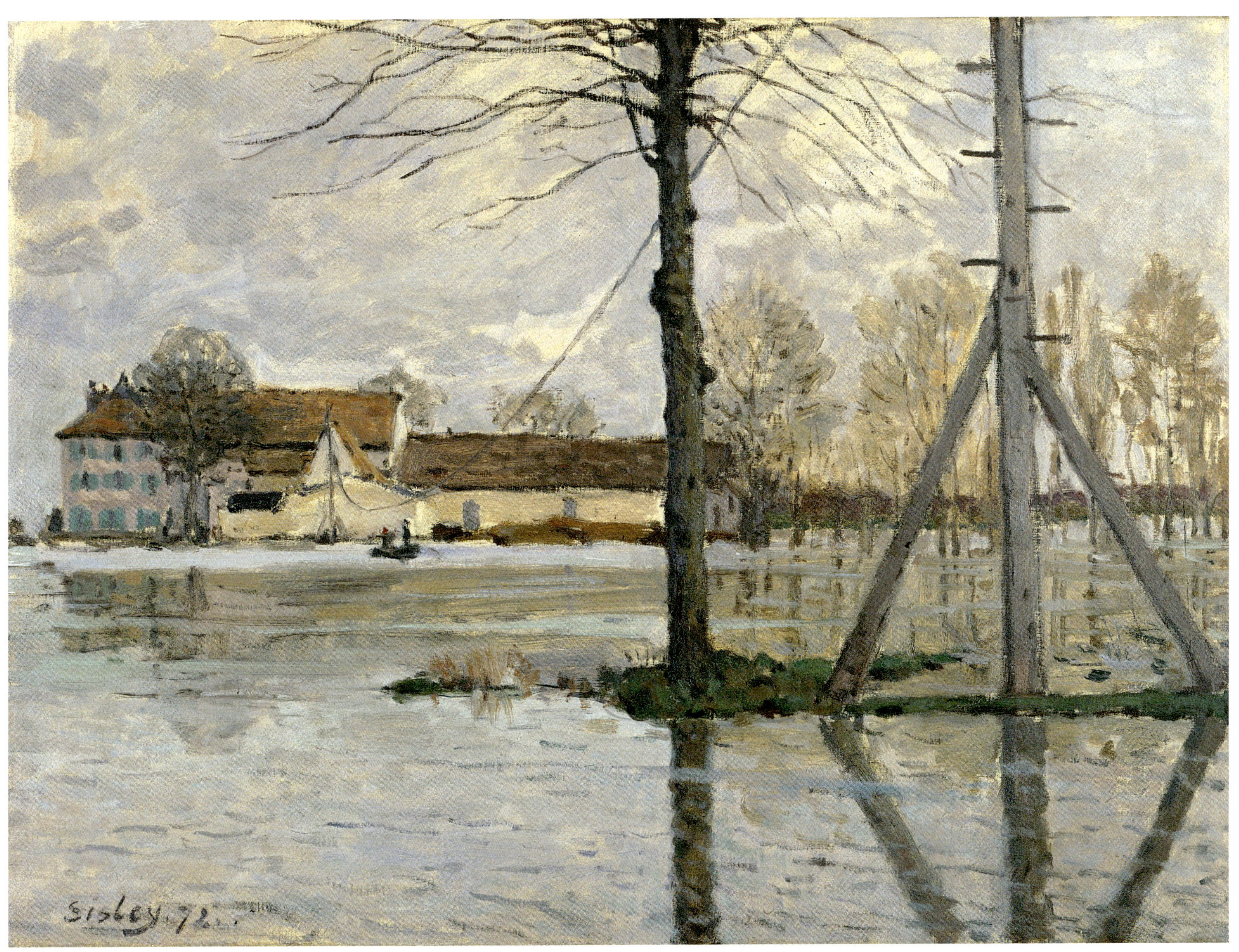

only chance to link itself to tradition,[16] and when Fromentin criticised the avant-garde for being impersonal and stuffed with conventions, Duranty was able to counter this by maintaining the same about the Academy's uncritical cult of Antiquity.

The question of individuality is part of a larger issue; an artist's worth (and therewith his individuality *as an artist*) must always depend on his ability to let his own time appear through his work, however at the same time Duranty's perspective concentrated on the unity. Thus he writes, "I am less concerned with this exhibition [the Second Impressionist Exhibition] than its *cause* and *idea*". The issue for him was to see the attempt to paint without "formality, optimistically and without holding back", on a fundamental naturalistic/romantic image of the surrounding world. Duranty's text links elegant and individualistic self-awareness to his own texts about art from many years before in the short-lived pro-Courbet periodical *Réalisme* (1856). The critic links painting with a literary-cultural dream about art which depicts life as it is lived, an art which "... carefully expresses a country's everyday life — weddings, christenings, births, the continuation of life from generation to generation, festivity and family life".[17]

Nevertheless, he could assert shortly afterwards that *the new* as such was the unifying element: "With very few exceptions one must admit that everything in this new movement is new or wants to be free". This applied not least to the technical sphere, but Duranty found occasion in his last lines, however, to warn against a specific tendency: "In France, especially, the inventor is eclipsed by the one who perfects and patents the invention — virtuosity takes precedence over naive clumsiness and the popularizer reaps the reward of the innovator".[18] The sentence is a striking, laconic description of how tradition works in figurative art.

Duranty also settled accounts with the individualism in the Prix de Rome system and the general prevailing attitude in the French Academy as such: "Les nouvelles peintres" would not submit works to the Salon, because "their painting is not some form of examination, and because we have to rid ourselves of all official ballyhoo, the awarding of prizes as if to schoolchildren, the whole university system for art". A natural art, an art free of artifice, simply had to win: "La Nouvelle Peinture" was only a beginning. Duranty's background in the naturalistic literary tradition broke through in his physiologically-superposed metaphors — he prefigures the *apology* to the public, that this type of art in its infancy has yet to reach the articulated expression of its talent. The Impressionists are some sort of stammerers, but only because the world at that point has not yet caught up with them. They are, in other words, *ahead of their time*, and it is at this point that avant-garde modes of thinking are consolidated.

The Pygmalion Effect

The Impressionists were not the only people who related to time and history. Such constellations of the history of ideas are one thing: it was quite another issue when it came to the much more concrete relation to what was the everyday, what was actually lived, which was breaking through with Manet and Courbet, Bastien-Lepage and Daumier. For some, there was a clearly distinguishable driving force behind the work which wanted to show everything, as mercilessly as possible — in the last instance, that desire was intimately bound up with the artistic process as such, and this is where the question of the relation between style and representation breaks through with a vengeance: one of the problems experienced by Salon art or the "late classicising" tradition, at least when seen through modernistic eyes, could be formulated thus: is what the work of art expresses still compatible with its medium, or: is the *style* getting in the way of the thought? Many of the contemporary critics involved themselves in the problematic; when Paul Dubois exhibited his *Florentine Singer* in the summer of 1865, the Salon was enchanted, because, as one critic put it, here was a work which combined historical/thematic complexity with a clear sense of how to present life. The artist had, in other words reached a synthesis of narrative and verisimilitude: "M. Dubois has said in this figure all he could have wished to say, and this result seems to us to be considerable, in these days when so many artists, otherwise skilled, have all the trouble in the world to express half of their thought. The *Narcissus* [Salon of 1863 — the same year as the Salon des Refusés — cat. no. 26, fig. 31] was only a happy encounter; but the *Florentine Singer* is a reasoned and intentional work".[19]

Everything has been said, nothing is left to chance (still art's worst enemy). Underneath we can still detect the whining of Mantz' fear of the evil practice of the time, namely the same decadence which Gérôme and Thoré, each from his respective standpoint and forty years apart, warned against: that *in spite* of their evident abilities the nation's artists would be led astray by ideas which were too big, and crippled by their demanding work. The two Dubois sculptures moreover come across as essentially different; *Narcissus* is a decorative, somewhat arabesque-like exercise in style of the type which illustrates best why late Neo-Classicism has been disdained. Nevertheless the figure, as though lost in its own thoughts, has become enclosed in a form in the movement described by the drapery, a reflective introversion which suggests a sculptural meta-dimension. With Dubois of course *Narcissus* becomes a sculptural meditation on the artist's relation to the life it reflects — the concept's posing of the youth so that he stands "inside" his drapery, cuts him off from his surrounding world (of which the brook or stream in which he is reflected is only suggested — the rest must be provided by the observer) and makes the stance itself a metaphor for Narcissus and/or narcissism in every work and its relation to the observer. The more classical-allegorical aspect of the narrative is supported by the narcissus flower, Dubois has incorporated into the surface of the base, to the left of the figure. This is an extra dimension, which contemporary observers, including Mantz himself, would have noticed, as well as being that attribute which Ovid gave the figure in his *Metamorphoses*; in Ovid, the body of the youth is white and flawless as Parian marble — another instance of the medium and the theme uniting in a higher unity, and polychromy is excluded.

On the other hand the *Florentine Singer* in bronze seems to build towards a possible "colouring from life" purely by virtue of non-classical realism in the costume, which means that each individual part is clearly and sharply defined in relation to each other. The surface is at centre stage, as it tends to be more in fifteenth-century Florentine painting than that age's sculpture, which was Dubois' model for this work.[20] There was, however, more "literature" in *Narcissus*, than in *Florentine Singer*, in which Dubois, without restricting himself to any strict scheme of recognition permitted himself to go his own, freer way. This may, in addition, make this work more distinctive and realistic than its predecessor.

Jean-Léon Gérôme's master stroke — and something which won him both honour and popularity in his time — was the wholly individual use and reuse of motifs of his own, which, in the final third of his career he put into play in a most "modern" way. Around 1875–76 Gérôme could no longer be satisfied by painting alone and threw himself with fervour into sculpture. From this time to his death he worked equally in both media. His principal theme had long been in place in his painting: the oriental, historical pictures and mythological or literary themes were the artist's most important genres, and it was particularly in the latter that he now drew certain

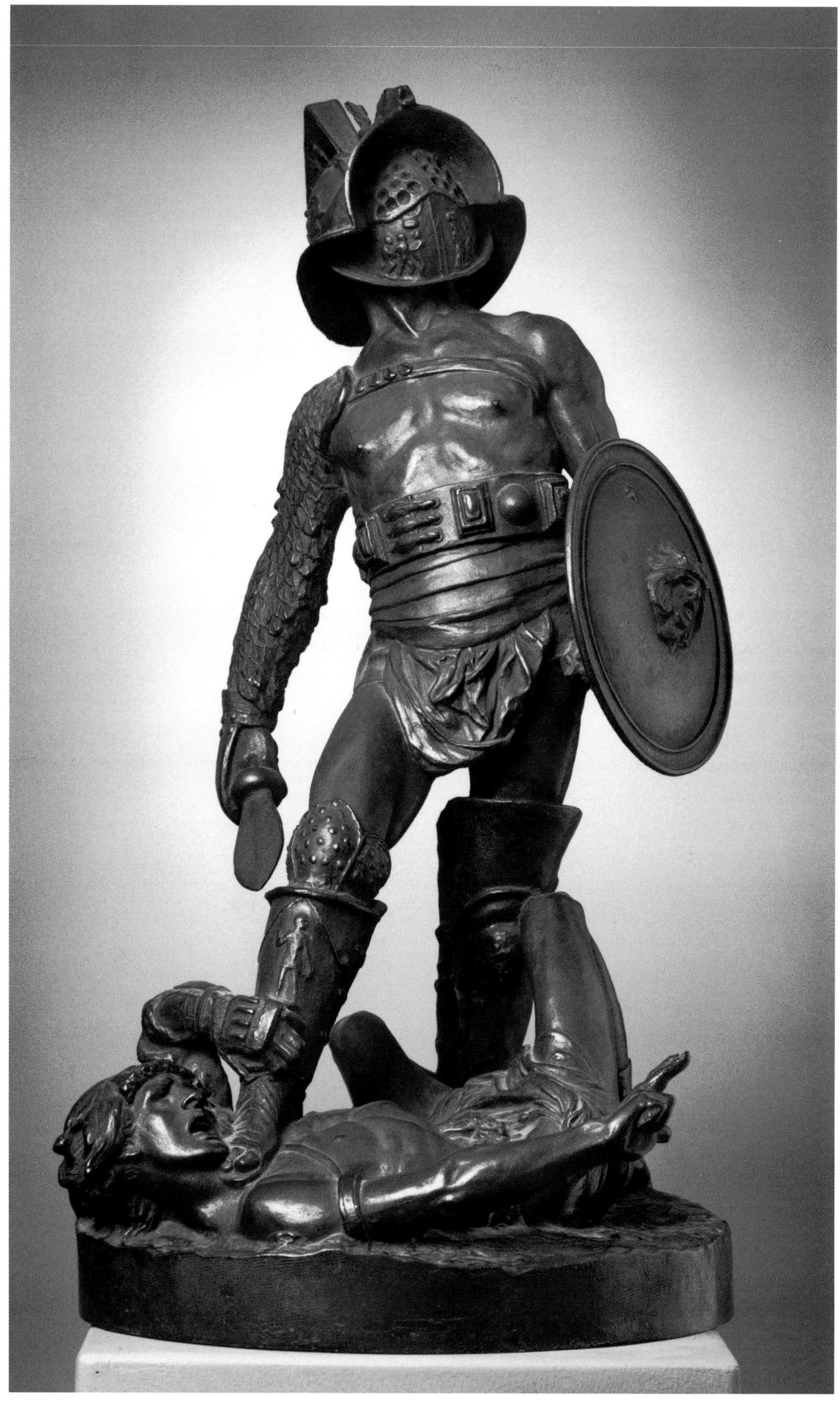

7
Jean-Léon Gérôme
The Gladiators (1878)
Bronze, h. 50 cm
Copenhagen, Ny Carlsberg Glyptotek
(cat. no. 33)

The gladiator is placing a foot in triumph on his fallen opponent, who is struggling to free himself and making signs to the audience begging for mercy. Gérôme has taken his group of gladiators from one of his own paintings, for he loved to play painting and sculpture off against each other. The figures in Gérôme's paintings often seem to be endowed with a statuary rigidity, while on the other hand his sculptures have features testifying to a painter's interest in the surface. This also applies to *The Gladiators*, where the account of the two opponents' dress and armour accumulates so many surface details that the volume of the sculpture almost seems to dissolve.

subjects from which great sculpture could arise. An unusually large number of Gérôme's works deal with the role of the artist, ideals and myths, and a large part of his oeuvre presents the observer with a historical gaze, which shows how the Ancient Greeks and Romans lived — either as a cultural elite or in a violently dramatic presentation as a cruel, but nevertheless just (or justified) master race. In the sculpture *The Gladiators* (1878, cat. no. 33, fig. 7) which the artist bequeathed to the founder of the Glyptotek, Carl Jacobsen in 1885, he has "borrowed" the motif from himself[21]; in one of his numerous paintings of the Roman arena with gladiators in combat (*Pollice Verso* [Thumbs Down], 1874, Phoenix Art Museum, Arizona) he found this group with a net fighter (Roman term: *retiarius*), who has been defeated by a *mirmillo* (fighter armed with a sword and wearing a Gallic helmet). The victor looks up to the public around the arena awaiting their judgement whether to end his opponent's sufferings or let him live. The vanquished gladiator gesticulates wildly, screaming his appeal to the public for mercy, but the painting's title indicates the episode's foregone conclusion.

As a sculpture, the group gains an extra dimension from the observer being put in the role of the judge (critic), an effect of which Gérôme could hardly have been unaware. *The Gladiators* stands as the artist's first monumental sculpture, and it won him a medal at the World Exhibition in Paris in 1878. At the Musée d'Orsay the work can be seen in yet another context — constituting a third recycling — where the group forms an integrated component of a monument executed by the sculptor A.-J. Morot (1850–1913) to Gérôme himself; here the full-figure statue of the artist can be seen in the process of modelling the two combatants. In *The Gladiators* Gérôme was primarily concerned with the presentation of as accurate a study as possible of this aspect of ancient Roman civilization, and he spent a great deal of time in finding the right sources for this depiction. He was particularly preoccupied with the accurate rendition of the armour and weapons of the various types of gladiator, and the artist wanted to show the greatest possible authenticity. To the oil painting and the gladiator group must be added a series of studies in watercolours, oils and wax,[22] all dealing with the epoch Gérôme had chosen to depict. Here the legacy of Neo-Classicism's at times fanatical studies of the ancient world manifests itself to the full: but the relation between the individual works, media and genres in the case of Gérôme, is, at all events, much more far-reaching than that. His establishment of a substantially complex, internal structure of references at the centre of his artistic work, reveals the painter-sculptor to be extremely conscious of the concept of tradition in both its "classical" and its "modern" manifestation. Thus his alibi as far as the academic-idealising tradition is perfectly sound, while at the same time he establishes a totally self-referring field of works whose thematic and visual familiarity to the public becomes an important factor in their function within Gérôme's art, enhancing the potential for success of each individual work of art. To be any more meta-artistic than this would be really difficult.

To manage to simultaneously follow tradition, while at the same time creating a niche into which one can insert the fruit of one's labours (cunningly disguised as an antiquitising motif) had long been a principle element in Gérôme's painting. In one work in particular, the painter-sculptor reflected on how painting relates to sculpture, the artist to the work of art, and art to reality. This work was one of the many contemporary depictions of Pygmalion and Galathea, (others include cat. nos. 53 [Rodin] and 43 [Marqueste], figs. 38 and 37). Gérôme has chosen to depict a sculptor, logically himself or his alter ego, in his atelier in the process of modelling the female figure as in the classical myth about art being given life by the force of her creator's wishful thinking and just a touch of divine intervention. We are at that magic point where the (self-?) love-struck artist is united with his work in a kiss, and Gérôme has chosen to show it as a metamorphosis — the marble of sculpture becomes flesh and blood, starting at the head and moving downwards while we watch: the life-giving kiss melts the barrier between art and life, and the weight of the stone drains out of the figure, so that for a brief while yet the lowest part of her legs and feet are still cold marble.

In refined style the artist plays on the characteristics of his metier to make concepts and thoughts "real" and dress the ideal in the flesh of reality on the canvas, yet, concurrently these Frankensteinian endeavours remain in the two dimensions of the painting.

All reality is, in fact, in the process of becoming an artistic expression in a new way. This happens through a complex exchange situation between *artificiality* and *realism*, not least in the idea of "life as it is lived". Where once marble represented the lofty, spiritual ideal for the academics, whereas to modern eyes it has come to mean a decrepit decadence, everything polychrome for most of the twentieth century has been viewed as a vulgarisation — precisely because of its intimate relation with reality as something which can be materially apprehended. This process had nothing to do with sculpture, which was supposed to be capable of subduing the material aspect of the world's manifestations, aspiring beyond the ordinary and the everyday, towards a purified and sharply-focused expression of spirituality. The Belgian sculptor Paul de Vigne hit the nail on the head with a definition of sculpture which, at the same time, indicates the power and status relationship between colour and whiteness in the twentieth century: "Art should express none but the most noble thoughts; the principles of sculpture exclude vulgarity".[23]

At this point in time sculpture was still an affair of ideals, and in such an undertaking colour detracts from the ideal because it is: a) earthly (as opposed to "heavenly" — spiritual) by way of its connection with the "dirty" *hyle*, matter devoid of form, matter in its least refined state; b) sensually erotic, eroticising, because the coloured body is not a "pure" idealisation; c) "vulgar" in the sense that it is used in the context of popular culture — amplifying effects, an essentially sensational contrivance.

"Sensation" in its French sense has a precise connection with the immediacy of the sensory impression. The "sensational" occurs in such environments as the travelling freak show, where garish effects were an essential part of the presentation, and it could be particularly clear in the use of wax works. During this period wax mannequins were used as instructional models for the teaching of anatomy, but a new use for wax figures emerged with Madame Tussaud's Waxworks in London, which, despite their clownish form, came across as a valuable producer of sensations; permanent waxworks achieved a rank superior to that of the travelling theatres of illusions by being (at least partly) historical, and thereby educational. As anatomical models or as part of a "historical" tableau, colour had a legitimate function as a mimetic guarantee of the authenticity of what was artificially presented; it had a purpose, it pointed beyond the colour itself, it was, in fact, instruction. Colour gave verisimilitude by way of its close link with that reality which created an illusion but was, anyhow, something else, namely a product with a quite definite, "purified" or ideal objective. The multicoloured work of sculpture in wax, however, was never to be confused with that ideal's true product of artistry one continued to desire of a real work of art in stone, and colouring of sculpture could not be regarded as artistically defensible until much later in the century.

The sculptor Eugène-Louis Aizelin (1821–1902) exhibited his *Mignon* (cat. no.

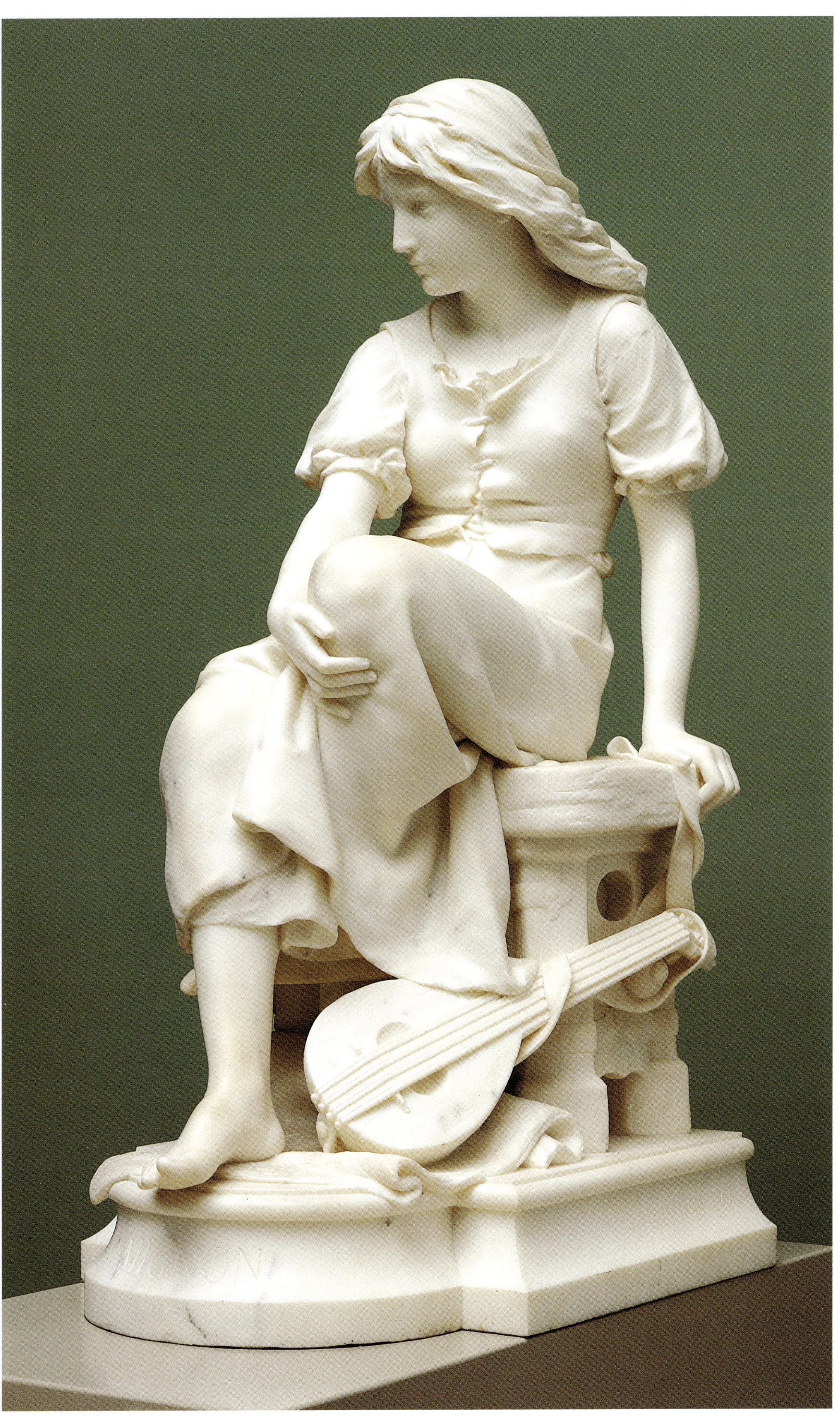

8
Eugène-Louis Aizelin
Mignon, 1881
Marble, h. 137 cm
Copenhagen, Ny Carlsberg Glyptotek
(cat. no. 1)

The figure of Mignon is taken from Goethe's novel *The Apprenticeship of Wilhelm Meister* (1794–96). Goethe describes her as a figure reduced to a life split between a real and an ideal world. This dualism is reflected in Aizelin's sculpture. With its detailed rendering of skin and clothes, the sculpture competes against reality itself. But the white, ethereal quality of the marble at the same time links it to an idealistic, academic tradition. *Mignon* thereby becomes a metaphor for a fundamental condition for sculpture: the dichotomy between the reproduction of reality and the ideal.

1, fig. 8) at the Salon of 1881, and at first glance it appears to be yet another of Academicism's many virtuoso depictions of a figure from literature. Mignon is a character from Goethe's *The Apprenticeship of Wilhelm Meister* (1794–96) and is therefore evidence of the relation between contemporary art and classic literature. The girl is, however, an uncharacteristically complex figure as a subject for a sculpture; in Goethe's work Mignon assumes a key position between two worlds — on one hand, the world of reality, on the other, a soundless world of ideals. She is therefore a paradox; every aspect of her is, by definition, double or ambivalent, from her sexuality (she is a girl, but androgynous, cf. the boy's clothes and the strapped down bust) to her speech (she is barely able to talk, but manages to sing perfectly). The distinguishing feature of her character is longing, a longing which has no object. As Per Øhrgaard writes, "Mignon is a memory of an original state, which is unavoidably lost in upbringing and education; she is 'das Unbehagen in der Kultur' (Freud), the eternal reminder that civilization is not solely development, progress and fulfilment but there is always an attendant loss and bereavement. What is brilliant in Goethe's drawing of the character is that Mignon is as special as she is. She is not an idealisation of beauty, truth and goodness set against a warped reality — no, she is herself warped because she is compelled to live in a society that has distanced itself to such an extent from the original. Only in Paradise will Mignon be beautiful and graceful; out of it she must of necessity be a kind of Kaspar Hauser before her time".[24] When she dies all the characters in the novel grieve over the loss of such a voice, artistic but at the same time, displaced by time and place. She is embalmed and "survives as a memory in art".[25] In Aizelin's work she is art herself: by providing her with a cithar he is referring allegorically to her artistic nature. In this sculpture the idea of the greatest possible realism in the execution fuses with the theme of the work. Through his virtuosity, the sculptor approaches a hyperrealistic wholeness, in which even the smallest details are minutely reproduced: Mignon's clothing, the grain of the wood in the stool on which she is sitting, the strings of the instrument, etc. And even the marble is so undercut that the stone threatens to dissolve before one's eyes.

With *Mignon* Aizelin seems intent on defying the nature of sculpture by virtue of an extremely illusionistic rendering of the human body — let us call this the Pygmalion effect — and partly with making art as such the central theme of this sculpture. The sculpture casts the spectator in the role of one who looks in wonder as the work "becomes life itself" via an almost supernatural mimetic process. The work's unconscious is its display of a thorough artificiality as the essential artistic parameter. At the same time, virtuosity itself deconstructs the stone's materiality (and thereby the whole concept of sculpture), and moves the sculpture's mode of operation in the direction of painting; a figure such as Mignon becomes purely two-dimensional — we are invited to follow the enticing representation of skin and clothes, and this sensual dwelling on the materiality links the ideal of art with our own human reality. Only Aizelin's insistence on the marble's white ethereal aspect keeps the sculpture in an academic, idealistic tradition. It is the same insistence on the ideal clinical white which supports the massive resistance to polychromy for so long in the nineteenth century — a resistance which succeeded in supplanting the archaeologically-based (and historically much earlier) indication that the body in Greek sculpture was not, in fact, white, but as many-coloured "as life itself".

Polychromy in figurative art thus has two principal characterisations in the history of the Modern, which are tendentially mutually opposed; on one side there is the attitude that polychromy is an integral part of the new *par excellence* — on the other, no modern investigation will deny that polychromy is an

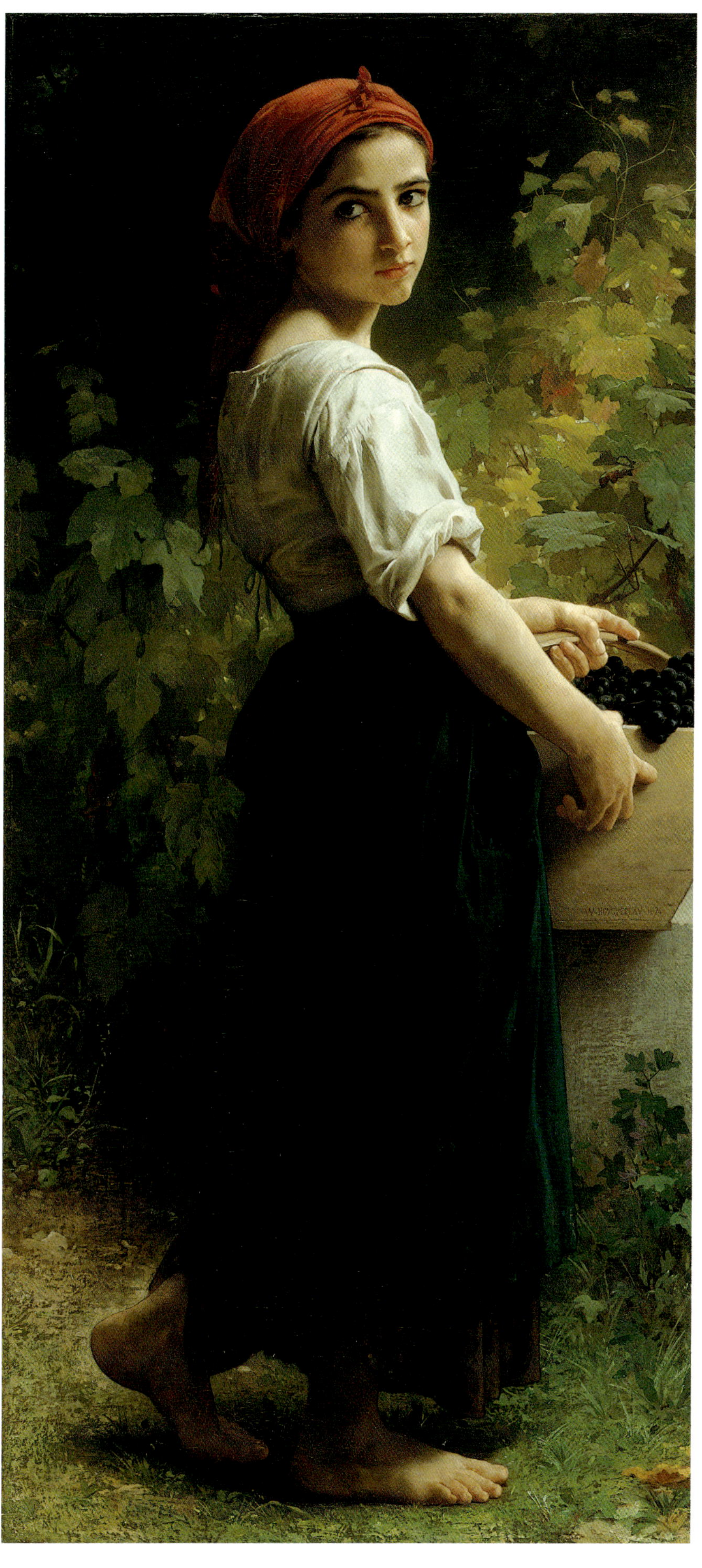

9
Adolphe-William Bouguereau
Girl with Grapes, 1874
Oil on canvas, 140 × 62 cm
Copenhagen, Ny Carlsberg Glyptotek
(cat. no. 7)

Bouguereau was one of the most famous and sought-after artists of his day, and he enjoyed great success in the Salons of the period. This genre painting was executed the same year that the Impressionists held their first exhibition. The simple composition, the idealised portrayal of reality and the smooth manner of painting are typical of his popular, academic style. The Impressionists were critical of Bouguereau's efforts to smooth out any trace of the brushwork. They found his style "slick and artificial". When Renoir started to wear glasses, he is said to have cast them aside with the words: "My God! They make me see just like Bouguereau".

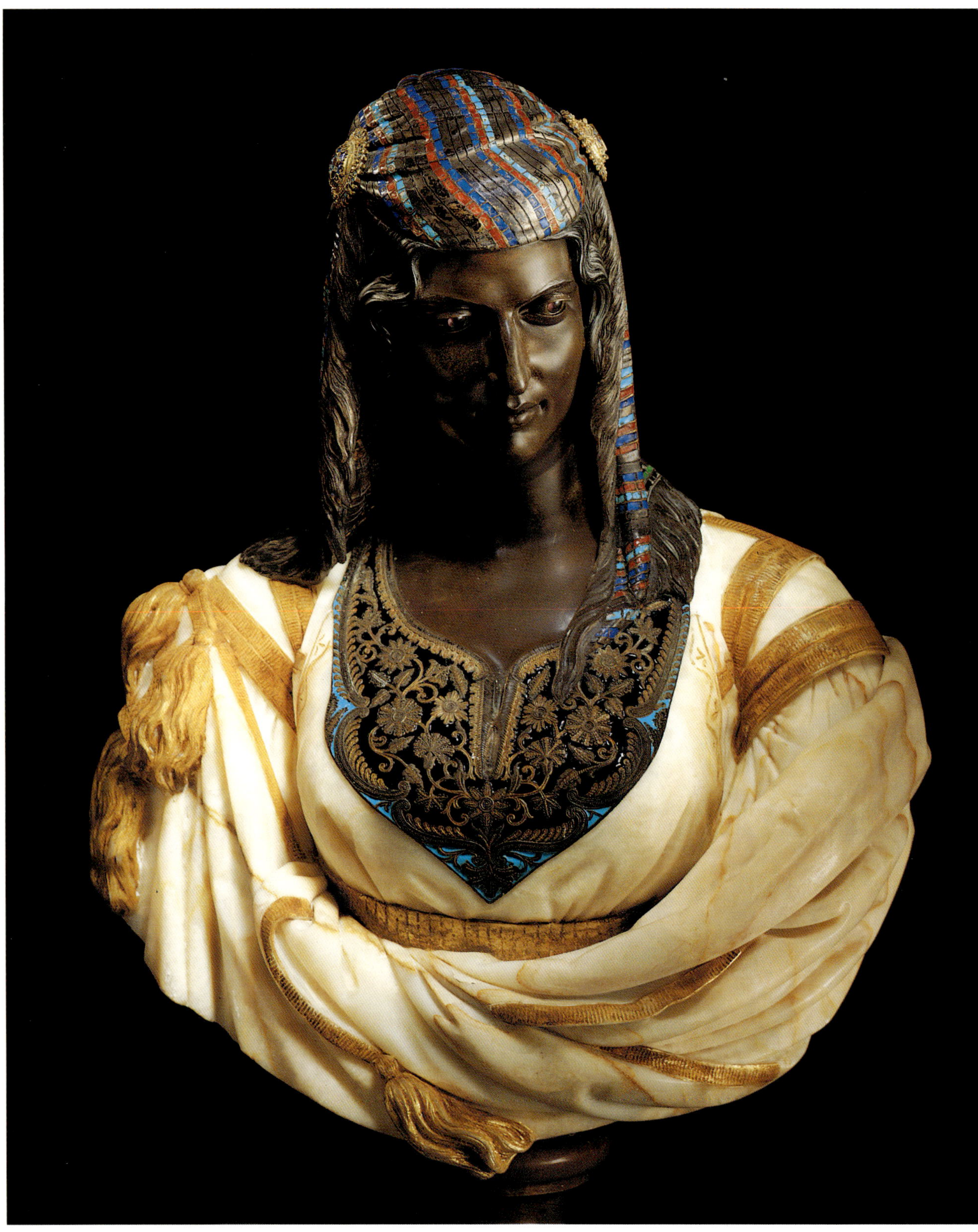

10
Charles Cordier
Jewess from Algiers, ca. 1862
Onyx, partially gilt, bronze, silvered bronze, enamel, semi-precious stones, h. 92.8 cm
Amsterdam, Van Gogh Museum
(cat. no. 17)

Cordier created this bust for a gallery dedicated to the depiction of the world's different ethnic groups. While travelling in North Africa he had studied the local populations and applied his knowledge to sculpture. He highlights the "exotic and alien" character of the Jewish woman's face by his use of many colours and sumptuous fabrics. The woman's "ethnic" look and the opulence of the materials appealed to the upper classes in Paris, who commissioned copies in more or less luxurious versions. This sensuous work was Cordier's greatest success. Both the subject, the materials and the variety of colours betokened a breach with the neo-classical ideal and its white marble.

artistic practice which is thousands of years old. Hargrove, for example, sees polychromy as a regular attack on the status quo, and thus presents that which is coloured as a "progressive" modern practice.[26] It appears that it will take considerable effort to purge sculpture of every tendency to the Classical — if modern sculpture, crafts or pottery uses strong colours, or colour at all for that matter, the inspiration is always alleged to have come from outside the art of Classical Greece.

The fact is rather that the many sources of polychromy — Pre-Columbian art, "primitive cultures", etc. together with the principal European source, archaic Greek culture all run together in an extreme consciousness of tradition in the period 1860–1900. The expansion of the cultural world-picture in the same period through colonisation, travel and charting in terms of the history of ideas or typology may have opened a greater artistic consciousness around the common, the historical and the human than there had been room for in nineteenth century European culture, dominated as it was by one particular concept of what was classical, beautiful, good and ideal. This particular idea of great confluences in a kind of almost mystical common humanity, of which Symbolism was an expression, and in which it was a firm believer, is an offshoot; every rigid insistence on white marble and its tonnage of classical culture must automatically be put in the shadow by an ideal of form and colour, which puts *the human* (back) in the main role. Against this background the idea of depicting "life itself" in an art, which never manages to get out of its narrow context with the generally human, normal and everyday, becomes the logical champion in a "new" cultural picture.

The same year that Aizelin carved his Mignon in marble, Degas exhibited a sculpture with which, in some circles, it has been compared. At the Sixth Impressionist Exhibition in 1881 Edgar Degas scared the daylights out of a lot of people with his *Dancer with Ballet Skirt, Fourteen Years Old* (cat. no. 22, fig. 36)[27] by doing a mime of life that came too close. After all, it is civilization which is up for grabs, when the critic reads this little girl literally and calls her an ape or a degenerate delinquent beanpole; she is *the other* in relation to the pleasant, bourgeois public, a foreign interloper in the culture. The attitude which dictates the condemnation of the little ballet dancer, is on the other hand totally consistent with the idea that the human psyche or soul can be read from the exterior. This period also witnessed the heyday of phrenology: the teaching which asserted that by measuring the circumference of the skull, and the relation between the various parts of the head (the eyes, nose, mouth and ears) was a kind of physiological pendant to the ideas of emergent psychoanalysis concerning charting the interior of human reason.

The little dancer is an intense attempt to be of her own time and to present her own sculptural "ideals". Degas' rendition of the childlike girl's body in starkly contrasting materials, fabric, real hair, wax in several colours — provoked a scandal whose echoes continue into modern history: here we have a piece of reality, without prettifying additions, and, it was thought, equally devoid of charm. She was called ugly, angular, socially and morally tainted, audacious and sick no less. Much of this was due to how the small figure relates to her genre, full-figure sculpture, and its tradition. The ballet girl is the re-entry of the human form into the Modern, and its problem, as far as its public was concerned, was that it violated a carefully-drawn boundary between life and art. It becomes a kind of effigy, a transitional stage between the living and the dead. Perhaps the little figure has another aesthetic dark side, on an unconscious level, which was not mentioned by any of the contemporary critical voices, but which did, perhaps, contribute to the public unease, namely the mummies of saints in Catholic countries, which, to this day, are regarded and treated as holy relics. The ballerina, when set against the reverence shown such processional figures, has something of the blasphemous.[28] In any case, Degas' reasoned choice of his materials and subject drew reality into the exhibition in a more concrete way than any Impressionist painting could have done, and this extract of Paris life was anything but heroic and sculptural in the classic academic sense. That the sculpture, its presentation and function in the exhibition, were, at the same time, handled in a new and dramatic way (with Degas' usual flair) is yet one more, important aspect of the same story; it had been announced that Degas was intending to exhibit a sculpture at the Fifth Impressionist Exhibition in 1880, but when the doors opened there was only an empty glass case, where the figure should have been. Degas had not managed to finish the work on time. Whether it was the artist's genuine intention to show the figure in 1880 we will never know, but now the stage was set for the presentation of the following year.

The little ballet dancer went on show at the exhibition of 1881 in her case, surrounded by photographs taken by Degas of various outcasts of society, particularly criminals and the mentally ill. The critics and the public read a context into the issue, and Degas' corner became a kind of artistic contemporary freak show, not unlike the "encyclopaedic" typifications of which the nineteenth century was full. Degas' work with human types can be set alongside Charles Cordier's commissions for the large gallery of races in the Jardin des Plantes — the Paris Zoo — which had been started in the 1860s, and for which the artist's *Jewess from Algiers* was one of the sculptures commissioned (cat. no. 17, fig. 10). Where Degas was regarded as pushing good taste to the limits by choosing the ugly as his theme, Cordier went down well with the critics so many years before. One reason for this was, naturally, that Cordier's way of depicting people was consistent with a well-established typological series of genres which had a didactic end in view. The other reason was that sculptures like the *Jewess* were, quite simply, beautiful, attractive in their materially composed sensuality. It was not sensuality itself which was the problem.

The *Jewess* remains in her ghetto as a depiction of a type first and foremost — the notion of race or hierarchy which lay behind the contingent notion of showing other (implicitly inferior, but exotic and as objects interesting ethnicity) has its own history and here Cordier's work should simply be fitted into a distinct context around surrounding sculpture's opportunities and limitations. The bust of the Jewess became a great success for Cordier when he exhibited at the Salon of 1862 and it was produced in a long series of versions and sizes, often with a male pendant to complete the impression of another world, removed from the Parisian drawing rooms.[29] The work is an assembly of extraordinary virtuosity, with two different patinations of the bronze for the hair and the face and inlayed semiprecious stones for eyes. The glance, which manages to be shy but coquettish at the same time gives the figure even more vitality.

On the other hand, Cordier was not as fortunate when in the following year of 1863, he chose to exhibit a polychrome portrait bust of his benefactor the Empress Eugénie. Paul Mantz wrote in the *Gazette des Beaux-Arts* that the artist had sunk even deeper than the level of waxworks, a scathing criticism, consistent with the view of wax as impure and cheap-sensational struggle for effects. Cordier was also reprimanded for his use in the Empress-bust of both enamel and metal (bronze) which at that time was regarded as the combination of two essentially unrelated materials; it had been acceptable the year before with the *Jewess from Algiers* but there should be a difference between people, in sculpture too.

The debate over polychromy versus white marble had in fact flared up in 1862 when the English sculptor, John Gibson (1790–1866) had exhibited his *Tinted Venus* (modelled in 1851) at the International Exhibition at Crystal Palace in Sydenham, where it provoked great outcry. This was a life-size figure in painted marble, but could hardly be judged shocking by modern standards — and it should not have been in relation to neo-classical standards and customs. It would be difficult to imagine a more Greek theme than Venus with the apple, and the polychromy was confined to the love goddess's golden hair, red lips and a gilding of Paris' apple from the famous beauty contest, which Gibson has placed in Venus' hand. The pose draws substantial inspiration from Canova, and the figure was installed in a pavilion of its own, designed by the architect Owen Jones in the style of a Doric temple. What was perhaps more shocking was that the entire surface of the marble body was coated with a fine layer of wax (probably coloured),[30] creating the illusion of skin — long before Degas had conceived his ballerina. Moreover Degas did the same as Gibson; despite her combination of materials and her non-ideal appearance the artist coated his entire statuette with a thin layer of wax — is it a struggle to bring the figure into a unity (the classical homogeneous surface, a contour inducing uniformity, as in Ingres), or is it an attempt at the ultimate artifice by fixing life through art's own materiality? Gibson went some distance in the opposite direction with his *Venus* when he applied wax to the sculpture to draw it away from the cold of the marble and closer to the "naturalness" of (real) life.

Dancer with Ballet Skirt, Fourteen Years Old remained the only one of Degas' numerous modelled figures to be exhibited in his lifetime, and with the edition of some thirty casts in bronze, the story of this figure's private modern breakthrough is complete. Its modernistic potential is given free rein by mass production whether with few minor variations and in one edition, which made it possible to sell the little girl as a luxury item in a solid, durable, and most of all modern, material, bronze (in the sense that mass production of metal goods is characteristic of the industrial age). But the question is whether sculpture has thus negated some of its own essential character; Degas' own, unique (and thus essentially unmodern) example depended on the reality effects in the selection and combination of his materials so as to be able to function as the artist intended. The complete workability of wax brought what was modelled closer to the skin, bones and skeletal structure in a human being, and silk and tulle introduced a fabric really pendant to the body of the sculpture. A careful colouring in various tones distanced the figure from the classic uniform unity and fixation of contour, and offered, moreover, its own radical solution to the eternal problem of the portrait sculpture: nude or clothed, in "antique" or modern costume — not only was the girl in contemporary dress, effort had been expended to draw attention to the differences in texture in every piece of clothing. Finally the work was crowned with real hair — a real piece of a human being, extrapolated and used in a sculpture of one.

Seen side by side, Degas' and Aizelin's sculptures are both virtuoso works, and both attempt to present reality "sensationally" — in the French meaning of the word in each case. Seen from the perspective of art history, Degas' figure far surpasses Aizelin's in terms of "realism" — marble cannot compete with coloured wax, real hair. The question is whether the demarcation between their respective modes of functioning is extremely fine: the closely interrelated development of the subject and the execution, which should spontaneously support the Mignon figure becomes, in fact, its greatest problem — the material leaves the figure mired in the established order from which it pines for a bygone, better era, towards the ideal world, from which Mignon was banished by Goethe. Degas' ballerina is burdened with no such longing, she is of her time, and that contemporary quality was something which Modernity was quick to identify. Finally it is the dimension of the disturbing which Degas

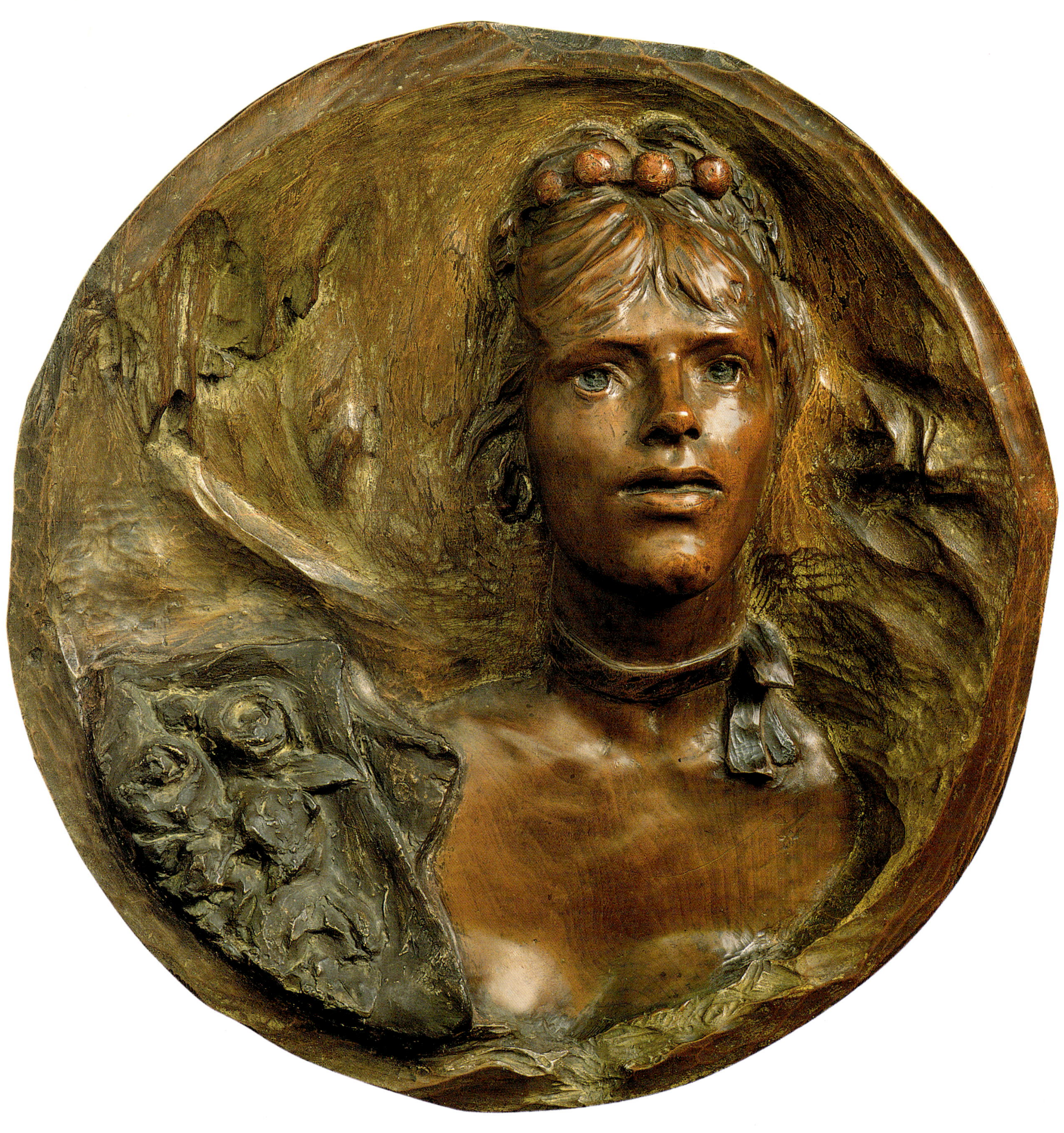

11
Paul Gauguin
Chanteuse, 1880
Mahogany, plaster, paint and gilt, Ø 53 cm
Copenhagen, Ny Carlsberg Glyptotek
(cat. no. 31)

This work is a portrait of a well-known cabaret singer, Valérie Roumy, who was a source of fascination to the Impressionist artists. Gauguin has captured her at the moment she receives the applause of her audience. But the distant expression on her face is in contrast with the atmosphere one associates with the occasion. Gauguin has been more concerned to depict the singer's state of mind than to register what is seen in an "Impressionistic" manner. The work thus strikes the Symbolist tone that Gauguin developed in his later works. *Chanteuse* was included in the Sixth Impressionist Exhibition in 1881, which also featured Degas' *Dancer with Ballet Skirt, Fourteen Years Old* (cat. no. 22, fig. 36).

(quite intentionally, no doubt) presses forward together with his little waxwork, namely the exhibition situation itself. In her bell jar, surrounded by photographs of the outcasts, the body of the ballerina had to come across as contrived and strange, as a specimen in formaldehyde. She shares the fate of Goethe's embalmed Mignon, preserved as a piece of real life, uprooted and exhibited without any such mitigating agency as Aizelin's tinge of idealisation.

The meta-dimension is something the two sculptors have in common, and that is itself a significantly modernistic distinguishing feature. Both sculptures are an attempt to thematise the relationship between realism and the effect of realism, but the effects are put right in the front line by Degas. It was those features which provoked the public disgust. Here, at a stroke, the artist revealed the artificiality of art — something on which Aizelin also drew, even if in *Mignon* he hides behind the virtuoso and the beautiful, from which standpoint it is possible to keep art and reality separate under the banner of the ideal. But the modern potential *is* there: as spectators our first duty is to admire the finish, the mawkish treatment of each armhole and the attention to the details of the dress, we shall be moved to follow the sculptor with our gaze. In this labyrinth we are clear, all at once, why this is Mignon and how her whole story is spun out of Aizelin's sculpture.

This is the crucial difference between Degas' original sculpture in wax and her mass-produced sisters, of which the Glyptotek's example is one.[31] In the bronze editions Degas' ballerina was taken over by the aesthetic of the mass-produced object, which — although the edition was not especially numerous — came to subsequently dominate the passage of the work through the history of art. *Dancer with Ballet Skirt, Fourteen Years Old* is one of the icons of the early Modern, but of all its differences from "the traditional" all that remains in the bronzes is the idea of *the realistic* — this is the result, moreover of the retrospective quality of the various colours in the bronze's patina. That quality which in its day represented the crucial fight between the materials over reality, on both sides of a tradition of sculpture, has been drained from the figure which stands in museums the world over today.

In addition to Degas' ballerina, the public at the same exhibition could experience Paul Gauguin's relief in wood *Chanteuse* (cat. no. 31, fig. 11) carved in mahogany the year before the Sixth Impressionist Exhibition. This work was, inherently, also part of the contemporary debate on polychromy, so that this theme developed together with the new ideas about depicting the everyday, modern life in all its many aspects. *Chanteuse* is one of the earliest examples of the modernistic technique of using a variety of materials, which was later given the term "mixed media", a mixing technique which was first used by Gauguin in this very work.[32] The piece of mahogany is, however, combined with plaster to form the bouquet, probably out of considerations more practical than aesthetic — Gauguin has coloured the plaster in the same brownish red as the rest of the work, i.e. he has not marked the differentiation from the rest of the work — and perhaps, in reality all it is is an attempt to patch up an unsuccessful or difficult part of the sculpture. It has also been suggested that Gauguin may have wanted to work more deeply and with a freer hand on the modelling of the flowers than the wood permitted him.[33] The Danish Gauguin scholar Merete Bodelsen has identified the singer as one Valérie Roumy, a popular cabaret chanteuse, who was also acquainted with Degas, and whom many of the artists of the time had also portrayed (one was J.-L. Forain, in a pastel [ca. 1880] now in the Kgl. Kobberstiksamling, Copenhagen). Degas, Gauguin and Forain knew one another and remained in contact throughout these years, and this typically Impressionist subject held the interest of three. There is therefore a certain connection between the two sculptures, which Degas and Gauguin chose to present to the public in 1881. In any case, Gauguin's work has, as Fonsmark has convincingly demonstrated,[34] only a skin-deep affinity to "the Impressionistic"; it is enough that the subject can be fitted into a modernistically suffused context of the shimmering, high-speed, big city and its life of pleasure, but that which depicts the situation in *Chanteuse* is not the most important thing in the work. The female figure seems rather more introvertedly dreaming or "symbolistic" in the distance her glance creates between what happens around her and her performance — she strikes one as displaced in relation to her simple, exterior reality.

Gauguin became rapidly aware of the signs of crisis in Impressionism, in that it seemed superficial as far as "lived life" was concerned. It is this scepticism over the new painting's eternal landscapes, which emerges from a letter to Pissarro from the late summer of 1881, in which Gauguin grows increasingly irritated over the many landscapes being produced, as if that were the only proper subject for an artist; to him, this behaviour put Impressionism and art in general at risk of the worst fate imaginable to wit, becoming a mass-produced article, with a hackneyed ideal of landscape at the centre of things.[35] In any case the artist was somewhat flattered at the fulsome praise offered by the famous critic Huysmans about his second contribution to the Sixth Impressionist Exhibition of 1881, the large painting *Woman Sewing*, cat. no. 30, fig. 12 which conformed to the Courbet definition of nearness to reality and thus "pure realism" for Huysmans. That it was by no means the inward-looking or literary which had been Gauguin's intention in the picture emerges from his reflections on Huysmans' enthusiasm in another letter to Pissarro, in 1883 (the year Huysmans' review was published): "He understands it only from the literary side, and therefore he can only see them [the Impressionists] through Degas and Rafaëlli Bartholomé and co., *because they paint figures*; the bottom line is, that he is flattered by Naturalism. I am still completely blue in the face from the incense he threw at me, and despite the implicit flattery I can see that *he is solely concerned with the literary aspect of my nude woman, not that of the painterly*".[36] The two sets of italics are mine and should indicate how Gauguin distinguishes between the painterly and the literary content of a painting; in his reality *Woman Sewing* is not a figure painting so much as a painting with a figure in it — Gauguin does not disallow the picture's "literary side", he simply gives it a lower priority in relation to the purely painterly elements. Gauguin was repelled by the attitude to art which regards painting and sculpture as simply the staging of a literary content, whether in the form of the literary naturalism Gauguin detected in Huysmans' piece, or as a one-sided "moral" focus on an everyday story — modern life for good or evil, as a narrative in its own right.

Something in the wording suggests that Gauguin associated the figurative in Degas and his like with this trap or erroneous inference, and that he was angry that the figurative got in the way of the painterly and the experience of that in itself precisely as it applied to his painting of the family servant, sewing on her bed. But what does he mean about the painterly side? Probably the same stuff which was at issue in the chanteuse relief — a strong focus on the decorative elements of figurative art, patterns and complexes in the surface, which all combines to form a unity of considerable expressive power; in such a unity the subject — although recognisable in figurative terms — finds itself in a certain abstraction, which detracts from the purely figurative. Instead of dividing things up into, respectively, expression and content, figure and abstraction, Gauguin seems to strive towards a synthesis in which the extremely outwardly-directed (the decorative, colour/form combination) comes in-

12
Paul Gauguin
Woman Sewing, 1880
Oil on canvas, 114.5 × 79.5 cm
Copenhagen, Ny Carlsberg Glyptotek
(cat. no. 30)

Gauguin's meticulous and realistic depiction of a nude woman sewing is devoid of erotic and "beautifying" undertones. As though she were part of a still-life the woman is given the same status as the other elements of the interior. The public found the work provocative on its first appearance, which was at the Sixth Impressionist Exhibition in 1881. The critics were displeased with the way Gauguin had combined the traditional nude study with the depiction of a scene from everyday life. The author and critic Huysmans was, however, more positive: "... among the artists of today nobody has presented such a powerful impression of reality..."

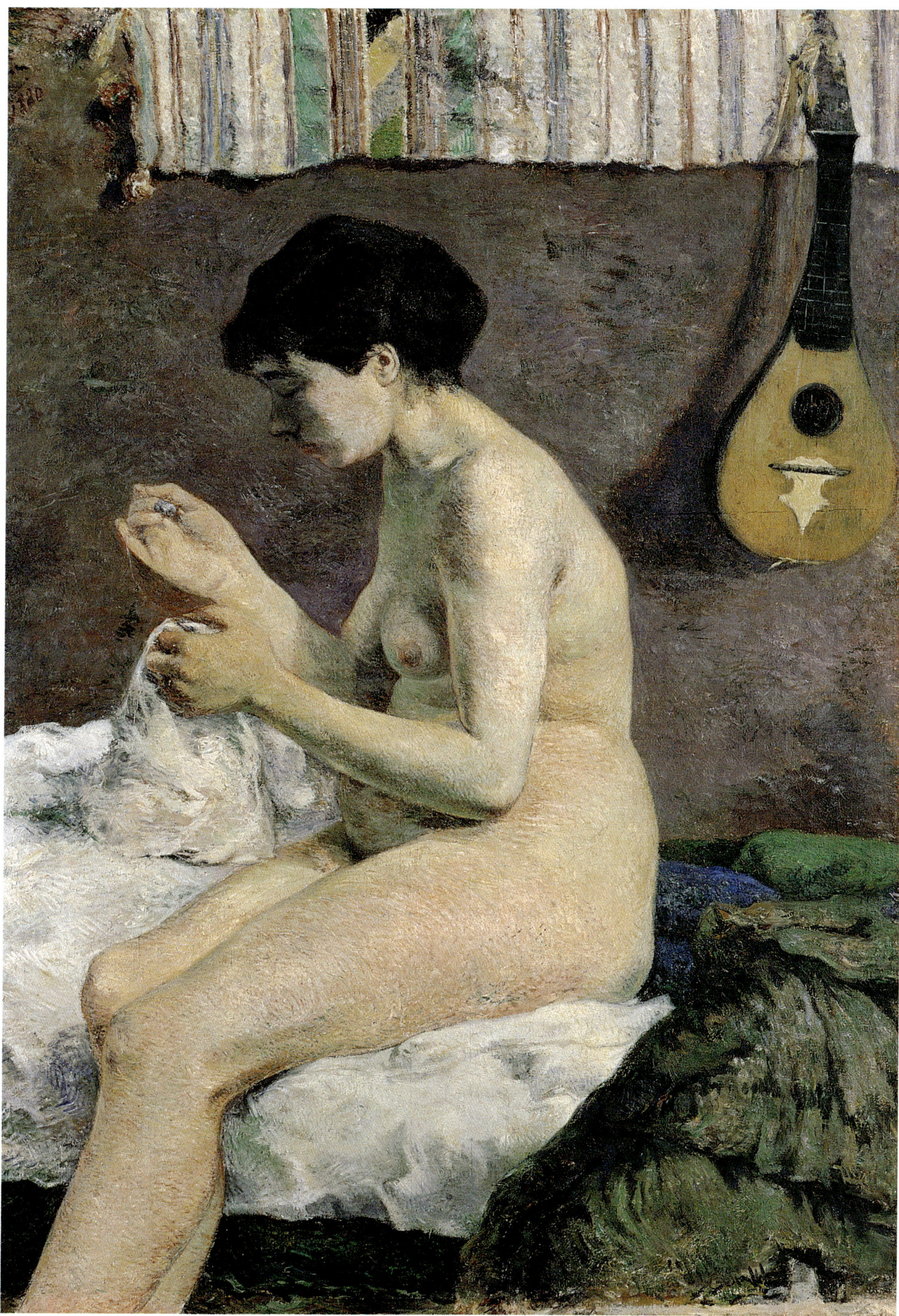

separably together with the inwardly directed (the human soul's primitive, natural or instinct-suffused depths). It is a clear symbolism to come, which is at work here in Gauguin's painting.

Substance and Artifice

The texture of a work of art came to play an increasing role in the art criticism of the nineteenth century — at the beginning, the presence of physicality in a work of art was seen as an indication of aesthetic decline, a decadence. At the Salon of 1857, the critic Maxime du Camp was able to conclude his book-length "review" of the paintings and sculpture in the exhibition with the assertion that "To judge things correctly it is sometimes necessary to sum up one's opinion as if an evil were at hand: supposing fire had utterly destroyed the Salon of 1857, would this have been any loss to art? No. No object exists which cannot be easily reproduced [...] this is a healthy sign, since as long as everyone knows his metier, we have cause to hope that he will settle down to producing art".[37]

To be able to practise one's *métier* was important, but art could only come into existence once the requisite skill was acquired. Du Camp, who was, in addition, to become one of Manet's firm supporters, dismisses in his introduction to that year's Salon all entries by Gustave Courbet. His grounds for this behaviour were that Courbet was merely "a painter", not an *artist*. Art could and must strive for higher things, and not remain content with simply copying and proceeding in a cocksure fashion to paint everything without any higher aspirations — in our age, claims Du Camp, the *métier* is supreme, and the hand is mightier than the spirit. The critic laments the increasing materiality in art, a dangerous tendency to over-emphasise the physical, until it takes over.[38] It is in itself problematic, because an excess of physicality tends to combine with sensuality and thus — once more — moral chaos. The full-bodied colour and the concentration in the drawing are the material out of which the subject must emerge, but even in the romantic notion of art a strict discipline prevails; the material must never subjugate the ideal which art is to express. Courbet is pure material, while, for instance Millet, with his "sublime sense of the objective of art", as Du Camp put it, succeeds in lifting painting above and beyond its basic materiality.

Sensualism is a distinguishing characteristic, not merely of a Salon art of boudoir eroticism, but also, in the widest sense, of the struggles of avant-garde artists. Meanwhile, sensualism steals the entire show. Courbet's triple portrait *Three English Girls at a Window* (ca. 1865, cat. no. 20, fig. 13) is a combination of portrait and Nature Morte, a still life with people — where the main theme is not one of individual or group portraiture at all, but the actual *hair* of the girls, a sensual-erotic motif with which Courbet was almost obsessed. Both in his series of portraits from the same period of a red-haired beauty (e.g. *Portrait de Jo, la belle Irlandaise*, Nationalmuseum Stockholm) and the large *The Source* there are examples of a fetish with red hair — and the latter picture demonstrates a clear debt to a painting with bacchantes and nymphs *(Bacchanal*, Sterling and Francine Clark Art Institute) by none other than Bouguereau, whom the progressive painters otherwise affected to hate. In the Glyptotek's *Three English Girls*, the composition is assembled around the tallest girl's long red hair, which flows down the painting's surface, the back of the chair and the bright red jacket in the centre of the picture. The story of how this picture came to be painted is as follows: in the summer of 1865, Courbet was painting in Trouville, Normandy: in the atelier of his colleague and rival, Alfred Stevens, he met the three daughters of a wealthy Englishman, the wall-paper magnate, John Gerald Potter, who had commissioned Stevens to paint the three girls. Courbet apparently made a great show of wanting to paint them himself, and although he received no official commission to do so,

13
Gustave Courbet
Three English Girls at a Window, 1865
Oil on canvas, 92.5 × 72.5 cm
Copenhagen, Ny Carlsberg Glyptotek
(cat. no. 20)

In several of his paintings, Courbet exhibits a fascination with the sensual qualities of women's hair. The same is also true of this group portrait, where he combines different types of painting: a still life with three girls whose hair undulates towards the observer. The space in the picture is only reproduced summarily with a little sea, a brief expanse of sky and a green-painted shutter. These elements frame the three girls in a network of horizontal and vertical lines. They are caught in a decorative, two-dimensional system in which the preponderance of colour and shape is the central feature. A later owner painted over one of the girls and the dog, possibly because he took issue with Courbet's concept of space.

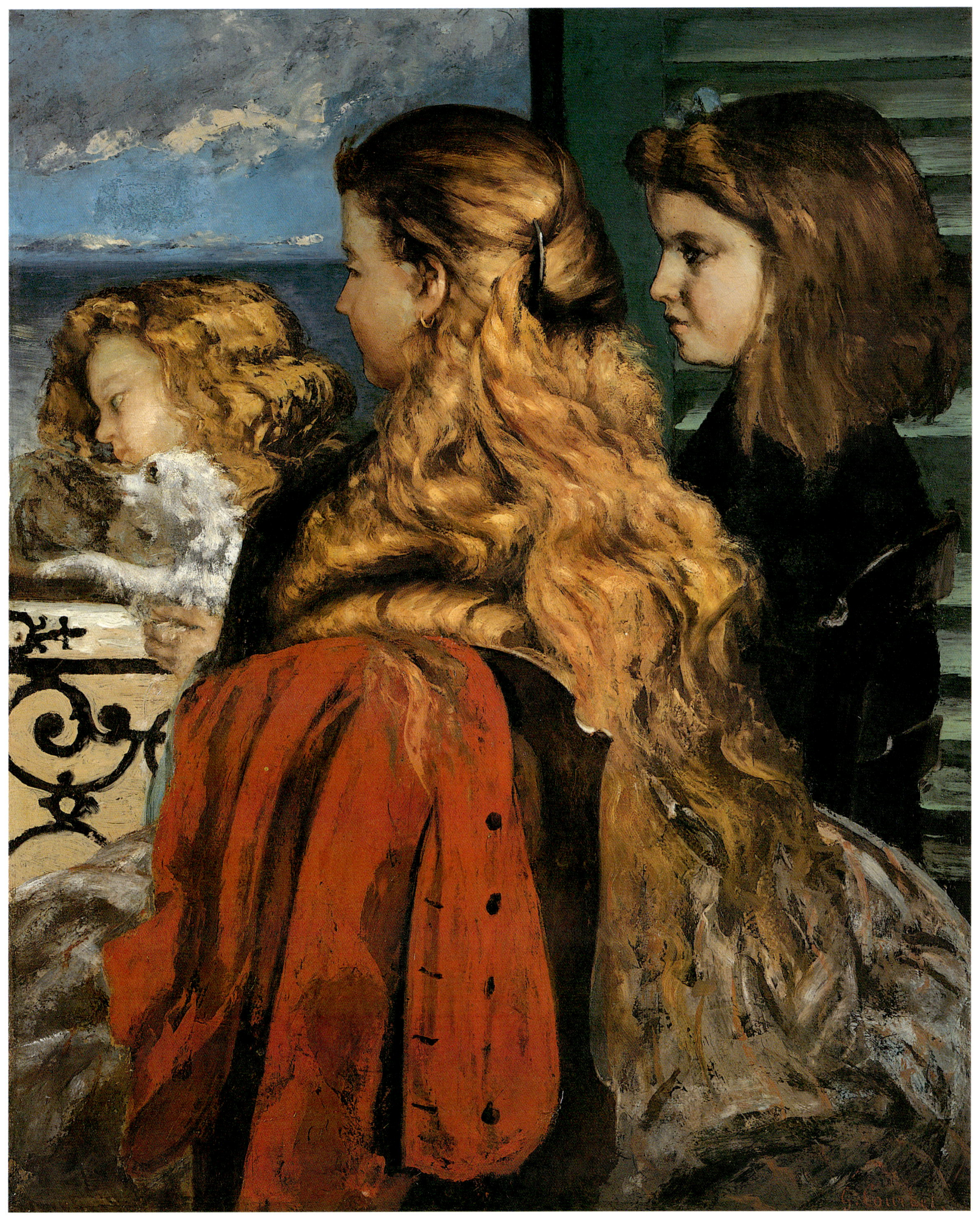

went ahead with his own portrait. It became a fantastic construction: in an extremely summarily rendered picture space with a modicum of sea, a bit of sky and a mighty green-painted shutter, the three girls are seated at an open window, neither inside nor out, or possibly on a balcony, confined within an intricate network of horizontal and vertical lines. They are positioned so that they are lifted up and over each other as though they are set pieces in a puppet theatre. The cast-iron bars are reduced to a flat ornament which seems to prefigure the compositions of Matisse, and together with the shutters has become the decorative frame around the rendering of physical and all too strong sensual phenomena. Hair, skin, fur (notice the small poodle in the arms of the smallest girl), clothes and the almost hypnotic play of the colours themselves are what is at issue here. There is little room for the depiction of human beings in this symphony. The three girls hardly appear in the likeness of human beings at all in this still-life-like picture, where their individuality and whole "humanity" is enclosed in a painterly-sensual space of reflection, which is, above all else, that of the painter — there is therefore nothing surprising about the refusal of the girls' father to have anything to do with the painting when Courbet showed it to him. It remained in the artist's possession until he died in 1879: avant-garde art tends to bury its mistakes.

A concluding, important, part of the painting's story is the fact that for a long time it was known as *Two English Girls at a Window*. In 1931 the then head of the Glyptotek's modern collection, H. Rostrup, discovered that the latest inventory of Courbet's oeuvre (list of works and details of the auction of his possessions after his death) referred, however, to three, rather than two English girls. In the museum's painting there were, however, only two, and no other use of the motif from the hand of the artist was known. From that point it was only a short step to scraping away a little of the top layer of paint to reveal the third girl in the composition, hidden under a bad piece of overpainting in the middle ground to the left, directly above the iron railings (fig. 3, detail). The starkly compromised, abstract picture space obviously gave a former owner the pretext to paint over the head of one of the girls, clear indication that he had taken it upon himself to "correct" the painter's transgression against the accepted theory of perspective. In this way Courbet's triple portrait becomes part of a modernist narrative — the collector's "disfigurement" was all of a piece with the idea that a picture space should conform as closely as possible to space in reality. Seen in that light *Three English Girls* was such a provocative aberration of this that one former owner had decided to put matters right.

Renoir's *Boy with a Cat* (cat. no. 50, fig. 54) is a reflection of the sensuality of the materials themselves. The painting depicts the encounter of skin, hair, fur and silk, all handled with a meticulous regard for each material's individual character and presented as if it were a full-figure portrait in the tradition of the Spanish Baroque. Here the legacy of Manet is clear, perhaps one might even be justified in identifying his *Olympia* (fig. 55) as the prime reference for the boy and cat. The shy, but at the same time self-conscious glance (which also reveals a consciousness of the observer) is the mark of somebody putting himself on exhibition to quite the same degree; the boy's demonstrative affection for his cat thus becomes a clear erotic signal. However, the slender body of the boy is perhaps a disavowal of the professional selling himself which was embodied by Olympia's pose and her entire being on the canvas, and pulls in the direction of the "modernist experiment" with genre, style and material with which both Manet and Renoir were preoccupied at this point in time.

A comparison between Renoir's boy and Gauguin's sewing woman, painted barely twelve years later, shows a marked difference from the afore-mentioned, observing painterliness. Renoir's picture is of a fundamentally different persuasion: moreover in that it was, in itself, unusual to choose a naked boy for a motif in preference to the pure image of the model — and, in addition — to represent the motif in large format — it is clear that Renoir's paramount concern was with the intricate interplay of different sensations of the real, as such an interplay can occur on the canvas. Gauguin lets his gaze, and ours, pass, uninterested, over the woman's nude exterior, inscribed in a decoratively suffused unity, which gives what is seen as a mask of realism — and it is understandable that the artist was less satisfied with Huysmans' positive response, feeling that he himself had also failed in part. As far as the "merciless" ("un-beautiful" or "un-classical" in other words) revelation of the female form and all the social and human connotations of the picture were concerned, at least as the review saw them, Gauguin risked losing a substantial part of his undertaking, namely the "smoothing out" of the figure to the point where it becomes part of the painterly on the same level as reality's dead or inanimate things. This smoothing out was a necessary step on the road to Gauguin's Pont-Aven paintings, and remained central to him.

Throughout this period, however, Renoir was working with a completely different concept of what is seen; the coolness in *Boy with a Cat* derives from the colour, not from any intentional neutrality towards the subject — on the contrary, Renoir seems to have been deeply interested in all of its widely differing elements, which are held together by compositional juxtaposition alone. Gauguin's woman sewing is presented as *observed* (thereby, according to the review "revealed") in her far more natural, homogeneous space than Renoir's nude boy, who so clearly "signals" the composition — and thus, perhaps also a thematisation of tradition in art with Manet as the latest link invoked by Renoir. In *Boy with a Cat*, neither the identity of the boy nor of the commissioner of the work (assuming there was such a person) is known; it stands alone in Renoir's oeuvre, and very little is known about it. As far as the post-*Olympia* element is concerned it is hard to relate to the picture without focusing brutally on its erotic implications, not just the sensuality and the mawkishness generally and literally, but to an even higher degree because of the subject's paedophile connotations; the pose of the boy and his glance which offers for sale a peculiar blend of vulnerability and calculation. Is it perhaps only the painter who gives himself away around the painterly project, not a boy who has self-consciously put himself forward as an object for our inspection?

In this same early period Renoir is involved in establishing his own brand of open-air painting, for whose modernity he strives in company with artists such as Monet: their excursions take them to the large restaurant and functions room "La Grenouillère" on the outskirts of Paris where both of them painted the picturesque and lively encounter of the Parisians on outings with idyllic natural surroundings. The figure — the human body — is naturally subject to a different form of control in the context where the landscape and sensuality go hand in hand around a more superficially fixated painterly vision in the work of Renoir. His *La Grenouillère* from 1869 (cat. no 49, fig. 53) can be reckoned one of the most distinct expressions of early Impressionism — a foretaste of what was to come. The contemporary *Boy with a Cat* departs so forcefully from this undertaking that one might easily believe it was painted by a different artist.

The self-portrait genre enables the artist to concentrate on his own physiognomy and thus shut out the rest of the world; he can focus on the overriding questions of this type of painting — identity, self-analysis and the presentation of oneself. This partial exclusion of literature, mythology and anecdotal narrative

14
Gustave Courbet
The Wounded Man, 1854–55
Oil on canvas, 81.5 × 97.5 cm
Paris, Musée d'Orsay
(cat. no. 19)

Here, Courbet portrays himself dying in a scene suggesting a drama which has taken place immediately before a duel or a suicide. The work can also be interpreted as the portrait of an artist's tormented soul. In this way, Courbet was making himself the subject of the myth of the artist which had been appropriated from Romanticism. The dark colours and the classical composition recall the great portraitists of the Renaissance and the Baroque. The picture was painted immediately before Courbet staged his exhibition *Le Réalisme* in Paris (1855), which was a veritable declaration of war on the Salon.

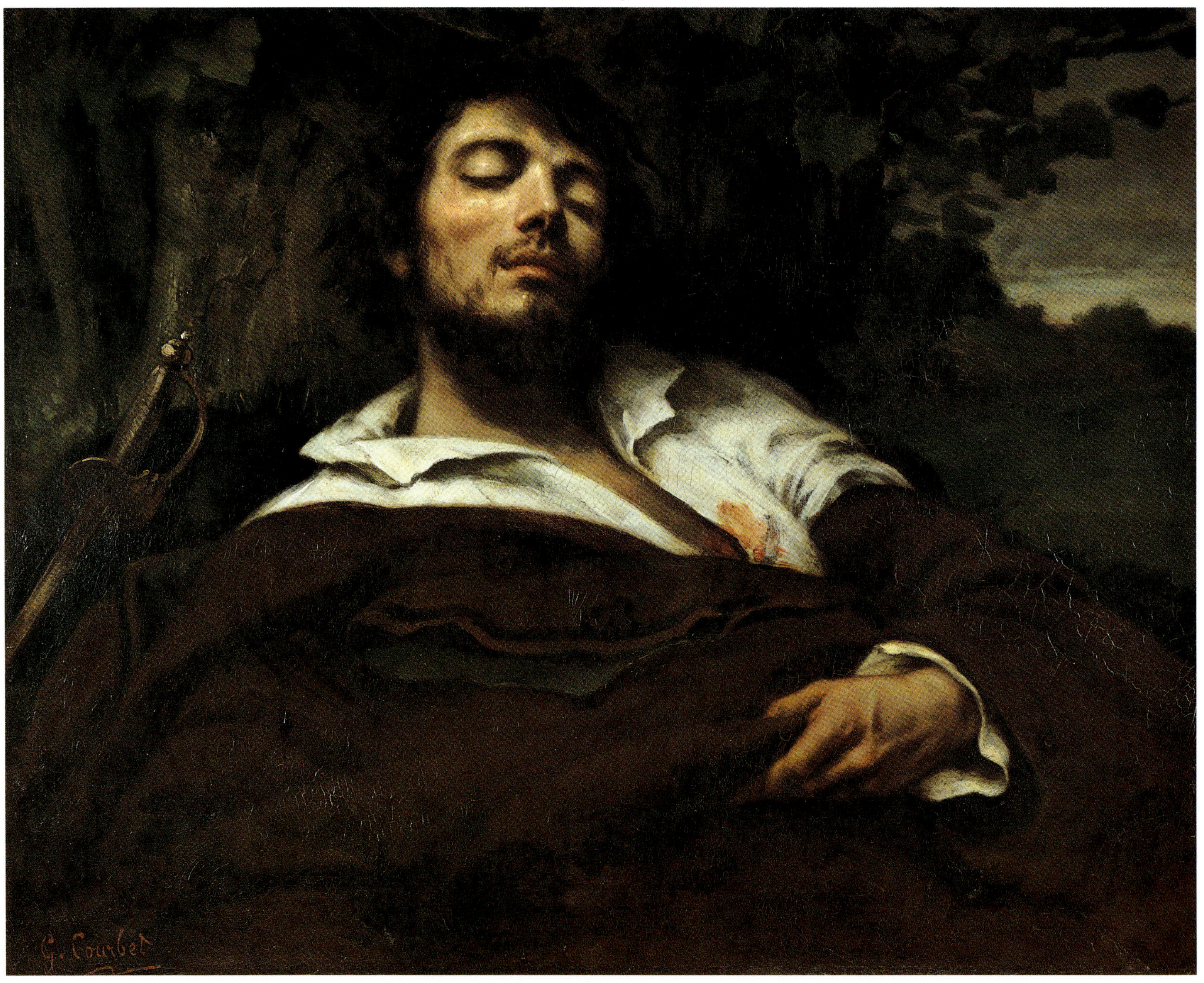

is normally credited to the Modern: therefore, the self-portrait, although as old as art itself has become one of the favourite genres of Modernism. The painter's handling of his material is an important factor in this context. The two Courbet self-portraits shown here were painted at almost exactly the same time as Du Camp made the above observations, but there is a marked difference between the two. The Musée d'Orsay's *Wounded Man* (cat. no. 19, fig. 14) seems to be, chronologically, the earlier of the two, to judge from a "natural" logic of development the painter reconnoitres tradition, paints himself into it and thereby discovers himself and his own independent, "masterly" style. However the dating of the work is uncertain,[39] and Courbet himself was unsure on the occasions in the course of his career when he needed to show it in exhibitions. Be that as it may, the painting was exhibited together with the Glyptotek's self-portrait from 1850–53 (cat. no. 18, fig. 15) and it was probably reworked around 1854–55. Courbet's self-portrait as wounded ("dying" according to the artist), is thematically related to "the Romantic"; the presence of the sword tells a tale of dying for love and/or honour, but the motif can also be interpreted as a portrait of the artist's tormented soul — here Courbet comes very close to Bonnat's sensitive and dreamy self-portrait from 1855, in whose eyes the spectator is invited to cast himself away (cat. no. 6, fig. 16).

The wounded man purely by virtue of his title and the presence of the sword registers the painter — whom we happen to recognise, just as the audience of the time would have — in a form which stylistically draws on tradition (Rembrandt, Titian, Rubens) and, as regards narrative, on a drama, the rest of whose actions lie outside the painting. This picture is pathos-filled, but not pastose; it is thinly glazed as tradition requires, layer upon layer in a creation of an illusion. The second, smaller, but radically truncated painting is purged of all romantic mythomania, but there is no mistaking the self-esteem. Here the painter displays himself in a different role — as a man of the people, in a parallel work to the well-known *Bonjour M. Courbet* (1854, Musée Fabre, Montpellier). Courbet has his shirt open, not in order to proclaim his calling or the stigmata of his feelings, but purely to express his solidarity with the peasantry and nature, the surrounding landscape. The latter is otherwise reduced to a background which manages to be both diffuse in terms of motifs, and at the same time a solidly-painted *verdure*. Now the painter is acting a part, naturally for himself and for the rest of us, without pathos, but in a pastose and densely-painted texture. We are left in no doubt that this is a painted presentation of oneself, and that it is a construction, whose immediacy is very contrived. The tradition is something he makes for himself — via the link with earlier works in the same genre, with himself as the chief protagonist — and its means of presentation, in their turn, entail a result which is unfinished and hasty. The idea of the sketch is mobilised as a very conscious element of style in this respect: it indicates *the new*.

Cézanne's self-portrait from 1885–86 utilises the principle of non-finito in another respect; it is quite possible that the picture is a preliminary study for a more finished, possibly quite intimate, self-portrait with the same characteristics (1886, private collection), but it appears, according to the aesthetic of the sketch, to be finished. Cézanne worked extremely consciously over the issue of finished versus unfinished in his painting, and, after Van Gogh, he is *the* painter of the period who produced the greatest number of self-portraits. The black, penetrating gaze comes across powerfully, and remains the only feature to communicate with the observer, the painter is putting himself up for inspection, an object for his gaze and ours.

What comes across as even more stylistically conscious is the portrait by Carolus-Duran of his friend Manet (cat. no. 9, fig. 17)

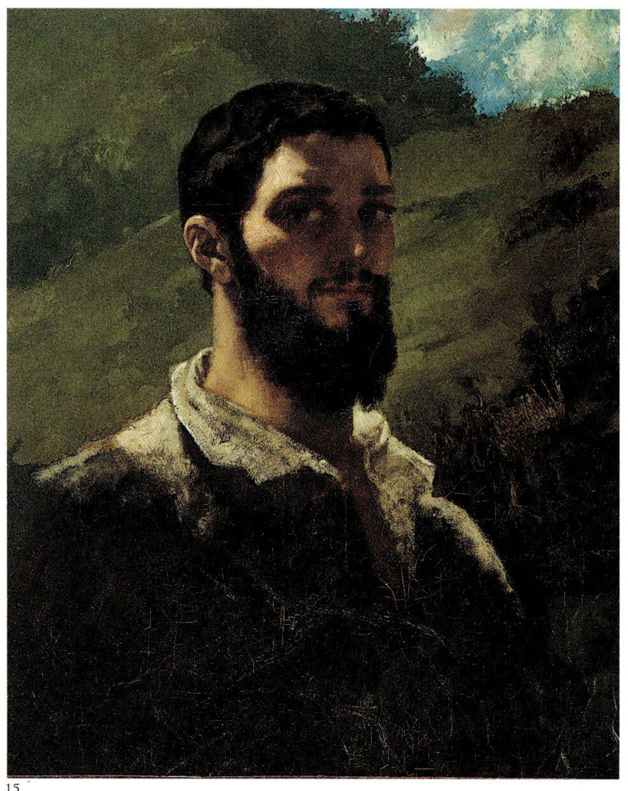

15

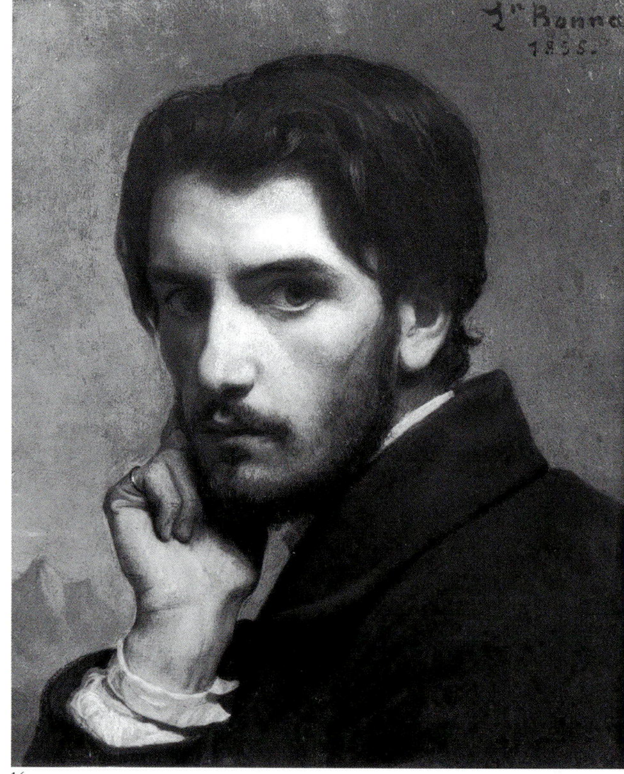

16

15
Gustave Courbet
Self-portrait, ca. 1850–53
Oil on canvas, 71.5 × 59 cm
Copenhagen, Ny Carlsberg Glyptotek
(cat. no. 18)

Like many other artists of the time, Courbet often used himself as his model. He was fond of playing parts in these self-portraits and appeared in various guises and poses. In this work he presents himself as a simple man in shirtsleeves, surrounded by a diffusely rendered landscape. In doing this, Courbet is identifying himself with the people and rural society, which was consistent with his socialist convictions.

16
Léon Bonnat
Self-portrait, 1855
Oil on canvas, 46 × 37.5 cm
Paris, Musée d'Orsay
(cat. no. 6)

This early self-portrait shows Bonnat as a dreamy young man who is shyly meeting the eye of the observer. The sensitive face makes the painter look delicate, almost feminine. The grave, melancholy tone is intended to demonstrate Bonnat's serious artistic temperament. It also testifies to his understanding of the role of the portrait as a character study. The picture shows clear signs of being inspired by Velázquez, whom Bonnat had eagerly copied during his early years in Madrid. But he also acknowledges the legacy from the neo-classicist Ingres. The self-portrait is thus Bonnat's romantically-coloured presentation of himself and his calling, styling himself a direct descendant of the greatest painters in this tradition.

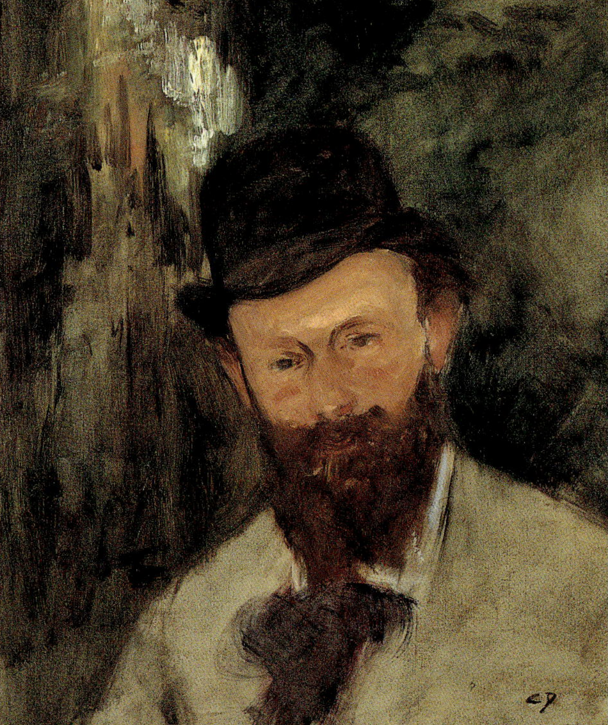

17

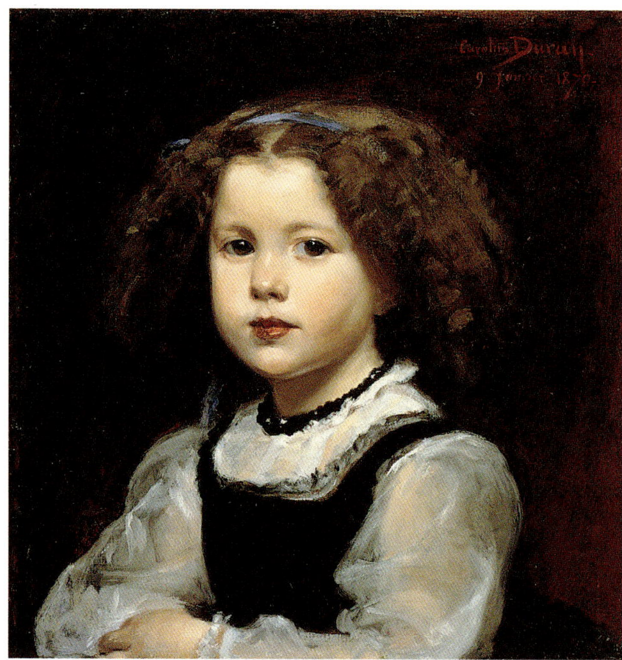

18

17
Emile-Auguste Carolus-Duran
Edouard Manet, 1880
Oil on canvas, 65 × 54 cm
Paris, Musée d'Orsay
(cat. no. 9)

Carolus-Duran was the friend of several Impressionists and moved in the same circles. However, he chose not to take part in their exhibitions and instead tried to become accepted by the Salon. Carolus-Duran adopted some of the Impressionist devices without seriously breaking with the academic idiom. In this portrait of his friend Manet, however, he allowed himself a certain stylistic latitude. By emphasising the sketch-like quality, he was perhaps amusing himself by painting Manet in Manet's own style. The picture was a gift from Carolus-Duran to his artist friend.

18
Emile-Auguste Carolus-Duran
Portrait of a Little Girl in Spanish Costume, 1870
Oil on canvas, 41 × 39 cm
Copenhagen, Ny Carlsberg Glyptotek
(cat. no. 8)

Carolus-Duran knew how to adapt his style of painting to the subject. In the *Portrait of a Little Girl in Spanish Costume* he has drawn inspiration from the Spanish master Velázquez' dark palette and rich use of colour. In portraits of his fellow artists, on the other hand, Carolus-Duran chose a realistic style. In this way, European tradition acted as a painterly repertoire from which the artist could make his own selection. Thus Carolus-Duran could at once permit Velázquez to add lustre to his portrait of a little girl while at the same time paying homage to him as one of the great masters in the history of art, truly deserving to be remembered.

which — despite looking as if it left the painter's hand unfinished — if only by its sketchiness seems to link itself to the character of Manet and the new painting in a peculiar manner. Carolus-Duran was a friend of many of the Impressionists and moved in the same circles as they did, but chose to absent himself from the exhibition circuit. He adopted some of the Impressionist devices but in a constant exchange with the academic language of forms, especially in the genre of portraiture, which was his bread and butter. The small portrait of Manet comes across as almost humorous in its style consciousness — is it really a sketch, or does it only exhibit a tendency towards the sketchy in its portrayal of the very man who to some was the patriarch of the new painting? The latter would, at the same time be a kind of tribute to Manet — to be painted as his own "children" would paint him. In any case, with this picture, Carolus-Duran has strayed a considerable distance from his customary path (cf. the *Portrait of a Little Girl in Spanish Costume*, cat. no. 8, fig. 18).

Carolus-Duran's pupil Jacques-Joseph Tissot (1836–1902) was already a known figure in French painting, when in the summer of 1871, he went to London in the immediate aftermath of the Commune. He had already been bought and acclaimed by the French state as far back as 1861, as a 25 year-old, after his debut at the Salon in 1859, and as a medal-winner he was now entitled to bypass their jury and submit work to the Salon directly. *The Meeting of Faust and Marguerite* (cat. no. 59, fig. 19) was one of six paintings exhibited by Tissot at the Salon of 1861 — and one of a total of three pictures at the same exhibition with themes from Goethe's *Faust*. The critical reception was overwhelmingly negative and dwelt on the archaism in Tissot's work as well as the considerable attendant dependence on his former teacher, the romantically inclined history painter, Henri Leys (1815–69); it was not long before Tissot changed his style in the direction of a more historically up-to-date depiction of *la vie moderne* — particularly in his portraits, the genre with which he was primarily involved. Normally he is compared with Alfred Stevens, another of the period's leading portrait painters (see cat. nos. 56–58, figs. 80, 22 and 25), but Tissot is far less traditional and draws on a much wider variety of references in his language of form. It is clear that he remains faithful to the ideals of academic painting. In 1870, with the input he received from the world around him, his art discovered new elements which drew him in the direction of the new painting.

The English capital and its artistic life appealed to Tissot: by the 1860s he had already been in London several times, probably first in connection with his participation in an exhibition at the Royal Academy in 1864.[40] Tissot's return to England in 1871 was a success, and he subsequently divided his time between Paris and London. He now devoted his energies to painting prominent citizens and works with anecdotal figures, sporting such titles as *Waiting for the Ferry* and *London Visitors*. The French critic, Edmond de Goncourt, made the following perceptive comment summing up the painter's character and life-styles: "this ingenious exploiter of English idiocy, was it not his idea to have a studio with a waiting room where, at all times, there is iced champagne at the disposal of visitors [...]?"[41] Goncourt talked somewhat differently when among Tissot's friends and in 1881–82 commissioned him to illustrate his novel *Renée Mauperin*, a project which suited Tissot's fashionable style admirably.

Goncourt was also capable of summoning up the Baudelairean vitriol as in the following description (which is partly in admiration) of his friend Tissot: "this complex being, a blend of mysticism and phoniness, laboriously intelligent in spite of an unintelligent skull and the eyes of a dead fish, passionate, finding every two or three years a

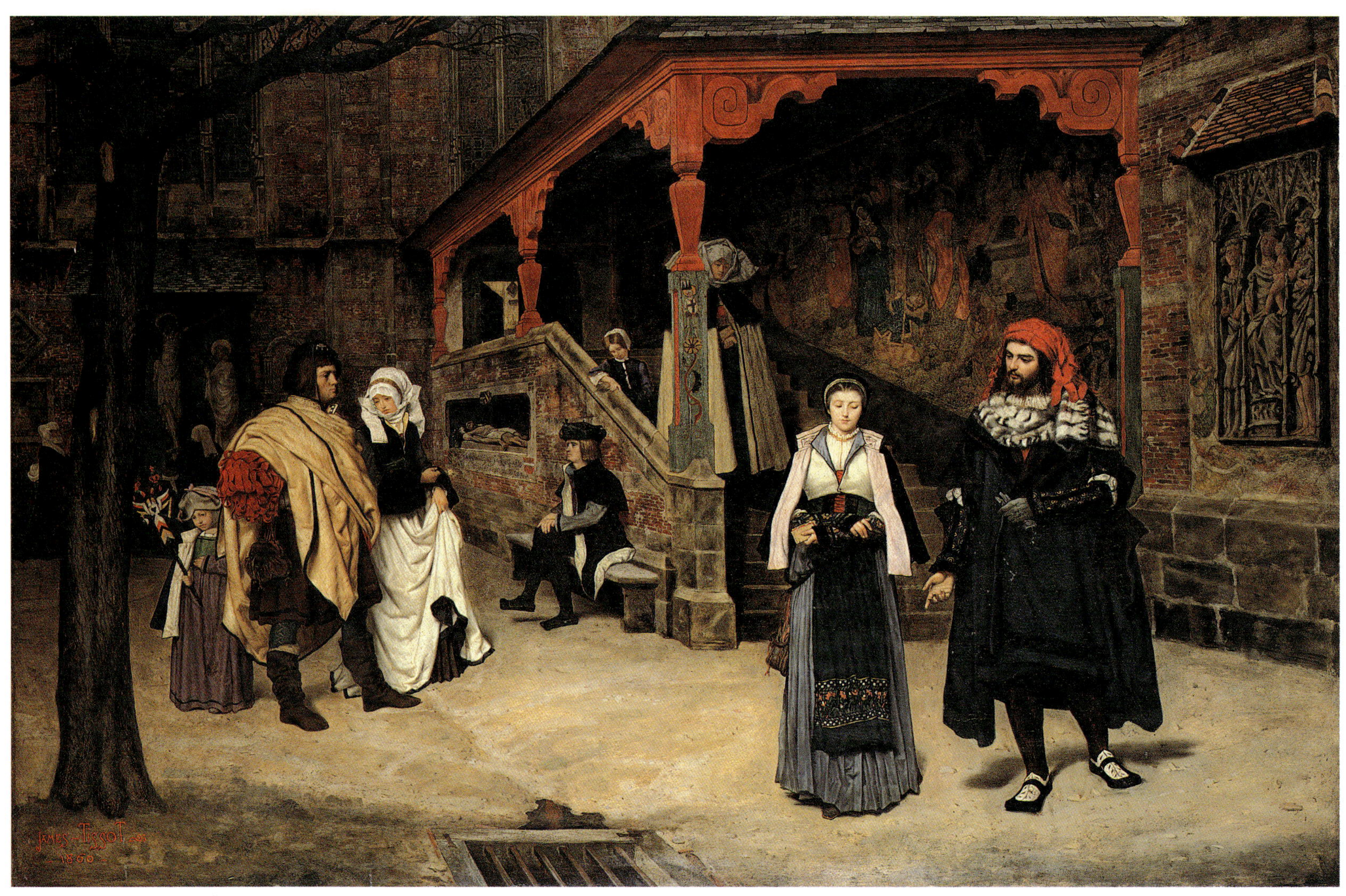

new *appassionnement*, with which he contracts a new short lease on his life".[42] (Note the undertones of "phrenology"!) Here Tissot is indirectly credited with all the attributes which had come to be associated with bohemianism, and, combined with the previous Goncourt commentary, this constitutes a portrait of an artist who knew his way around and a virtuoso juggler with technique and effects. A dandy, bon-vivant and a bit of a swindler — in *Chrysanthemums* (cat. no. 60, fig. 20), Tissot moves in the direction of the Modern in a way which might have caught the attention of the avant-garde.

The picture was executed in the English capital around 1874–75, i.e. roughly contemporary with the First Impressionist Exhibition, during a period of the artist's life when he was fascinated by the work currently being done by Manet; the two artists were together in Venice during these years and Tissot bought Manet's *Venice Bleu*, painted during their stay.[43] Courbet also attracted Tissot and several of the female portraits, for which he was best known in his time, make clear reference to Courbet's portraits of women — whether depicted alone or in a group. Tissot had probably met Degas as early as around 1858 in Flandrin's atelier at the Louvre and the Impressionist was later to paint Tissot's portrait (Metropolitan Museum of Art, New York). It was also Degas who, in a long letter to Tissot, challenged him to participate in the First Impressionist Exhibition in 1874 — an invitation which Tissot declined. Despite close friendships with many of the avant-garde painters he stubbornly abstained from the forum of their exhibitions.

left
19
Jacques-Joseph Tissot
The Meeting of Faust and Marguerite, 1860
Oil on canvas, 78 × 117 cm
Paris, Musée d'Orsay
(cat. no. 59)

The motif is taken from Goethe's literary classic *Faust*, which enjoyed great popularity at the time. Painters were looking to literature to find new themes in a period when figurative art found itself in the doldrums in the wake of Neo-Classicism. The Faust legend, however, was by now a somewhat hackneyed subject. Marguerite had been portrayed so often that one author termed her "the eternal, banal victim of the painters of our time". But Tissot tried to imbue the motif with a special original quality by drawing on a Nordic medieval tradition. This brought him success when the painting was exhibited at the Salon of 1861, and on that occasion it was bought by the French state.

20
Jacques-Joseph Tissot
Chrysanthemums, ca. 1874–75
Oil on canvas, 118.4 × 76.4 cm
Massachusetts, Sterling and Francine Clark Art Institute
(cat. no. 60)

In this work Tissot seems to have fused his fascination for contemporary life with that of photography and Japanese art. The woman's leaning body is caught in the moment, as in a photographic snapshot. However, this effect is competing with the decorative and nature-morte-like rendering of the flowers, inspired by Japanese art. The overall dynamic tension is stressed by the considerable difference between the degrees of sharpness in the painting. This "modernist" awareness of his medium shows Tissot as a painter intent on the possibilities of depicting modern life. In fact, his friend, Degas, encouraged him to participate in the First Impressionist Exhibition. But Tissot declined and was to "stay clear" of the narrow circle of Impressionists.

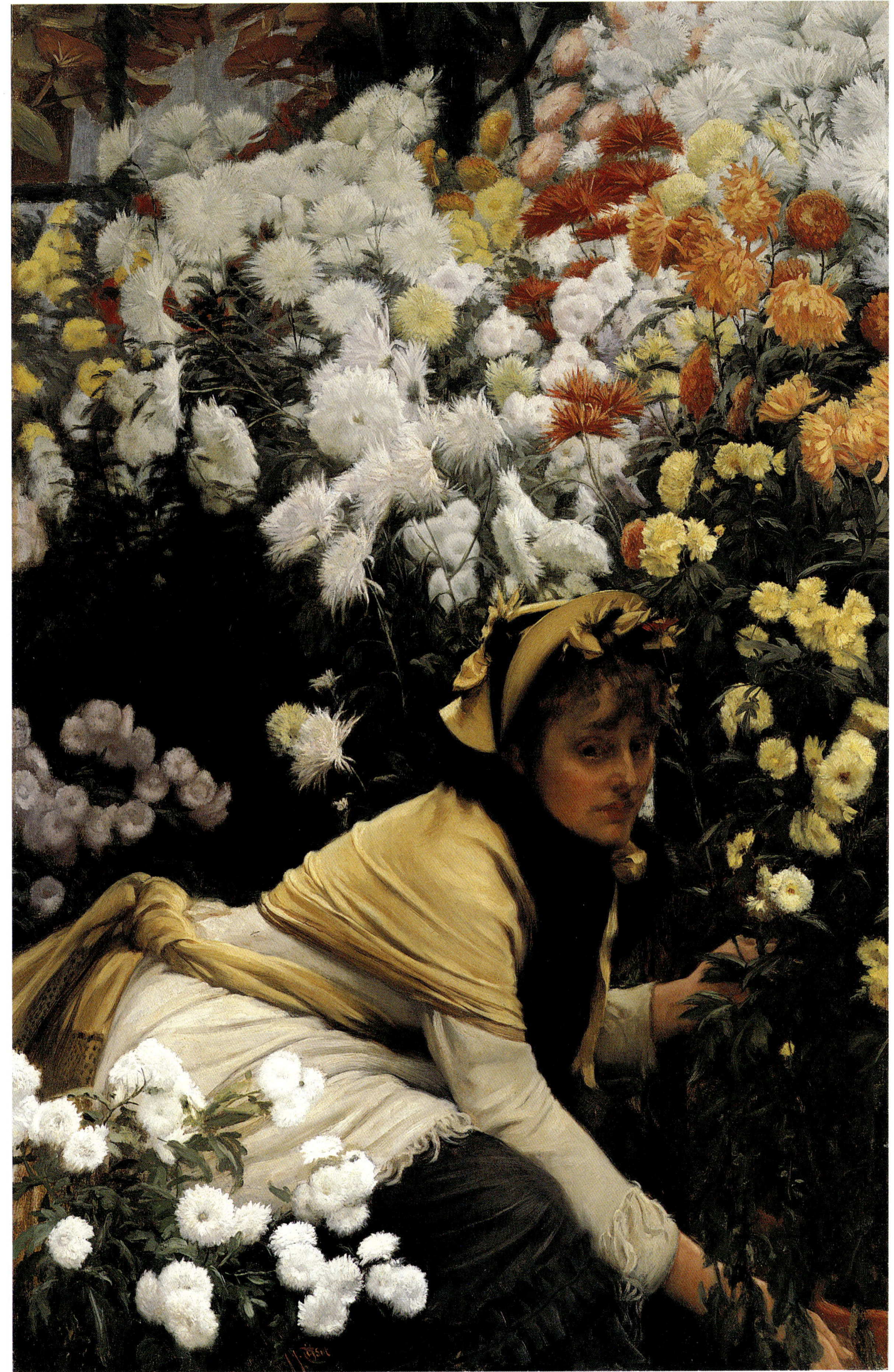

Taking *Chrysanthemums* as a point of departure, it is possible to say that Tissot would rather have devoted himself to his own mode of examination of the range of "modern" optical and painterly aspects than do so in the manner advocated by groups of painters such as the Impressionists. It may also have been the case that the events during the Commune had the effect of making Tissot want to distance himself from a group of artists who, in the eyes of many, were synonymous with the uprising — even though far from all of them had participated in the fighting. Tissot had to remember that he already had a reputation as a painter, and this may have influenced his distance from the group. But it did not mean that he was not interested in artistic questions; like Degas and Monet, Tissot was fascinated by Japanese woodcuts, of which he had a collection, and he was one of the first to discover the possibilities of perspective and composition they offered. The decorative effects, achieved with sparse painterly methods certainly appealed to him.

Chrysanthemums is thus closely related to both Japanese woodcuts and "modern life" as well as photography. The remaining third of the picture bears witness to the Japonising element, just as the picture's dramatic zigzag line from the ornamental group of flowers in the lower-left corner above the thigh and the back of the kneeling woman to the fully-unfolded chrysanthemum blossoms over her head stands in debt to Japanese art's principles of composition.

Tissot seems to be intensely preoccupied with the relation between surface and depth; there is a considerable difference in sharpness in the picture — the blossoms vibrate against each other in a way impossible for the painter's gaze (and thus, too, that of the spectator) to fix them on the surface in uniformity and bring them into focus. Steven Kern[44] has drawn particular attention to the white blossoms immediately above the woman's hat band as markedly heterodox or unfocused in their rendition; the grainy character of these is consistent with the rendition of the woman's face, which Tissot has chosen to show with the unfocused quality one associates with a snapshot. This creates the impression that by a sudden turn of the head towards someone coming into the greenhouse, the woman has disrupted the tranquillity of the situation. This feature of the picture introduces a pronounced photographic dimension; the woman has been assigned a position somewhere between being observed and observing, where the composition is sundered by nothing less than the glance of both the artist and ourselves. It is a relation of substantial complexity between reality and artifice. Here we see the incursion of the decorative (reinforced by Japonism), but everything which has to do with the two-dimensionality of the surface is held in check by the photographic depth of perspective, which, at the same time, gives the picture its animated momentary and portraitly character.

Photography turned out to be the device of which Tissot made most use, and a series of his figure compositions from the mid 1870s were directly linked to photographs, taken either by the artist himself (occasionally with himself as one of the figures, taken with a time release) or by professionals, paid for the work; his English girlfriend Mrs. Newton, with her two children by her first marriage, thus appears in a picture in an arranged composition, where the artist is given a prominent place — it was this grouping which became Tissot's painting *Waiting for the Ferry* (private collection, United States).[45] Mrs. Newton, a divorcee who became Tissot's wife in 1879, died in 1882, still only 28. She frequently modelled for the artist — and it is perhaps she who posed for the girl in the greenhouse in *Chrysanthemums*.

Tissot's *Chrysanthemums* may have an anecdotal or symbolic content — this particular flower blooms in the autumn, and is, in addition, often seen in churchyards, and the woman's slightly shy — perhaps even submissive — glance has prompted a tentative

21
Jules Bastien-Lepage
The Beggar, 1880
Oil on canvas,
193.5 × 180.5 cm
Copenhagen, Ny Carlsberg Glyptotek
(cat. no. 3)

Here, Bastien-Lepage portrays a meeting between the secure middle class and one of the outcasts of contemporary society: a little girl is nervously shutting the door after a beggar. The most expressive parts of the motif are represented with great attention to detail, while other areas are more sketch-like. Bastien-Lepage has thereby united the academic manner of painting with a technique inspired by the Impressionists. When the work was exhibited in the 1881 Salon it received applause and was praised as "... a fantastic piece of realism".

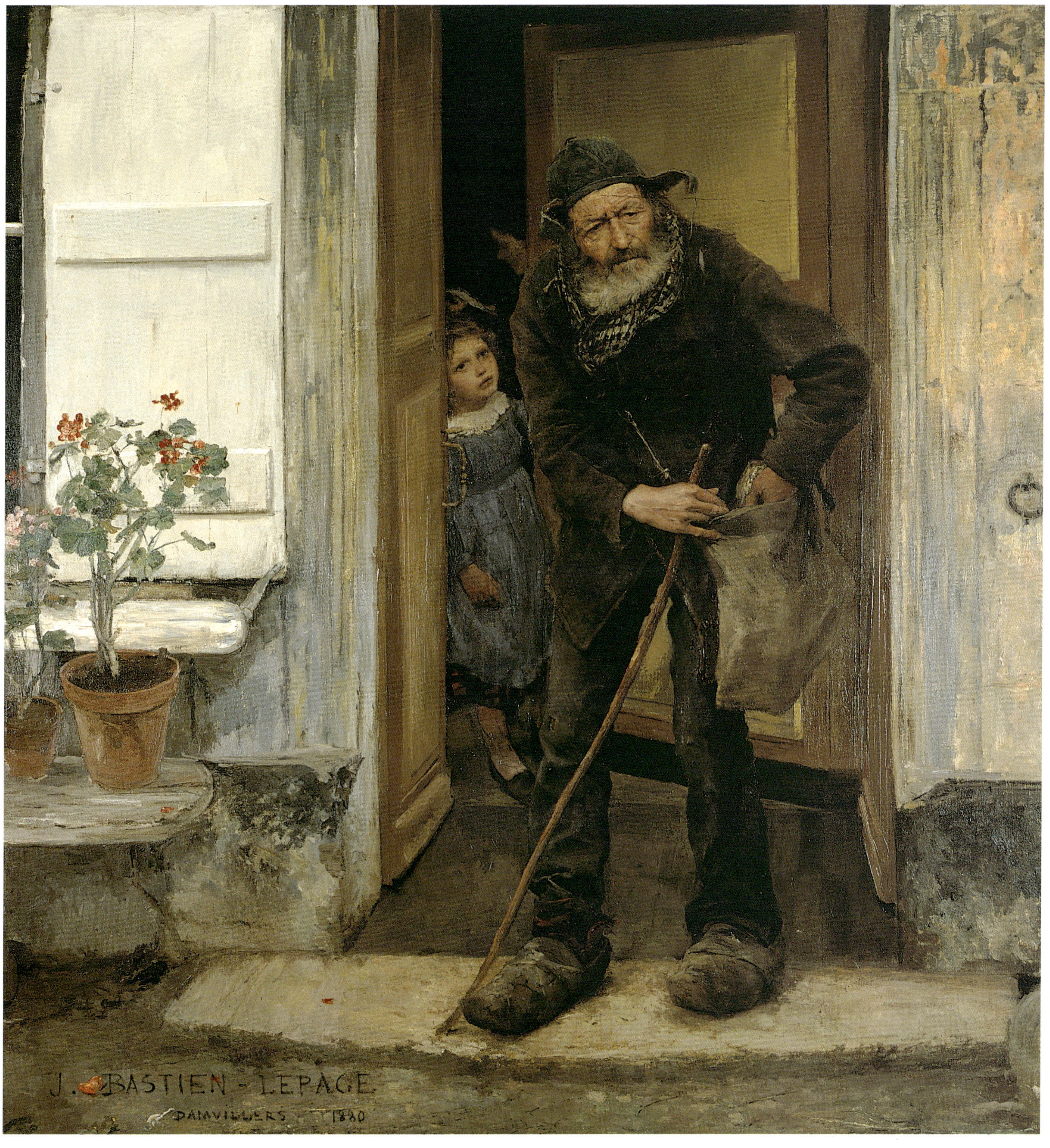
J. BASTIEN - LEPAGE
DAMVILLERS 1880

interpretation in the direction of the melancholy. The deliberate neutrality of the title could however suggest that Tissot has planned his effects with great care; to refer to a quality in his painting — the classification of a flower — without the object one would otherwise regard as the most important in this portrait (for the picture is *also* a portrait), can pull the spectator in both directions — both towards a symbolic interpretation of the meaning of the flower in a human context (autumn, death), but also towards a down-to-earth arrangement of flowers, another kind of "death", which one finds in still lifes. Zerner has expressed surprise that Tissot never explored that genre in his painting, and the same point could be made vis-à-vis landscapes — they only ever appear in contexts where figure painting is the foundation of the work.

Most of all, perhaps because of their "arranged" quality, chrysanthemums are associated with the work of art *past and present*. Most clearly prevalent in this picture are the "modernistic" elements, which demonstrate that a more contemporary depiction of life and reality in painting was a preoccupation which extended beyond the immediate circle of the Impressionists. In Tissot's work everyday life receives a totally different tone than the one given it by genre painting of street people, a variety of art which throve at the Salons of this period, despite the fact that there can be no doubt that what was being produced was not real Impressionist painting. But the picture contained an extremely calculated (and thereby modern?) intensification of the painting's power of utterance as it relates to photography and tendencies to "Japonising". Here we see the effortless meeting of Modernity and Tradition, by virtue of the artist's clear awareness of the means of painting.

The artists of the period had significantly varied concepts of "the outcast". Manet made his tramp in *The Absinthe Drinker* the object of an art historical masquerade with references to the Spanish Baroque (Velázquez, Ribera), while Bastien-Lepage made *The Beggar* (cat. no. 3, fig. 21) a piece of sentimental-romantic genre work, which quite clearly depicts a scene from contemporary life, but one in which the realism is mostly concentrated in the care with which it is painted. Manet's *Absinthe Drinker* (cat. no. 40, fig. 49) is modern in the sense that the realism seems to lie in the painter's attitude to his subject. It is a piece of harsh reality which might otherwise feature in painting only as part of a genre work (of the "poor, carefree gypsies" variety or something like that) or as a result of a consciously articulated moral standpoint — a warning of how one can go astray in life if one does not keep to the straight and narrow. Manet steps outside this tradition but he presents his subject in another, more "painterly", style, i.e. that of the Spanish Baroque portrait. This was ignored at the time: the general reaction of the public prevented them from noticing such a detail, bemused as they were by the mode of painting itself. There was the picture's "singularity"; people were confused because the various elements did not seem cohesive: they were also sketchily "loose" in execution. Posterity was to see art history appreciate Manet's realism as the most realistic, precisely because it is primarily to be found on the "painterly" level, while in the work of Bastien-Lepage it is still embodied in the sentimental. This hierarchy of development is perhaps an unsuitable device to characterise the complex circumstances attendant on "Realism" in the nineteenth century. Lepage's *Beggar* is a much later work than Manet's *Drinker*, but despite it being typical of a long tradition in Salon genre painting, not all contemporary progressive forces would have categorised such works as reactionary according to any self-respecting idea of the avant-garde in art. These circumstances are reflected in the story of the acquisition of *The Beggar*. The Glyptotek's founder, Carl Jacobsen (1842–1914) bought the large Lepage picture through P.S. Krøyer — one of the Danish artists we tend to see as related to the Impressionists — in 1888. Jacobsen, however would hardly have characterised them in such terms, hating as he did the Impressionists, whose style he regarded as ugly and mannered. Lepage's influence was to create a school for a whole series of Danish artists (one of whom was L.A. Ring) principally through the agency of Krøyer, who brought the Frenchman fame in Denmark as the man who continued and furthered the development of Impressionism — a point of view hardly reconcilable with either Impressionism or Bastien-Lepage's artistic endeavours. How could Krøyer from his vantage point in time make out Bastien-Lepage as a painterly successor to and perfecter of impressionistic ideals?

Perhaps his point of view holds precisely the same critical notion regarding Impressionism's superficiality or outwardness in its themes and subjects that Gauguin was voicing in the same period — Krøyer, who had been taught by Bonnat, had been inside French painting and had drawn on both the academically virtuoso and Impressionism in his own work, but may have been interested in a greater variety of attitudes to a painter's theme and role than he had yet found anywhere. He never became a Realist in either the unashamedly moralising or the sentimental style, but remained on the safe side of the concentrated symbolism, which was a far, but obvious relation to the style of painting employed by artists such as Bastien-Lepage.

Realism and Realities

There is a certain obstinate inference about the theory of the development of the Modern which haunts even the most sceptical of research: the myth about the popular versus the unpopular. The avant-garde is traditionally seen as an eternally unpopular troublemaker, a mechanism which plays hell with the status quo. The condition of things is automatically seen as something diametrically opposed to the avant-garde, and it becomes a question of attempting to isolate the elements in avant-garde art, which have the most "revolutionary" potential — in other words that place in the new art where *precisely* the new is given its most concentrated expression. By the same token, in a period such as the last quarter of the nineteenth century it has seemed logical to identify the most anti-progressive ("reactionary") elements in the existing culture with the general progress of the bourgeoisie — and the petit-bourgeois in its wake. Baudelaire settled accounts with *la petite bourgeoisie* and the entire political-cultural mendacity of the era but at the same time set this "unavoidable class" on the pedestal of modern life for every real artistic struggle to find the truth about life as it was lived exactly at this point in time ("Combien nous sommes grands et poétiques dans nos cravates et nos bottines vernies", i.e. How grand and poetic we are, in our bowties and laced boots).[46] In a similar way, Daumier lampooned the figures of authority and the bureaucrats in the new power elite, etc. etc. — the history of art has frequently indulged in the uncritical, and systematic appropriation for its own purposes, of far more than whatever there is a reasonable support for in the works of art themselves. Baudelaire can be considered to have been correct in as far as there is an intimate connection between the new middle class and the development of modern painting. But an unconditional upgrading of everything which was not bourgeois in the period 1850–90 tying it too narrowly to the new movements in art is problematic; some of the way this holds — many of the artists associated with the new painting exhibited a definite solidarity with the non-bourgeois element of humanity — the peasants, the workers, the outcasts, but just as many obviously regarded the "outcasts" simply as good material; it could become a cause in itself to focus on the negative side of life (a good, romantic piece of genre work, such as Delac-

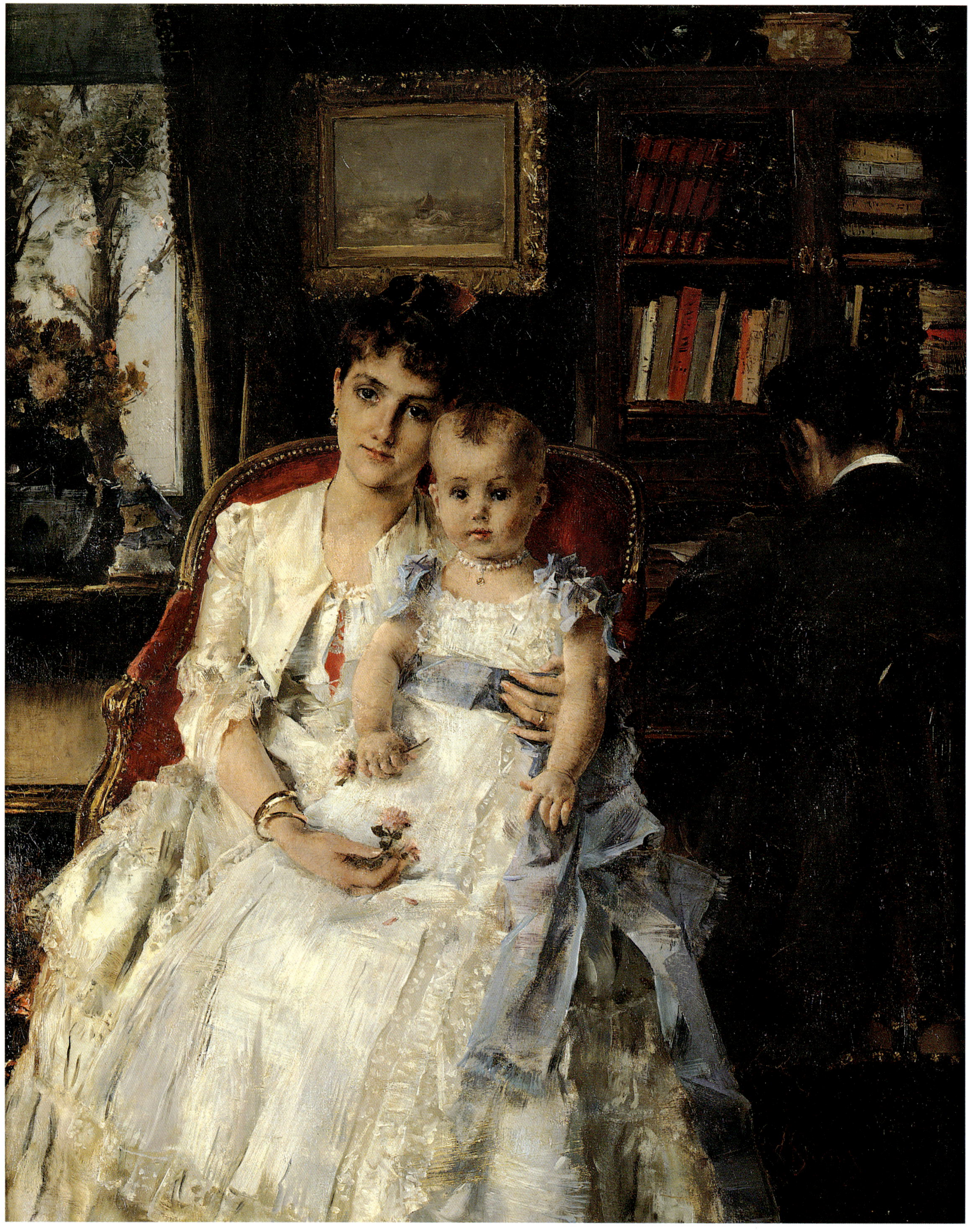

22
Alfred Stevens
The Joys of Family Life,
ca. 1900
Oil on canvas, 65.5 × 51.5 cm
Paris, Musée d'Orsay
(cat. no. 57)

The popular Salon painter Alfred Stevens here presents an idyllic family scene. Mother and child are introduced, and seem to radiate the complacency associated with comfortable bourgeois life. Though Stevens in this case has employed Impressionist techniques, i.e. the loose or "free" manner of painting, the total vision is consistent with academic principles giving equal emphasis to each component of the work. Thus the sketch-like element becomes an effect intended to indicate immediacy and realism. The picture demonstrates how short a time elapsed before Impressionist features were appropriated by their "rival", academic painting. In the hands of painters like Stevens, elements from the new painting were easily assimilated into the taste of the day.

roix and Géricault's portraits of the insane), and this luxuriously observing standpoint was not confined to the Bastien-Lepages of the Salon. Degas was only one artist who used the depiction of representatives of the lowest orders of society as a novelty in itself in his art.

Courbet is one of the first to take the realism of the everyday, as seen, for instance in Millet, further, without any literary or moral preamble, and Van Gogh was to elevate poverty to a modernistic state of holiness in his pictures of Dutch peasants and workers.

A comparison between, say, Gauguin's *Woman Sewing* and *The Joys of Family Life* by the celebrated Salon portraitist and rival of Courbet, Alfred Stevens, demonstrates how mastery of the glance and the painting's relation to the observer work together in a "realistic" painting. The Stevens picture is an idyllic depiction of what it is like to have everything; a family scene without discord, where two of the principal people of the household, mother and daughter look out happily at us; they are in complete control of their space — it becomes clear why Courbet's picture of the three English girls could be so provocative in its *otherness*, which rests primarily on the painting's turning away from the game of the idyllic — and it clearly marks out those who are well-to-do. A portrait can be two things: either an expression of the varying degrees of self-consciousness of the subject(s), or an expression of the painter's ambition to show a particular aspect of the human in a definite context. This kind of categorisation lends itself to both of the portraits in question; the sewing woman is shown in a situation, which, at this point in time approaches the genre of the nude study, i.e. an intimate relation between the painter and his model. It could never be a commissioned work, and neither the painter nor the model behave as if it were a chance occurrence — the uniform and consistently meticulous rendering of all the elements in the composition, animate or inanimate bears witness to Gauguin's distanced relation to his subject, an attitude which draws the work closer to still-life painting than to any other genre. The disinterested gaze includes, as implied in connection with the analysis of *Woman Sewing*, some painterly possibilities which a conventional portrait could not provide; Gauguin's large canvas becomes a kind of modern version of Chardin or Vermeer's "intimate world" whether or not the women are dressed, a fixing of the seen in timelessness. Stevens' family scene, on the other hand, has pretensions to the photographic, where the figures pose in a momentary picture — one among many happy moments, here even with the husband and father present, although relegated to the background, where he is at work at his desk. The rapid lightness in execution underlines the fleeting sense of the moment, in which Stevens, in virtuoso mode, puts down the essentials for the success of his sketch as an immediate presentation of happiness. Stevens is late with this vision, seen in a modern perspective, and maybe the work is best characterised as one of several new ways of turning Impressionism in on itself by making it chique — similar elements are at stake in Gervex' portrait of *Madame Valtesse de la Bigne* (cat. no. 34, fig. 23).

A critic is alleged to have said of Impressionism that in its pictures it is always Sunday. There is something fundamentally carefree and unconcerned about these depictions of the landscape, and this is also, of course, a substantial precondition for Impressionism's predominating popularity in the twentieth century. F. Orton has, sharply, and with feigned surprise noted that old Monet at the bottom of his fantastic garden in Giverny never once painted that scene of present reality, which moved past on the railway lines immediately on the other side of the boundary of his property: the endless series of trains carrying troops and supplies to the total destruction of the Western Front.[47] Monet certainly never did so, but perhaps his painting was not as purged of elements of contem-

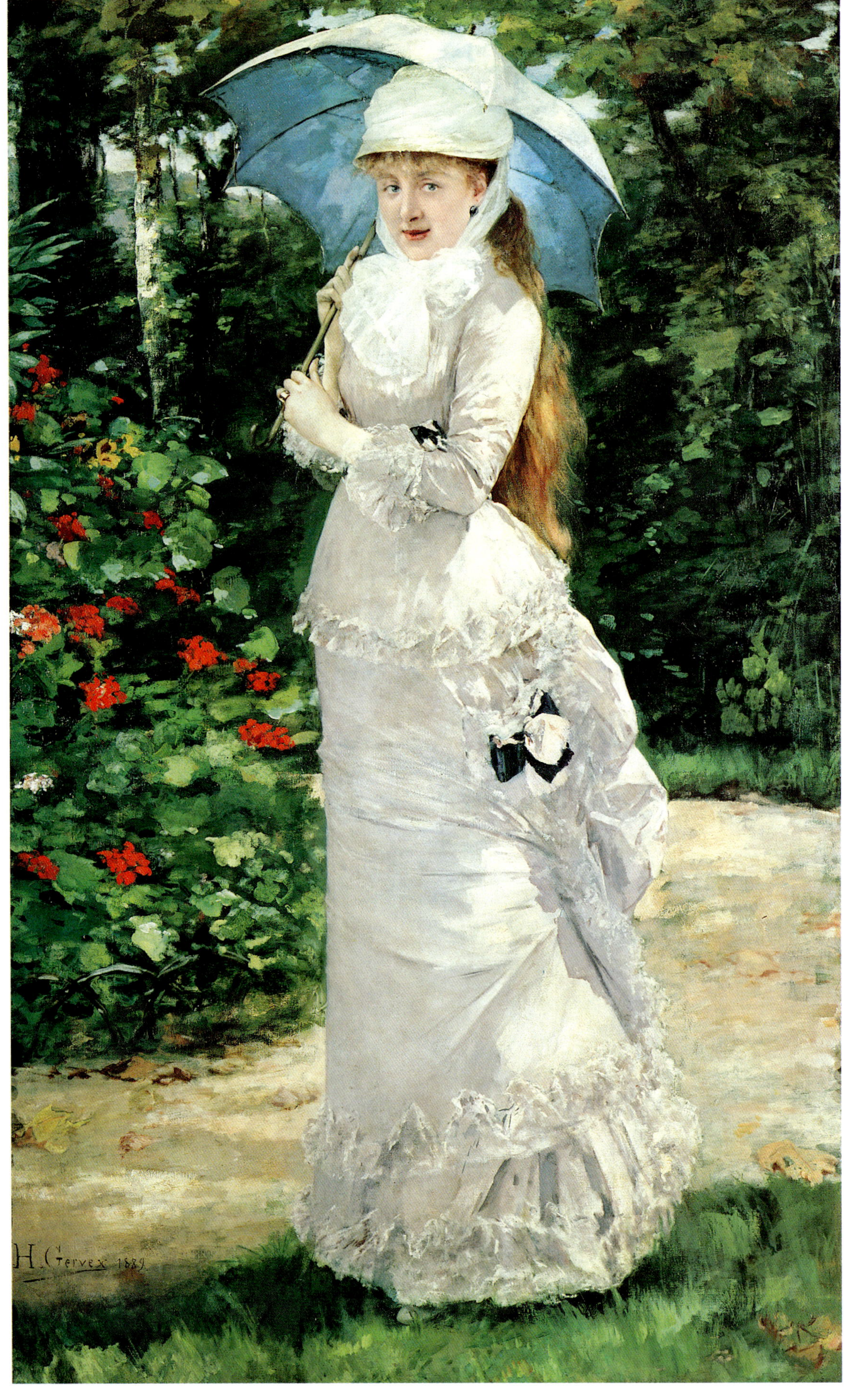

23
Henri Gervex
Madame Valtesse de la Bigne, 1889
Oil on canvas, 200 × 122 cm
Paris, Musée d'Orsay
(cat. no. 34)

The popular Madame de la Bigne held literary salons in which many of the artists and authors of the time participated. Among these was Zola, who chose her as the model for the courtesan, Nana, in the novel of that title. In Gervex' portraits she appears as a member of one of modern life's *demi-mondes*, who for a moment has coquettishly adopted a pose in the surroundings of a park for the benefit of the observer. The detailed reproduction of her face is in contrast to the more impressionistic areas of the painting. This flexibility was typical of Gervex, who adopted various styles in his painting as required. The portrait was given a positive reception in the 1879 Salon.

24
Claude Monet
Windmill and Boats near Zaandam, Holland (1871)
Oil on canvas, 48 × 73.5 cm
Copenhagen, Ny Carlsberg Glyptotek
(cat. no. 47)

Monet spent the years 1870–71 in Holland. While there, he painted a series of pictures of the estuary of the River Zaan. On his return in 1871 his teacher, Boudin, wrote: "Monet has returned from Holland with a series of magnificent pictures. He will undoubtedly come to play a leading role in our movement". Monet's use of the brush in this early work is inspired by Manet, whom he met in 1866 and for whom he had a great admiration. Whereas the left foreground shows an old windmill, the horizon in the right part of the painting appears to be a more modern, industrial area, seen in silhouette. The drifting smoke from the chimneys in the distance is a sign of the new epoch. In this way, the picture can be seen to be dealing with the changes of the modern era.

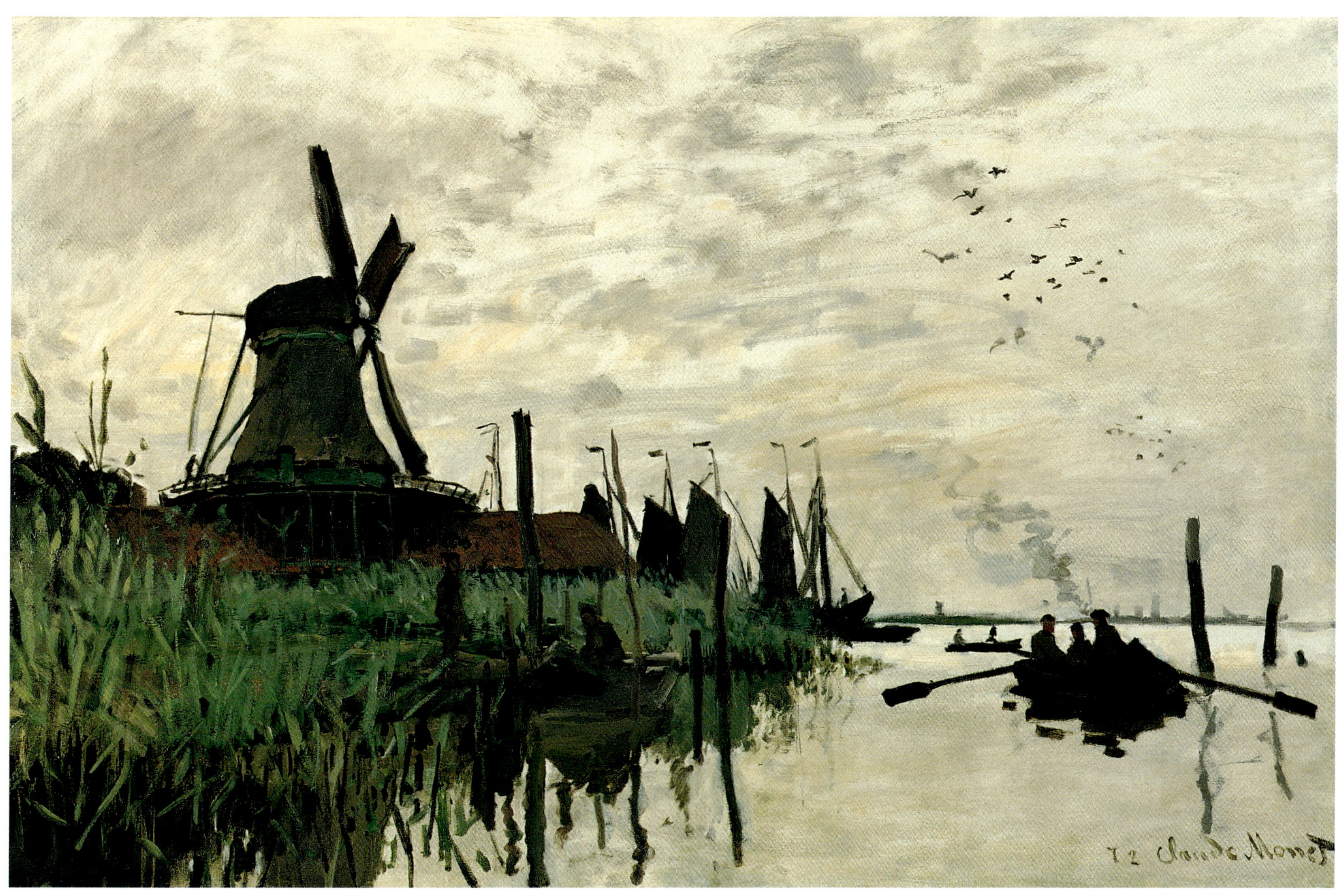

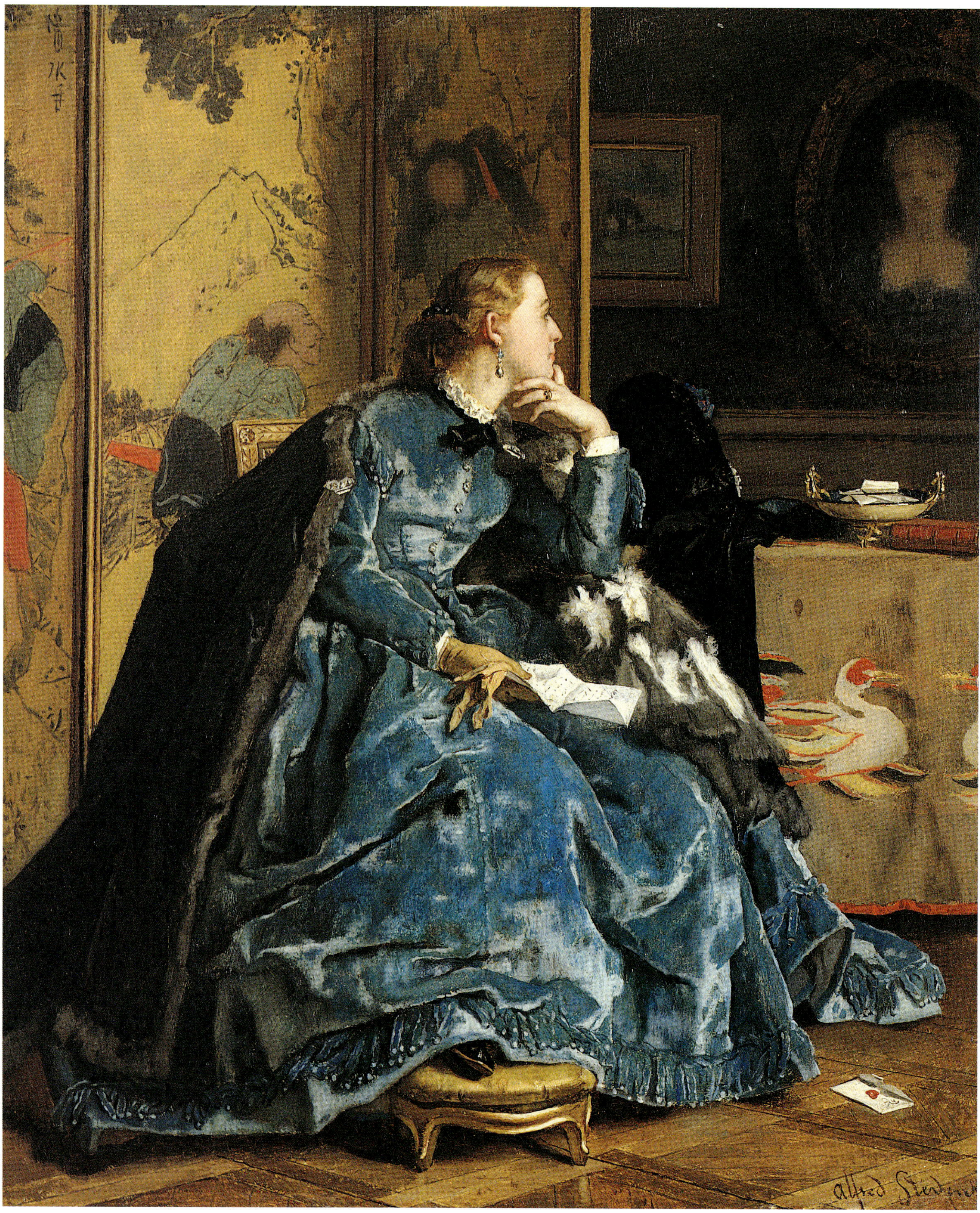

25
Alfred Stevens
The Blue Dress, undated
Oil on panel, 31.9 × 26 cm
Massachusetts, Sterling and Francine Clark Art Institute
(cat. no. 58)

The interest in Asian art and crafts was not solely the province of the Impressionists. Stevens' painting shows that Japonism also made its appearance in Salon painting in its own way. The brightly coloured, but matt, lacquered screen forms an effective contrast to the virtuoso rendering of the woman's shiny dress. In this way the portrait forms a decorative unity, emphasising the dress, rather than the woman: hence the title. Stevens worked between 1880 and 1900 with Japanese-inspired elements both as ornamentation and as an influence on the actual composition of his paintings.

porary social and political reality as one might immediately think. Probably his most famous picture, *Impression: Soleil levant*, the very painting which, the history of art likes to claim, gave Impressionism its name, can thus be interpreted as something more, and other than merely an "empty" landscape painting with its exploration of the meeting of land and sea as its principal theme. P. Hayes Tucker has offered another very interesting and plausible interpretation of this modern icon as an attempt by Monet to make his painting join the throng of voices around 1871–73 exhorting France to rise again, spiritually and morally, following her ignominious defeat at the hands of the Prussians.[48]

This resurrection kept the nation fully occupied on all fronts for the following years. One was thought to have believed that the battle was lost, but now there was a new fight to win. France put every shoulder to the wheel to rise again: the colossal war reparations to Prussia were paid off as early as 1873, and while the reconstruction of both the country and French self-esteem was under way substantial areas of the artistic community rallied round the dithyrambs in honour of the fatherland. There was, once again, a serious demand for official art; historical paintings and monuments to the fallen proliferated (Mercié: *Gloria Victis*, cat. no. 45, fig. 30). The war had prevented any Salon of 1871, but the following year art was to be called upon for spiritual support on a grand scale. Sculpture had — possibly because of its traditional value as a commemorative art-form and its more direct orchestration of the political — the least trouble in catching the spirit of the times, and the subsequent years' French sculpture worked consciously on the mobilisation of French virtues. As regards themes and motifs, this was brought about in close kinship with Classicism's most heroic and pathos-suffused ideas. Conservatism seems to be inherent in such works and their reception. But there was perhaps an additional approach. The subject of the harbour at Le Havre may be Monet's own way of saluting his country and his faith in a resurrection of a prostrate France; it was both the painter's hometown and the place which had directed his earliest years in forays in painting when he had studied with the marine painter Boudin: it was, in addition, one of the nation's most important ports and industrial centres. To a considerable extent it was here that healing and progress on the economic front were thought to be possible, and it was a worthy task for a young painter to depict his country's programme of rebirth — or at least that's Tucker's thesis.[49] He himself sees Monet's choice of the port as a subject more patriotic than uncomplicatedly idyllic. That idea is also consistent with a series of slightly earlier pictures by Monet of harbour and sea subjects, particularly the twenty-odd works which are known from the painter's stay in Holland from 1870–71. In 1987 the Glyptotek acquired one of these, *Windmill and Boats near Zaandam, Holland* (1871) (cat. no. 47, fig. 24) — a painting which both refers back and looks forward within Monet's oeuvre. In 1871 Monet painted more than 10 pictures with windmills and the sea in the rather secluded, friendly seaport area around where the River Zaan flows into the sea. Monet's first mentor, Boudin, who was also an art dealer, wrote, on the homecoming of his pupil at the end of the year, "Monet has returned home from Holland with a series of marvellous paintings. He will doubtless come to play a significant role in our movement".[50] Prophetic — but what was the promise Boudin could have seen in such a picture as this? It is most likely its unconcealed freshness and strength in the tension between the atmospheric in the green reeds, the driving smoke and the quite effortlessly rendered water, against the brown and brick-red hues of the rowing-boat and the mill buildings.

There is in addition a thought in this characteristic Dutch relation of land to water, which is not quite at home in Monet's lat-

26
Pablo Picasso
Spanish Lady in Crinoline, 1901
Oil on wood, 51 × 64 cm
Copenhagen, Ny Carlsberg Glyptotek

In his early years Picasso painted his way through virtually all the Western artistic styles. From 1900 to 1901, he lived, in turn, in Paris, Barcelona and Madrid, drawing extensively in this period on French Impressionism and Post-Impressionism, as demonstrated by this painting from 1901. Later that year, however, he abandoned this style to move in the direction of Symbolism. He thus appropriated from earlier painters whatever he could use. In this way he demonstrated his considerable technical skill and self-confident mastery of the artistic expression of previous eras. Picasso is without doubt the leading figure in Modernism — the brilliant creator with the entire history of art at his command.

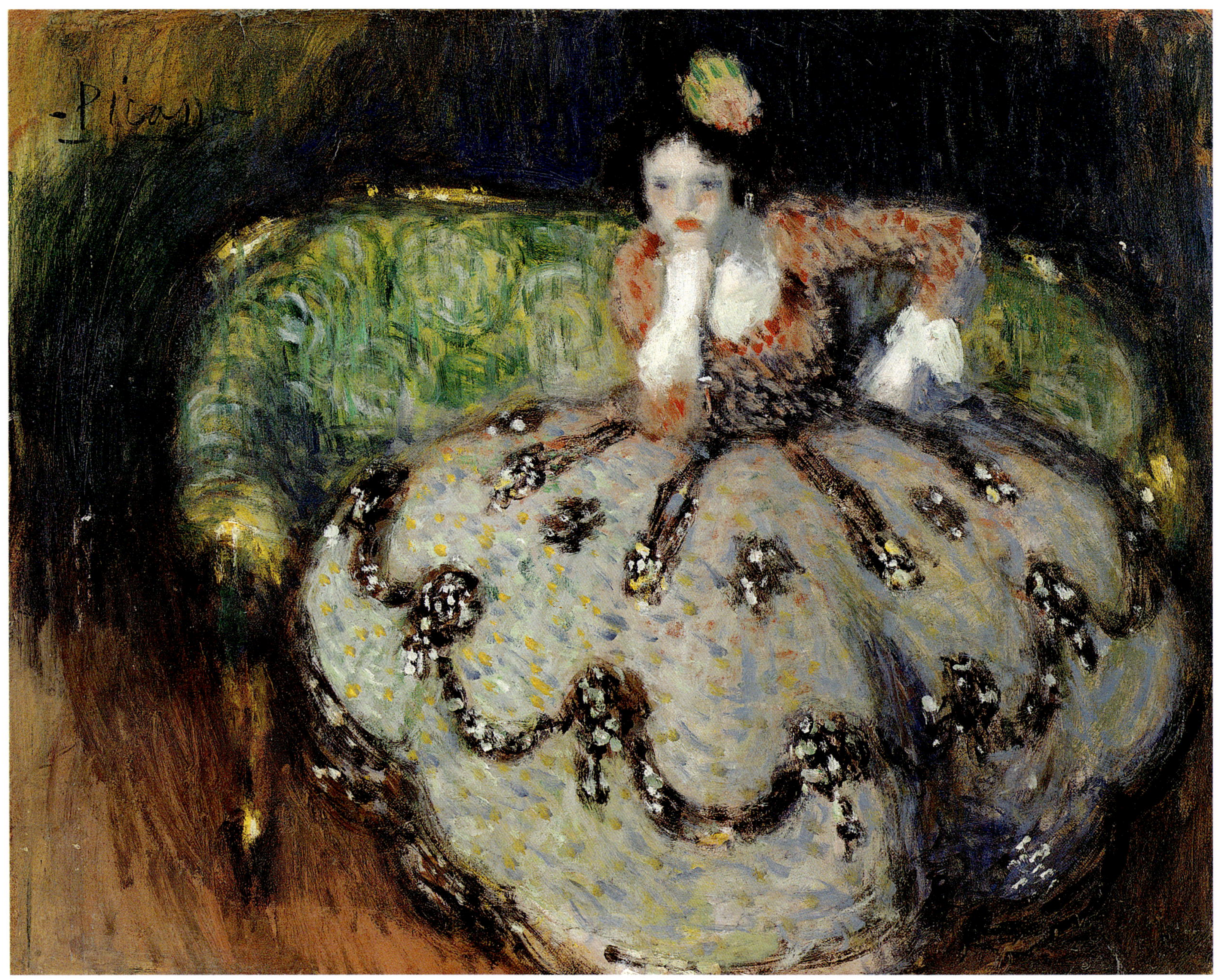

27
Vincent van Gogh
The Sheep-Shearers, 1889
Oil on canvas, 43.5 × 29.5 cm
Amsterdam, Van Gogh
Museum

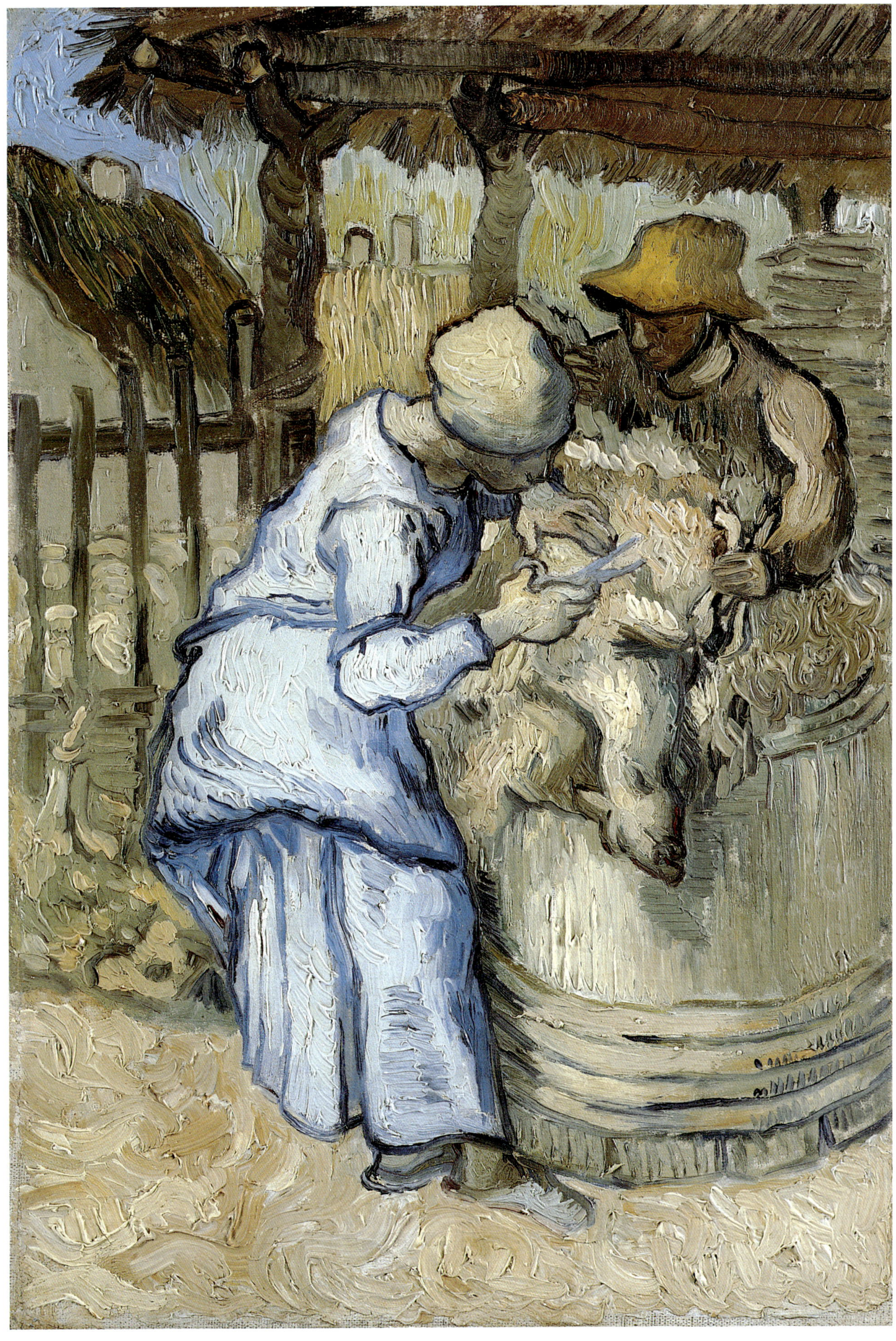

er eternal cycle over the water's alternating reflecting transparency and its material side — its substantiality in the choppy sea and the white caps (*"Les Pyramides" at Port-Coton, Belle-Île-en-Mer*, cat. no. 48, fig. 52); it is perhaps also in Holland that Monet finds his interest in the Japonising reinforced. The colonial power Holland offered rich opportunities to see Asiatic art, also in the museums of Amsterdam, and tradition has it that Monet acquired the basis of his extensive collection of Japanese woodcuts on this trip, but this may be something of an overstatement.[51] Another factor was that many people of that time — including the French travel writer Henry Hevard, whom Monet knew and with whom he travelled in Holland, felt drawn to the East, and wrote about it: the canals, the narrow fragile wooden bridges and the posts for pound nets and mooring, which also stick up out of the water in the Glyptotek's picture, have all contributed to the formation of this dream picture which has a close affinity with all the aspiring avant-garde generation's desire to find the new and paradisiacal in the exotic *per se*. But the Dutch idyll had another side, even for Monet in this painting of the old windmill "Het Oosterkattegat"; it can be seen as a principal component in a composition built upon two thematic contradictions, the old and the new — the second constituent is the silhouette of the industrial area on the horizon, where the drifting smoke from the chimneys, a sign of a new epoch, is in stark contrast to the old mill, whose sails are stilled in the evening after the day's work.[52] It may be this modern allegory on the mutability of time, which drives the picture, and thus puts it into a context, which fully unfolds in the slightly later *Impression: Soleil levant*.

Some fifteen years later we find Monet on the French coast, where, in five or six canvases he works through a sequence of a motif of sea and cliffs, namely the famous group of rocks, *"Les Pyramides" at Port-Coton, Belle-Île-en-Mer*. Painting for Monet is now a dense mass of colour, light and form, which sets this work apart from the earlier pictures. But the most striking thing about this cliff motif is the tilt of the horizon, which plays hell with the original perspective — and the spatial relationship, causing the motif to stand out as quivering individual shapes encapsulated in colour and held fast on the edge of focus. The shape of the cliffs which stick up out of the water become fields of darkly-glinting structures in the middle of the green sea, which is crowned by drily applied areas of white, where the waves break against the rocks. The figure and abstraction continue to shift between each other in the pulsation which is synonymous with Monet's painting as such. Here the paint becomes a matrix for vision and visibility, whose construction brings painting to rival traditional pictures of verisimilitude — not merely in figurative art's rendering of what is seen, but as reality in itself: Monet works towards a manner of painting which appears intended to replace reality with art. We are approaching Cézanne's great battle with all and everything, with himself and with truth in the painting's way of depicting things.

The Grand Style?

Art in France in the nineteenth century is, for the most part, highly conscious of surrounding reality and its related manifestations. The political and cultural world picture was presented and reflected continuously by art, including that of the Academy and the Salon. It has been joyfully asserted, with that cocksureness so characteristic of Modernism, that the best art, on the other hand, is always *critical*, which, paradoxically, denies Impressionism every critical potential.[53] With Cézanne we witness the final attempt to unify the great narrative of *the human being in relation to nature* in a single medium — the painting (see *The Bathers*, cat. no. 15, fig. 75). Cézanne radicalised the Impressionist experience in a painting which became so massive in terms of colour and

28
Aristide Maillol
Desire, 1904
Terracotta, 115 × 106 cm
Copenhagen, Ny Carlsberg Glyptotek
(cat. no. 38)

In this relief, Maillol has appropriated a Classical Greek idiom. When it was exhibited in the Salon d'Automne in 1907, the relief was proclaimed by one critic, André Pératé, to be a modern counterpart to the ancient metopes on the Temple of Zeus at Olympia. Maillol has framed the figures in a harmonious and decorative unity, thereby achieving a static, monumental presentation which tones down the expression of desire in its carnal sense. Maillol himself was enthusiastic about this structural firmness and considered the work to be one of his most successful.

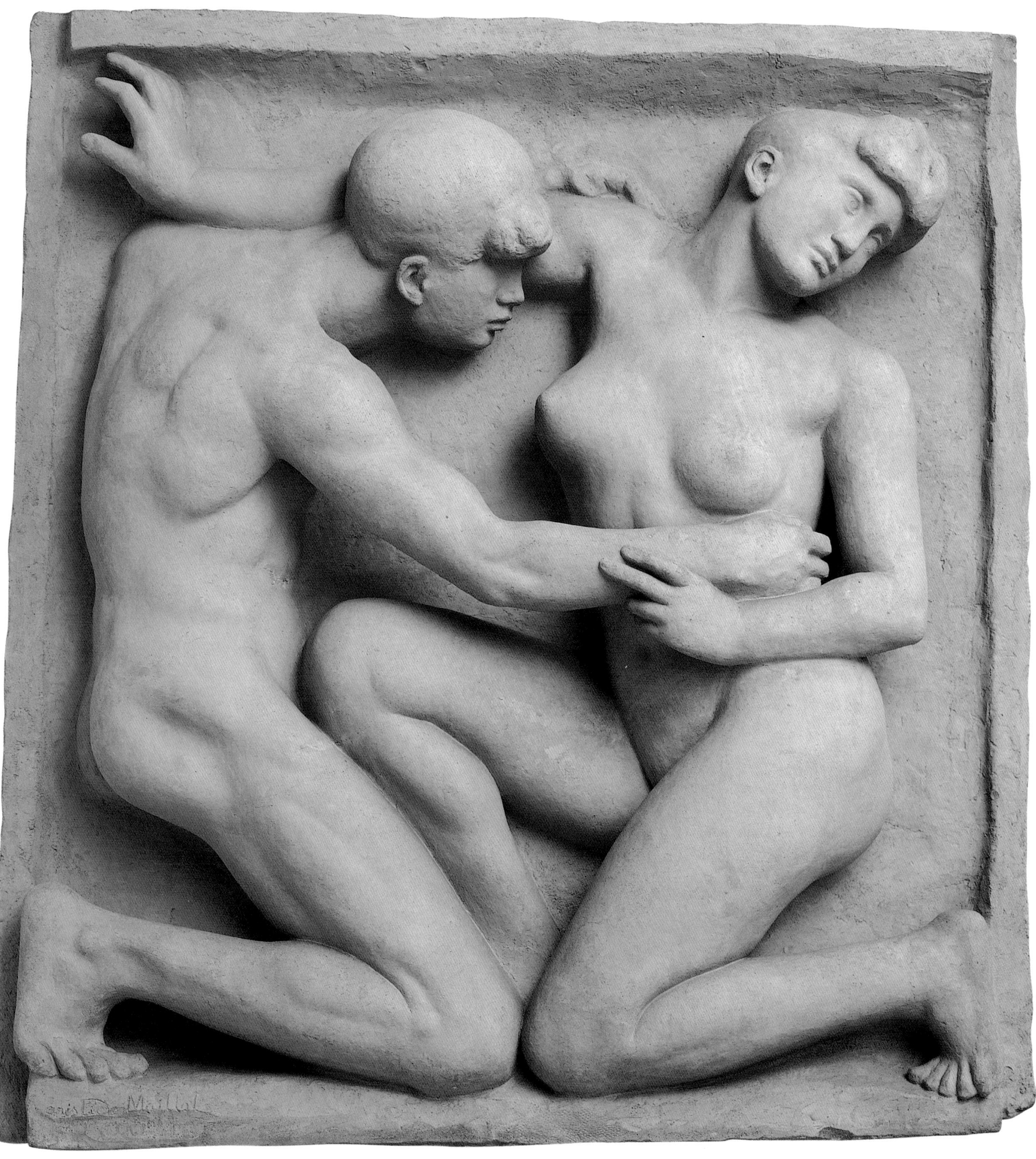

substance, that it was generally misunderstood and subsequently ignored. By virtue of its solidity it was on the point of becoming a body or a sculpture. Picasso is supposed to have stood bewitched by a Cézanne landscape, and, after a long pause, struck an area of particularly heavily-painted sea with his hand: "Look, it is completely set and solid". Through the strivings of Gauguin, Van Gogh and Emile Bernard towards a simple, "primitive" (in the sense of original or natural) artistic expression, painting advances in the direction of decorative strength in colour and form, retreating from the narrowly figurative relation to the surroundings.

Cézanne was only "rediscovered" some ten years after his death by a school of criticism following in the wake of early Cubism's formal language — a language essentially Cézannian. Cézanne himself is now recognised as one of the twentieth century's greatest artistic founding fathers: thus, as early as just after its presentation the Glyptotek's great *Bathers* sent a groundswell into the next generation of painters: Picasso used the large central female figure in the exact same pose as Cézanne in what may well be his most important painting, *Les Demoiselles d'Avignon* 1907, and Matisse, shortly before, had borrowed the same figure for his *La Joie de Vivre* of 1905–6. Cézanne had become the Tradition, a guide, Inspiration and an example to the artists of the Modern.[54]

Around the time of the initial forays into Cubism (ca. 1907–10) a number of sculptors develop a figurative artistic expression of a certain monumentality. This builds partly on the work of Rodin, but in a much more focused, closed form and without the painterly problematising of contour and outline, which Rodin's work tended to present (*The Shade*, cat. no. 52, fig. 40). The figuratively-formal disintegration and impermanence make way for a solidity in the structure which combines the plastic form with the ornamentation of the surface. Apart from Rodin's pupil Bourdelle, and Henri Laurens, the most significant artist working in this direction is Aristide Maillol. His *Desire* from 1904 (cat. no. 38, fig. 28) has been seen as an expression of a decorative-architectural simplicity, whose evocative power drove one sculpture expert into rhapsodies and caused him to proclaim the relief a modernist pendant to the figures on the Acropolis, among which, unlike most modern works, it could immediately have been inserted.[55] Besides such "classical" endeavours stands the contemporary *Decorative Figure* by Matisse (cat. no. 44, fig. 44). The neutral "modernistic" cadence of the title is rendered ridiculous when juxtaposed with the standing nude model's posture, leaning against its base — we have, at one and the same time moved both nearer and further away from the *real* and the *natural* in this form of sculpture; the female figure's classically sculptural mass is undermined by the posture, which, because it is overdone, reduces itself to an ornament — a decorative character, which is transferred to the entire figure.

The anecdote about Maillol's relief and the Acropolis figures discloses a plurality of style, which now set in; that is perhaps the most striking effect of the Modern — and that which above all characterises this "movement" in art. *Contemporaneity* has, at least in principle, superseded the most rigid of thinking about tradition, or assumed a position alongside the continually active idea of the history of the different schools in painting and sculpture. The academic masters at the Salon and modern avant-gardistes were in fact contemporaries, but it is only recently that the history of art and taste has examined the far from simple relationship between the two.

[1] P. Mainardi, *Art and Politics of the Second Empire* (New Haven and London, 1987), p. 142: "... Manet was simply ignored. In this Exposition year, Manet seemed too insignificant to receive much attention".
[2] Théophile Thoré, *Exposition Universelle de 1867*, II, p. 385.
[3] Mainardi, 1987, p. 152.
[4] *Ibid.*
[5] *Ibid.*
[6] For a very thorough presentation of Courbet's involvement in the Commune and its aftermath for himself, see: *Courbet et la Commune*, exhibition catalogue (Paris: Musée d'Orsay, 13 March – 26 May 2000).
[7] G.M. Ackerman, *J.L. Gérôme*, p. 128.
[8] *Ibid.*
[9] Paul Hayes Tucker, *The First Impressionist Exhibition and Monet's Impression, Sunrise: A Tale of Timing, Commerce, and Patriotism*, in *Art History* (vol. 7, no. 8, December 1984), pp. 465–76; Stephen F. Eisenman, *The Intransigent Artist or How the Impressionists Got Their Name*, in C.S. Moffet (ed.), *The New Painting: Impressionism 1874–1886* (Oxford, 1986), pp. 51–59.
[10] Tucker, 1984, p. 469: "... of the nineteen reports on the show [...] five were notices or announcements".
[11] Eisenman, 1976, p. 51 ff.
[12] Tucker, 1984, p. 468.
[13] N. Bryson, *Vision and Painting. The Logic of the Gaze* (London, 1983), pp. 1–66 (on "perceptualism" and "natural attitude", art history's ideas of how painting and tradition work — in Bryson's case, as related by Gombrich).
[14] Jules Castagnary, in *Le Siècle* (29 April, 1874); quot. after A. Dayez (ed.), *Le centennaire de l'impressionisme* (Paris: Grand Palais, 1974), pp. 264–65.
[15] L.-E. Duranty, *La Nouvelle Peinture* (1876), p. 39.
[16] *Ibid.*
[17] *Ibid.*, p. 45.
[18] *Ibid.*, p. 47.
[19] Paul Mantz, in *Gazette des Beaux-Arts* (19 July, 1865), pp. 35–36.
[20] I.e. primarily Benozzo Gozzoli's fresco of *The Adoration* in Palazzo Riccardi, Florence.
[21] The small bronze is a miniature repetition of the full-scale sculpture, probably out of a special "artist's edition".
[22] Among which are two figurines or miniature sculptures, cast in bronze (cf. NCG M.I.N. 565 & 564; gift of the artist to Carl Jacobsen, 1885, together with the aforementioned).
[23] Paul De Vigne (1843–1901), quot. after A. Yarrington, *Under the Spell of Madame Tussaud; Aspects of "high" and "low" in 19th-century polychromed sculpture*, in *The Colour of Sculpture* (Amsterdam: Van Gogh Museum, 1996), p. 83.
[24] P. Øhrgaard, *Goethe - et essay* (Copenhagen, 1999), p. 248 ff.
[25] *Ibid.*, p. 247.
[26] J. Hargrove, *Painter-sculptors and polychromy in the evolution of modernism*, in *The Colour of Sculpture*, pp. 103-117.
[27] See also S. Søndergaard, in this volume.
[28] My thanks to MA Charlotte Christensen of Copenhagen, who suggested this extra aspect to me.
[29] *The Colour of Sculpture*, p. 174.
[30] *Ibid.*, p. 122. Contemporary photographs are not trustworthy as to this. The sculpture was reproduced in several editions, in varying sizes and hues of wax, from the gilt to the reddish.
[31] As to the different casts and versions, see Musée d'Orsay, *48/14 La Revue du Musée d'Orsay* (no. 7, 1998), pp. 68–72.
[32] A.-B. Fonsmark, *NCG MedKøb* (1987), p. 33 and note 8.
[33] *Ibid.*, p. 34.
[34] *Ibid.*, p. 38.
[35] Gauguin to Pissarro, August or September 1881, in V. Merlhes (ed.), *Correspondance de Paul Gauguin. Documents, témoignages* (Paris, 1984), p. 22, letter no. 17.
[36] Gauguin to Pissarro, 1883 (*ibid.*; the italics are mine).
[37] M. du Camp, *Le Salon de 1857. Peinture – Sculpture* (Paris: Librairie Nouvelle, 1857), p. 175.
[38] *Ibid.*, pp. 5–6.
[39] Musée d'Orsay: "ca. 1854–55".
[40] *Ibid.*, "an untitled medieval subject".
[41] H. Zerner, *Introduction, James Jacques Joseph Tissot 1836–1902. A Retrospective Exhibition* (Providence: Museum of Art, Rhode Island School of Art and Design, 28 February – 29 March, 1968; Toronto: The Art Gallery of Ontario, 6 April – 5 May, 1968; no pagination).
[42] *Ibid.*
[43] *Ibid.*
[44] S. Kern on Tissot's *Chrysanthemums*, in *The Clark - Selections from the Sterling & Francine Clark Art Institute* (Williamstown, Mass., 1996), p. 84.
[45] Shown in Zerner, 1968, pl. 31.
[46] Charles Baudelaire, *Curiosités Esthétiques (Salon de 1845)* (Paris: Garnier, 1962), p. 45.
[47] F. Orton, *Reactions to Renoir Keep Changing*, in F. Orton and G. Pollock, *Avant-Gardes and Partisans Reviewed* (Manchester and New York, 1996), p. 100.
[48] Tucker, 1984, p. 470 ff.
[49] *Ibid.*
[50] *Monet in Holland* (1986), p. 43.
[51] H.E. Nørregård-Nielsen, *Monet i Holland, MedKøb* (1987), p. 16.
[52] *Ibid.*, p. 10.
[53] Eisenman, 1986, pp. 56–57.
[54] See also J. Toft, in this volume.
[55] A. Elsen, *The Origins of Modern Sculpture* (New York and London, 1969), p. 138.

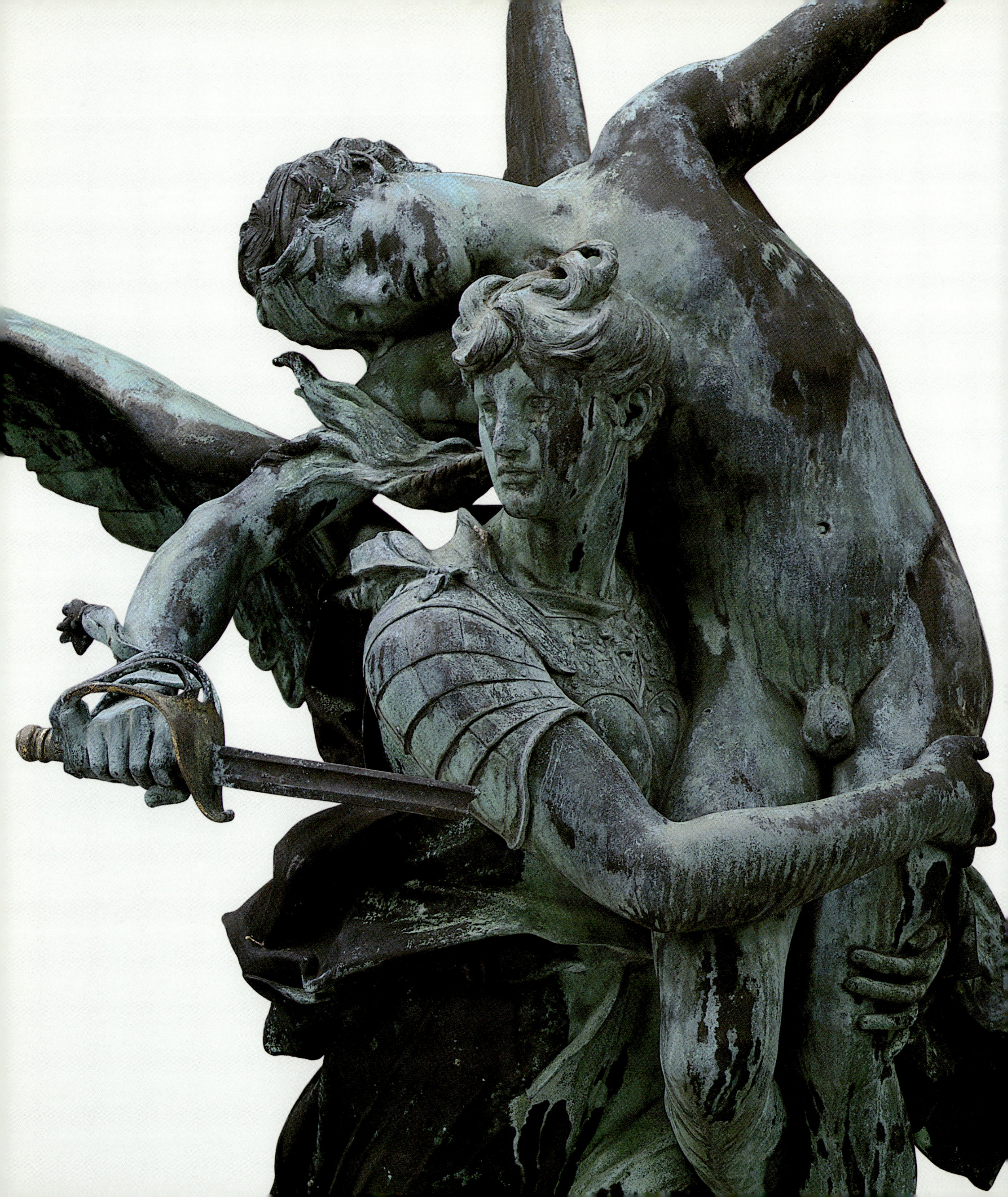

Sidsel Maria Søndergaard

When Tradition Becomes Modern

The dialectic of repetition is easy, for that which is repeated has been — otherwise it could not be repeated — but the very fact that it has been makes the repetition into something new. When the Greeks said that all knowing is recollecting, they said that all existence, which is, has been; when one says that life is a repetition, one says: actuality, which has been, now comes into existence. If one does not have the category of recollection or of repetition, all life dissolves into an empty, meaningless noise.[1]
Søren Kierkegaard

French sculpture from the second half of the nineteenth century draws extensively on its forerunners, presenting a myriad references to works from almost every period in the past: Classical Antiquity, Hellenism, the Mediaeval era, Renaissance, Baroque, Mannerism, Rococo, Neo-Classicism. Realism, however, did not make its true breakthrough in sculpture until the close of the century, i.e. in this respect it lagged considerably behind painting.

Overwhelmingly it seems to have been Italy which was the focus of such references: the French sculptors showed a particular interest in the *non-finito* of Michelangelo and the slender adolescent figures by the master of the Florentine Renaissance, Donatello. Michelangelo's famous work *The Dying Slave* was the object of special admiration and borrowings, with Auguste Rodin's early work *The Age of Bronze* (cat. no. 51, fig. 34) from 1875–76, as the best-known example. Baroque dynamics were also popular and present in many Salon sculptures. One example of this is Antonin Mercié's figure group *Gloria Victis* (cat. no. 45, fig. 30) which has provided the title for this exhibition.

Mercié linked his work to the French defeat in the Franco-Prussian War of 1870–71. With his winged figure *Fame*, which like a Valkyrie bears a fallen soldier aloft, he wanted to give his slain countrymen a symbolic resurrection. Mercié did not stint himself, but orchestrated all the devices at this command in a host of references to the European sculptural tradition, from the *Nike of Samothrace* to the iconography of rape.[2] Thus *Gloria Victis* illustrates how different influences can vie for attention within a single work, and it is a typical example of the eclecticism which was popular in contemporary Salon sculpture.

This particular eclecticism has given rise to the widespread tendency to interpret sculpture from the second half of the nineteenth century as something which destroys style rather than establishing it. This view is based on a concept of art history as a consec-

29
Antonin Mercié
Gloria Victis, 1874, detail
(full fig. 30)

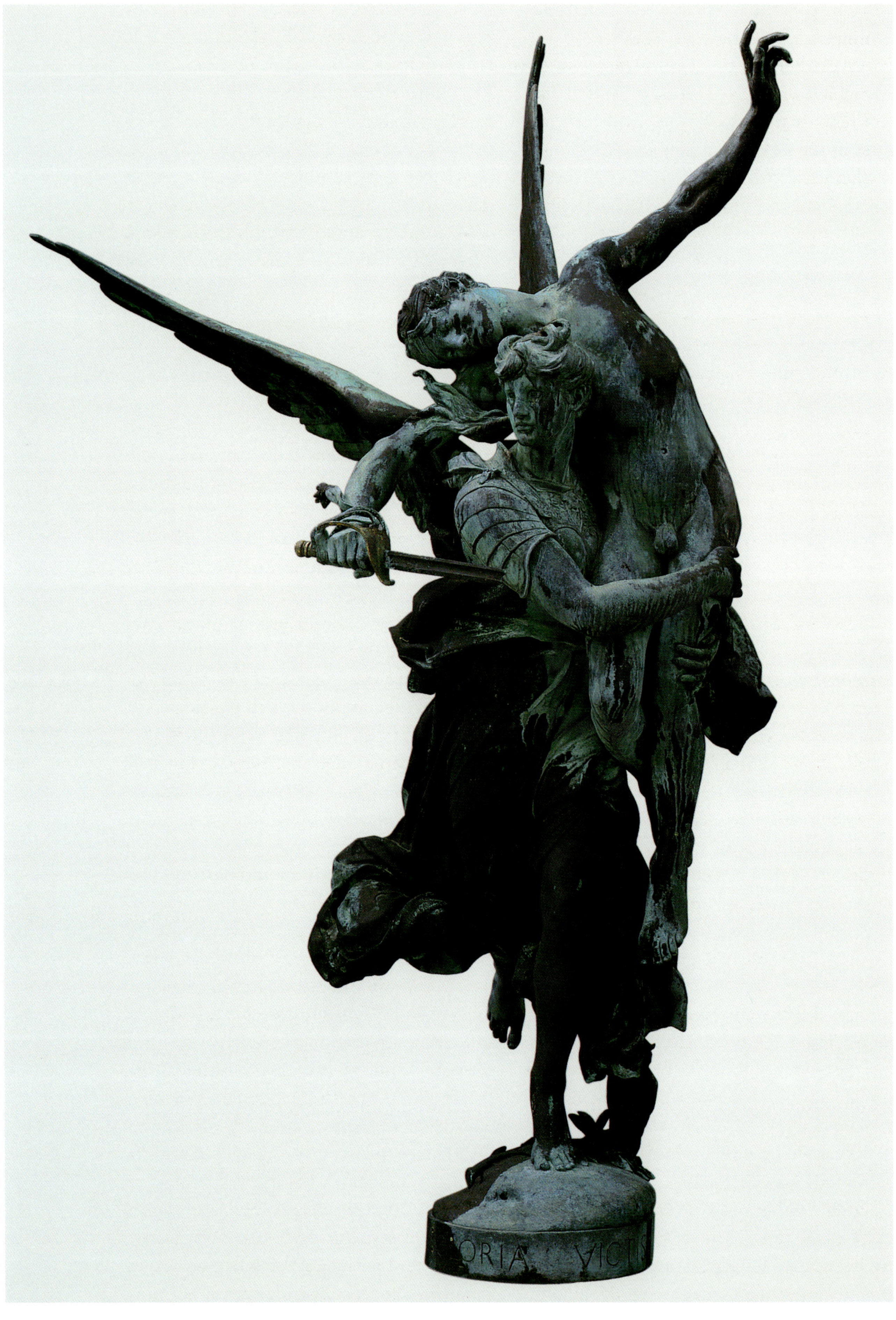

30
Antonin Mercié
Gloria Victis, 1874
Cast in bronze (1905),
h. 309 cm
Copenhagen, Ny Carlsberg Glyptotek
(cat. no. 45)

Gloria Victis means Glory to the Vanquished. The title underlines the work's paradoxical tableau of a heroic defeat. With the winged Fame bearing aloft a fallen soldier, Mercié sought to give the French defeat in the Franco-Prussian War of 1870–71 a symbolic redress. This re-writing of France's crushing defeat was the source of the sculpture's enormous success. Bronze casts of the work were set up all over France as monuments to the fallen. The group echoes various styles in the European sculpture tradition: we find the measured elegance of the Renaissance as well as a Baroque dynamic. The work is thereby a typical example of the eclecticism that was in vogue in the Salon sculpture of the period.

utive sequence of developments of style, each distinct from the next. This is probably one of the reasons that sculpture from the second half of the nineteenth century has been overlooked by art historical research with the result that much of the French sculpture from the period between Neo-Classicism and Rodin is largely unfamiliar outside France.

The history of art has, in reality, treated the greater part of the nineteenth century as *terrain vague*, as far as the history of sculpture is concerned. The period between Neo-Classicism and Modernism tends to be regarded as merely a transitional phase for sculpture, a sort of Dark Ages with Rodin as the only star in the heavens to light the way for posterity. In consequence, we have made the simple messages speak for themselves and have regarded Rodin as the Great Redeemer: the first sculptor to make a serious break with the dogmas of Neo-Classicism and bring sculpture into the modern age.

It is still difficult to avoid duplicating the conventional, contradictory relationship between Neo-Classicism and Modernism, but in the last fifteen years there has been — particularly with the opening of the Musée d'Orsay in Paris in 1986 — a new light cast on this liminal zone in the history of sculpture. At the Musée d'Orsay, as at the Ny Carlsberg Glyptotek, the famous sculptures of Rodin are presented side by side with others of the era's most celebrated works, thus inviting a more subtle analysis of the situation.

However, from a modernist or post-modernist perspective it is by no means easy to pinpoint what is particularly contemporary about the sculpture of the period. The analysis has been hampered by the close relation of the works to the tradition of sculpture. What has happened is that the eclectic consciousness of tradition and modern contemporaneity have been simplistically treated as diametrically-opposed entities, and quotations and references have been read as an expression of how the sculptors concerned were mired in tradition. This article is, however, motivated by the thought that the modern position is not, of necessity, restricted to a break with tradition, but, instead, is formed in a constant exchange with the older masters, which an artist cultivates as part of his visual frame of reference. Furthermore the article suggests that the attitude of the contemporary critics towards the question of tradition in sculpture was by no means a simple one, i.e. this article problematises the widespread tendency merely to contrast modernist perspectives with more conservative outlooks.

The question is, thus, whether it is not precisely Salon sculpture's use of the tradition, which can be said to mark a modern position. As such this tradition of sculpture is linked to a modern consciousness of history, a consciousness born with the French Revolution: that moment when the whole notion of progress made a serious impact for the first time. It was precisely in this age of upheaval that artists, taking their cue from the archaeologists, looked to Hellas, and the formation of the neo-classicist style became a reality. The idea of progress thus became part of a double structure, in which its companion was retrospective cultural consciousness.

A Well-head of Cultural Formation

The neo-classicist perspective on Antiquity was a self-conscious gaze reflected in the greatness of former times; the gaze permitting its artistic practitioners to assume the role of rightful heirs to the proud traditions of Western Civilization. As far as sculpture is concerned, this took concrete form with the first major attempt to construct a tradition with Neo-Classicism's highly influential manifestos written by J.J. Winckelmann (1717–68) and G.E. Lessing (1729–81).[3]

The neo-classicist precepts were an attempt to impose order on the Renaissance Cult of Antiquity and formulate a rational Theory of Beauty[4] which might contain the epoch's dream of the ideal, free complete subject.[5] Thus Winckelmann, taking as his point of departure the sculpture of Antiquity, produced a theoretical analysis of the characteristic form of perfect beauty.[6] He emphasised the sculpture's whole, perceptible form mediated by a clear and supple contour as the very image of pure beauty. He stressed that white marble was the sublime material for sculpture as much as the uncoloured stone gave the form the optimum conditions to render the essence of beauty, as Neo-Classicism understood it: "It is not colour, but form, which brings forth the essence of beauty, all enlightened spirits are easily of one mind on that question. Since the white is the colour which best reflects light, and, accordingly is the most sensitive, so a beautiful body will appear more beautiful the whiter it is".[7]

The smooth surface of marble, it was thus implied, did not only possess a pronounced sensual appeal, it was also, in itself, an ideal vision of human skin, devoid of wrinkles and veins, and, by the same token, a vision of mankind without suffering or passions. Karin Sander has expressed this very precisely: "The surface of the statue, which resembles the human body, and yet is spared the problem-filled interior of a real body of flesh and blood, constitutes an ideal surface onto which aesthetic, ideological or philosophical ideas can be projected".[8] The flawless marble skin of the sculpture was thus inextricably linked with a kind of metaphysical transparency, which could serve as a metaphor for the utopian totality of existence; and perhaps as an adjuration that unity and cohesion were possible.

Winckelmann was of the conviction that by studying the ideal forms of ancient Greek sculpture it was possible to find one's way back to the Platonic link between the beautiful, the true and the good. The sculpture of ancient Greece could, in other words, be morally uplifting, and it was therefore the duty of neo-classicist sculptors to imitate Antiquity, thereby learning to create works which could continue to disseminate the notion of the beautiful physique as the proper dwelling place of the healthy, moral soul. Neo-Classicism's "re-launch" of the ancient classical tradition of sculpture was thus a way of keeping faith with an ideal of edification, and it was one of the reasons that Winckelmann's successors in France continued to advocate the imitation of the original classical model: in sculpture this didactic ideal was able to assume a material form.

The neo-classical tradition was carried further by the aesthetic theorists Quatremère de Quincy (1755–1849) and Victor Cousin (1792–1867) as well as by such critics such as Henri Jouin,[9] Charles Blanc (1813–82) and Paul Mantz (1821–95). Last, though by no means least, was the sculptor and theorist Adolf von Hildebrand, (1847– 1921) who, as late as 1893, published a particularly influential tract on figurative art which was based on the ideals of Neo-Classicism.[10]

The Winckelmann credo was thus to demonstrate its efficacy throughout the nineteenth century, and its role cannot be underestimated. It did not merely exert an all powerful influence on all public training of sculptors which proceeded at both the Ecole Gratuite de Dessin in Paris, also known as the "Petite Ecole",[11] and at the Ecole des Beaux-Arts. It was also the determining factor in the verdicts of the Salon juries. Theoreticians, critics and academicians all vaunted the sculpture of Antiquity as the ultimate standard against which a sculptor should measure himself; although slavish imitation of a work from the ancient world would be regarded as a failed attempt.[12] The result was the classicising, academic sculpture which dominated the Salon exhibitions in Paris.

At the Ecole des Beaux-Arts it was an article of faith that a training in draughtsmanship was the basis of all artistic creation — and that applied equally to prospective sculptors[13] — their drawing skills were to be honed in their encounter with classical sculpture, of which the students were to copy either two-dimensional representations or plaster casts. Since the classical canon put considerable emphasis on outline, the students were exhorted to concentrate on the contours and apprehend the shapes as flat surfaces.[14] The prime consideration was the understanding of the relationship between planes, as emerges from the entreaties of Paolo Emiliani Giudici in the *Gazette des Beaux-Arts* in 1859: "If you want to apprehend the truthful imprint of reality [...], indicate your planes boldly and draw square rather than round, because from planes result relief and planes do not emerge from the round. In sculpture it is a question of reliefs and it is therefore necessary to take heed of profiles".[15]

The same year, in another issue of the journal, he emphasised the point that sculptors were not to supplant the tranquil worth of sculpture with reckless choices of pose or go to extremes on the other hand by permitting the intrusion of the tangible human physique. Instead one should strive for, "... lines which collide and harmonise, conflict with each other and balance. [One must also have] an understanding of planes [and] a deep knowledge of anatomy, but not one which recalls the model, nor its vulgarities, weariness, nor convulsive poses..."[16]

The watchword for both neo-classical and Salon Sculpture was thus *mastery* of form. The tool of the sculptor was the line, which often dominated the three-dimensional object to such an extent that it had no active relation to the surrounding space; rather its orientation involved a front and a back, indicating a relatively fixed location, from which the spectator can best apprehend the work visually.[17]

Modernist Critics Reconsidered

The academic sculpture of the nineteenth century had, therefore, clear theoretical guidelines, with, as its supreme goal, the ideal depiction of "the standing human figure, nude or draped à l'antique".[18] No such clear theoretical writings existed to support any alternative position, which might have been labelled "modern". There were, however, several sporadic modifications of the academic method and ideals. As David Scott has shown, it is in fact possible retrospectively to construct a rudimentary aesthetic for the Modern in the sculpture of the nineteenth century from the writings of critics such as Victor Cousin, Théophile Gautier, Emile Zola, and the Goncourt brothers.[19] It might be interesting to widen the perspective and examine the attitudes of both modernist and conservative critics. One reason for this is that among the critics who helped shape the avant-garde movement one can also find "conservative" tendencies. In the same respect, side by side with the conservative professions of faith in the writings of neo-classicist inspired critics, one finds utterances which, from our perspective, can be interpreted as an openness to a more modern approach. Thus in 1810, despite his neo-classicist affiliations, we find the statesman and historian François-Pierre-Guillaume Guizot (1787– 1874) appealing to sculptors to put a higher priority on their modelling in clay and wax. More radical was the critic Gustave Planche (1808–57) who, in 1831, lamented the tendency of such sculptors as Pradier to continue to pursue ideas that were more closely associated with painting rather than with sculpture itself.[20]

As early as 1817, Stendhal (1783–1842) had formulated an aesthetic of "Romanticism"[21] where he described "a desperate thirst for violent emotions" and hoped that this "thirst for energy will take us back to the masterpieces of Michelangelo": "If we were vouchsafed a Michelangelo [...] of what would he not be capable? Perhaps he would create a modern sculpture, perhaps he would force this art to express passion".[22] These meditations on sculpture were followed up when in 1824 he sighed "The statuary art is on the eve of a revolution: need it servilely copy the Antique like most French sculptors?"[23] Stendhal hoped that sculptors would surrender themselves to passion with Michelangelo as their supreme model and thus cause the romantic "revolution" to redeem sculpture. At the beginning of the nineteenth century the word "romantic" was synonymous with "modern" in the widest sense of the term[24] and "the Romantic" was regarded as the artist's interpretation of the passionate encounter with his contemporary world.[25] In the formulation of this aesthetic, Stendhal was distancing himself from the classical, ideal concept of beauty and offering in its place the mutable present: "The beauty in each century is merely the expression of the qualities which the age finds useful".[26] Thus he posits the idea of beauty as a relative concept, which has as its focus the particular and not the universal. But as a means to reflect a contemporary artistic expression, a parameter of "modern" art, he — like many of his contemporaries — invoked one of the greatest masters of the past. Stendhal opted for the Renaissance over Antiquity as the focus of his tradition.

At the Salon of 1833 works by Antoine-Louis Barye (1795–1875) and Auguste Préault (1809–79 and making his debut) gave substance to a renewal in French sculpture; a renewal, which the critics Gabriel Laviron and Bruno Galbaccio immediately welcomed in their *Le Salon de 1833*.[27] The hegemony of academic sculpture seems therefore to have been challenged; however, in the years 1834–48, Préault was to have almost every work he submitted to the Salon rejected.[28] When he was fortunate enough to return to the good graces of the jury in 1849 he was lauded by his friend, the poet and critic Théophile Gautier (1811–72) in his review of the Salon of that year as a leading romantic sculptor.[29] Gautier set the "insipidity" of the contemporary mythological works in contrast with an agonized and passionate quality in Préault's works, which was, "... of an extraordinary newness in sculpture", the result, he says, was that, "the classical tradition was broken and the revolution accomplished throughout all of art".[30] For Gautier this "break" with the classical tradition was the watershed which must precede the renewal, and this separatist notion was to become the core of that understanding of Modernism as a counter culture which was subsequently to gain such widespread currency.

Gautier himself was to assume a dominant position among the critics of the age. Under the Second Empire he was selected to be the "official critic"[31] and from this position he fostered the growth of Romanticism. But as far as sculpture was concerned Gautier's art criticism embodied several contradictions which were characteristic of the period. Although he was predominantly the champion of Romanticism and thus was on the lookout for emotionally-charged expression, a legitimate violence, taking his stand in relation to his era, he was also capable of writing as follows: "Nudity is the essential condition of sculpture [...] ; the representation of the human body divorced from all particularity and chance constitutes the beautiful ideal".[32] Like the neo-classicists he found that physical ideality had received its definitive form in Classical Antiquity, and therefore every subsequent evaluation of beauty must take place in relation to the art of Antiquity or Neo-Classicism. However, his own preference was for such sculptors as Préault and Carpeaux because they cultivated the expression and the effect rather than the ideal.

In 1872, when the romantic "revolution" was long past and Gautier had been a witness to the way official art had swallowed up every tendency to the heroic or romantic, he wrote: "Of all the arts, assuredly none lends itself less to the expression of the romantic idea than sculpture. It [sculpture] seems to have received its definitive form from Antiquity [...] Of what is statuary capable without the gods and heroes of mythology who furnish both the nudes and

31
Paul Dubois
Narcissus Contemplating His Reflection in the Spring (1863)
Carved in marble (1899),
h. 185 cm
Copenhagen, Ny Carlsberg Glyptotek
(cat. no. 26)

According to the Greek myth, Narcissus rejected all his admirers and was punished for his arrogance by Nemesis, the Goddess of Fate. She made him suffer in a state of unrequited love for his own reflection in the waters of the spring. Dubois shows Narcissus looking down into the water; introspective and self-indulgent, he stands contemplating his naked body. The statuary calm and the polished surface of the marble belie the tragic dimensions of the temptation. Instead, the beholder sees an ideal male figure, infatuated with himself, oblivious to all else.

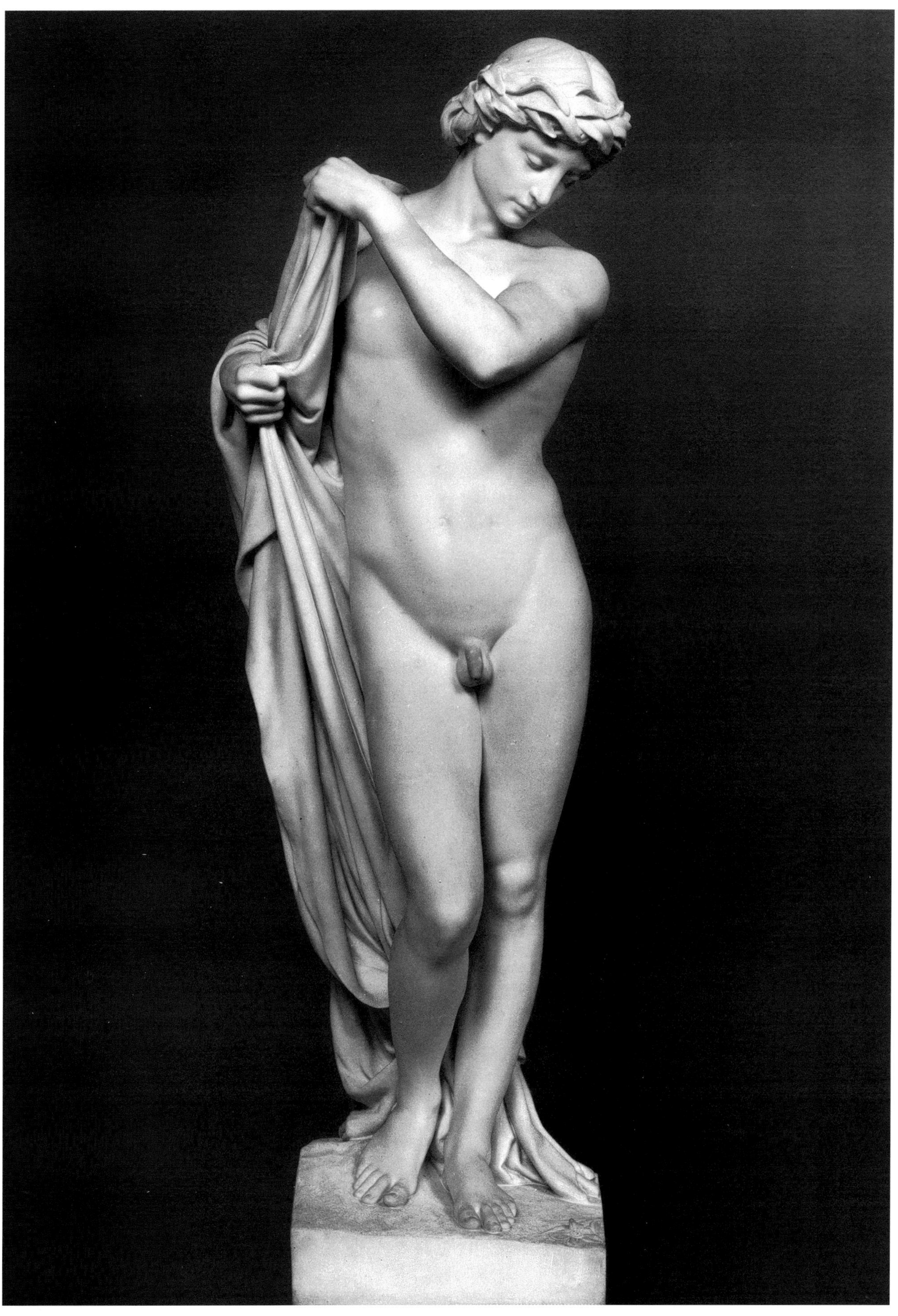

the drapery with the plausible pretexts they need?"[33] Thus, with quiet resignation, he managed a final, indirect criticism of the sculpture of his age, which, to a great extent, was doing little more than trading on the classical legacy in the latter's depiction of languorous nude bodies. It was as if Gautier thought that all Antiquity still had on its side was beauty itself.[34]

Gautier himself did, however, cultivate the sensual qualities in sculpture and went beyond Winckelmann's teaching in his preoccupation (bordering on obsession) with the female body. Sculpture for Gautier was not only ideal, but, simultaneously, the most complete expression possible of the tangible reality of the human body. This aesthetic paradox is expressed in his commentary on Clésinger's famous *Woman Bitten by a Serpent* (Paris, Musée d'Orsay), which was a great success at the Salon of 1847. Gautier was enthralled by Clésinger's "boldness quite unheard of in the age in which we live, in exposing, without any mythological title, a masterpiece which is neither goddess, nymph nor dryad [...] but utterly woman..." He believed that this female nude was "a shining image possessed of a beauty which is utterly modern".[35] Gautier thus drew a distinction between beauty ancient and modern yet cultivated them both.[36]

It is also possible to detect Gautier's interest in both the idealized vision of Woman and her tangible sensual aspect[37] in his poetic analogies between sculpture and the female body.[38] David Scott has drawn attention to Gautier's evocation of Woman as sculpture. Firstly, this was symptomatic of the academic conventions of the nineteenth century; secondly it is an expression of sculpture's potential as an object onto which can be projected desires and fantasies of more or less erotic nature which are reflected in both poetry and "mid-century aesthetic writing".[39] An example of this, as Scott has pointed out, was the widespread tendency to refer to a sculpture as a "marble" — i.e. giving the word "marble" the function of a synecdoche[40] for sculpture. This marks an emphasis on the material sensuality of sculpture itself and points toward its metaphorical displacement to the skin of the human being.

Thus, Gautier exemplifies the era's increasing fascination with sculpture's actual materiality, especially among the critics who cultivated the present and the Modern. However, a main aspect of this materiality seemed also to be the source of a fundamental scepticism about sculpture as such. This view found its clearest expression when Gautier's pupil, the poet and critic, Charles Baudelaire produced his *Salon de 1846*. Under the superscription *Why Sculpture is Boring*, he castigated the medium for being tedious and inextricably bound up with the primitive worship of idols: "Sculpture has several disadvantages, which are the inevitable consequence of its ends and means. Although it is, like nature, both brutal and positive, it is also, simultaneously, both vague and ambiguous because it has to display too many facets at the same time".[41]

For Baudelaire it was not merely sculpture's "natural palpability" which was problematic (because it made it impossible for the spectator to apprehend the work at a single glance). It was also suspect because, as opposed to painting, it did not involve any deep contemplation. To put it simply, Baudelaire harboured doubts as to how far sculpture could ever be "elevated above" its palpability and so become a forum for the reflections he considered worthy of attention — reflections on the conditions of the modern human being.

Although Baudelaire's anti-sculpture diatribe was, even this far, controversial, it is indicative of an ancient and widespread concept that it was sculpture's innate material nature which frustrated any sophisticated artistic communication. This prompts the assumption that sculpture is too closely bound to its material, to all that is material, and thus, in a quite fundamental sense, is further removed from spiritual concerns than, for example, either painting or poetry.[42]

The widespread tendency of Salon sculpture clearly to quote and refer to past masters can hardly have awakened Baudelaire's interest in sculpture either, for Baudelaire (in *Salon de 1846*) also had an outspoken antipathy to eclecticism: "Eclecticism has at all periods and places held itself superior to past doctrines, because, coming last on to the scene, it finds the remotest horizons already open to it; but this *impartiality* only goes to prove the impotence of the eclectics. People who are so lavish with their time for reflection are not complete men: they lack the element of passion. [...] The eclectic does not know that the first business of an artist is to protest against Nature by putting Man in her place. This protest is not made coldly and calculatedly, like a decree or a rhetorical exercise; it is spontaneous and urgent, like vice, passion or appetite. Thus an eclectic is no man".[43] Baudelaire found any explicit reference to sources undesirable, because, in his opinion, it compromised the originality of the work in question.[44]

However, Baudelaire's *Salon of 1859* shows that his attitude to tradition was far from simplistic. Accordingly in 1859 he defended a work by the sculptor Franceschi thus: "... this figure has given rise to several criticisms which in our opinion were too facile. [...] It has been called a plagiarism, and M. Franceschi has been accused of simply taking a recumbent figure by Michelangelo and standing it upright. This is not true. [...] the paradoxical elegance of these limbs are clearly the doing of a modern artist. But even if he should have borrowed his inspiration from the past, I would see in this a ground for praise rather than for rebuke; it is not given to everyone to imitate what is great..."[45]

It would be unwise to underestimate the effect Baudelaire's categorical verdict on sculpture had on both the contemporary and subsequent evaluation of the sculpture of the nineteenth century. Equally, one should be aware of how Winckelmann's concept of sculpture as a medium for the idealisation of human emotional life has acted like a filter on the understanding of the subtleties of neoclassical sculpture.[46] Accordingly, David Scott points out that with Baudelaire, as one of the most important theorists of Modernism, we witness not only the development of a state of conflict between Neo-Classicism and Modernism. More specifically, his disapproval of sculpture has also instilled a fundamental doubt as to how far sculpture is even capable of modernity — at least in the terms he has defined. And this is a concept embodying a demand for present temporality, which appears to exclude any systematic comparison with the past.[47] This fundamental notion of a break with all that has gone before has, roughly speaking, functioned in a normative capacity, which has contributed to changing the concept of the eclectic art of the nineteenth century in a negative manner. That Baudelaire's imperative — that art must be modern — has been used as an artistic and theoretical dogma for the concept of Modernism in the twentieth century demonstrates in an ironic fashion a parallel to the method used by critics and theorists who cultivated the teachings of Neo-Classicism in the nineteenth century.

Like Stendhal and Gautier, Baudelaire seems to harbour inconsistencies in his analysis, which contribute to the thesis that any purely simplistic view of tradition and the modernists as two exclusive armed camps is untenable.

An Irritating Prelude to the Dissolution of the World

The modernists were not alone in their cultivation of the sensual and material in sculpture. These were central aspects of the controversies over decadence; a notion accompanying the idea of modernity and progress in the nineteenth century.[48] In art these two entities were closely linked to the argument over the relation between materiality and spirituality in art, between formalism and morality, which flared up around the time of the romantic "revolution", and remained a perennial theme in the art criticism of the age.

The influential art historian, administrator and theorist, Charles Blanc, who founded the *Gazette des Beaux-Arts* in 1859,[49] adhered firmly to the classical theory of an ethic and universality of beauty, and involved himself in the debate. In the art of the time he detected a dilution of the Classical Tradition, and thereby a decadence, which, to his mind, was attributable in equal parts to the enfeeblement of the artists' training, an uninformed public, and the insufficient support and impotence of the state.[50] Blanc insisted on the ethical demands in art and disparaged the rising tendency to concentrate on the material, formal and sensual aspects of art with the following words: "Moral beauty has been forgotten, the sublimity of depth escapes us". The romantically-minded critics, including Gautier, he denigrated with the phrase "les matérialistes de l'art".[51]

Blanc advanced his views, especially those on aesthetic and formalist values, in his tract *Grammaire des Arts du Dessin*, which was published in several parts in the *Gazette des Beaux-Arts* in the course of the years 1860–66. It was here that he put forward an elaborate code of rules for figurative art. An example of this is his in-depth prescription of how movement should be rendered in sculpture; above it was the superscription, "A moderation in movement and a sobriety of gesture constitute the first law of sculpture".[52] Although Blanc displayed a subtle understanding of the limitations imposed on the sculptor by sculpture's own materiality,[53] and thus came to modify this dictum so that it applied primarily to sculpture in marble,[54] Neo-Classicism remained for him far more than a formalist code of conduct.

Blanc's friend, the critic and civil servant Paul Mantz, who, in the period 1859–72 covered the annual Salon Exhibition in the *Gazette des Beaux-Arts*, was, however, less preoccupied with the moral aspects. His more pragmatic view conceded that there were such things as eternally valid aesthetic rules, and that these decreed the norms for how line, colour and plane were to interact in one harmonious and rational whole. Just like Blanc and Giudici, he too believed that the sublimity peculiar to sculpture carried with it some restriction on how much liberty sculptors might affect with regard to gestures and gesticulation.[55] However, as long as these rules were observed, he was prepared to be open-minded about "progress" within art, and he refused to countenance the idea that art could descend into decadence.[56] This formalistic outlook was the recurring theme in Mantz's criticism, where in sculpture he championed the ideals of Neo-Classicism and demanded of sculptors a sense of overall beauty and rhythm of lines.

One expression of Mantz' classical-formalist position and openness to innovation was his review of the Salon of 1863, which included the debut of the young sculptor, Paul Dubois (1829–1905) with his works *John the Baptist as a Child*,[57] and *Narcissus Contemplating His Reflection in the Spring* (cat. no. 26, fig. 31). Mantz went into raptures in his description of how Dubois was made a sculptor in Rome under the influence of, "the eternal masters".[58] He continues: "... there is in *Saint Jean-Baptiste* and *Narcissus* such an excellent feeling for beautiful lines and such considerable taste that criticism can only joyfully salute such a fortunate debut. The little *Saint Jean-Baptiste* standing, with his hand raised, advances with that ardour both youthful and inspired, which is entirely appropriate for forerunners; the head is poetic, the entire figure has movement, slenderness and an elegant energy that defies belief. However in preference to this, admittedly remarkable figure, we would put forward *Narcissus*, who is more truly conceived in the terms of grand sculpture, and

32
Paul Dubois
Florentine Singer from the Fifteenth Century, 1865
Cast in bronze (1897), h. 155 cm
Copenhagen, Ny Carlsberg Glyptotek
(cat. no. 27)

Dubois was one of the principal exponents of the Neo-Florentine style that derived its inspiration from the Renaissance and came into fashion in the 1860s. His *Florentine Singer* is clearly inspired by the Renaissance sculptor Donatello's famous work *David*. Dubois' version of the slender boy's figure was a huge success and brought him a Gold Medal at the Salon of 1865. It moved the contemporary critic Paul Mantz to proclaim Dubois one of the hopes of modern sculpture. Other critics instead saw the work as an expression of the decline of sculpture because it showed a more "charming" masculine model than the lofty classical ideal.

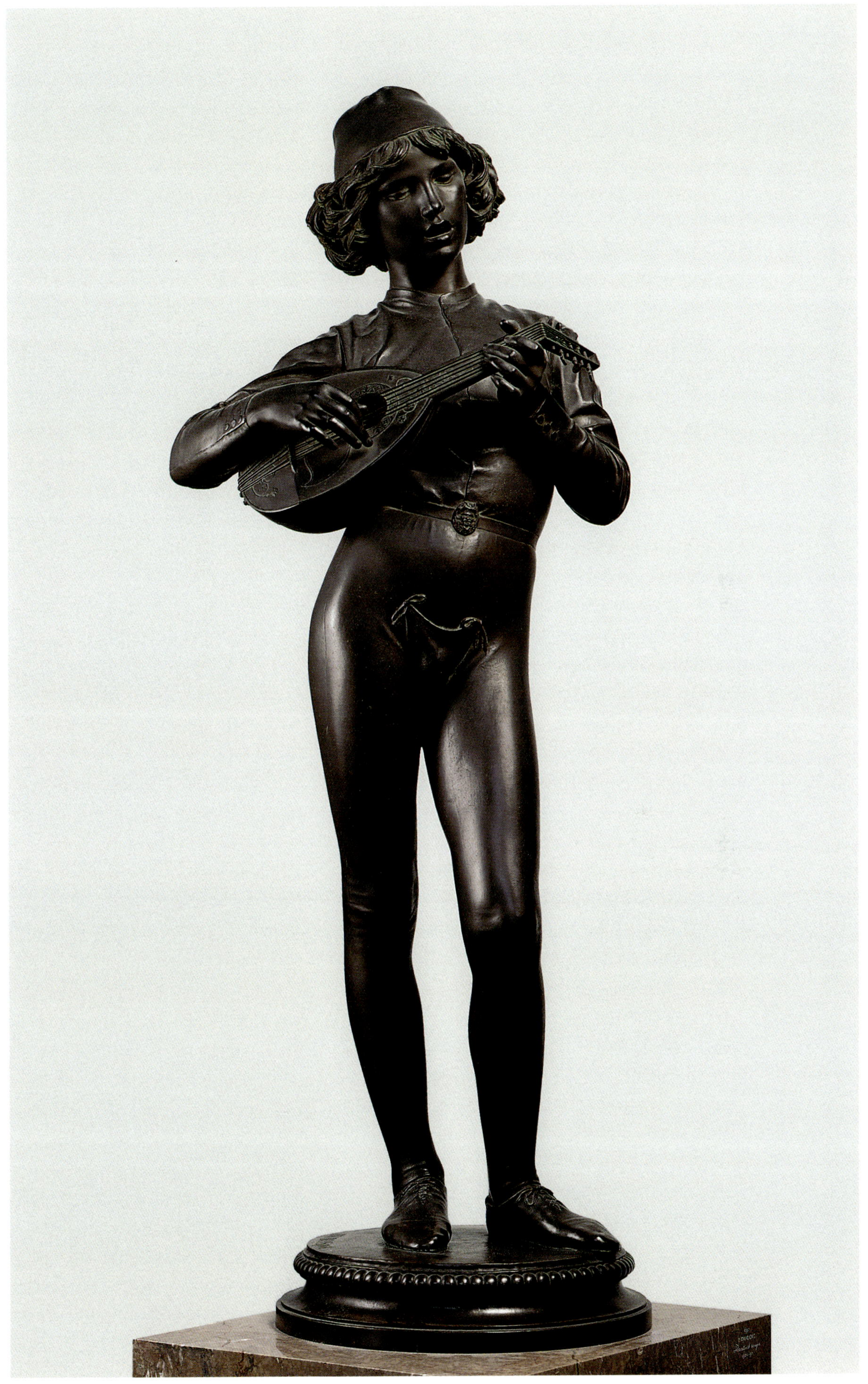

whose attitude is full of both serenity and nobility. Can this really be the mythological Narcissus who has been so frequently abused? No, without doubt, and in this we must congratulate M. Dubois, who has brought new life to the old fable in generalising the type. His figure is that of a young ephebe, who, finishing his toilette, inclines his head in a movement filled with grace, and seems less preoccupied with contemplating his floating image in the water running at his feet, than with pursuing the course of a vague reverie. Taken altogether, M. Dubois' statue unfolds before us in one pure, harmonious line; there is no more than a hint of violent projection or deplorable angle; instead there is a series of shapes and curves engendered both logically and musically one on another. [...] The work is, moreover, we could not say it too often, of one of the most distinguished sentiments; [...] and, without reproducing antiquity, without imitating the statuary of Florence, it has the exquisite savour of that body of work".[59]

Thus Dubois achieved his breakthrough at the Salon of 1863. He followed this up with *Florentine Singer from the Fifteenth Century* (cat. no. 27, fig. 32) which won him a Gold Medal at the Salon of 1865 and caused Mantz to proclaim Dubois one of the hopes of modern sculpture.[60]

Mantz described the *Florentine Singer* as "a boy of fifteen years old, a child in terms of the gracefulness of his limbs and the slenderness of his body, but already mature in terms of art and shortly to be so as far as love is concerned".[61] With a naivety which is typical of the ecstatic enthusiast, he continued by pointing out how "the clothes, so simple as to hardly exist, unite the forms of the young singer, and give to this dressed figure the charm of a nude".[62]

Mantz thus had no problem with Dubois' handling of the sculptural, nor the masculine ideal, because the harmonies and the clear course of the lines were, according to his own credo, exactly as they should be. Although the slender physique of both *John the Baptist* and *Florentine Singer* was greatly inspired by the David statues of both Donatello and Verrocchio from the fifteenth century, Mantz' judgement was that Dubois' work was free of imitative features, just as surely as in *Narcissus* Dubois had managed to avoid plagiarising the sculpture of Antiquity. He omitted to elaborate on the fact that the slight curve of the hip of the *Florentine Singer*, in an interplay with its virtual nudity seems to eroticise the figure to a degree remarkable in a representation of a member of the male sex — in this respect one is tempted to write the work off as a semi paedophile sentimentality. Neither did he notice that the depiction of *Narcissus*' mawkish self-indulgence illustrates precisely how the classical ideal in contemporary sculpture was being increasingly subject to a marked sensualisation. This process was gradually transforming the concept of the classical from its Platonic context of the balance between the beautiful, the true and the good into a lubricious, voyeuristic orgy of soft lines and nude flesh.

There were however other contemporary sculpture critics who, like Blanc, were prone to regard deviations from the classicising ideals as backsliding, a sign of decadence. This was particularly the opinion of the critic Léon Lagrange, who, in his "Le Salon de 1864" was only reluctantly and slightly sceptically prepared to accept the young generation's handling of the sculptural ideal: "It is in this familiar art of our era that all the finesse of French genius shines out. Why must one pay for this superiority by abandoning more elevated qualities which brought about the grandeur of previous ages?"[63] Lagrange was not merely lamenting the enfeeblement of the monumental, he went as far as to maintain that the talented sculptors seemed to have been paralysed. He also bewailed the decay of style and morals: "... to talk about inspiration, ideas, style, moral value, would obviously be a waste of one's time".[64]

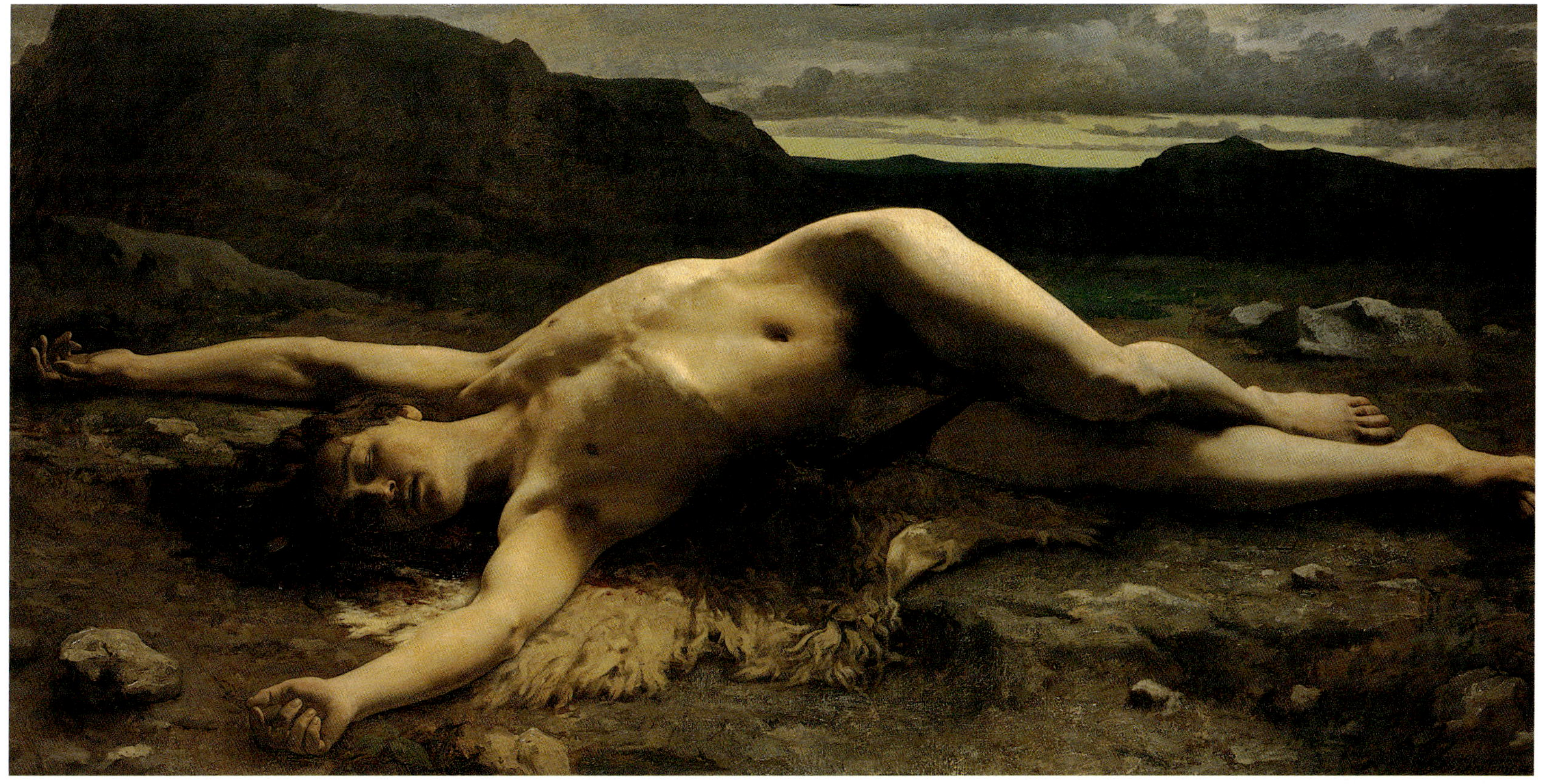

33
Camille Bellanger
Abel, 1874–75
Oil on canvas, 110 × 216 cm
Paris, Musée d'Orsay
(cat. no. 4)

The motif is taken from the Old Testament story of Cain who slew his brother Abel out of envy and thereby demonstrated the depravation of mankind after the Fall. Abel becomes the suffering innocent victim and thus the model for true believers. Bellanger shows Abel lying dead, naked and stretched out in the landscape as an easy prey to the eyes of the observer. The slender, sensual male body was an aspect of the masculine ideal of the time. Bellanger has thus used the religious story as a pretext for a portrayal of the naked male body as a sensual object. It has almost become a necrophiliac perspective. The painting was a great success when it was exhibited in the Salon in 1875.

For him the worst thing was the predominant preference for depicting young boys rather than mature men: "The tendency to the over-imaginative is not the only general characteristic of modern sculpture. I perceive another, no less evident and no less dangerous. Instead of accepting the human form when it is in full bloom, at the age when it presents the spectacle of mature male beauty, i.e. between the ages of twenty and forty years old, I see an excessive number of sculptors preferring a more fleeting period, a nature less developed and a beauty less perfect. [...] Where should we look for the source of this predilection if not in the general tendency which drives all French art to set less store by beauty than by charm? These immature natures, these delicate forms have charm [...] Enough of this charm, we say to these infantile sculptors, enough of this art which softens, enough of these flowers whose perfume enervates. Bite the fruit, attack beauty and be men".[65] On this occasion Lagrange's criticism was directed specifically at works by Dubois, as well as those by Carpeaux and Falguière.

The testimony of Mantz and Lagrange bears serious witness to the overwhelmingly complex attitudes then prevalent to questions of tradition, modernity and decadence. They both represented the more conservative position, which cultivated the classicising, formal rules for sculpture. Mantz and Lagrange were in agreement that Dubois was a modern sculptor in the sense that his works went beyond the boundaries of the traditions of which he was nevertheless so obviously a part, namely both "the standing man, nude or draped in the antique manner" and the decorative and charm-evoking predecessors of the Renaissance. But the salient point was the moral dimension which Lagrange saw as irrevocably linked to the depiction of the male body, which, apparently — and to his dissatisfaction — could encompass a wide spectrum, ranging from the more feminine to the archetypically masculine. Lagrange saw this as a sign of a decline, which, in a broader sense was one of the symptoms of the crisis in representation developing in

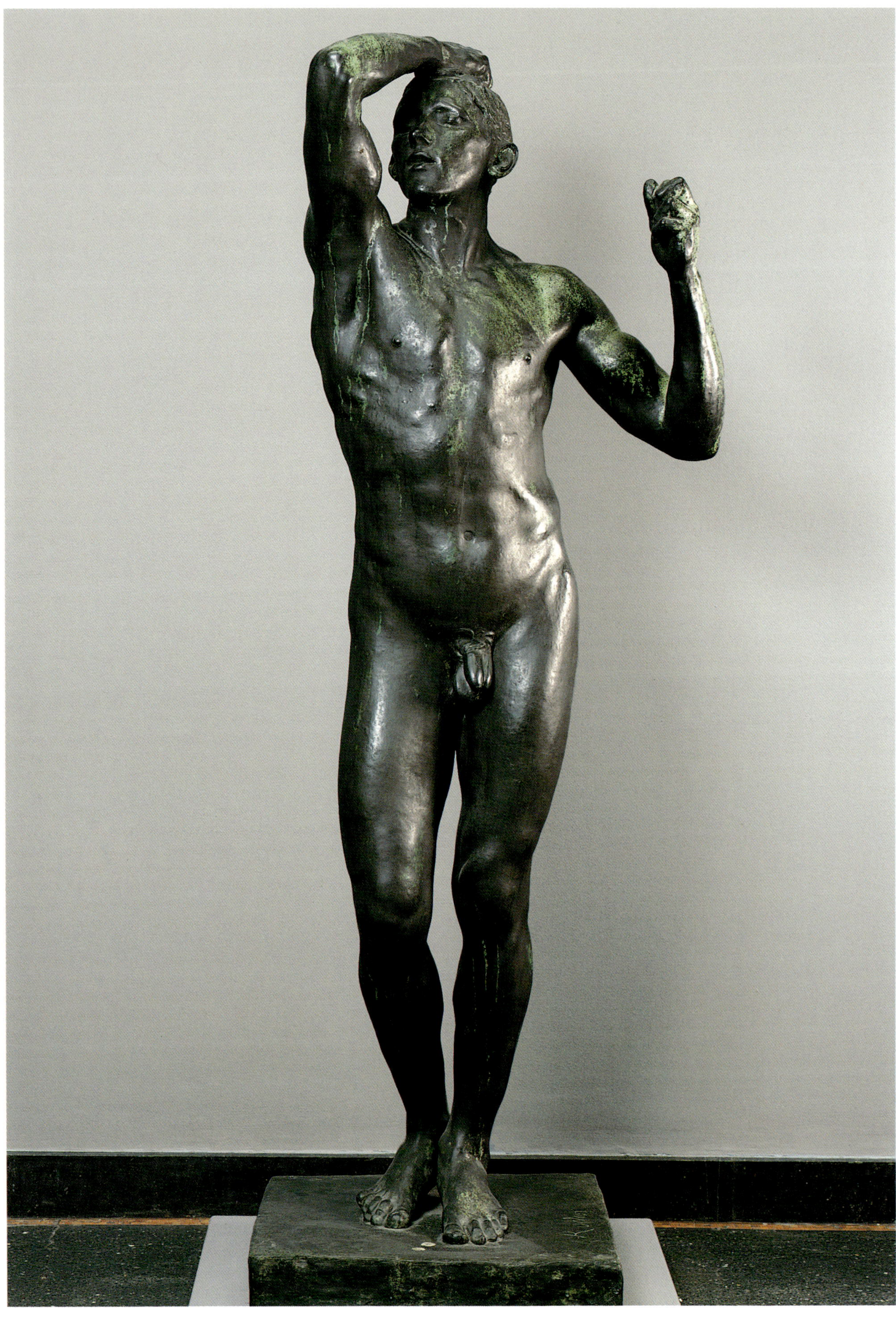

34
Auguste Rodin
The Age of Bronze (1875–76)
Cast in bronze (1901),
h. 180.5 cm
Copenhagen, Ny Carlsberg Glyptotek
(cat. no. 51)

From the beginning of his career, Rodin was deeply fascinated with Michelangelo. *The Age of Bronze* was thus inspired by the Renaissance master's famous work *The Dying Slave* (Paris, Louvre). Rodin used the pose for a motif suggesting awakening and described his figure as, "one of the first inhabitants of our world, physically-speaking perfect, but at the childhood stage of understanding and only in the process of waking up to the meaning of the world". In his modelling, Rodin had tried to get so close to nature that he was accused of having moulded the sculpture directly from a live model. He refuted these assertions with the help of photographs of the model.

sculpture in the second half of the nineteenth century, in the course of which the formal neo-classical rules became a hollow shell enclosing an ideal of culture which was passing away. The sculptors tried to continue operations within the academic paradigm, but the metaphysical dimensions were being supplanted by the charming and sensual in a kind of sculpture which was also concerned with the quest for a new, more naturalistic or realistic relation to reality.

Reality as an Effect

The human factor, the sensual and the immediately perceptible became an important indicator for the displacement undergone by the neo-classical ideals in the nineteenth century. The neo-classical teaching was indeed regarded as an aesthetic law, which in many ways was used as a rigid method of training by the various academies of art. However, in the course of the nineteenth century, the academic dogmas, to a great extent, assimilated the new tendencies so that there was not as violent a confrontation between the old schools and the new as happened in the case of painting. In addition this "renewal" often appeared in works which simultaneously evidenced a pronounced awareness of tradition.

A perfect example of this is Rodin's early work, *The Age of Bronze* (cat. no. 51, fig. 34) from 1875–76 which illustrates the gradual shift in paradigm. Here we see the resurrection of Michelangelo's *Dying Slave* in the modern epoch in a decidedly naturalistic setting. As such the work is part of the cult of Michelangelo, which was given its impetus by Carpeaux in the 1860s. In addition it is a salute to the greatest sculptural ideal of all time: the standing nude male figure. However, in its naturalism, the body is emptied of any contemporary academic codes to such a degree that on its first appearance, Rodin was accused of casting the work directly from a living model. The fact that Rodin made the figure first and only arrived at a title later, also shows that he was not plundering the attics of mythology or anything else of the kind as a pretext in his creative process. In his endeavours to find a human, as distinct from an ideal physicality, in *The Age of Bronze*, Rodin went far beyond the boundaries of neo-classicist and academic teaching. But the work is simultaneously a salute to the tradition Rodin was proud to hand on — the legacy of Michelangelo.

Another significant aspect of these sculptural considerations was the sculptor's predilection for virtuoso "life-like" effects. One instance of this is *Music* (cat. no. 23, fig. 35) from 1878 by Eugène Delaplanche, a work created for the Opéra Garnier in Paris. The opera house was to be decorated with allegories related to the building's function. Delaplanche's daring response to the challenge extrapolated the conventional allegorical personification by equipping the idealised female figure with "real" attributes — this extended to a meticulously-represented violin complete with real strings and a bow strung with real horsehair. This was yet another work which flirted with the sensual qualities, since the woman's body is barely covered by the soft drapery, held in place by a ribbon secured under the bust — a piquant way of emphasising the body's smooth marble skin and the clean contours of the figure rather than concealing them. *Music* is thus a synthesis of idealised sensuality and meticulous realism, and it attracted considerable attention when the plaster original was exhibited at the Salon in 1877; the majority of the critics were enchanted, and some went to so far as to compare the sculpture with the works of Raphael.[66]

The work's characteristic combination of the idealisation and over-accentuated realistic details is symptomatic of the "crisis of representation" into which Salon sculpture had manoeuvred itself at the end of the nineteenth century. Firstly Delaplanche's attempt to revitalise the allegory ironically emphasises that the genre was an outmoded convention. Secondly he demonstrates a significant

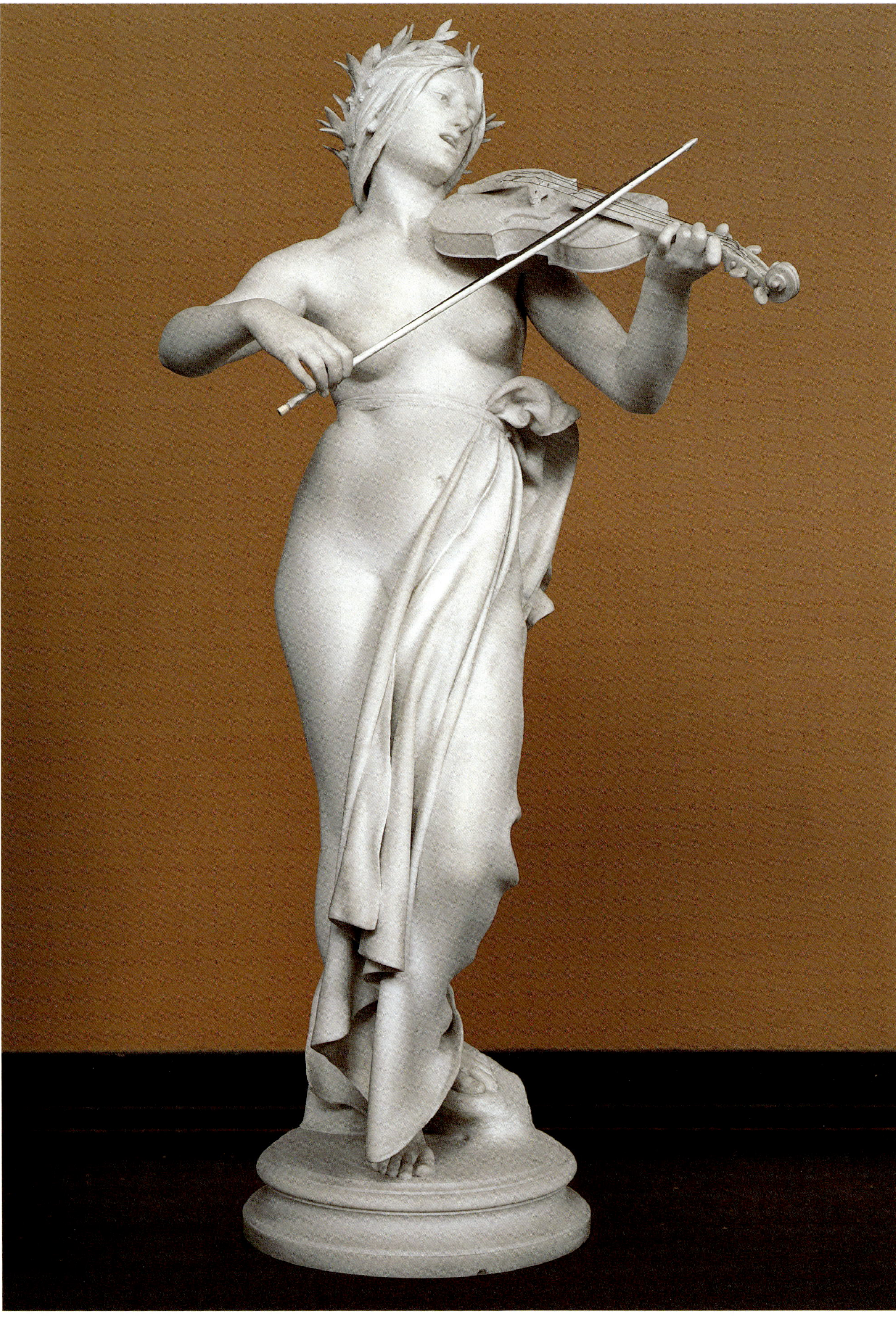

35
Eugène Delaplanche
Music, 1877
Carved in marble (1878),
h. 172 cm
Copenhagen, Ny Carlsberg
Glyptotek
(cat. no. 23)

This allegorical sculpture was originally created to form part of the ornamentation of the Opéra Garnier in Paris. Delaplanche was trying to inject new life into the tradition of allegory by letting the woman play with a bow strung with real horsehair on a violin with real strings. The work thus became a synthesis of meticulous realism and idealised sensualism, causing a stir when it was exhibited at the Salon of 1877. The bold challenge to the boundaries between art and reality was just acceptable because the female figure reminded the critics of the works of Raphael. Carl Jacobsen was enthusiastic and bought the work as the first piece of French sculpture in his collection.

36
Edgar Degas
Dancer with Ballet Skirt, Fourteen Years Old (1879–81)
Bronze, tulle and silk, h. 99 cm
Copenhagen, Ny Carlsberg Glyptotek
(cat. no. 22)

This dancer attracted great attention when she was shown at the Sixth Impressionist Exhibition in 1881. Degas had originally created the figure in wax and furnished it with real hair, a tulle skirt and silk ribbons. With its realistic effects, the curious figure of a girl was a pioneering attempt to make the sculpture more lifelike — and the public was shocked at the sight. Many critics found the sculpture ugly. But the author Huysmans had a sharp eye for the new qualities and called Degas' bold figures, "the only really modern attempt I know in modern sculpture".

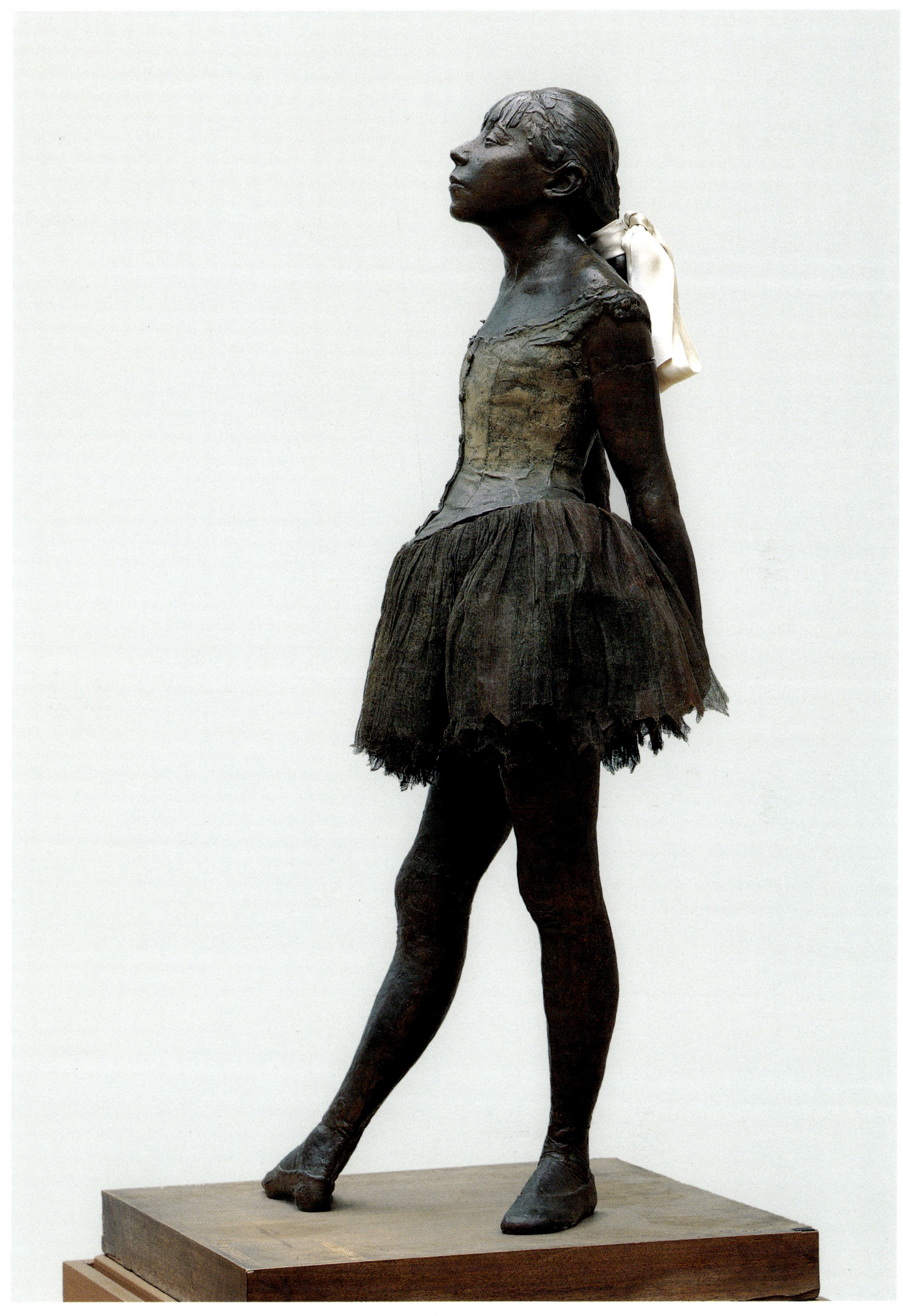

characteristic of this crisis: that academic sculpture in its eagerness to deny its artificiality in fact emphasises that very quality. Actually Delaplanche demonstrates how verisimilitude may be achieved through a variety of effects, in fact he seems to give us *reality itself* by the device of the violin bow. In so doing he shows how Salon sculpture tries to deny its material, thereby, at first glance, setting it in opposition to modern sculpture which is conventionally defined by advertising its own materiality. However, Delaplanche achieves something very similar because it is precisely the man-made quality of *Music* in its totality, which is emphasised.

Where Delaplanche, to a certain extent, attempted to revitalise Salon Sculpture within the frame of an academic paradigm, Edgar Degas took a more radical approach when, in 1879, he modelled his *Dancer with Ballet Skirt, Fourteen Years Old*, in wax (cat. no. 22, fig. 36) regarded by many as the first modern sculpture. Degas' original intention was to show the work at the Fifth Impressionist Exhibition in 1880, but he then opted to exhibit merely the empty glass case, only finally bringing in the sculpture itself for the Sixth Exhibition the following year — actions which are ample testimony to Degas' sense of presentation and showmanship. When the sculpture finally was exhibited, it attracted great attention because of its realistic effects, real hair, tulle skirt and ballet shoes. As such, *Dancer with Ballet Skirt, Fourteen Years Old* has a number of sculptural elements in common with Delaplanche's *Music*, but, nevertheless it is Degas' work which is regarded as a truly modern sculpture. Without doubt one explanation is the more radical nature of Degas' approach. He flirted with the aesthetic of ugliness and made the enigmatic figure of the girl adopt a stance which is directly opposed to the classical tradition. Its unconventional choice of materials linked the figure to the waxworks which enjoyed much contemporary popularity while the glass case recalled specimens prepared in the course of zoological research.[67] The figure can therefore be regarded as a prism for a series of the epoch's renderings of the Other. With his use of reality effects, Degas made his sculpture approximate life itself, but by the use of the glass case, he established a border between the work and the public which, at a safe distance would provide the frisson in fascination combined with fear.

The *Dancer*'s rough treatment at the hands of the critics also contributed significantly to isolating the figure from other works with similar realistic effects. J.K. Huysmans was one of the few to admit to a positive interest and wrote that the work was, "the only really modern endeavour I know of in sculpture".[68]

The Imagery in the Pygmalion Legend: the Hand of God versus the Hand of Man

The story of Pygmalion, rendered by Ovid in his *Metamorphoses*, and enjoying considerable popularity in the nineteenth century, contains the period's ideal artist myth. Briefly, it concerns the sculptor Pygmalion, who was lonely and made himself a female figure for a companion, the beautiful Galathea. Aphrodite took pity on the artistic soul and caused the statue to come to life, following which Galathea was passionately united with her creator. Jean-Léon Gérôme, Laurent-Honoré Marqueste and Auguste Rodin all drew inspiration from the legend for their work. In contrast to Gérôme and Rodin, however, Marqueste chose to omit Pygmalion from his sculpture, focusing entirely on *Galathea* (cat. no. 43, fig. 37). Her stance is a coquettish contrapposto with the hands behind the head and the eyes closed — a posture which clearly refers to both Michelangelo's *Dying Slave* and Rodin's *The Age of Bronze*. Like Rodin, Marqueste renders the actual pose a motif of awakening: Galathea is coming to consciousness, quite literally quickened by Pygmalion's life-giving kiss. Simultaneously her pose gives the spectator unrestricted access to the body's invit-

37
Laurent-Honoré Marqueste
Galathea, 1884
Carved in marble (1904),
h. 180 cm
Valby, Carlsberg Museum
(cat. no. 43)

In the Greek legend of Pygmalion as retold by Ovid in his *Metamorphoses*, the sculptor Pygmalion fell in love with a female figure he himself had created. Aphrodite took pity on the artist and one day caused the statue to come to life when Pygmalion kissed her thus uniting the pair. The myth is about the artist-genius who, with the aid of divine inspiration, creates life from the barren stone. It also deals with the role of desire in the encounter of the spectator with the work. Marqueste has chosen to omit Pygmalion himself, thereby permitting the spectator to take his place. In this way Galathea's inviting shape and rhythmic lines tempt the spectator exactly as they tempted her creator.

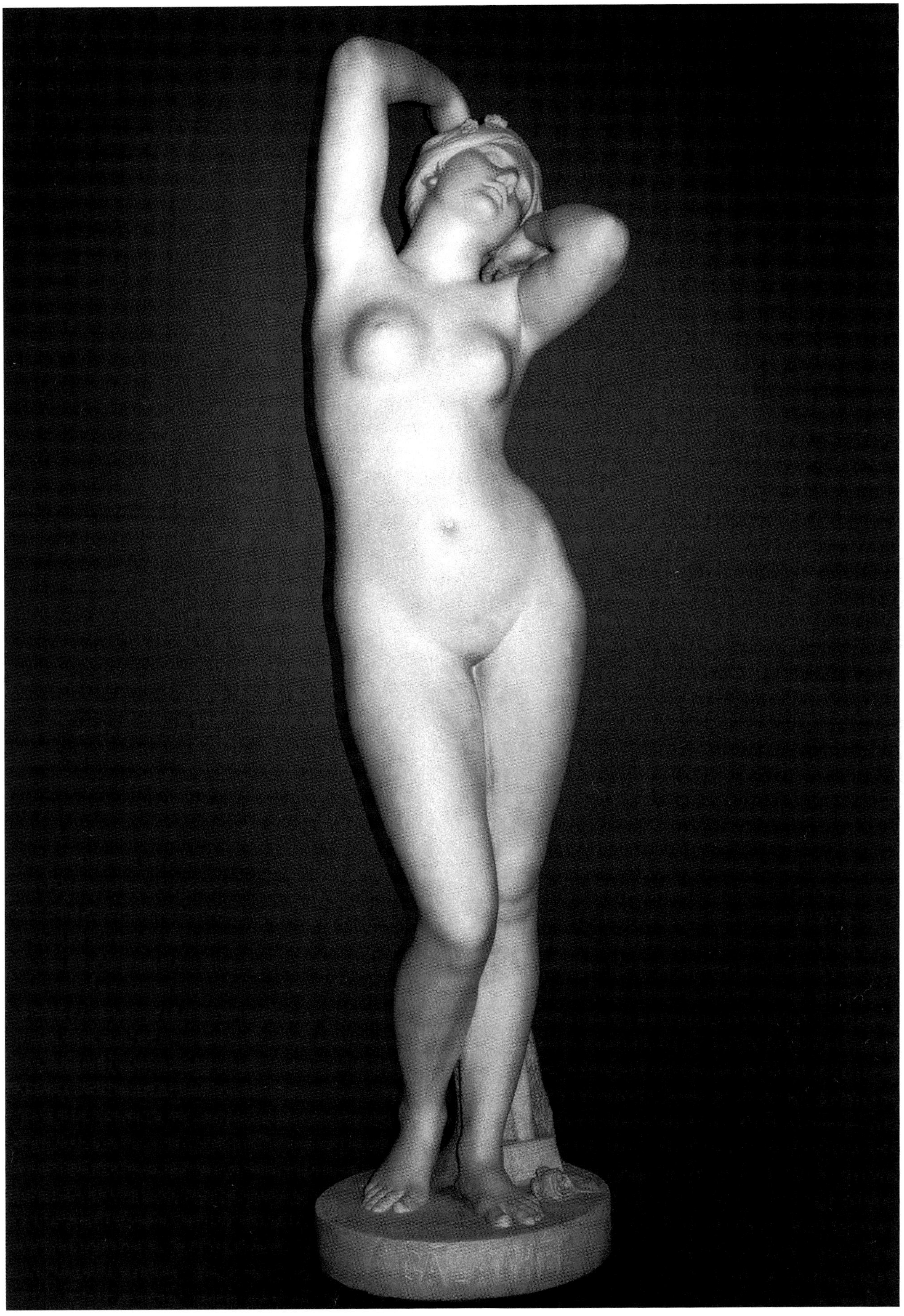

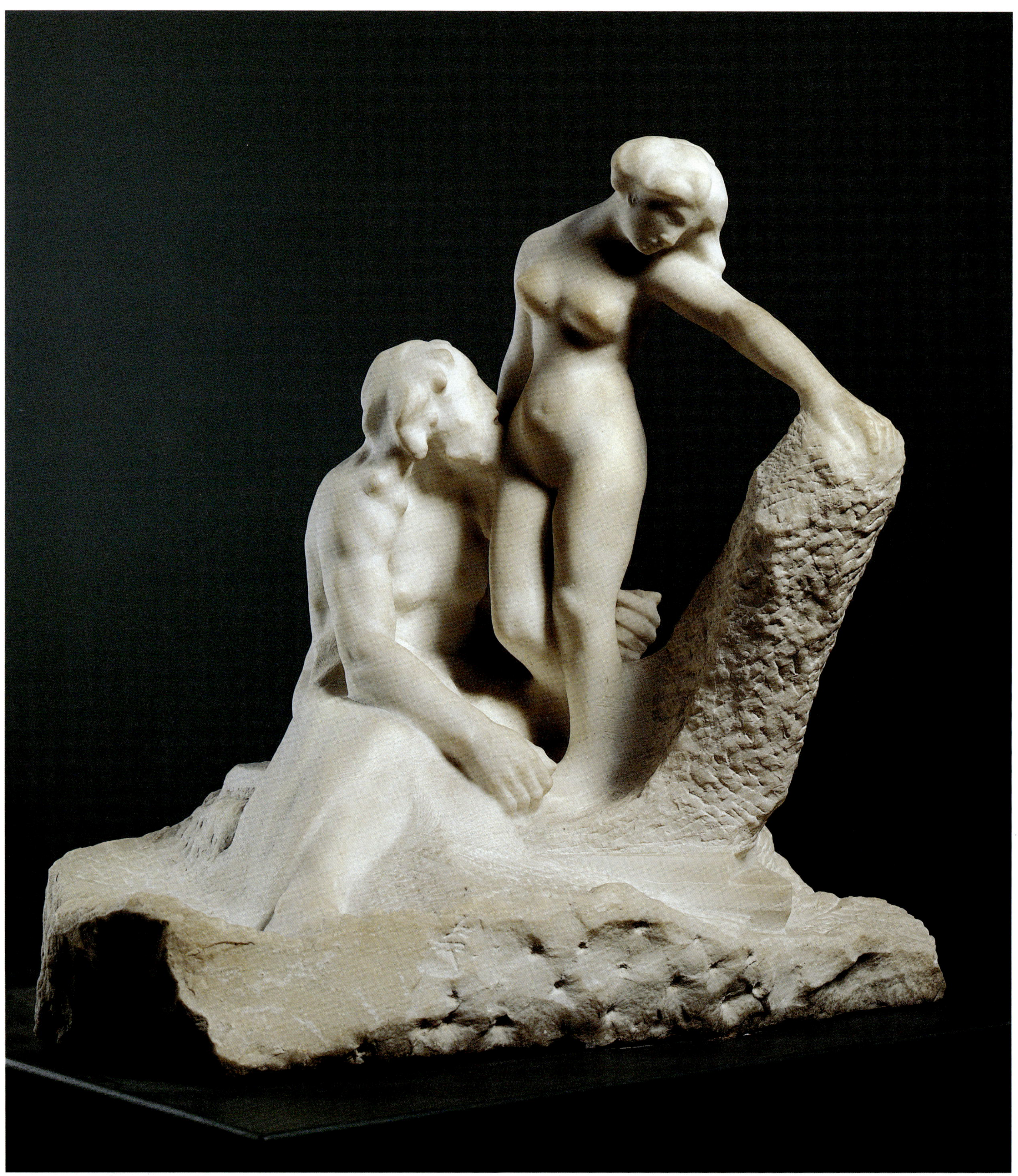

38
Auguste Rodin
Pygmalion and Galathea
(1889)
Carved in marble (1907–10),
h. 76.9 cm
Copenhagen, Ny Carlsberg
Glyptotek
(cat. no. 53)

Rodin takes as his point of departure the Greek myth about Pygmalion, who falls in love with Galathea — the sculpture of a woman he himself has modelled. With the aid of Aphrodite, Galathea is brought to life before the eyes of her creator, after which they are passionately united. Rodin has chosen to depict the very instant in which Galathea is transformed by Pygmalion's life-giving kiss. With this focus on the process of creation, Rodin symbolically portrays the artist-genius liberating the figure from the stone by virtue of divine inspiration. In this way, the work also becomes a kind of "self-portrait" of Rodin's own creative power.

ing shape and rhythmic lines. By bearing witness to Galathea's metamorphosis, the spectator virtually becomes a stand-in for Pygmalion, thereby sharing his desire for the unconcealed sensuality of his own creation.

The popularity of the theme is probably due to its multifaceted metaphorical aspects and the fact that the myth unites what are arguably the three most important demands made on the sculpture of the nineteenth century. Firstly it is possibly the oldest myth concerning art as the ideal imitation of life, precisely the ideal to which academic sculpture should aspire. Secondly it gives sustenance to the romantic notion of the nineteenth century which represents the artist as a genius, who, through divine inspiration, brings forth a figure from the barren stone. In conclusion the myth is also about the fact that desire has a role in relation to the work of art — not only in the process of creation, but also in the encounter between the work and the spectator. It is precisely this aspect Marqueste has chosen to emphasise in his interpretation of the myth. The work points quite specifically to the desire which can be awakened by a naked woman — and exemplifies how sculpture of that period was able to cater for male fantasies, i.e. it reflects the voyeurism typical of the time.

Rodin began work on the theme in 1889 from a different angle to that of Marqueste. Rodin's version of *Pygmalion and Galathea* (cat. no. 53, fig. 38) is meditation on the actual principle of the process of sculptural modelling in a double sense. While Pygmalion, according to the myth, was creating Galathea with the help of Aphrodite, the work's pronounced stamp of *non-finito* emphasises how the raw material becomes something formed by the hands of the artist. *Pygmalion and Galathea* is like Adam and Eve, shaped, not by God but by Rodin, and is, in other words, almost a self-portrait of the artistic power of creation.

That is at least how it looks on the face of it. Adolf von Hildebrand, however, was more sceptical about Rodin's use of the *non-finito* treatment of the stone. Hildebrand was a confirmed admirer of Rodin's talent, but he was, at the same time, irritated that Rodin never strove for, "complete, thoroughly-structured works". In 1917 Hildebrand wrote a rejoinder to a review by the art critic Heinrich Wölfflin, and chose to focus on precisely this quality in Rodin's work: "… beyond his astonishing feeling for organic life, he employed means that were to create an effect, and that these means came from a process that did not take place in the work of art itself, but that were employed artistically to stimulate, indeed, to delude the viewer. Everybody who has ever worked directly in stone must realize that Rodin perceived the traces of work in Michelangelo's partially hewn marbles in a purely superficial manner, and that he used it in and for itself. The way he did so immediately proves to the expert that Rodin never cut anything directly in stone himself. He works in a manner that cannot originate through a natural process. I am only drawing attention to this deceit, which is surely completely unconscious because it shows how a superficial appearance can be made to look as if it had meaning, that is, to look as if it is an expression of a process of life and of creation. It can also be seen as a superficial stimulus for the eye, as a component, just as a word might be taken purely as a sound without considering its meaning".[69] The puritanical Hildebrand thus regarded this *non-finito* effect as a falsehood in Rodin's works: "His works were only realised in clay and his marbles were fakes stated in an untrue language. In this he was most naïve. Others have also had to resort to such means, and in the end, perhaps Rodin was the most courageous of deceivers".[70]

When Hildebrand characterises Rodin in a mixture of admiration and belittlement as "the most courageous of deceivers" it is naturally consistent with Hildebrand's own classical standpoint which is expressed in his tract *Das Problem der Form in der Bil-*

denden Kunst, in which he attempts to develop a theoretical approach to the relation between form and appearance.[71] For him the central problem in figurative art — both for painting and sculpture — was the question of the work's *unity*. This was a unity, which, in Hildebrand's mind was a condition resulting from the interplay of work and spectator. In Hildebrand one encounters, therefore, a significant recognition that form, and thereby meaning, come into being in a dialogue between the work and the spectator. The spectator has no *a priori* control over the object. Hildebrand found this so problematic for the sculpture, however, that he reached a conviction that the work should be created in such a way as to overcome its three-dimensionality and take into account the limitations in a single viewpoint. It is therefore the business of sculptors, so to speak, to meet the spectator halfway and adjust their work so that it would be possible to retain a single, firm, viewpoint and yet, at the same time achieve a clear picture of a unity in terms of both form and space. For Hildebrand the ideal solution was a relief, which clearly meets the spatial demands of the work on the framework of a picture; the ideal, to his mode of normative thinking was the ancient Greek relief. The sculptor should, therefore, like the painter, work with an illusory space, having a viewpoint which was predetermined and fixed.[72]

Thus the modernist Baudelaire was not alone in finding the three-dimensionality of sculpture problematic: fifty years later he would paradoxically find an ally in the classicist Hildebrand. Each reached his own radical conclusion. Where Baudelaire "gave up" and called sculpture stupid and primitive, Hildebrand was quite ready to circumvent sculpture's "dimension problem" by making reliefs; this was not only a way of coming towards the human way of seeing, but also because the object, according to his reasoning, would, otherwise remain real and thus the artistic idea would be lost. Hildebrand's concept of art had this emphasis on the artistic construction in common with Baudelaire. But Hildebrand's demand that sculpture should make it easy for human beings to see — the process of identification should not be made more complicated — went against the increasing tendency of contemporary art to encourage the spectator to take a more active part in the process. This applies both to the sculptures of Rodin and the shimmering surfaces of Impressionism. Although Hildebrand appropriated his age's concern with the problem of form and had a relatively modern understanding of this interaction, he was, at the same time, unmistakably a classicist, who, in his demand for unity and a cohesive silhouette, firmly positioned himself in the slipstream of Winckelmann's ideal of the pure contour.

It was therefore against this background that Hildebrand distanced himself from Rodin with the words: "As soon as he follows his own path however, Rodin becomes modern in the bad sense: he is French. Whether it is the Monument to Victor Hugo... or any of his many-figured groups, most of them fall apart. We cannot find the angle from which to grasp them in their unity. And in those cases where he strives for a spiritual frame of mind, we find a forced superficial appendix, as in the case of a bad actor".[73] In this way Hildebrand points out a feature which is absolutely central to Rodin's works: a use of effects which function on the surface of the work in such a way that they challenge the classical dictum that the outer surface of a work should be an expression of the order within. This can clearly be seen in the monument to *Balzac* (cat. no. 54, fig. 39) where the writer is swathed in a cape, seemingly possessed of an expressive life of its own, which does not reveal any structure which we might imagine to be underneath. Balzac's genius is to be communicated by the expressive, visual effect and not by a structure dictated by logic.

39
Auguste Rodin
Balzac, 1891–92
Bronze, h. 106 cm
Zurich, Kunsthaus
(cat. no. 54)

This portrait of the famous author was exhibited at the Salon of 1898. There it provoked a scandal and was rejected on the grounds that it was neither a beautiful nor faithful portrait of the national laureate. People regarded the sculpture as a twisted and unfinished depiction of the novelist. Rodin's tendency to caricature was, however, a conscious choice in his quest to express the essence of Balzac both as a human being and as an artist. The figure became an immovable monolith growing straight out of the ground, and crowned with the expressive head. With this vision of Balzac's personal strength and creative power Rodin broke away, in every sense, from the traditional concept of the monument.

40
Auguste Rodin
The Shade (1880)
Cast in bronze (1902),
h. 192 cm
Copenhagen, Ny Carlsberg Glyptotek
(cat. no. 52)

Rodin created *The Shade* as an image of one of the damned souls in Hell. It was one of the many independent sculptures emerging from his unfinished lifetime work *The Gates of Hell*. Rodin has given physical substance to a shadow, which is, strictly speaking, a visual phenomenon. The play of the light on the monumental body gives life to the surface. Rodin has created the visual effect so that at a distance the silhouette of the work looks like a shadow. The prominent musculature is inspired by the ancient *Belvedere Torso*, but the broken figure of *The Shade* is decidedly anticlassical in its tense pose.

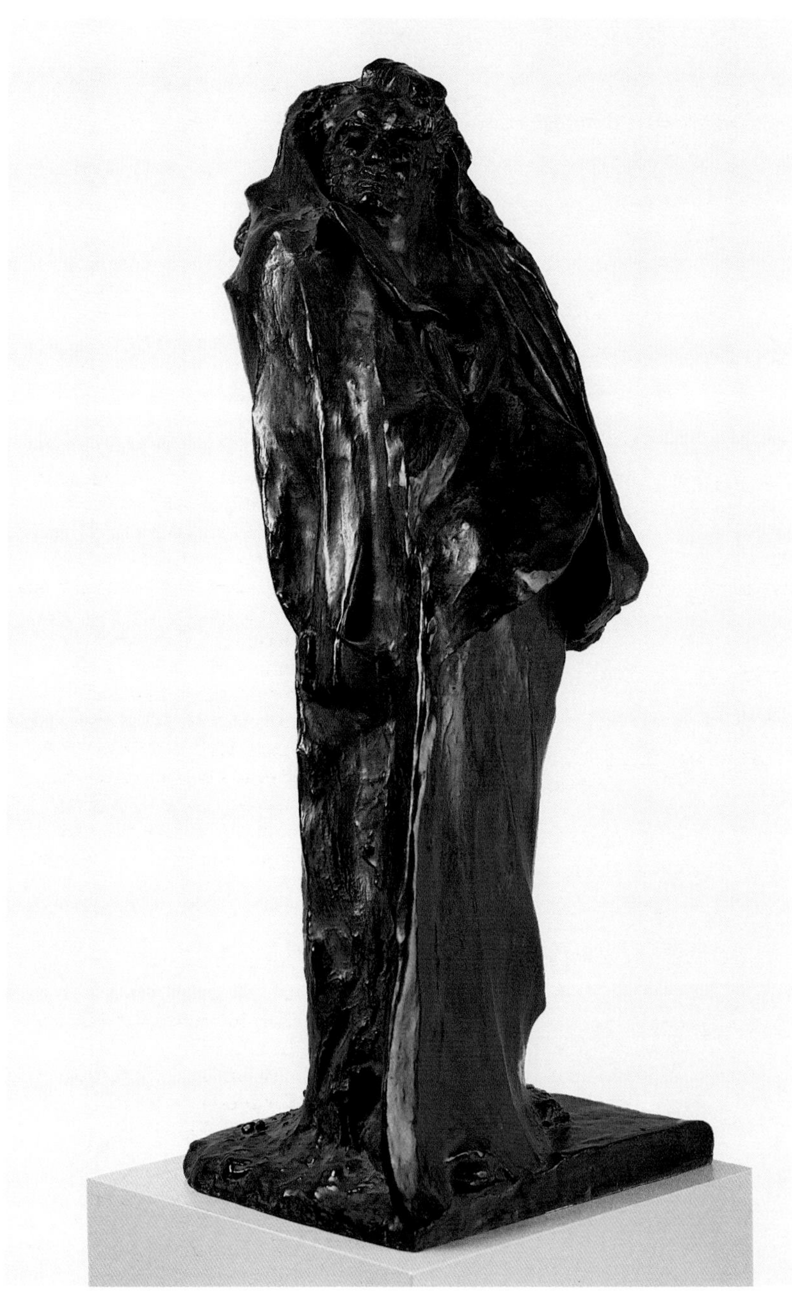

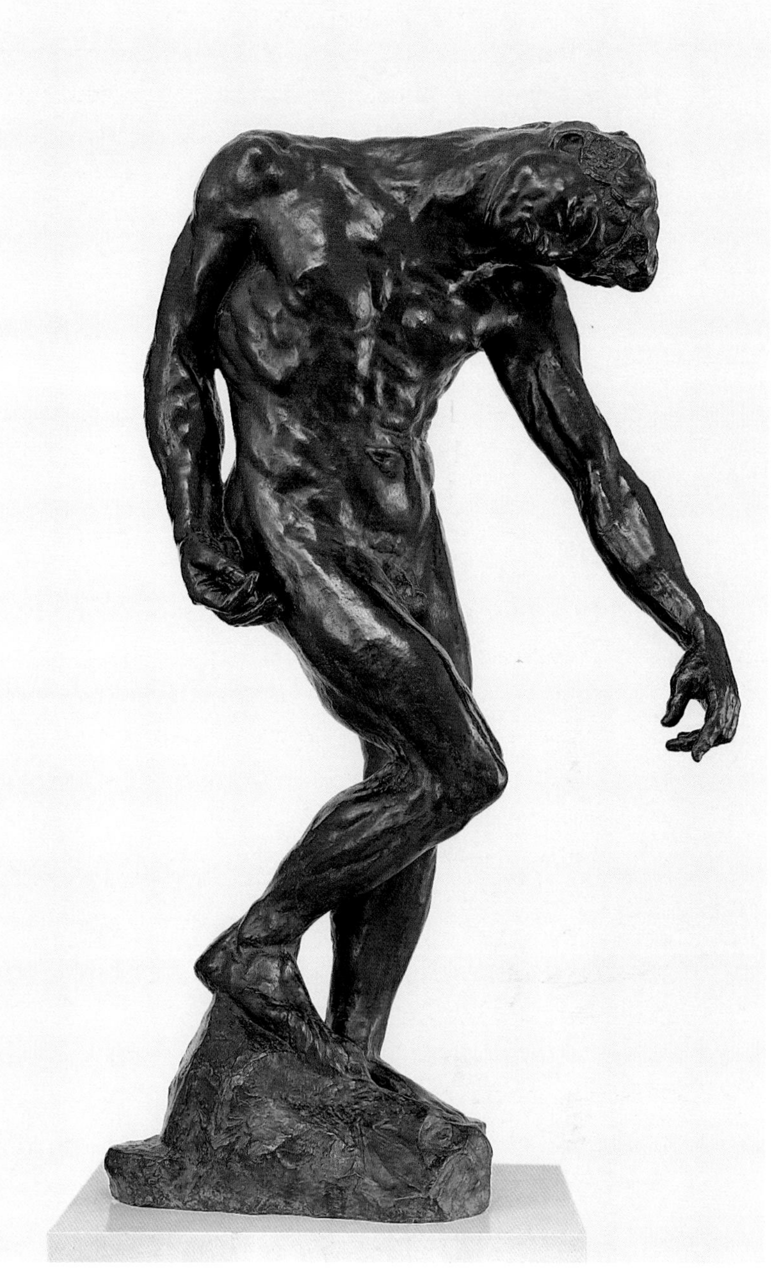

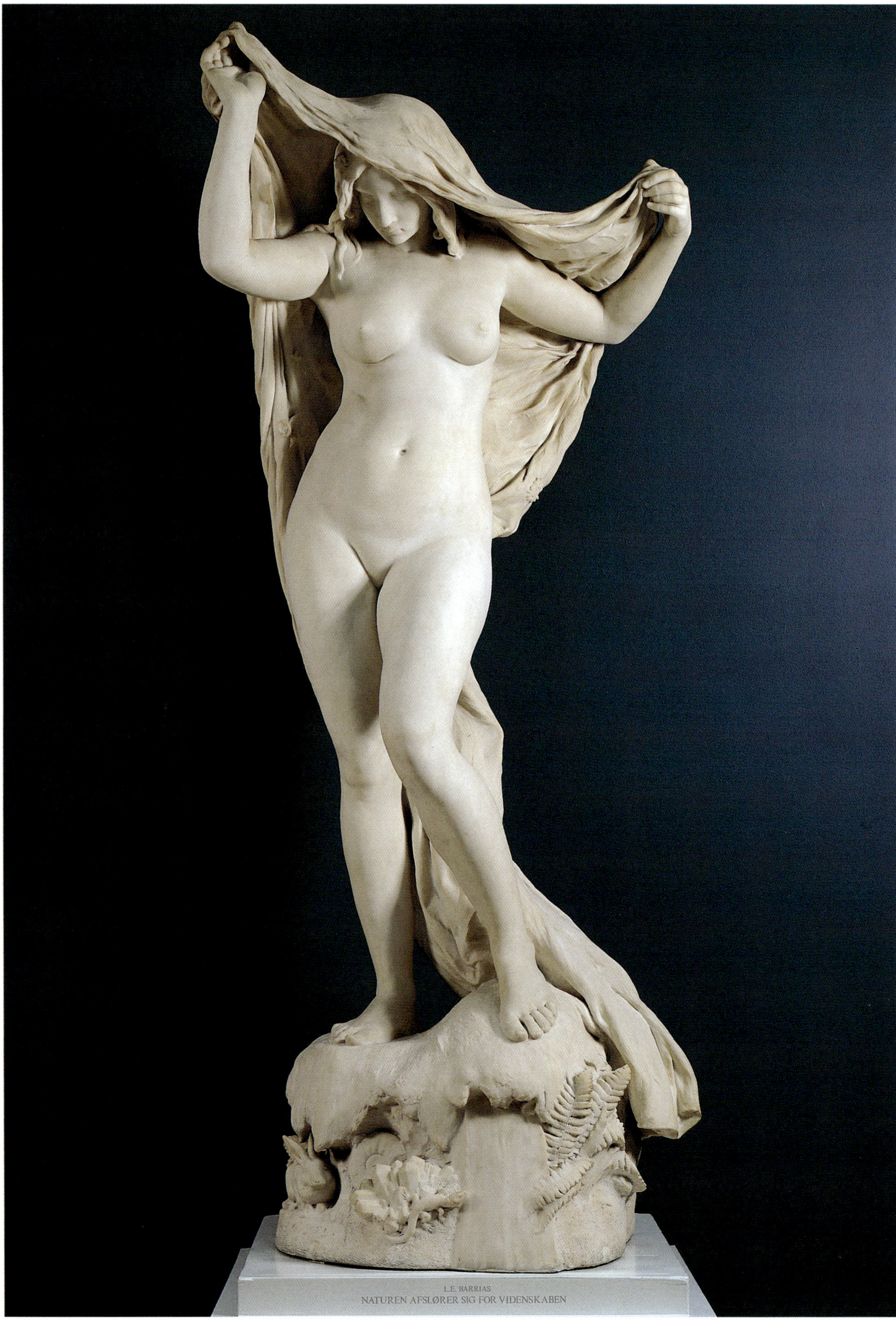

41
Louis-Ernest Barrias
Nature Revealing Herself to Science (1893)
Carved in marble (1895–97), h. 253 cm
Valby, Carlsberg Museum (cat. no. 2)

Barrias had the task of creating a work concerned with scientific progress which, at the time, seemed capable of solving all the mysteries of the world. As he said, it was only a question of time before nature revealed its last secrets. The sculptor accomplished his task with this allegory — a veritable striptease in which Nature reveals her naked body. But rather than prompting thoughts of scientific investigation, the work fuels fantasies of an erotic nature. In this, it is typical of the sensualism that was making itself felt in the Salon sculpture and erasing any allegorical connection. This sculpture became famous in its time and was, however, seen as an allegory of the epoch of progress when it was shown in the World Exhibition in 1900.

Seen in this way, Rodin's *The Shade* (cat. no. 52, fig. 40) can almost be interpreted as an artistic acknowledgement of the visual effect as such: the rendering of a visual phenomenon in solid form. In his attempt to accomplish the task, which is, in theory, beyond the abilities of any sculptor, Rodin has given the body of the colossus a wavy surface, which seems to wipe out the outline of the form, thereby giving the figure, when seen from a distance, the effect of a shadow.

Towards the end of the century, Louis-Ernest Barrias (1841–1905) set himself a task which seemed, likewise, beyond the capabilities of sculpture when he began work on a figure which would express the progress of science; a phenomenon which, it was then believed, would solve all the world's mysteries. It was, as he said, only a question of time before nature revealed her ultimate secrets. Thus, in *Nature Revealing Herself to Science* from 1893 (cat. no. 2, fig. 41) Barrias attempted to give solid form to the modern, positivist principle of inquiry through the figure of a woman who puts aside her veil and thereby disclosing the secrets of her body. The result is a veritable striptease, which, far from directing one's thoughts towards natural science's objective methods of inquiry, provides sustenance for fantasies of a decidedly erotic character. In this way Barrias' work is symptomatic of the sensuality which managed to penetrate the Salon and made cuckolds of every allegorical association and literary forerunner. In other words, in the case of Salon sculpture, allegorical sculpture found itself with a serious credibility problem.

It is, however, interesting that in 1899, Barrias produced a second version of the figure in polychrome marble, onyx and ivory with details in lapis lazuli and malachite. This version was hailed at the Salon of that year as a modern work — presumably on account of its multicoloured choice of materials, thus rejecting the neo-classicist stipulation of the purest of white marble. The sculpture achieved considerable contemporary fame and was seen as an allegory of the progress of the epoch when it went on show at the World Exhibition of 1900.

That posterity has elected to hail Rodin as the first modern sculptor, while relegating Marqueste and Barrias to obscurity may be ascribed to Rodin's ability to make his work formulate a multifaceted materiality which puts the process of artistic creation right in the centre. However, Marqueste's *Galathea* and Barrias' *Nature Revealing Herself to Science*, are equally authentic expressions of the sculptural preoccupations of the time. Barrias' sensual-erotic marble version of the idea of the naked truth is paradigmatic for the efforts of Salon sculpture to encapsulate Modernity in an academic language of forms, which had stretched its naturalism to the extreme. The formal demands for wholeness and statuary volume are preserved, but all that remains of the classical ideal is nudity itself.

A Masquerade of Quotations

Closer examination makes it apparent that it is not too easy to differentiate between the traditional and the avant-garde in sculpture. Salon sculpture's relation to tradition is actually quite subtle, and moves within a spectrum which can be characterised by such words as copying, imitation, influence, quotation, reference, inspiration, allusion and incorporation.

One important factor is that traditions of sculpture other than that of Classical Antiquity manage to find their way in and are subsumed into the academic canon, just as, to an increasing degree, academic sculpture assumes typical contemporary features — among them realistic and sensual elements. However it is precisely these features which force academic sculpture into a crisis, which, so to speak, comes from within. In addition, and of particular interest, is the mobility which seems characteristic of the choice of references made by sculptors. They are ap-

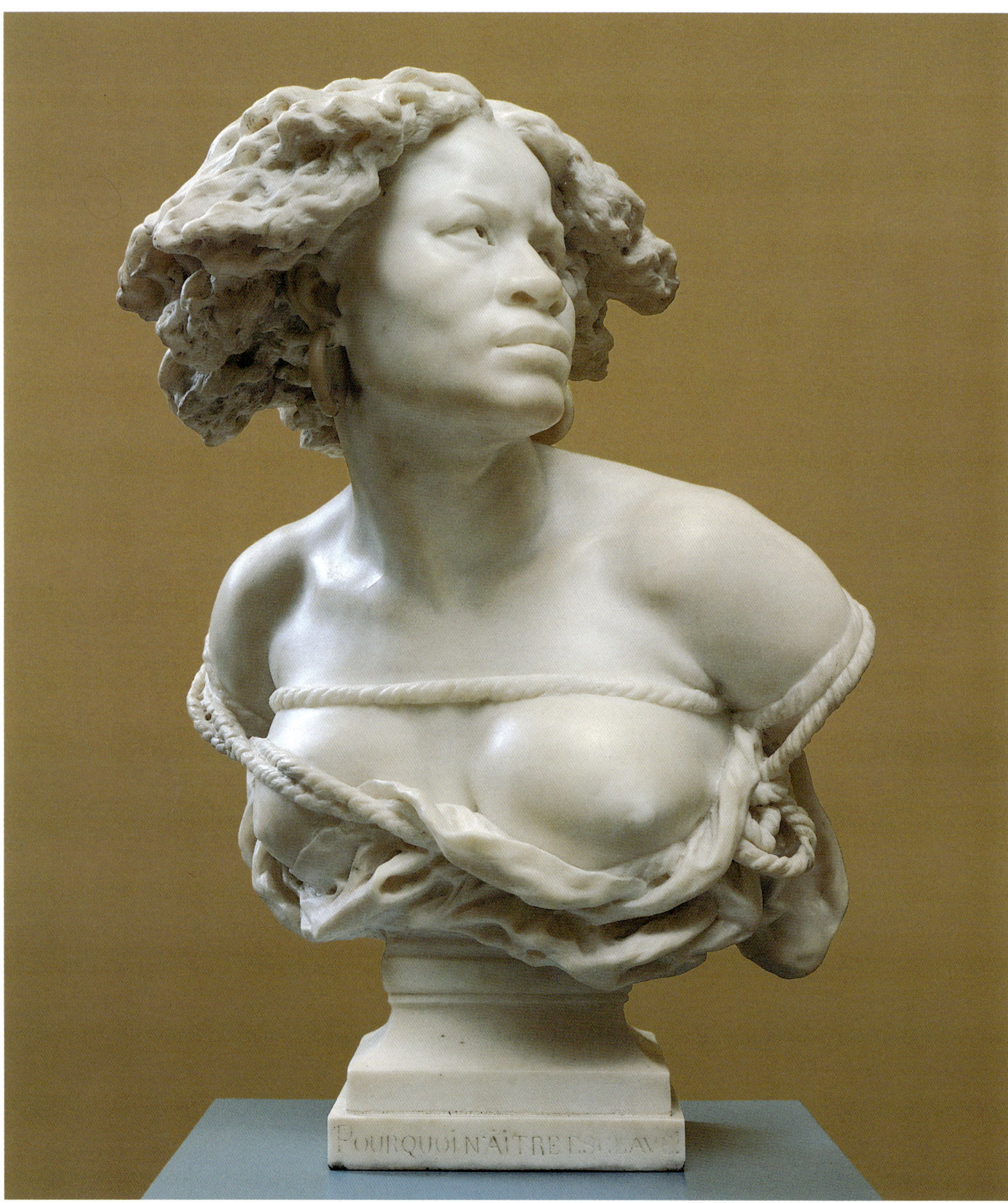

42
Jean-Baptiste Carpeaux
Negress (1868)
Carved in marble (1869), h. 67 cm
Copenhagen, Ny Carlsberg Glyptotek
(cat. no. 10)

With *Negress* Carpeaux wanted to remind his public of the horrors of slavery. He sculpted this "savage" and "ignoble" figure on the basis of precise ethnographical studies. However, he questioned the existing social hierarchy by using the aristocratic form of the bust and adding the inscription *Why be born a slave?* What was, in fact, a moral issue became the point of departure for the figure's sensuous play between rope and body — and the public loved it. Carpeaux treated the exotic, piquant motif with a feeling for both decoration and statuary exuberance. In consequence the work came to consist of equal portions of political indignation and decadent seduction.

43
Jean-Léon Gérôme
Sarah Bernhardt, 1895
Painted wax, h. 69 cm
Amsterdam, Van Gogh Museum

44
Henri Matisse
Decorative Figure (1908)
Bronze, h. 73 cm
Copenhagen, Ny Carlsberg Glyptotek
(cat. no. 44)

The title of this work draws attention to what was a prime concern for Matisse: form as ornamentation. The figure is not standing erect in the manner of a classical statue, but has stepped down from his plinth and is posing nonchalantly for the spectator. As a result, the square shape of the plinth counteracts the flowing lines of the body to form a decorative whole. The figure has thus become an ironic commentary on the Classical sculptural tradition.

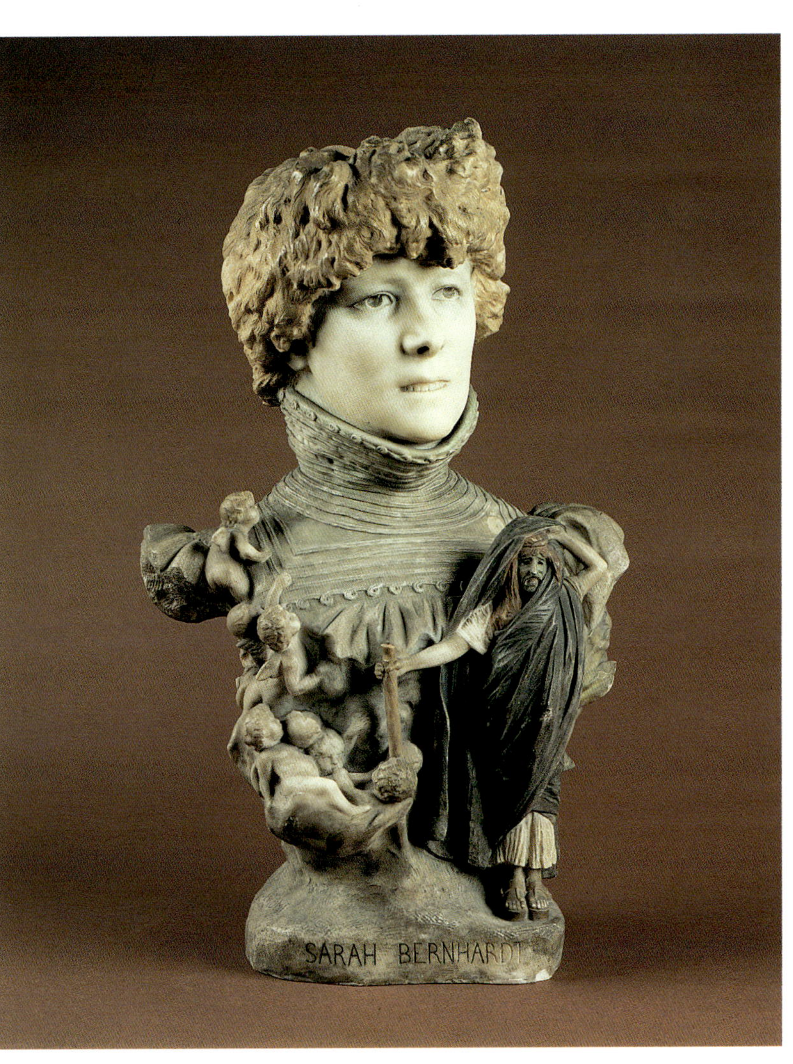

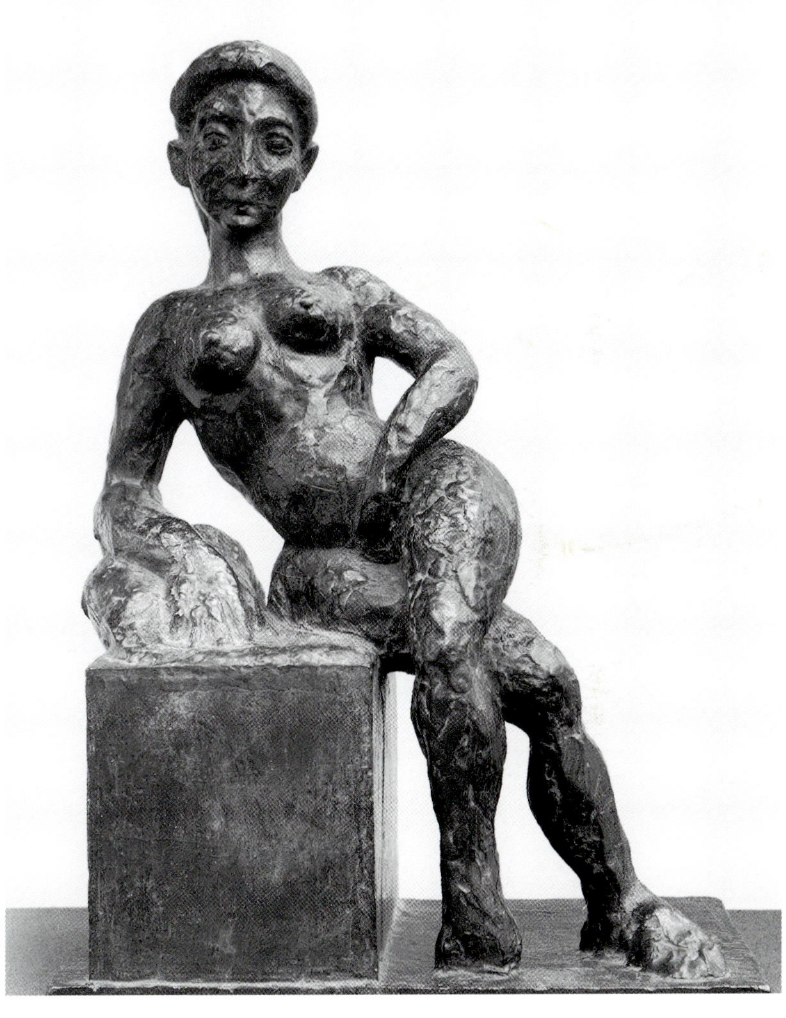

parently free to choose whether to be inspired by Antiquity, the Renaissance, the Baroque, the Rococo, etc. Many opt for the Renaissance.

The sculptors' educational journeys to Rome were without doubt crucial to this predilection for the Renaissance, but it is probably also significant that Renaissance sculpture is, in itself, testimony to how it is possible, as a sculptor, to avoid becoming paralysed by one's admiration for the masterpieces of Antiquity.

In other words, the attitude of the Salon sculptors to tradition derives from a panoptic view of the European tradition of sculpture, which permits the artist to dominate his past through his ability to juggle his quotations. In this respect it is as if the Salon sculpture from the second half of the nineteenth century reproduces itself within a structure of repetition, rendering the tradition a matter of continuous recycling: a phenomenon also encountered in the painting of the era.[74]

The question is, however, whether the crisis of representation prevailing in the Salon sculpture is not a central element in its articulation of the Modern. One aspect of this crisis is a concept of tradition which permits multiple references — as though tradition has become a "self-service menu", or a costume one can clothe sculpture in according to the occasion. Another aspect of the crisis is the quest for effects and the sensualism which, in time, erode the link with tradition.

If one were able to discard the modernistic filter, it might be possible to interpret this articulation in Salon sculpture, this wrestling with matter, as just as "authentic" an expression of the modern position as the kind of sculpture we traditionally regard as modern — particularly considering the fact that this relationship is not exclusive to Salon and academic sculpture, but also features in the sculpture, which, based on the conventional criteria of Modernism — the fragmented and the unfinished — we have labelled "modern".

The experience of modernity is thus greater than, and different from the experience of tension and schism, as which it is frequently presented. It also includes an active, historical consciousness, which is crucial to the eclecticism to be found not only in sculpture, but throughout the entire aesthetic field in the nineteenth century. The distinguishing feature of modern self-awareness is transformation. To be modern is therefore, not merely a question of attracting attention to the transformation from subject matter to work of art, but it also involves a protean capability within a tradition.

There are, however, many nuances in this consciousness of tradition. Fundamentally, we must assert that a tradition is always defined in retrospect — it is a historical construction. As such consciousness of tradition is a way of locating oneself in relation to history, a way of creating a context — just like the writing of the history of art, is context-creating. And one of the most important narratives in the history of art deals, as is well known, with finding references in Classical Antiquity. In her article, "The Venus Pudica: uncovering art history's 'hidden agendas' and pernicious pedigrees", Nanette Salomon deals with precisely this relationship: "Writers are not the only ones to produce and reproduce these coherent narrative histories. They are also worked through artists, who consciously or unconsciously operate within prearranged historical tropes so that their work can easily be inserted into these well-valued discourses. Classical references can, of course, come in a variety of different shapes and sizes. These involve a sliding scale from explicit to implicit connection with ancient art: for example mythological subject-matter, classical form, classical pose or classical disposition. Such connections do much more than validate any work by placing it within a recognizable, and highly prestigious, historical genealogy. They bestow an instant sense of knowledge and mastery upon the viewer who sees the connections and place him/her in the league of a cultural elite".[75]

Artistic awareness of tradition, quotations, references or whatever else one might call it, are, in other words, a coded language, which can be read without difficulty by the initiated. And just like the writing of history, the artistic quoting from tradition plays an active part in creating an ideological narrative of a certain cultural development, which actively promotes the myth of western culture's universality and ability to survive — complete with all the Eurocentrism, colonialism, male chauvinism, etc. etc. involved. Thus the awareness of tradition has the potential of being understood as an implicit defence against modern progress and in the last instance an anti-nihilist life-belt. To return to Søren Kierkegaard's concept of repetition, with which I commenced my introduction, it is however possible to add an aspect to the awareness of tradition. Then repetition provides the opportunity for the individual to take up an authentic position in relation to modern reality. This becomes an undertaking which seeks the now and the absolutely immediate. Within Kierkegaard's frame of reference the sculptors' complex use of quotations — ideally seen — becomes a much more marked way of representing a modern position. When the sculptor quotes, and thereby draws attention to works of earlier masters, his own peculiar nature (or lack of such) stands out all the more clearly, and thus he simultaneously points out that his own works are contrivances — they are even theatrical (though not necessarily in Michael Fried's understanding of the concept). The presentation thus becomes an act, a drama with tradition as the scene: a play just like the modern presentation of oneself as described by T.J. Clark in *The Painting of Modern Life*.[76]

In conclusion, one might say that the sculpture of the second half of the nineteenth century becomes, in one and the same gesture, a sign of the great narrative of civilized cultural formation, as well as of the consumer's ideology together with his social and sexual aspirations. Towards the end of the century it seemed as if this surfeit of meanings and technical finesse forced Salon sculpture to go into a spin. Works such as Delaplanche's *Music* mark this demise of the academic paradigm. One can interpret this flexible transformation of the sculptural tradition — which over a prolonged period was given increasingly realistic and sensual features — as an expression of the enduring power of bourgeois ideology, or it can be read as an expression of a particularly modern masquerade. As far as I can see, the answer lies somewhere in between.

[1] Søren Kierkegaard, *Fear and Trembling. Repetition*, edited and translated, with Introduction and Notes by Howard V. Hong and Edna H. Hong (Princeton: Princeton University Press, 1983), p. 149.

[2] See Anne-Birgitte Fonsmark, Emanuelle Héran and Sidsel Maria Søndergaard, *French Sculpture 2* (Copenhagen: Ny Carlsberg Glyptotek, 1999), pp. 226–27.

[3] J.J. Winckelmann, *Geschichte der Kunst des Alterthums*, 1–2. Teil (Dresden, 1764); G.E. Lessing, *Laokoon: oder über die Grenzen der Malerei und Poesie*, 1. Teil (Berlin, 1766).

[4] Matei Calinescu, *Modernitetens fem ansikten* (Ludvika: Dualis, 2000), p. 33. Translated from English: *Five Faces of Modernity* (Durham: Duke University Press, 1987).

[5] Alex Potts, *Flesh and the Ideal. Winckelmann and the Origins of Art History* (New Haven and London: Yale University Press, 1994), p. 146.

[6] *Ibid.*, p. 165.

[7] Winckelmann, 1764, Part One, Chapter Four.

[8] Translated from Karin Sanders, *Konturer. Skulptur- og dødsbilleder i guldalderlitteraturen* ([Contours. Images of Sculpture and Death in the Literature of the Golden Age], Copenhagen: Museum Tusculanum, 1997), p. 23.

[9] Charles W. Millard, "Sculpture and Theory in Nineteenth Century France", in *The Journal of Art Criticism*, vol. 34, 1974–75, pp. 15–20 (p. 16). Winckelmann and Lessing were indeed their inspiration: Quatremère's response was the most conservative, Cousin had a more moderate view, that sculpture was the high point in the history of European art, while Jouin held an "orthodox academic position". See Quatremère's *Le Jupiter olympien, Essai sur l'idéal* and *Considérations morales sur la destination des ouvrages de l'art*. See also Henri Jouin's *Esthétique du sculpteur*. Millard also mentions some less familiar names: Émeric-David, author of *Recherches sur l'art statuaire*; Seroux d'Agincourt, author of *Histoire de l'art par les monuments*, v. II as well as Paillot de Montabert, author of *Théorie du geste* and *L'Artistaire*.

[10] See Adolf von Hildebrand, *Das Problem der Form in der Bildenden Kunst* (Strasbourg, 1893). It was with this tract that sculpture be-

came the object of more systematic reflections on the problems of form and was incorporated in what can be called "proto-phenomenological" considerations vis-à-vis the interaction with the spectator and space. Rudolf Wittkower maintains in his book *Sculpture* (1991), p. 233, that Hildebrand's book was the most read and most influential book on art in the period from its first appearance up to 1914. Its readership ranged from the general public to artists and students and influenced, among others the art historical method of Wölfflin.

[11] Anne M. Wagner, "Learning to sculpt in Nineteenth Century France. An Introduction", in *The Romantics to Rodin*, exhibition catalogue (Los Angeles, 1981), pp. 9–20 (p. 10). At the Petite Ecole where sculpture was taught as one of the decorative arts, the students were taught anatomy, drawing, modelling in clay and the techniques of carving, both from life and from casts of earlier works. The aim of such instruction was that students should learn to imitate, rather than interpret the original models. In the course of their training the students' abilities were regularly tested in competition assignments, e.g. the ornamentation of a fountain, where the goal was primarily to train them in the execution of decorative motifs for the growing building industry in a Paris which was now undergoing a rapid expansion. By virtue of its systematic programme, which equipped its students with the fundamental skills, the Petite Ecole also functioned as a kind of preparation for the Ecole des Beaux-Arts, where it was possible to continue one's training as a "proper" artist. This was the avenue chosen by Jean-Baptiste Carpeaux, and attempted by Auguste Rodin, all three of whose applications for admittance were, however, rejected.

[12] Calinescu, 2000, p. 33.

[13] Students at the Academy of Art were subjected to a stringent programme, their time being divided between so-called *études libres*, and the numerous competitions by which their abilities were evaluated. The professors chose the competition subjects very carefully, stipulating the specific number of figures, their specific attitudes and any specific attributes. The competitions were in fact building on the fundamental idea that for every problem there existed such thing as an ideal solution. And it was towards those solutions the students trained at the Ecole des Beaux-Arts were exhorted to strive. The actual training was, in fact, under the control of the Académie de Peinture et de Sculpture, founded in 1648. It was the Academy's department of sculpture which decided the theme of the assignment — most frequently a scene from mythology or history — for the competition leading to the prestigious Prix de Rome. It was also the Academy which was responsible for awarding the competition's crucial first prize (the Grand Prix), whereby the successful artist received a state travel bursary to cover a five-year period of study at the Ecole Française de Rome. On his return home the artist tended to be greeted with public commissions, which would guarantee work and thus income. When, after several years, he had made his reputation, the artist would himself be made an associate of the Academy, and participate in the awarding of the Grand Prix. This cycle ensured the perpetuation of the tradition within a relatively closed system. The ambitious sculptor of the nineteenth century was thus obliged to compete for the coveted Prix de Rome. See Wagner, 1981, pp. 9–20 (pp. 13–14), also Anne Pingeot, "Formation et apprentissage", in Anne Pingeot and others, *De Carpeaux à Matisse* (Lille, 1982), pp. 23–31. See Wagner, 1981, pp. 12–13 and Pingeot, 1982, pp. 24–25 for an account of the procedure in the Prix de Rome competition, which consisted of three tests.

[14] Millard, 1974–75, p. 16.

[15] "Voulez-vous prendre l'empreinte de la vérité [..], marquez résolument vos plans et dessinez carré plutôt que rond, parce que des plans résulte le relief, et que les plans ne résultent pas du rond. En sculpture, il s'agit des reliefs; il faut donc prendre garde aux profils..." Paolo Emiliani Giudici, "Correspondance de Florence: le sculpteur Dupré, ses bas-reliefs à la base de la grande coupe égyptienne" (Correspondance particulière), in *Gazette des Beaux-Arts*, 1859, vol. 1, Quatrième livraison, pp. 240–47 (p. 242).

[16] "... des lignes, qui se heurtent et s'harmonisent, se contrarient et se balancent, intelligence des plans, profond savoir anatomique, mais qui ne rapelle pas le modèle, ni ses vulgarités, ni ses lassitudes, ni ses poses convulsives". Paolo Emiliani Giudici, "Correspondance de Florence: le sculpteur Bartolini et ses ouvrages" (Correspondance particulière), in *Gazette des Beaux-Arts*, 1859, vol. 1, Deuxième livraison, pp. 111–16 (p. 116).

[17] Millard, 1974–75, p. 16.

[18] *Ibid.*, p. 17.

[19] David Scott, "Matter for Reflexion: Nineteenth-Century French Art Critic's Quest for Modernity in Sculpture", in Richard Hobbs (ed.), *Impressions of French Modernity* (Manchester and New York: Manchester University Press, 1998), pp. 99–117.

[20] Millard, 1974–75, p. 17.

[21] Stendhal, *Histoire de la Peinture en Italie*, 1ère ed. 1817.

[22] "... une soif ardente d'émotions fortes..."; "... soif de l'énergie nous ramènera aux chefs-d'œuvre de Michel-Ange". "Si un Michel-Ange nous était donné, [...], où ne parviendrait-il point? Peut-être crécerait-il une sculpture moderne, peut-être forcerait-il cet art à exprimer les passions". Quoted from Luc-Benoist, *La sculpture romantique* (Paris, 1928), p. 37.

[23] Millard, 1974–75, p. 17. Quoted from Millard, who quotes from Stendhal, "Salon de 1824", in *Mélanges d'art et de littérature* (Paris, 1867), p. 254.

[24] Calinescu, 2000, p. 42.

[25] *Ibid.*, p. 44.

[26] "La beauté dans chaque siècle n'est que l'expression des qualités qui lui sont utiles". Luc-Benoist, 1928.

[27] Gabriel Laviron and Bruno Galbaccio, *Le Salon de 1833* (Paris, 1833), pp. 38–39.

[28] Apart from one work in 1834 and one in 1837.

[29] Gautier acclaimed Préault as being for the Romantic movement in sculpture what Victor Hugo was for literature, Delacroix for painting and Berlioz for music. See Théophile Gautier, *Critique d'Art. Extraits des Salons (1833-1872)*, textes choisis, présentés et annotés

par Marie-Hélène Girard (Paris: Séguier, 1994), pp. 349–50.

[30] "… d'une nouveauté extraordinaire dans la sculpture: la tradition classique était rompue, et la révolution s'accomplissait dans tout le cycle d'art". *Ibid.*, p. 351.

[31] Patricia Mainardi, "Les premiers essais de synthèse d'une critique de l'art contemporain international", in Jean-Paul Bouillon (ed.), *La critique d'art en France 1850–1900*, Actes du colloque de Clermont-Ferrand 25, 26 et 27 (Université de Saint-Etienne, 1989), pp. 53–62 (p. 55).

[32] "Le nu est la condition essentielle de la sculpture…, la représentation du corps humain, dégagé de toute particularité et de tout accident, constitue le beau idéal…" Quoted from *L'Art en France sous le Second Empire* (Paris: Grand Palais, 1979), p. 253. Originally from Théophile Gautier, *Les Beaux-Arts en Europe, 1855* (Paris, 1855–56), 2 vols., t. I, p. 117.

[33] "De tous les arts, celui qui se prête le moins à l'expression de l'idée romantique, c'est assurément la sculpture. Elle [la sculpture] semble avoir reçu de l'Antiquité sa forme définitive… Que peut la statuaire sans les dieux et les héros de la mythologie, qui lui fournissent avec des prétextes plausibles les nus et la draperie dont elle a besoin". Théophile Gautier, quoted from Luc-Benoist, 1928, p. 35.

[34] Calinescu, 2000, p. 38.

[35] "Hardiesse, inouïe dans le temps où nous vivons, d'exposer sans aucun titre mythologique un chef-d'œuvre qui n'est ni une déesse, ni une nymphe, ni une dryade […] mais tout bonnement une femme"; "figure étincelante d'une beauté toute moderne". Quoted from Stéphane Guégan, "Modernités", in *Théophile Gautier, la critique en liberté* (Paris: Musée d'Orsay, 1997), pp. 38–58 (p. 44).

[36] In 1848 Gautier published an article entitled "Plastique et civilisation - Du beau antique et du Beau moderne", in *L'Evénement* (8 August, 1848). Reprinted in Théophile Gautier, *Souvenirs de théâtre, d'art et de critique* (Paris: Charpentier, 1883); see also Calinescu, 2000, p. 48.

[37] Scott, 1998, p. 101. As Scott puts it, "it was both spiritual or intellectual and physical or material".

[38] *Ibid.*, p. 102. "Gautier's evocation of the women in terms of sculpture is, however, not only an academic convention but also the expression of a deep fantasy".

[39] *Ibid.*, pp. 102, 104 and 107. He also points out how Gautier in his poetry makes use of a verse/marble metaphor, which became so integral a part of the period's poetic language (used also by such writers as Gautier's own pupil Baudelaire), that, in Scott's estimation it developed a crucial influence on the concept of contemporary sculpture.

[40] A synecdoche emphasises the quality of an object above the object itself.

[41] "La sculpture a plusieurs inconvénients qui sont la conséquence nécessaire de ses moyens, brutale et positive comme la nature, elle est vague et insaisissable à la fois, parce qu'elle montre trop de faces à la fois". Charles Baudelaire, "Salon de 1846: XVI. Pourquoi la Sculpture est ennuyeuse", in *Curiosités esthétiques* (Lausanne: Edition de l'œil, 1956), pp. 185–88 (p. 185).

[42] See Lessing's comparative analysis of the different aesthetic disciplines.

[43] Quoted from Charles Baudelaire, "The Salon of 1846", in *Art in Paris 1845–1862. Salons and Other Exhibitions Reviewed by Charles Baudelaire*, translated and edited by Jonathan Mayne (London: Phaidon Press, 1965), pp. 41–120 (p. 97). The original quotation in French: "L'éclectisme, à différentes époques, s'est toujours cru plus grand que les doctrines anciennes, parce qu'arrivé le dernier il pouvait parcourir les horizons les plus reculés; mais cette impartialité prouve l'impuissance des éclectiques. Des gens qui se donnent si largement le temps de la réflexion ne sont pas des hommes complets; il leur manque une passion. […] Un éclectique ignore que la première affaire d'un artiste est de substituer l'homme à la nature et de protester contre elle. Cette protestation ne se fait pas de parti pris, froidement, comme un code ou une rhétorique; elle est emportée et naïve, comme le vice, comme la passion, comme l'appétit. Un éclectique n'est donc pas un homme". Charles Baudelaire, "Salon de 1846: XII. De l'éclecticisme et du doute", in *Curiosités esthétiques* (Lausanne: Edition de l'œil, 1956), pp. 170–72 (pp. 171–72).

[44] Michael Fried, *Manet's Modernism, or The Face of Painting in the 1860s* (Chicago and London: The University of Chicago Press, 1996), pp. 164–65.

[45] Quoted from Charles Baudelaire, "The Salon of 1859", in *Art in Paris 1845–1862. Salons and Other Exhibitions Reviewed by Charles Baudelaire*, translated and edited by Jonathan Mayne (London: Phaidon Press, 1965), pp. 144–216 (p. 206). The original quotation in French: "Cette figure, généralement remarquée, a suscité quelques critiques selon nous trop facile. […] On a dit que c'était un plagiat, et que M. Franceschi avait simplement mis debout une figure couchée de Michel-Ange. Cela n'est pas vrai. […] l'élégance paradoxale de ces membres est bien le fait d'un auteur moderne. Mais quand même il aurait emprunté son inspiration au passé, j'y verrai la raison d'un éloge plutôt que d'une critique; il n'est pas donné à tout le monde d'imiter ce qui est grand…" Charles Baudelaire, "Salon de 1859: VIII. Sculpture", in *Curiosités esthétiques* (Lausanne: Edition de l'œil, 1956), pp. 372–83 (p. 375). Michael Fried suggests that Baudelaire preferred a work to recall in the spectator, in an unobtrusive manner, the memory of earlier works without him feeling coerced in any particular direction — i.e. as a more unconscious process. Fried, 1996, pp. 164–65.

[46] It is however possible to read something else in neo-classical sculpture: this is apparent in, for example, Mikkel Bogh's interpretations of Thorvaldsen, where Bogh demonstrates how Thorvaldsen's works of sculpture can be seen as the locus of a modern concept of the subject. In other words, Bogh makes Thorvaldsen modern. See Mikkel Bogh, *Bertel Thorvaldsen*, Dansk Klassikerkunst 3 (Copenhagen, 1997).

[47] Calinescu, 2000, p. 51.

[48] *Ibid.*, p. 142.

[49] Blanc began his career as a critic in 1839 and wrote his last review of the Salon in 1879. Neil M. Flax, "Charles Blanc: le moderniste mal-

gré lui", in Jean-Paul Bouillon (ed.), *La critique d'art en France 1850-1900*, Actes du colloque de Clermont-Ferrand 25, 26 et 27 (Université de Saint-Etienne, 1989), pp. 95–104 (p. 96).

[50] Jean-Paul Bouillon and others (eds.), *La Promenade du critque influent. Anthologie de la critique d'art en France 1850-1900* (Paris: Hazan, 1990), p. 153.

[51] "La beauté morale est oubliée, la sublimité du fond nous échappe". *Revue du progrès politique, social et littéraire*, 1839, t. I, p. 346. Quoted from Flax, 1989, p. 97.

[52] "La modération du mouvement et la sobriété du geste sont la première loi de la statuaire". Charles Blanc, "Grammaire des Arts du Dessin - Livre II - Sculpture (deuxième article)", in *Gazette des Beaux-Arts*, 1864, pp. 59–79 (p. 60).

[53] *Ibid.*, p. 62.

[54] *Ibid.*, p. 74.

[55] An instance of this is Paul Mantz's judgement that in his work *Ugolino* (about which Mantz tended to be critical anyway), Carpeaux overstepped the mark with regard to what was permissible in sculpture by presenting Ugolino with his fingers in his mouth: "Le geste de l'affamé portant ses doigts à ses lèvres arides n'est guère admissible en sculpture, il est plus bizarre que rationnel..." Paul Mantz, "Le Salon de 1863: peinture et sculpture", in *Gazette des Beaux-Arts,* 1er juillet, Première livraison. Cinquième année, tome quinzième (Paris, 1863), pp. 32–64 (p. 51).

[56] Bouillon and others, 1990, p. 19.

[57] See Jens-Peter Munk and Holger Reenberg, *French Sculpture I* (Copenhagen: Ny Carlsberg Glyptotek, 1993), pp. 176–77.

[58] Mantz, 1863, pp. 32–64. "L'exposition de sculpture nous a révélé le nom d'un nouveau venu, M. Paul Dubois, dont le talent, plein de jeunesse, s'est formé à Rome d'après les leçons des maîtres éternels..."

[59] "... il y a dans le *Saint Jean-Baptiste* et dans le *Narcisse*, un si excellent sentiment des belles lignes et un si grand goût, que la critque ne peut que saluer avec joie un aussi heureux début. Le petit *Saint Jean-Baptiste*, debout, la main élevée, s'avance avec cette ardeur juvénile et inspirée qui convient aux précurseurs; la tête est poétique, la figure entière a du mouvement, de la sveltesse et je ne sais quelle élégante énergie. A cette figure, déjà si remarquable, nous préférons le *Narcisse*, qui est mieux conçu dans les conditions de la grande sculpture, et dont l'attitude est pleine de sérénité et de noblesse. Est-ce bien le Narcisse mythologique dont on a tant abusé? Non, sans doute, et nous en félicitons M. Dubois, qui a rajeuni la vieille fable en généralisant le type. Sa figure est celle d'un jeune éphèbe qui, au sortir du bain, penche la tête par un mouvement plein de grâce, et semble moins occupé de regarder sa flottante image dans l'eau qui coule à ses pieds, que de suivre dans sa pensée le cours d'une vague rêverie. Prise dans l'ensemble, la statue de M. Dubois déroule au regard une ligne harmonieuse et pure; point de saillie violente, point d'angle fâcheux, mais au contraire une série de formes et de courbes musicalement et logiquement engendrées les unes par les autres. Dans les détails du torse et de la hanche, nous avons remarqué quelques maigreurs, quelques pauvretés, mais elles sont à peine sensibles, et le marbre réparera aisément les rares défectuosités du plâtre. L'œuvre est d'ailleurs, nous ne saurions trop le redire, d'un sentiment des plus distingués; elle est venue d'un seul jet, sans reproduire l'antique, imiter la statuaire florentine, elle en a l'exquise saveur". Mantz, 1863, pp. 32–64 (pp. 51–52).

[60] Paul Mantz, "Le Salon de 1865", in *Gazette des Beaux-Arts*, 1er juillet, Première livraison. Cinquième année, tome quinzième (Paris, 1865), pp. 5–42 (p. 36).

[61] "Un garçon de quinze ans, un enfant par la gracilité des membres et la sveltesse du corps, mais déja mûr pour l'art et bientôt pour l'amour". *Ibid.*, p. 34.

[62] "Le vêtement, si simple qu'il existe à peine, épouse les formes du jeune chanteur, et donne à cette statue habillée le charme d'une figure nue". *Ibid.*, p. 34.

[63] "C'est dans cet art familier qu'éclate de nos jours toute la finesse du génie français. Pourquoi faut-il qu'il paye cette supériorité par l'abandon de qualités plus hautes qui ont fait en d'autres temps sa grandeur?". Léon Lagrange, "Salon de 1864", in *Gazette des Beaux-Arts*, 1er juillet, Première livraison. Sixième année, tome dix-septième (Paris, 1864), pp. 5–44 (p. 39).

[64] *Ibid.*

[65] "La tendance à la fantaisie, [...] n'est pas seule que l'on puisse signaler comme un caractère général de la sculpture moderne. J'en aperçois une autre non moins évidente et non moins dangereuse. Au lieu d'accepter la forme humaine à l'heure de son épanouissement complet, à l'âge où elle présente d'une manière fixe le spectacle de la beauté virile, c'est à dire de vingt à quarante ans, je vois un trop grand nombre de sculpteurs préférer une heure plus fugitive, une nature moins arrêtée, une beauté moins parfaite. [...] Où chercher la cause de cette prédilection, sinon dans la tendance générale qui pousse l'art français tout entier à tenir moins de compte de la beauté que du charme? Ces natures jeunes, ces formes délicates ont le charme [...] Assez de charme, dirons-nous à ces sculpteurs enfantins, assez de cet art qui amollit, assez de ces fleurs dont le parfum fatigue. Mordez au fruit, attaquez-vous à la beauté, et soyez hommes". Lagrange continues: "Il y a des besoins plus vivants qui appellent la main du statuaire. L'art monumental ne saurait se passer de cet auxiliaire puissant. Il faut des statues pour nos édifices civils et religieux, pour nos places, pour nos sépultures". *Ibid.*, p. 34.

[66] Fonsmark, Héran and Søndergaard, 1999, p. 114. "La Musique, de M. Delaplanche, est une statue dont le charme dou et la grâce parfaite font penser à Raphaël". Roger-Ballu, "Le Salon de 1878", in *Gazette des Beaux-Arts*, 1er Août, Deuxième livraison (Paris, 1878), pp. 168–95 (pp. 191–92). Carl Jacobsen was also fascinated by the work: not only was it the first French sculpture he purchased, he also made it the axis about which his whole "programme notes" — published in *Ude og Hjemme* in 1878, was to turn.

[67] It is, however, interesting that it was painters such as Degas and Gérôme who started to use wax as a medium. For them it was probably not as great a sin as it would have been for a painter, who, throughout the whole of his train-

ing would have been exhorted to set white marble higher than any other material and only use wax for sketches.

[68] Joris-Karl Huysmans, "L'Exposition des Indépendants en 1881", in *L'Art Moderne* (Paris, 1883), pp. 225–57 (pp. 226–27).

[69] Adolf von Hildebrand, "Auguste Rodin", in Ruth Butler (ed.), *Rodin in Perspective* (Englewood Cliffs, N.J.: Prentice-Hall, 1980), pp. 139–43 (p. 140). "If I had but a torso or a leg from Rodin's hand, I would be filled with the greatest distress that there remained only this glorious fragment; how wonderful the complete figure must have been! Not since the Greeks or since Michelangelo would I have seen something that gave this kind of intense feeling for organic life. Of course, I would then have looked for a complete figure by Rodin. Then the disappointment would set in". *Ibid.*, p. 139.

[70] *Ibid.*, pp. 142–43.

[71] Adolf von Hildebrand, *Das Problem der Form in der Bildenden Kunst* (Strasbourg, 1893), pp. 3–4. "Wir müssen also die Räumliche Vorstellung im allgemeinen und die Formvorstellung, als die des begrenzten Raumes, im besonderen als den wesentlichen Inhalt oder die wesentliche Realität der Dinge Auffassen".

[72] Rosalind E. Krauss, *Passages in Modern Sculpture* (Cambridge and London: The MIT Press, 1977), p. 45.

[73] Von Hildebrand, 1980, pp. 139–43 (p. 141).

[74] See Fried, 1996, which includes his analysis of the general tendency to make references in contemporary painting. See in particular p. 162.

[75] Nanette Salomon, "The Venus Pudica: uncovering art history's 'hidden agendas' and pernicious pedigrees", in Griselda Pollock (ed.), *Generations and Geographies in Visual Arts: Feminist Readings* (Routledge, 1966), p. 69.

[76] T.J. Clark, *The Painting of Modern Life: Paris in the Art of Manet and His Followers* (New York, 1985). According to the deconstructivist credo, taking quotations is a subversive activity, since that which is quoted in and with quoting is refashioned and destroyed. There is thus no question here of progressive development, in which the artist carries on the work of his predecessor. On the contrary the artist repeats his predecessor's work in order to incorporate it, and take its place.

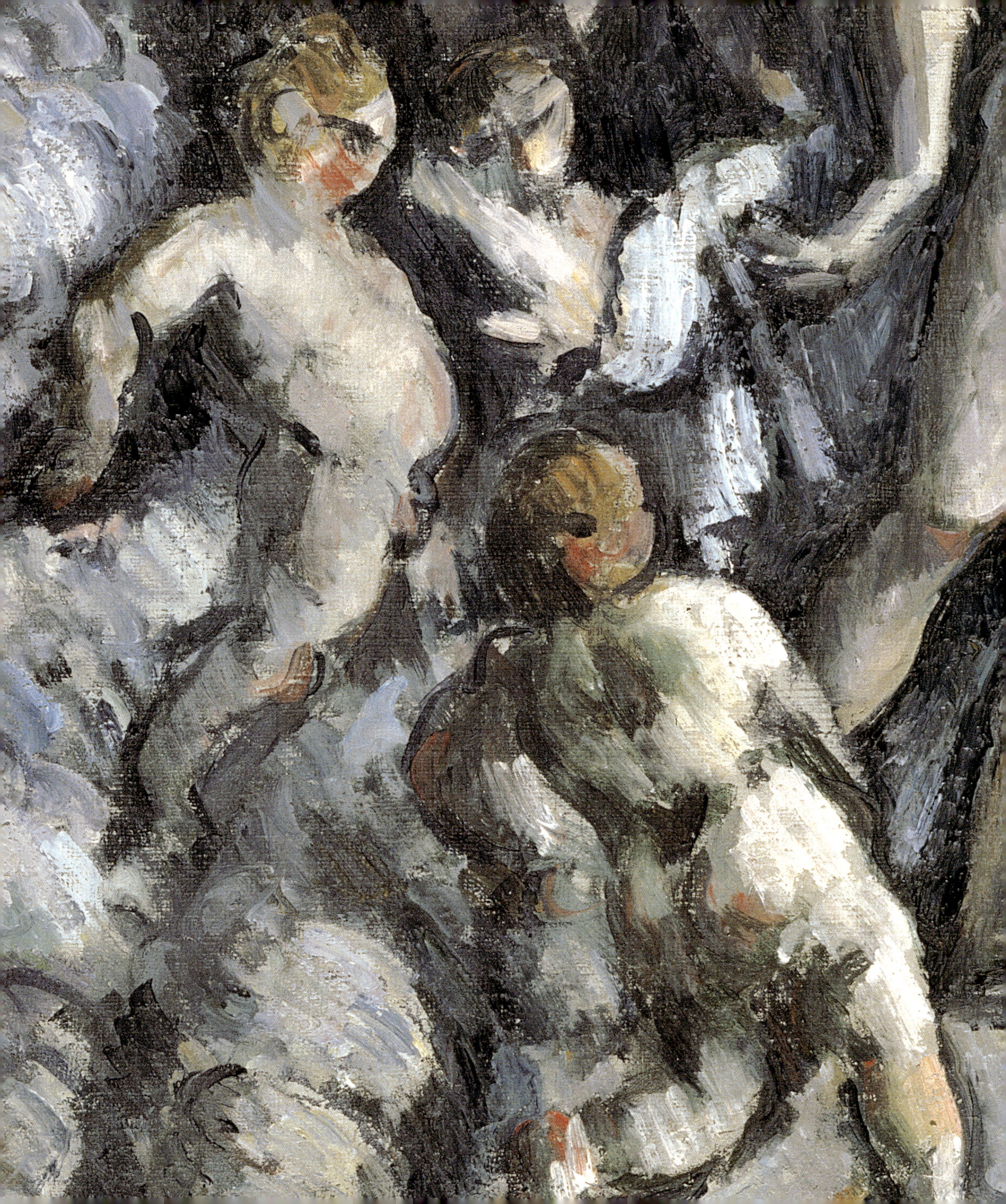

Jens Toft

Tradition, Burden and Force

45
Paul Cézanne
The Temptation of St. Anthony, ca. 1875, detail
(full fig. 56)

The greater one's involvement with French art from the crucial years of the middle and the last half of the nineteenth century, the more one is struck by the problem of tradition. Tradition appears to be *the* central issue with which art was so preoccupied during this period, as to possibly merit the word "obsession". Furthermore it is important to notice that the art which thus relates to tradition is art as a whole. Not only the body of work that was later anathematised and scorned as "Salon art", which is characterised almost everywhere throughout the literature of art history as the representative, perhaps even the victim, of tradition. The obsession of tradition includes the artists of the "avant-garde", of *la nouvelle peinture*, Manet and Cézanne not the least, but also, in their own way, both Renoir — who like Cézanne made himself a spokesman for a declared and demonstrative "Classicism" — and Gauguin, despite (or perhaps because of) his proclaimed wildness and "primitiveness".

The problematic of tradition is, therefore, much more complicated than a cursory glance might suggest. Tradition is not merely something of which one is a victim, or from which one must be liberated. On the contrary, it seems it is in the work of Manet and Cézanne, that we find the most profound reflections on the problematic of tradition. I hope that I shall be able to make that point clear in the following sketchy remarks. On the other side it appears that, on closer analysis, the painting so scornfully referred to as "Salon painting" is more than just the negative "other" in relation to which Modernism can stand out as a positive force. "Salon painting" is in fact struggling with the same kind of problems with which the modernists are struggling, not least those relating to tradition, renewal and "modern life".

Much obfuscation surrounding these matters is perhaps a product of inadequate understanding, or even downright misunderstanding, of the true nature of tradition and its effects. Tradition is usually characterised as something which is handed down: from father to son, from one generation to the next, as something on the shoulders of which an artist can stand, or against which he can take up arms.[1] It is that rhetoric figure which nearly always gives structure to the narrative on French painting of the period covered here, a narrative which identifies originality and artistic value with revolt and the break with tradition, and can do hardly otherwise, and, conversely reduces the lack of obvious breaks in tradition to traditionalism and plagiarism. But what if tradition functions quite differently? What if nothing is actually *handed down*, what if, instead, tradition is always *cre-*

ated? What if the work "in" tradition is always a *production of* this tradition? What if tradition is in no way "there" in an objective sense, but something which must always be constructed, what then?[2]

With this view on tradition and on the relation to tradition, it is hoped that we can give a more accurate picture of what is happening in French painting of the period. It is to be hoped that we can discern better the nature of problems as they have posed themselves to the artists and which they have tried to solve. It is to be hoped that we can more clearly discern their doubts and hesitations, the processes of which their works are an expression, instead of seeing them in the light of their results or "effects". For example: Gérôme has no "effect" in the history of art, he lost just like Stevens and Bastien-Lepage, and therefore he tends to feature merely as a curiosity, as part of all that had to be defeated. On the other hand, Manet, Monet, Cézanne, Gauguin and Van Gogh appear, along with Rodin and Maillol as heroes: they "won", inasmuch as they established a new tradition, Modernism — Matisse, Picasso, Expressionism, Constructivism, Abstract Art, etc. In both cases winners and losers are both reduced, or at least tend to be so, to, respectively, the new tradition which they created, or to the old tradition of which they are seen as the victims. In neither case are they understood on their own premises.[3]

Thus what this exhibition aims to present, along with this paper, is an alternative, and partly new, understanding of French art of the period considered. I will try to examine some of the artists and works in the exhibition, taking as my point of departure the assumption that each of them is attempting to construct a tradition *and* a position for himself in, or in relation to this tradition. In other words, by creating or defining (himself in relation to) tradition, each artist and each work of art is attempting to construct a context, art historical and broader, in relation to which they are productive and even meaningful.[4]

An understanding of French art of the period on these premises does not set out to deny the differences between traditionalists and modernists — nor is it an objective in itself to alter the hierarchy of the painters of the period. I still believe that Ingres, Courbet, Manet and Cézanne are greater, even much greater, than Gérôme, Stevens, Bastien-Lepage and Bonnat. But one might hope that the latter group will be regarded as more than just dead epigons outside of the valid artistic quest, and that the former will appear as a more integrated component of an extremely complex history, and not as its negation.

One need not hesitate to call the French art of the period "painting in crisis", at least in the sense that all the tendencies can be seen as a critical quest for a foundation for painterly representation. In spite of what I wrote above, tradition is, in one sense, something which *is there*: one can see it quite clearly, tradition, at, say, the Louvre, in the form of masterpieces of centuries — or even of millenniums. For a painter brought up in tradition — not to mention one who is not so, but who is nevertheless witnessing it, and is conscious of it — it is a case of something which is at once a terrifying superior force, of which one cannot help but be afraid, and at the same time an ideal of sublime perfection, which one can only desire. What one *cannot* do is to pretend indifference. One cannot just throw oneself into painting what one sees and feels. Were one to try, one would be crushed, paralysed by the gazes of Raphael, Poussin, Velázquez, Rembrandt and all the rest who look back and peer over the shoulders of the new with an inscrutable gaze, brought about by one's own super-ego and the critical gazes of the public.

Faced with such a superior force it should be no surprise if one's hand is paralysed. Where should the necessary strength come from to resist these gazes and insist on oneself, in a way parallel to the way in which *Olympia* (fig. 55) in Manet's painting of that

46
Jean-Léon Gérôme
The Cock-Fight, 1846
Oil on canvas, 143 × 204 cm
Paris, Musée d'Orsay
(cat. no. 32)

With *The Cock-Fight*, Gérôme experienced his great breakthrough in the Salon of 1847. He himself described the painting as a study of nakedness. But he tried to give the simple genre motif a nobler aspect by furnishing it with a lofty classical context: the marble-like bodies and the hard outline encapsulate and solidify a sensuality and a desire which are only vicariously unleashed with the fight between the vicious cocks. In his attempt to hide the desire, however, Gérôme ends up precisely by underlining the contrast between the stiffened outlines of Neo-Classicism and the physical presence. When Gérôme's attempts to mask this become evident, also the decadence contained in the painting becomes evident.

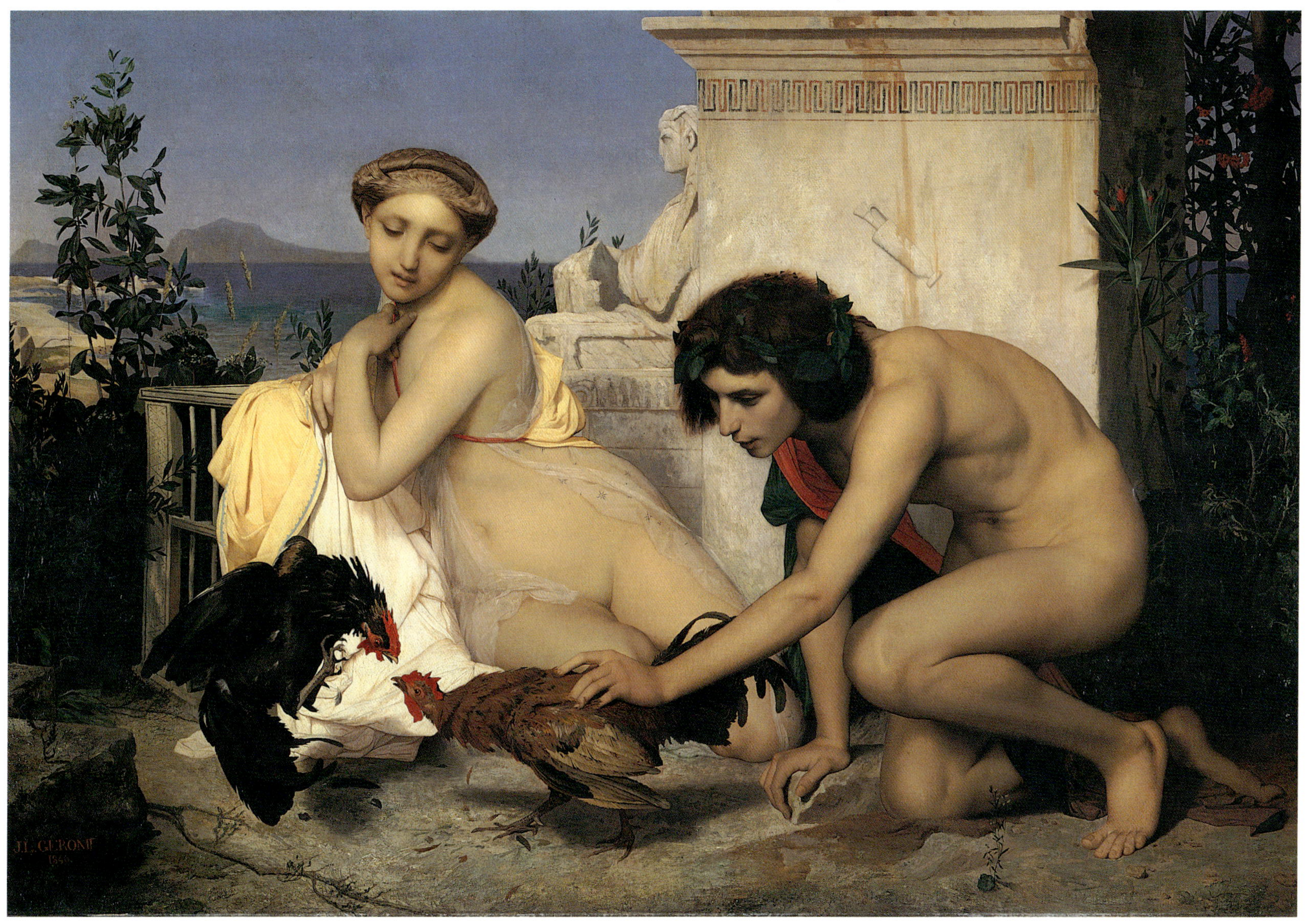

name defies the gaze on her and on the painting, the gaze which represents the Law in relation to which the painting acquires a meaning, and which will sanction it as viable: the social or symbolic order, tradition.[5]

In addition to the problems which are probably always associated with becoming a subject in tradition, it also seems to be the case, quite specifically in this particular period, France in the nineteenth century. Tradition now seems to have lost its power in many ways. Not as a crushing superior power, but as a living force from which the subject can draw strength, and in which contemporary painting can find its founding principle. The poet and art critic, Charles Baudelaire seems to be one of the first to understand the problem. In 1863 Baudelaire, in his famous essay *The Painter of Modern Life*,[6] defines the two aspects of art, the eternal and the modern, and connects beauty as ideal and form with the eternal, and beauty as force with modernity, with life — and also Raphael was modern once, and it was from thence, according to Baudelaire's formulation, that he derived his eternal strength and power.[7]

Perhaps the relation to tradition, as previously asserted, has, in reality always been something to be established through an active constructive process. Poussin's practise in the seventeenth century and the struggle between "Poussinists" and "Rubenists" suggest that, neither for them, tradition was something provided, and of which, without more ado, one might be a part, but rather something which was left to be defined. In any case, by the nineteenth century the problem becomes obvious, perhaps because modern life in the metropolis, as diagnosed by Baudelaire, renders signs artificial and superficial, devoid of intrinsic "essential" foundation, as it is said in other contexts and with almost identical words by Søren Kierkegaard and Karl Marx. It may be that tradition is incapable of connecting with the subjects living in the shock-aesthetic and fragmented space of the big city. Perhaps what is missing in relation to tradition is the intensity of big city life.

Tradition as precondition of meaning and as loss. And on the other hand subjectivity and modernity as fragmentation and intensity. How can intensity be given meaning, and how is meaning or tradition given intensity? These questions seem to define the problematic around which all the artists of the period, on all levels, and despite all mutual differences, appear to hover.

Ingres and Gérôme: Tradition as Loss and as Ideal

Gérôme's *Cock-Fight* (1846, cat. no. 32, fig. 46) is among the oldest paintings in the exhibition. Here I will look at it in relation to *The Source* (1820, reworked in 1863 with a pupil) by Ingres — *the* Ingres, who in his lifetime had an almost godlike status and was considered Classicism incarnate itself, which was held up against all the corruption of Modernity. This was the story at the time, and the supporters of Modernism have repeated it since, only in reverse.

The painting of two young Greeks, a man and a woman, seems, despite its all too obvious Classicism, to be far from being in harmony with tradition. Rather it seems to articulate a clash and incompatibility between the signs of Classicism and physical existence. Not only is the physical and erotic, in the best "Freudian" style, displaced from the human bodies to almost inorganic feathered tumult of the "bestial" cockerels. The landscape is filled with crumbling ruins and appears petrified in an almost photographically transfixed past which has no connection to the violent immediacy of the cockfight. This cockfight must, as asserted, be seen as a displaced metaphor for the body's desire, and it is thus, on one level, a smutty, limited device which, together with the displacement of the missing pubic hair to the opulent and almost mannered coiffure will permit the spectator to simultaneously live out his erotic fantasies and yet re-

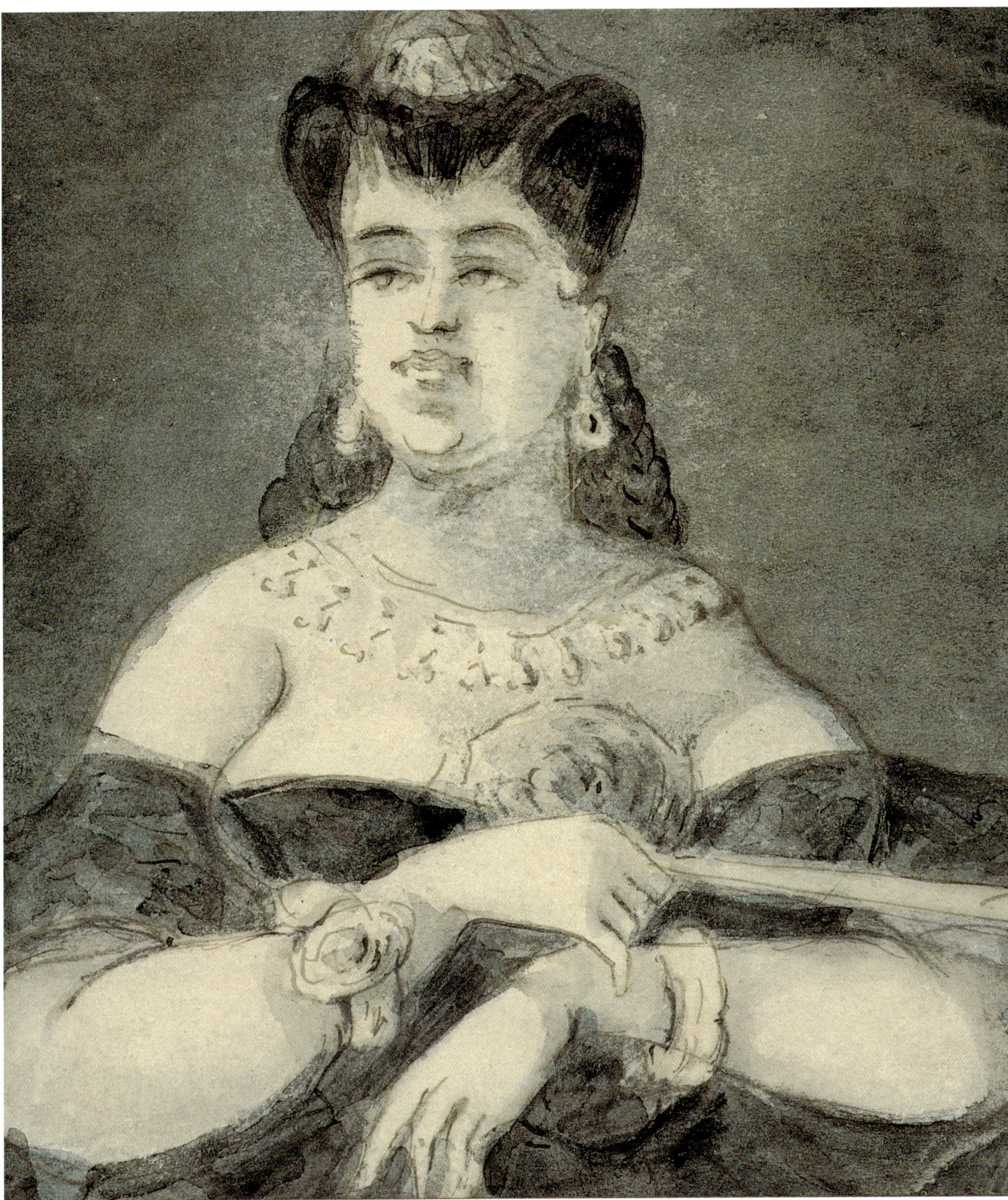

47
Constantin Guys
A Courtesan, 1850s
Watercolour, Indian ink and white body colour on paper, 17 × 15 cm
Copenhagen, Ny Carlsberg Glyptotek
(cat. no. 35)

Guys here employs a classical form of portraiture traditionally reserved for the depiction of members of the upper echelons of society. Its use in *The Courtesan* is an ironic comment on the attempts of the Second Empire to preserve their spurious respectability. While the academic artists of the time were considered to be defending morality through idealised representations of the world, Guys' no-nonsense approach to the subject and his sketch-like manner of painting were seen as a stylistic decadence. Baudelaire, however, praised him as "the painter of modern life" in his essay of the same title, and Guys' art was of great influence on Manet, who owned a large number of works by him.

main within the protective walls of tradition and high culture. But what seems to be of greater importance than the ideological content of these displacements — mediation between desire and socialisation — is the melancholy expressed by the bodies, particularly that of the girl, which is marble-like and statuesque, and, consistent with this, the mask-like character of her face. The human body as the classical symbol par excellence of ideal harmony, the delicate skin and the ideal proportions are drained and petrified, beyond a present whose substance is animal sensuality.

The classical body is therefore not (any longer) the outer expression of an original harmony within, the inner eternal presence of tradition and origin. It is, instead, a *sign*, which must seek to link the present with the lost origin, an origin which is perhaps always already lost, but which, in any case, can be articulated as such in the work of Gérôme. This is also possible with Ingres, twenty-six years previously, in such works as *The Source* (fig. 48), where the signs' emptiness and artificiality are no less pregnant than in Gérôme. One would certainly have to go a long way to find an artist in whose work there would be, and to such a degree, an equal insistence on the signs of Classicism and simultaneously on the atrophying and draining of these same signs into something whose harmony functions only on the picture plane, as picture, but emptied of any organic life: see the solidifying of the jet of water into a giant icicle, which seems to grow from beneath and upwards and therefore "supports" the jar, and see the smooth surface of the spring, which is more reminiscent of a mirror's surface with a Christmas decoration, which the girl can stand *on*, than a water surface with foam which she can stand *in*. And notice again the missing pubic hair, which, as always in Ingres, has been displaced into hair of the head, that however, in this particular painting is less luxuriant and opulent than is usual in his work. Notice likewise the sheen of the human limbs, exactly like porcelain or marble: could it be that what we're really looking at is a Venus in Furs?

My point here is no more than with Gérôme, to "reduce" an artist — in this case Ingres — to some possible social "use-value", pornographic or other. Nevertheless, my reference to *Venus in Furs* is more than merely fortuitous. *Venus in Furs* is, as some will know, the title of the 1870 novel by Leopold von Sacher-Masoch which describes masochism to which the author has given his name. In this novel the author analyses the power exercised by the perfection of the white, statue-like body, a power to which the adorant desires to submit. The association is thus an attempt on my part to read or interpret the classical body, as we encounter it in Ingres and his pupils of the period, with its precise boundaries, contours and surfaces — to read and interpret this body as an artificial — complete but empty — sign of the absence of an authority in which painterly representation can find its founding principle despite (or perhaps precisely because) it is perfectly closed around itself and at insuperable distance in its perfect inhuman beauty.

In the case of both Gérôme and Ingres, I have concentrated on the stiffening of the movements and the bodies, as well as on the draining or evacuation of the spaces. In addition, I have interpreted these features as an expression of the emptying of signs and meanings, i.e. as an expression of a modern crisis of consciousness. These analyses must, however, be modified or slightly adjusted, in that they have another side, something which manages to be in almost diametrical opposition, yet without there being any question of contradiction. On the contrary, the two things are connected — dialectically? Rather than being the expression of scepticism, this stiffening can, in fact, be read as a sign of desire, desire of holding on to and connect oneself to the vanished, to the origins, Arcadia, the authentic.

48
Jean-Auguste-Dominique Ingres, *The Source*, 1856
Oil on canvas, 163 × 80 cm
Paris, Musée d'Orsay

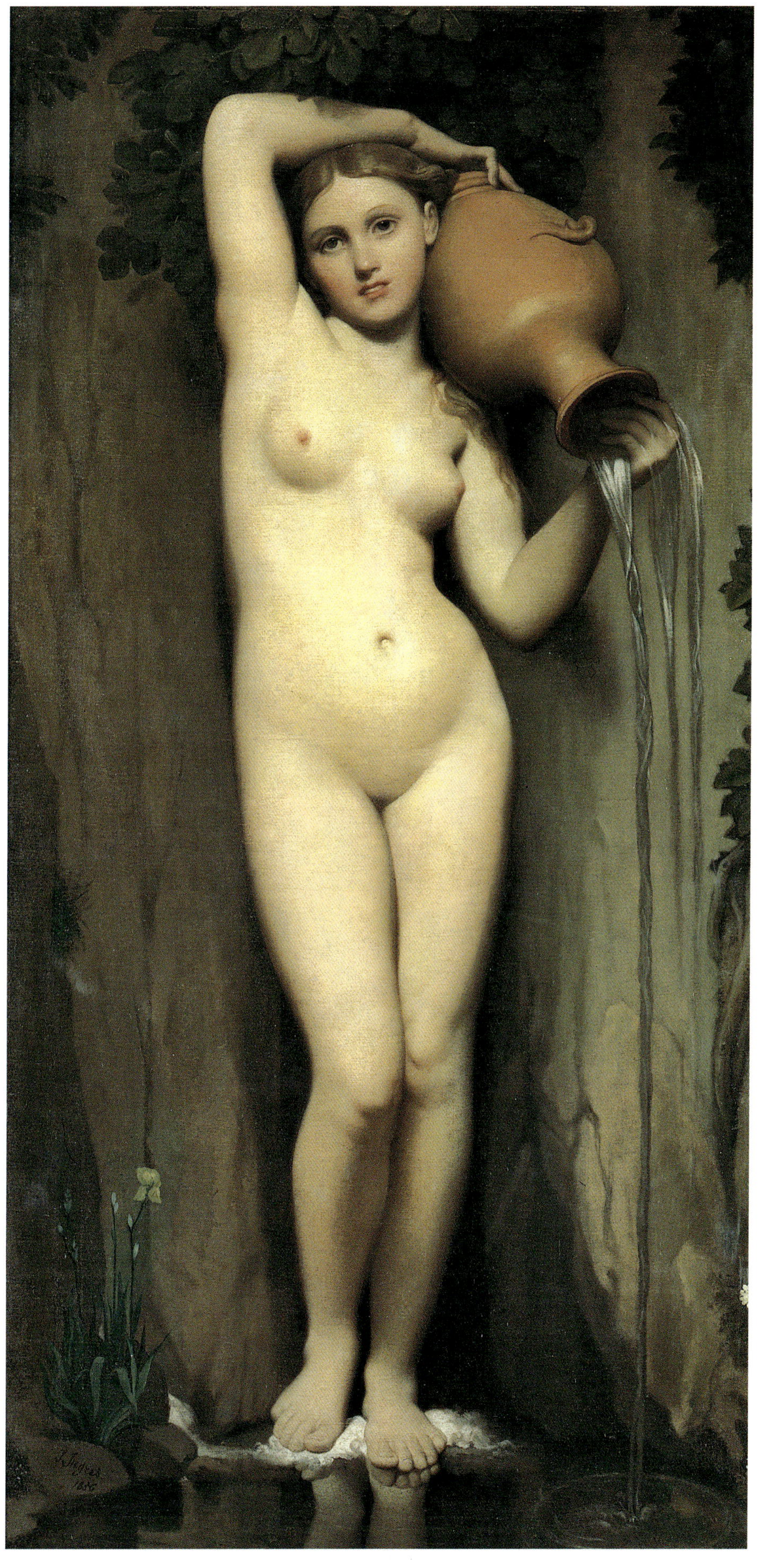

Are these paintings about either of these things? Do they represent connection with tradition and the origins, or do they stand for loss and separation? Both in fact, would be the answer, the paintings seem to produce a condensation[8] of different meanings and both in different ways and to different extents.

One level of condensation of these significations is given expression in a formulation I used above, although without having thought through its consequences. In my analysis of Gérôme's painting I talked about "an almost photographically immobilised past", playing with this around two aspects of the photographic principle. Photography, on the one hand consists in freezing a moment, i.e. in fixing and preserving it, but on the other hand its role is to tear it loose from the context or continuity, of which it is a part and in relation to which it has significance. To preserve the moment is, therefore, simultaneously to empty, drain or deprive it of meaning.

The notion that the photograph is both true and empty also formed the basis of Baudelaire's criticism of photography, as well as constituting the background for his rejection of it. Nevertheless, this conception of photography was a living reality in the Paris of the period. Photography was in fact invented in France, as far back as 1826, by Nicéphore Niepce, made public and becoming widespread from 1839, when Daguerre's invention, a further development of Niepce's own, was purchased by the French state, and put at the disposal of the public. The photographic mode of seeing was, therefore, not unknown at this time. On the contrary, it has later in a thoroughly convincing manner been argued that it was not so much photography that influenced painting. Rather it was a case of the painters' discovery of this photographic principle which led to the technical invention of photography,[9] which, if correct, means that there is no obligation to document an influence of photography on Gérôme to be able to talk of "photographic" structures in his paintings, or in those of Ingres.

The break with — or isolation from — the past, and the consequent "emptying" of the latter, yet also with the simultaneous fixing and preservation of it is both the principle of photography and of desire,[10] inasmuch as desire always is the effect of loss: we desire what we do not have, that which we have lost. And it is perhaps precisely from the loss of this bond that the desire to bind oneself to the past and to the origin of things, draws its strength.

Manet: The Absinthe Drinker (1858–59) and The Execution of Emperor Maximilian (1867)

The subject in *The Absinthe Drinker* (cat. no. 40, fig. 49) is not of some remote Arcadian origin, but a part of the reality of modern Paris. That reality is represented by the tramp Collardet, who was a denizen of the area round the Louvre and, therefore, would have been a familiar figure to the public at the Salon, to which the painting was submitted in 1859, and by which body it was rejected.

This tramp's appearance in the painting is, however, no more unambiguous than is Parisian modernity. In the first place, modernity itself is not yet a fact, it is only under construction. Baron Haussmann's massive building programmes are in their initial phase. Secondly, there is (as yet) no such thing as a "modern" nor "French" "language" of painting, something that would serve as a firm foundation on which to build the representation of this new reality in its specific character. Instead we are met by a series of enigmatic and unconnected signs: the figure's down-at-heel appearance is counteracted by its upright posture, the top hat does not match the cloak, which manages to appear at once shabby and elegant, cast as it is, with a nearly theatrical flourish over the shoulders; the attitude of the legs is remarkably artificial, which is seen by Michael Fried[11] as an indirect reference to

49
Edouard Manet
The Absinthe Drinker, 1859
Oil on canvas,
180.5 × 105.6 cm
Copenhagen, Ny Carlsberg Glyptotek
(cat. no. 40)

The Absinthe Drinker was rejected by the Salon of 1859, judged to be decadent both in choice of subject and style. To begin with, in a monumental portrait, Manet took the liberty of depicting one of the marginal figures of the time, who shamed the image the Second Empire had of itself, which was one of affluence and progress. Secondly, Manet eschewed the academic manner of painting and instead allowed his work to be centred on the surface, through his use of colour and the sketch form. In the eyes of the critics, this was the road to perdition, both as regards painting and morals. However the poet Baudelaire wrote to Manet: "You are only the first example of the artistic decline of your time", thereby underlining the fact that Manet was one of the first to dare seriously to defy tradition.

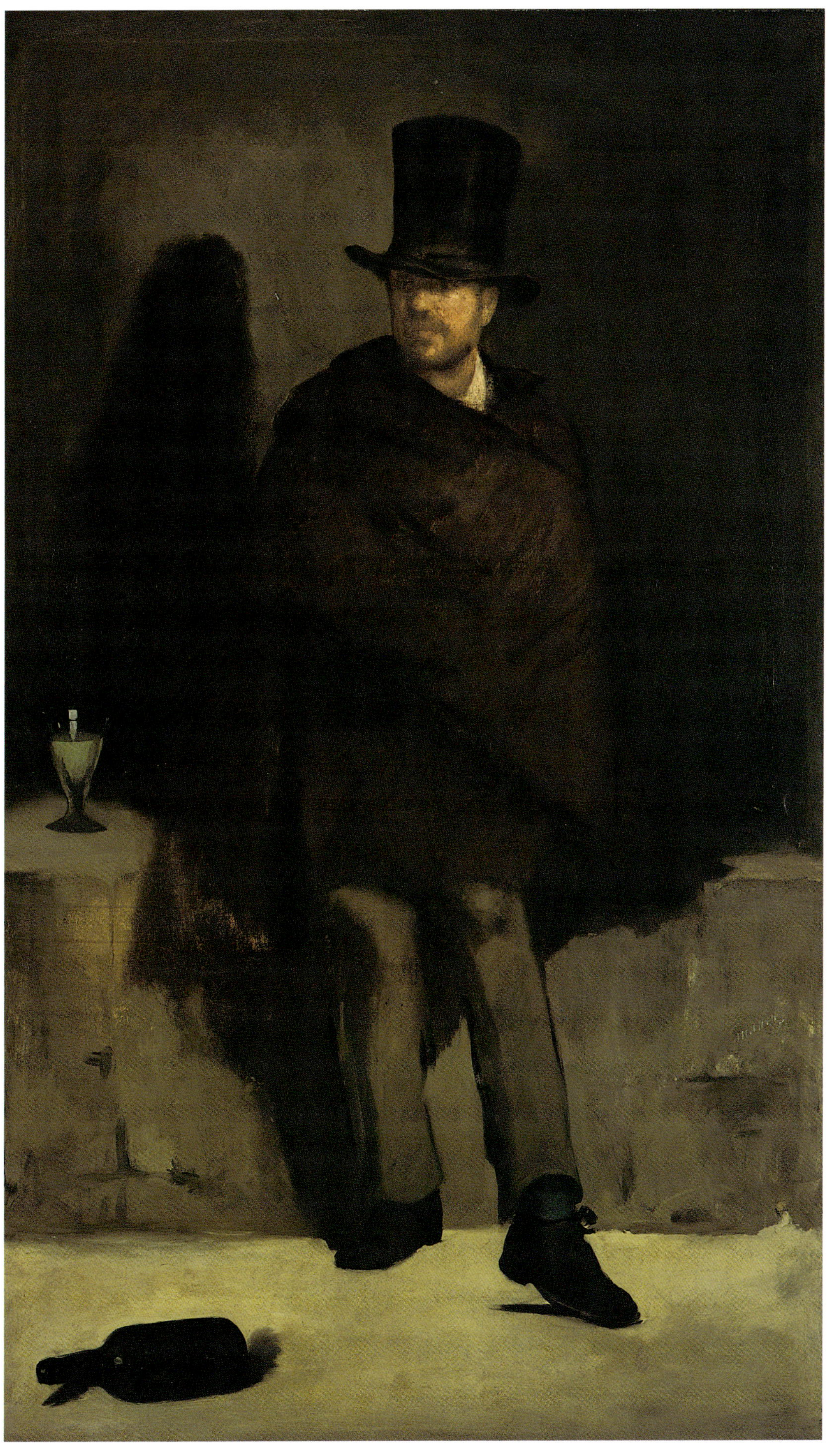

Watteau's *L'Indifférent* from around 1718. It is a case of superficial elegance, which is in stark contrast to the rags and also to both the empty bottle on the ground and the absinthe glass, but not at odds with the demonstratively virtuoso quality of its execution. One might go on to notice the way the figure, emerging from the gloom, is not even consistent with its own shadow, whose outline and the relation between the figure in the foreground and that in the background come across as a faint but inverted echo of Goya's *The Majas on the Balcony* from 1800–5. Finally, as Manet himself pointed out, the figure contains clear references to Velázquez' two "philosophers", *Aesop* and *Menippus* from 1636–40, just as, in the overall method of painting with the *clairobscur* of the dark colours and *non-finito* (unfinishedness, openness), there are clear references to "the Spanish Style", even though Manet's *non-finito* is far more radical and demonstrative than that of Velázquez, and without its metaphysical foundation. By the same token, Manet's *clairobscur* is, in any case, not truly "Spanish", but also an allusion to the artificial spotlight of the theatre or photographic studio.

Thus neither the figure nor the painting is in equilibrium. Both are almost demonstratively putting themselves forward in relation to the spectator. The figure's faint rigidity and generally contrived attitude seem, first and foremost, to express the consciousness of being observed, of being an object of (another's) gaze, a gaze which through interpretation of the signs endows the figure and the painting with their meaning.[12]

As with Ingres, we see in Manet that the signs are emptied of content, or are acknowledged as empty in relation to the reality they are supposed to represent. In the work of Manet it is not the distance of time which drains the signs of meaning. That, however, is still the case, since modern reality which is to be represented has (as yet) no signs of its own.That reality can only be represented or created in painting through those signs which are available, signs which by definition are old-fashioned in relation to the new reality — and there are no other signs. For the signs handed over from the past to become signs of modernity, they must be torn loose from the context of tradition and emptied of their conventional meaning. They must be presented in new configurations and thus, through these, bring forth new possibilities of meaning.

In other words, Manet intervenes radically in tradition. He turns the signs inside out, towards the spectator to force him to ascribe meaning to the work in the "fissure" between the surviving meaning of the signs and their heterogeneous, mannered appearance as demonstrative, but empty signs on the canvas.

That meaning is something which comes about through, and as a result of the relation of the signs to other signs, to tradition and its signs, to see signification as a productive process and not as an essence, to see meaning as something which is not "read", but is *created* through the encounter with the other signs, and thereby with the interpreter of the signs — that was indeed the experience of Gérôme and Ingres. But to draw attention to this fact and explicitly make this recognition the foundations for a new paradigm in painting — that is Manet's outstanding revolutionary contribution. It is an act, however, which does not distance him from, but rather binds him intimately with this whole episode of the painting tradition, in which he intervenes. In particular, it connects him, as already mentioned, with Salon painting, with Ingres, Gérôme and Couture, in whose atelier he was a pupil from 1850 to 1856, cf. the exhibition's sketch for Couture's large work *The Decadence of the Romans*, from 1847 (cat. no. 21, fig. 50, a 1847 sketch). All of them express the same experience of crisis in relation to tradition that we have seen in Manet. However what sets Manet distinctly apart from the other artists is that he seems to have recognised

50
Thomas Couture
The Decadence of the Romans
(sketch), 1847
Oil on canvas, 52 × 84 cm
Paris, Musée d'Orsay
(cat. no. 21)

The painting is a preparatory study for a much larger work that was the main attraction at the 1847 Salon. In both theme and style, Couture confronts classical tradition with decadence: he is pillorying the old Romans as debauchees, portraying them in unheroic attitudes and in "modern" bright colours.

In this way he contrasts them with the illustrious, classical statues in white marble forced to witness the degeneracy of the Romans. Some critics interpreted the portrayal of Roman decadence as a satire on the decline of the July Monarchy. In this way the picture was construed as a prophecy of the regime's fall.

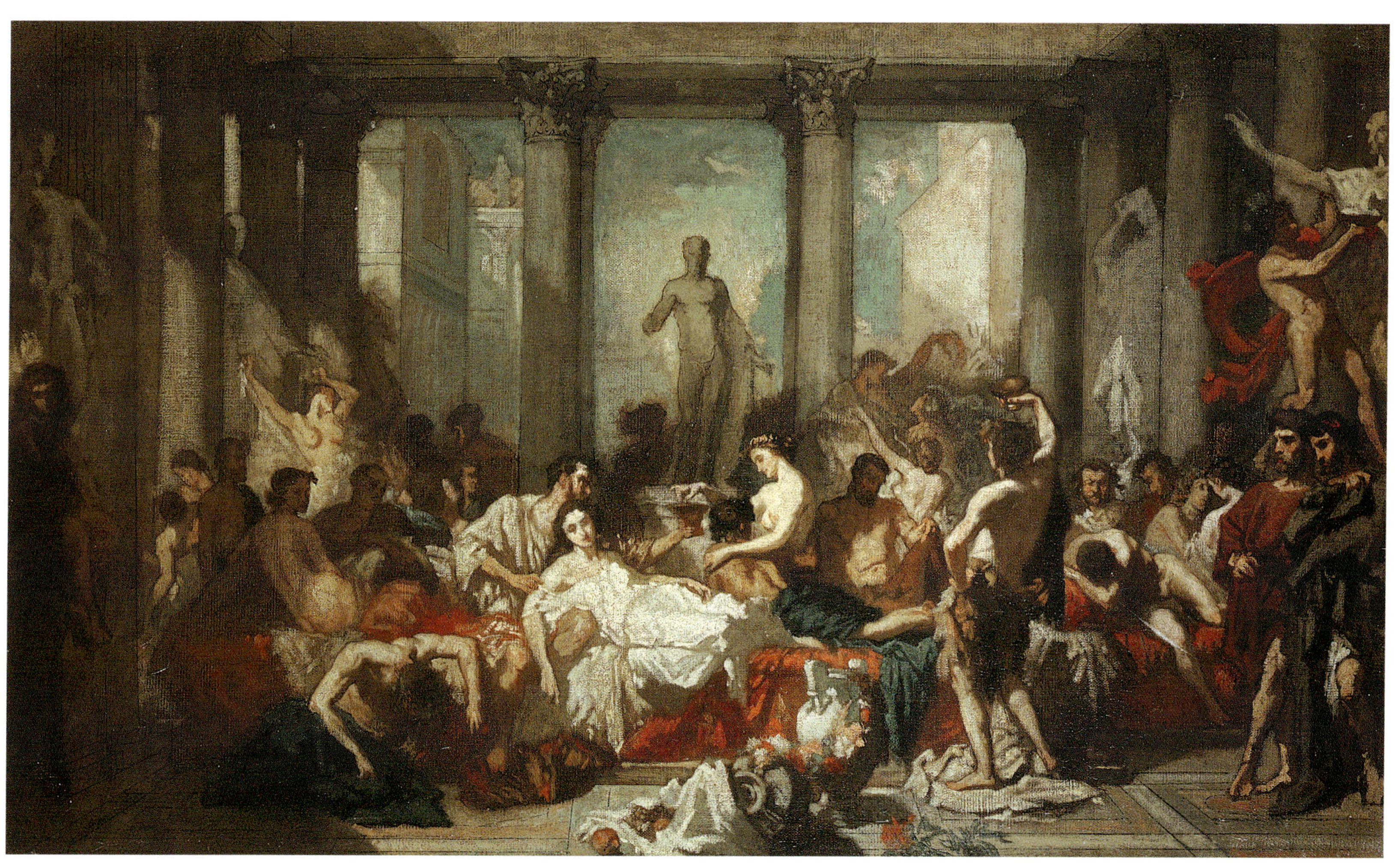

that the empty sign — i.e. the sign which is empty until it is filled or interpreted by the spectator — is itself *the* sign of modernity. It is not merely the *painterly* sign of modernity, it is the actual paradigm of modern life as such and modern subjectivity, which is constantly in the process of coming into existence and being transformed in a continuous exchange of signs. Is it really the tramp we see? Or is it an actor? One playing the part of a tramp, or of an actor? Or is it something completely different? And what is the connection between the French tramp and the Spanish signs? We are witnessing a circulation of signs without any foundation or founding principle. Existence, raw and naked is sundered from its meaning, which must be constantly created in relation to other signs, which are also, in themselves, empty.[13]

The emptiness of the signs, the nakedness of existence, the divorce of existence from meaning: these appear to be also the themes in *The Execution of Emperor Maximilian* from 1867 (cat. no. 42, fig. 51). There is a masquerade-like quality to the halo of the sombrero, an empty sign in a ritual, the observers of which are peering over a wall as a direct quotation from a bull-fighting picture by Goya. By the same token it is almost impossible to analyse or even "read" this painting without reference to Goya's famous execution picture, *The Fifth of May 1808* (1814). But whereas in the Goya picture the meaning of death as martyrdom remains intact, in Manet it is devoid of inner significance. Instead, it is yet again in the interval between the present work and those absent, that meaning is constituted or prevented: death as a meaningless reality.

A Brief Word about the Impressionists: Monet in Particular

The existence of things is one thing, their meaning another, and both something that must be constantly defined in relation to each other: that seems to be the experience which Manet passes on to the Impressionists, or at least what the latter extracted from Manet's oeuvre.

Some Impressionists seem to find it easier than others to accept this experience. Perhaps the only one truly capable of doing so is Monet. And by this I mean the Monet whose series of paintings of water lilies, poplars, haystacks, or, as in this exhibition, *"Les Pyramides" at Port-Coton, Belle-Île-en-Mer* from 1886 (cat. no. 48, fig. 52), can be regarded as a systematic exploration of the boundaries between things, as they are in themselves on the one hand, and as they appear to us on the other. And, not least of all, these series can be seen as a systematic attempt to develop painterly equivalents to the raw power of nature: whirlpools, cliffs, rocks, water in the lily pictures like a reflecting surface as distinct from that which is reflected in that surface, water as a surface as distinct from water as depth, etc. The paintings of Monet appear to be a systematic exploration of these differences, of the coming into being of these differences and thus also of the reciprocity of coming into existence of subjects and objects, of consciousness and matter.[14]

In the literature on Monet there is frequent discussion of the extent to which the late Monet should be regarded as a radical Impressionist, i.e. a kind of Realist, or whether, on the other hand he is to be seen as a Symbolist. This is not the kind of debate I could even pretend to resolve, as my own problematic in this area is rather different, even though I tend to lean most towards the Impressionist interpretation, and it is that view which is most consistent with the present problematic.

Perhaps, as I have suggested, it is only Monet who, together with Cézanne, can follow in the footsteps of Manet, i.e. accept the "inhuman" gaze, which is brought into being in the work of Manet, that very gaze which divorces existence and matter from meaning. This gaze can be read both as the gaze of meaninglessness or as a gaze, be-

51
Edouard Manet
The Execution of Emperor Maximilian (sketch), 1867
Oil on canvas, 48 × 58 cm
Copenhagen, Ny Carlsberg Glyptotek
(cat. no. 42)

Through the agency of Emperor Napoléon III, Archduke Maximilian of Austria was made Emperor of Mexico in 1864. In 1867, however, France withdrew her troops, whereupon the Emperor was executed by Mexican insurgents. Manet's depiction of the event is based on oral and written accounts. The result is a ruthless and unsentimental presentation of the cruel event and thus a realistic contribution to a debate on world politics. Manet's own political position is revealed by his rendering of the Emperor's sombrero as a halo.

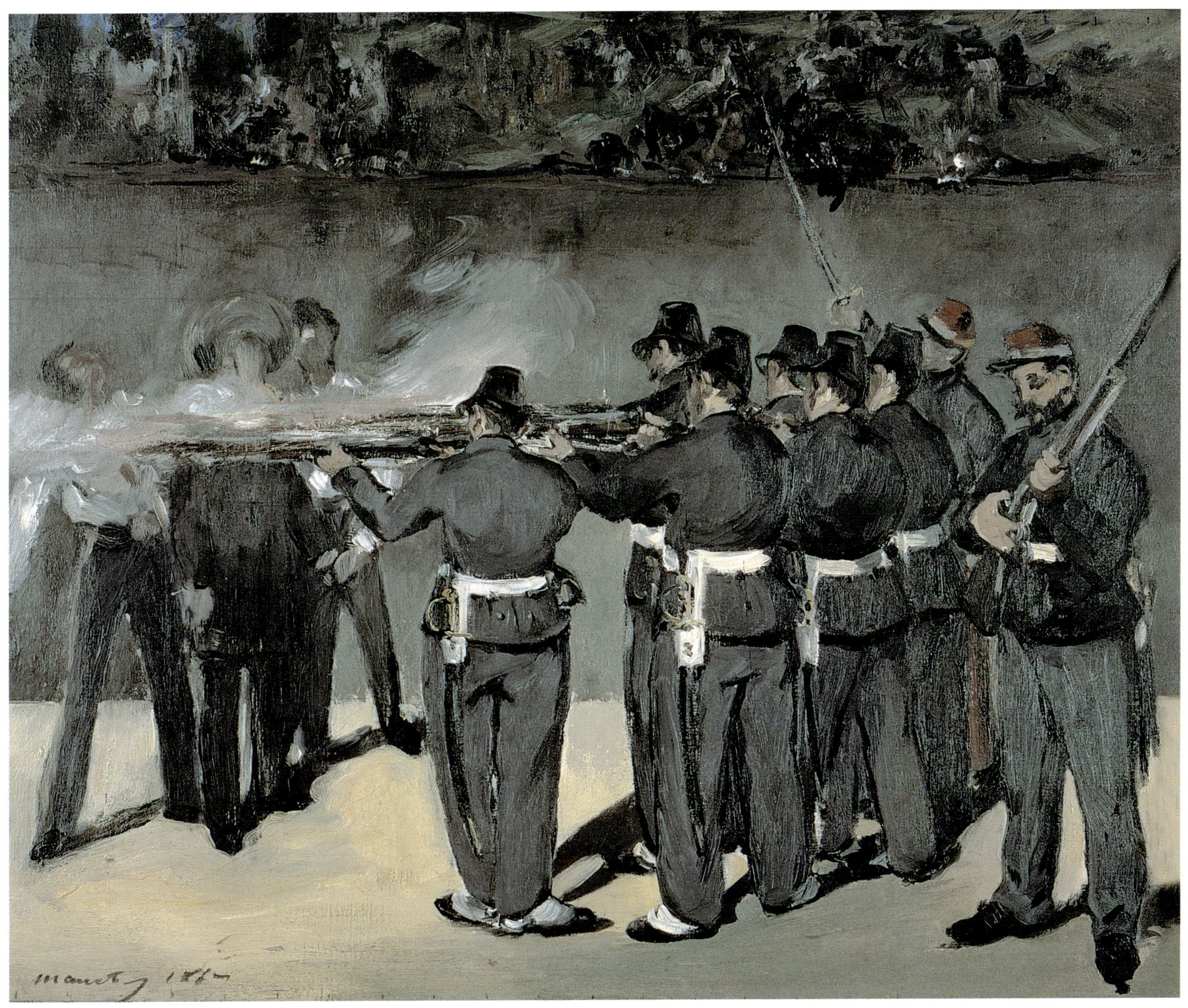

52
Claude Monet
"Les Pyramides" at Port-Coton, Belle-Île-en-Mer, 1886
Oil on canvas, 59.5 × 73 cm
Copenhagen, Ny Carlsberg Glyptotek
(cat. no. 48)

Monet began working with motif series around 1880. This painting is one in a sequence of views of the famous rocks "Les Pyramides" near Port-Coton in Brittany. The work exemplifies Monet's increasing tendency to render light and form through dense masses of colour. He challenges the traditional relationship between figure and ground as well as the laws of perspective, and makes the cliffs stand out as individual sculptural entities. These dark structures are offset by the green and white of the sea. Reality and abstraction alternate in the heavy-textured but vibrant light that is so characteristic of Monet's painting after 1880.

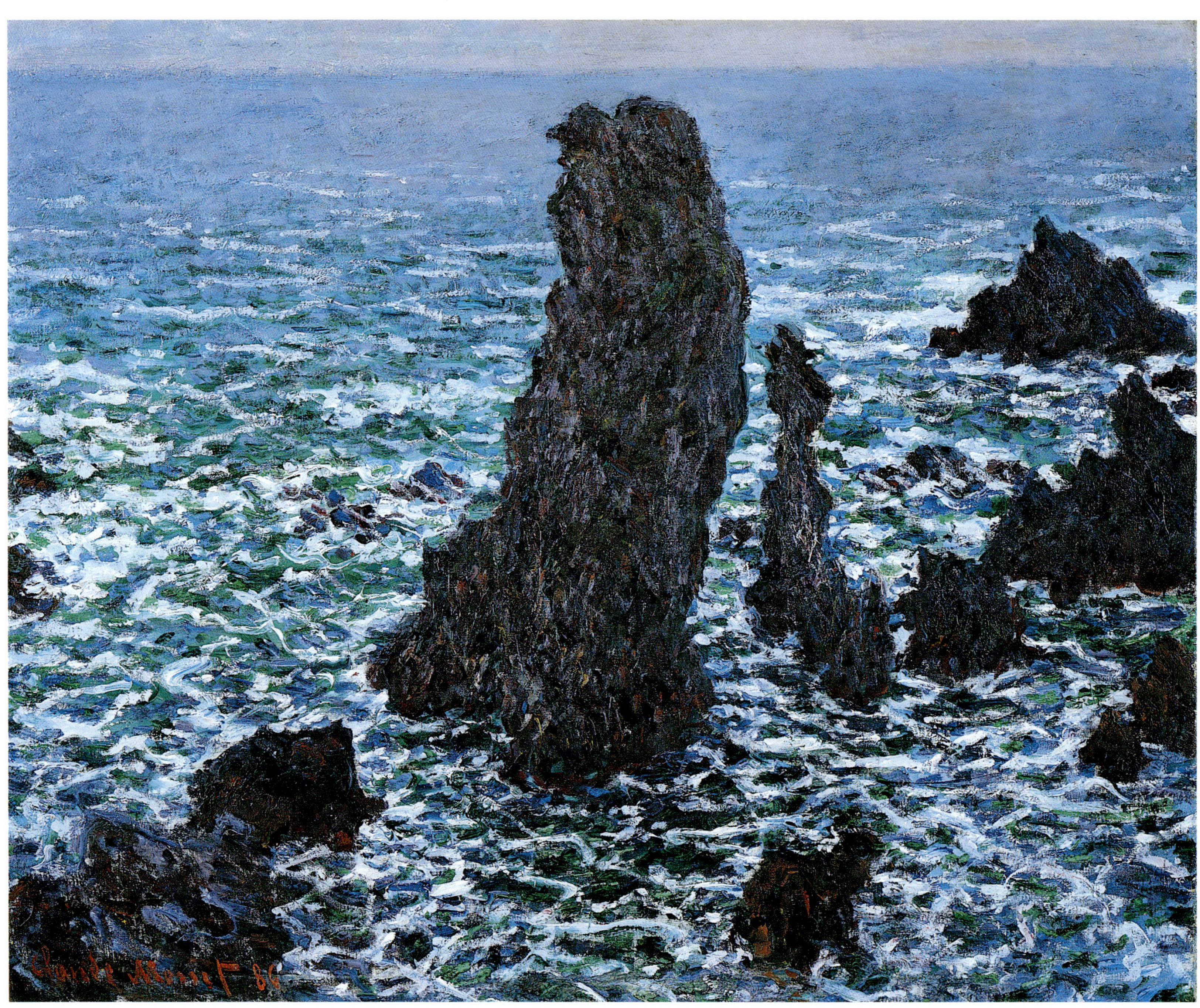

cause empty, of freedom and of open possibilities. It can be read as a revolt not against tradition as such, but against tradition as nature, as something given once and for all, to the advantage of an understanding of the same tradition as a system of differences, which means nothing in itself, but generates meaning, this being the prerequisite of signification. Perhaps it is only Monet who can do that, that Monet who was also, in the words of Cézanne "nothing but an eye, but what an eye!"

In any case, it is as if most of the Impressionists quickly experienced that gaze, as either too inhuman or as too superficial, all depending on how one looks at it. Almost right from the beginning Renoir tries to make a compromise between on the one hand Impressionism's radical gaze on the phenomenal world, a gaze that dissolves form and all that is solid and stable, and on the other hand form and stability; form and stability as they are defined not only by tradition but also by everyday experience, that tells us that things do have a certain identity and stability behind the phenomenal flux. The two Renoir paintings of the exhibition, *Boy with a Cat* (cat. no. 50, fig. 54) and *La Grenouillère* (cat. no. 49, fig. 53), executed almost at the same time, show how the two struggles coincide in the work of Renoir. The latter work is one of early Impressionism's best known and most typical masterpieces, while the first one exhibits what was, for Renoir, an unusual austerity and stringency.

It seems as though much of the new art of the period can be described as a quest for a new principle, one which gives a basis of meaning, behind the radicalism of both Manet and Monet: Gauguin's Synthetism and Van Gogh's "Expressionism" struggle, each in its own way, through examination of the painting's own qualities, which have been revealed by Manet and Monet, towards a meaning in nature or in subjectivity, something which can "heal" the wound or bridge the gap, which was introduced by the Salon painters and of which Manet took the consequences.[15]

Cézanne: the Restoration of Classicism

It seems to me, however, that it is Cézanne who offers the most radical challenge to Manet and does so nearly on Manet's own premises as he does not, as do Gauguin, Van Gogh and Renoir, seek to humanise Manet's inhuman gaze: quite the contrary, in fact. He reinstates difference as a rift, as doubt or as hesitation. He seems to let "the things in themselves" appear as a hesitation or rift or doubt between their different possible modes of appearing to us, through all the different possible viewpoints. Thus the circular form of the bowl in *Still Life with Apples in a Bowl* (cat. no. 14, fig. 79) flattens out, and tends towards an ellipse, and thus it will appear in one's perception, but without, in the picture, being a circle or an ellipse. Likewise, Cézanne's figures are always in a space, but never a space which exists prior to or independently of the object and the perception of it. Neither is the space ever purely the function of the subject's observation of the object. As in Monet, but far more radically so, it is rather the mutual coming into existence of the subject and the object as a difference, to which we are witness.

I call Cézanne more radical than Monet because he works more radically with the *difference* than Monet does. As already stated, and as can be seen in "*Les Pyramides" at Port-Coton, Belle-Île-en-Mer*, in Monet it is always a case of an eternally pulsating, almost formless energy which generates the *possible* differences: the line can be read now as spray, now as current and power in water, as a transition from one state to another in eternal motion. In Cézanne, on the other hand, it is rather a question of the *difference* than the transition and the pulsing. Identity is not, as in Monet, seen merely as flowing potentiality, but as a reality. But in contrast to what was the case in Ingres and

53
Pierre-Auguste Renoir
La Grenouillère, 1868
Oil on canvas, 66 × 81 cm
Stockholm, Nationalmuseum
(cat. no. 49)

"La Grenouillère", a restaurant and functions establishment on the Seine, was a popular destination for excursions of the Parisian bourgeoisie. Here Renoir captured an aspect of "modern life" as it unfolded before him. People and their surroundings are delineated with the same sketchy brushstrokes, which give the impression of the vitality of the situation. Because of this unconventional painting technique, Renoir did not submit the picture to the Salon jury, who would probably have rejected it. Today the work stands as one of the most characteristic expressions of early Impressionism.
During the same period Renoir was also exploring other approaches with the more monumental *Boy with a Cat* (cat. no. 50, fig. 54).

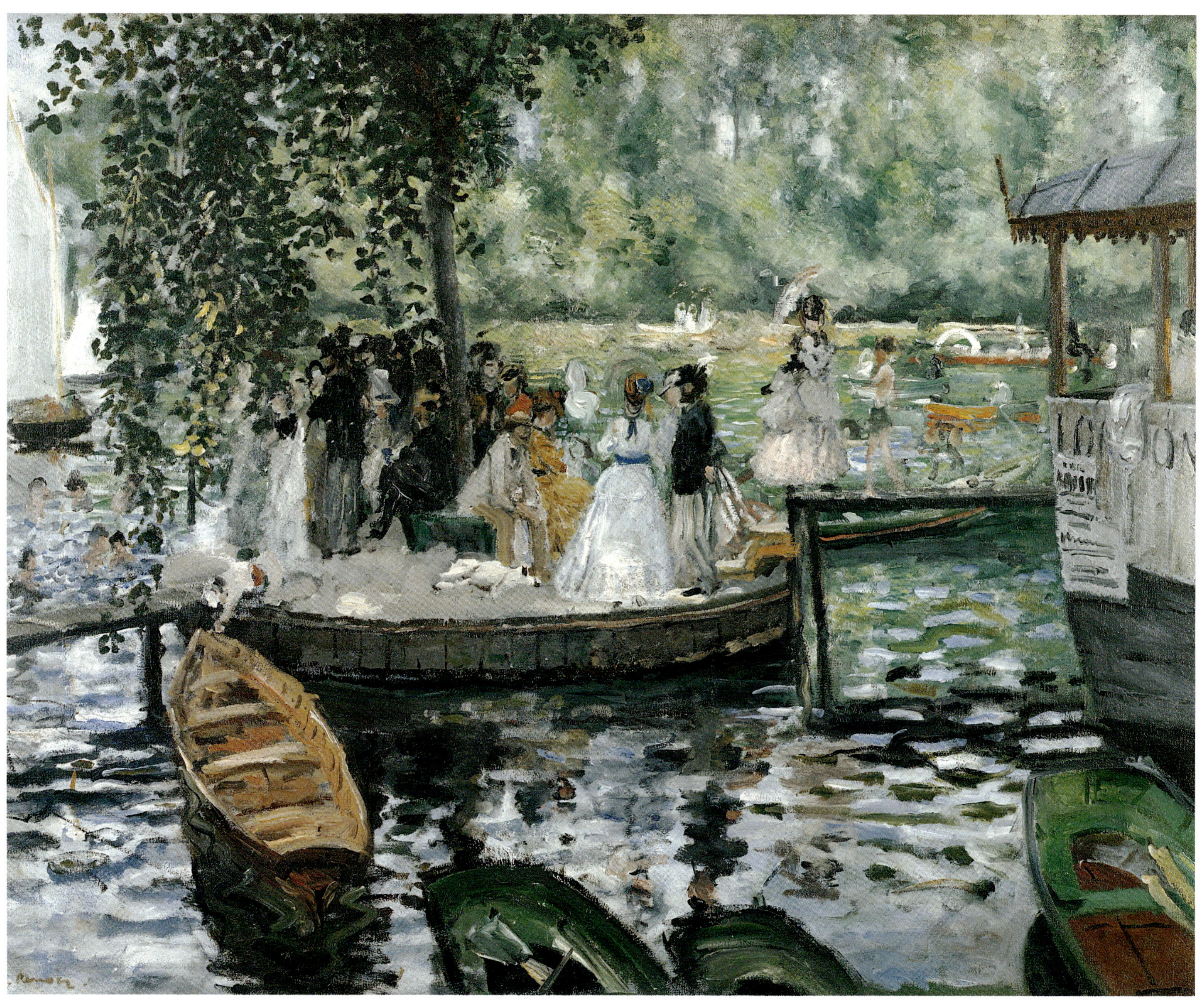

54
Pierre-Auguste Renoir
Boy with a Cat, 1868–69
Oil on canvas, 124 × 67 cm
Paris, Musée d'Orsay
(cat. no. 50)

At the end of the 1860s, Renoir concentrated on *plein- air* painting. Together with Monet, he painted at the resort of "La Grenouillère" on the Seine (cat. no. 49, fig. 53). During the same period, however, he also painted this monumental figure which is so unlike his other works. In his merciless depiction of the naked boy, Renoir seems to be influenced by Manet. With the cat and the boy's direct stare and white body the painting could be a male pendant to Manet's *Olympia* (fig. 55), which caused a scandal when it was exhibited in 1863. Renoir has rendered human skin, animal fur and cloth with a keen sense of the various textures. The painting thus becomes an intimation of sensual temptations on several levels.

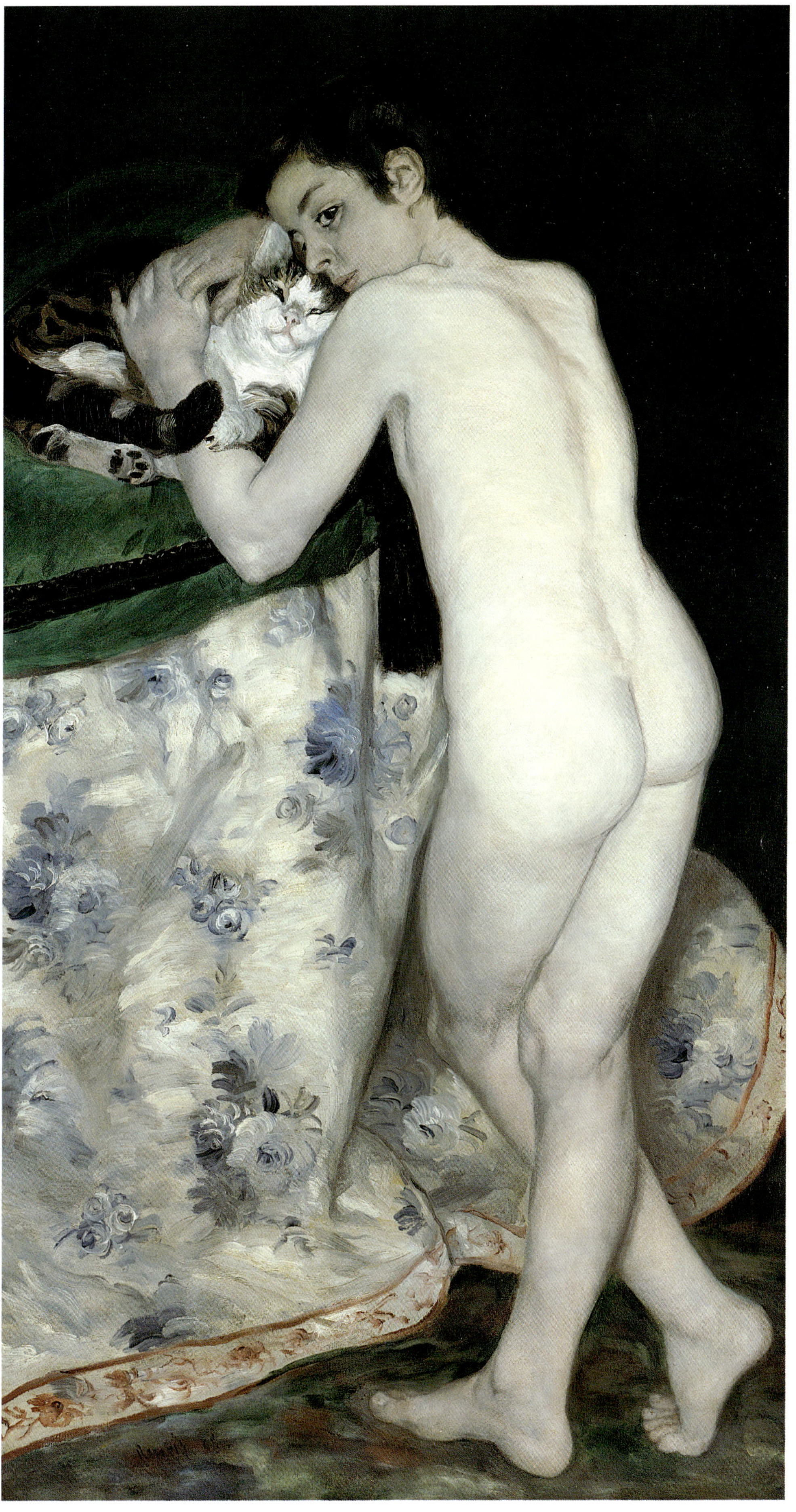

55
Edouard Manet
Olympia, 1863
Oil on canvas, 130 × 190 cm
Paris, Musée d'Orsay

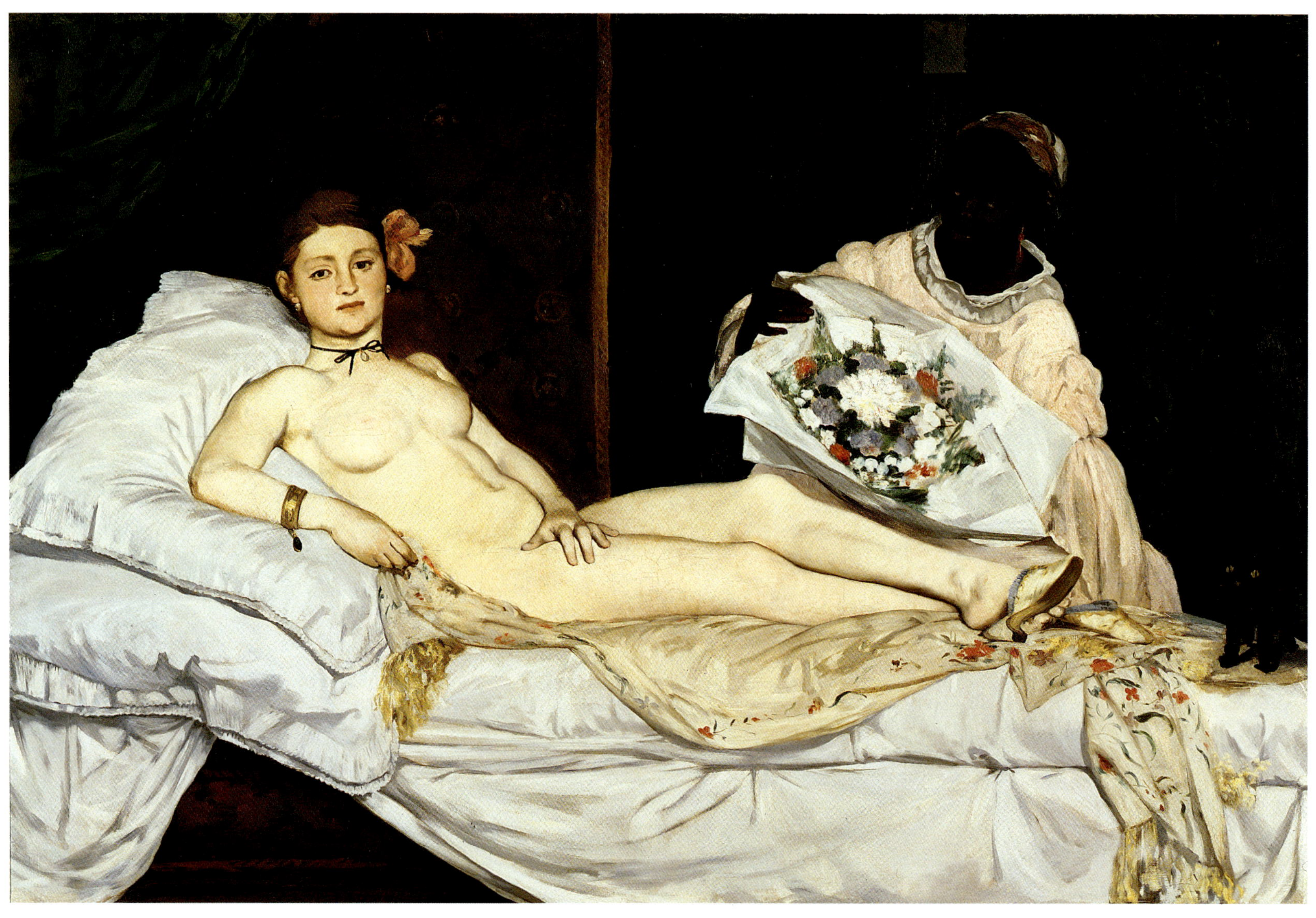

Salon painting, difference here is always a difference which comes into being, not a difference which is already established.

It is probably in this fashion that one should understand Cézanne's famous dictum about recreating Poussin from Nature. From nature's flux (Monet) we extract the — classicistic — order and structure. An order and a structure which is also part of reality but which was emptied, first by the Salon painters and subsequently by Manet. This order or structure is what Cézanne aims to restore, not as some postulated order already existing in the world, in a way which can be depicted, but an order which can be *created* in painting as Classicism, which, likewise must be recreated: with Cézanne's *Bathers* (cat. no. 15, fig. 75) we are back where we started, with the classical body in an Arcadian landscape, but now recreated as something which comes into existence in the painting's own medium: line, form, colour, space.

Let us take a closer look at this. The line is Classicism's fundamental principle of representation, a line which, however, in the work of Ingres and Gérôme, is almost invisible, a virtual or ideal line, that marks the transition between figure and space. It is not a part of either the figure or the space, but it is the figure's border itself, that which without being a physical component of the figure defines its identity — i.e an ideal or purely spiritual quality and demarcation.

In Manet, this contour line is radically redefined. It acquires a physical visibility and materiality, which it had not previously possessed, which creates not a little confusion as to its true significance. To extrapolate T.J. Clark's analysis of *Olympia* (fig. 55) in particular I would assert that it is precisely this confusion which is the issue in Manet's contour line. What he defines is a contour line never previously seen, a contour line which, precisely because it is unprecedented, has neither a fixed meaning — in that its meaning is a product of the difference — nor an inner essence, which is given external expression. This is at one and the same time, a fundamental semiotic premise for the analysis of the formation of meaning, and it is that premise which is the foundation of Manet's painting.[16]

With Monet the contour line is utterly suspended while Renoir and Gauguin attempt, in various ways, to reinstate it in accord with their Impressionist-critical tendencies, without there being, however, any question of a radical new kind of contour line. There is, rather a kind of "compromise" between the classical contour line and Manet's new one, i.e. a line which in its exterior appearance recalls Manet's but whose function in paintings's totality is reminiscent of the classical one, to represent an ideal order and identity.[17] Cézanne, on the other hand, seems to attempt a redefinition of the contour line by an approach every bit as radical as Manet's: it is a contour line which, on one side (and entirely in accord with his aim of "recreating Poussin from Nature") aims to restore order and difference as we know it from Classicism, but which, on the other side, extracts this order from the pulsating chaos we see in Monet. The result is a contour line which is a condensation of several different things, seen at its clearest in the *Bathers*, a contour line that seems to confirm the observation of Christian Metz (quoted above): "that which is born 'against' a feeling also is born 'in' it and does not permit itself to be separated from that, even if that is its purpose".

A closer inspection of *The Bathers* reveals that, for Cézanne, the contour line is not the fundamental principle of representation. In the landscape parts of the painting there are no lines at all, on the contrary, there is a genesis of forms, which seems to come "from within": the "constructive strokes" with which the foliage is painted seem to represent a transformation of what, in Monet, was pure pulsation, into form, or, at least, virtual form. In contrast the contour line in question is the relation to the

56
Paul Cézanne
The Temptation of St. Anthony, ca. 1875
Oil on canvas, 47 × 56 cm
Paris, Musée d'Orsay
(cat. no. 13)

Temptation was a highly popular theme around 1850, when religious art was undergoing a renaissance in France. The author Gustave Flaubert's description of the Temptation of St. Anthony was the starting point for this work. In it, Cézanne turns the story into a dramatic seduction scene with an autobiographical content. He has portrayed himself at the centre as the hermit Anthony, who is tempted by Woman and the Devil. Cézanne had previously portrayed himself in orgiastic and voyeuristic scenes, devoid of conventional perspective. But in contrast to those, this work returns to perspective as was understood in the Renaissance. It is also "classical" in the sense of the French landscape artist Poussin (1594–1665), whom Cézanne admired.

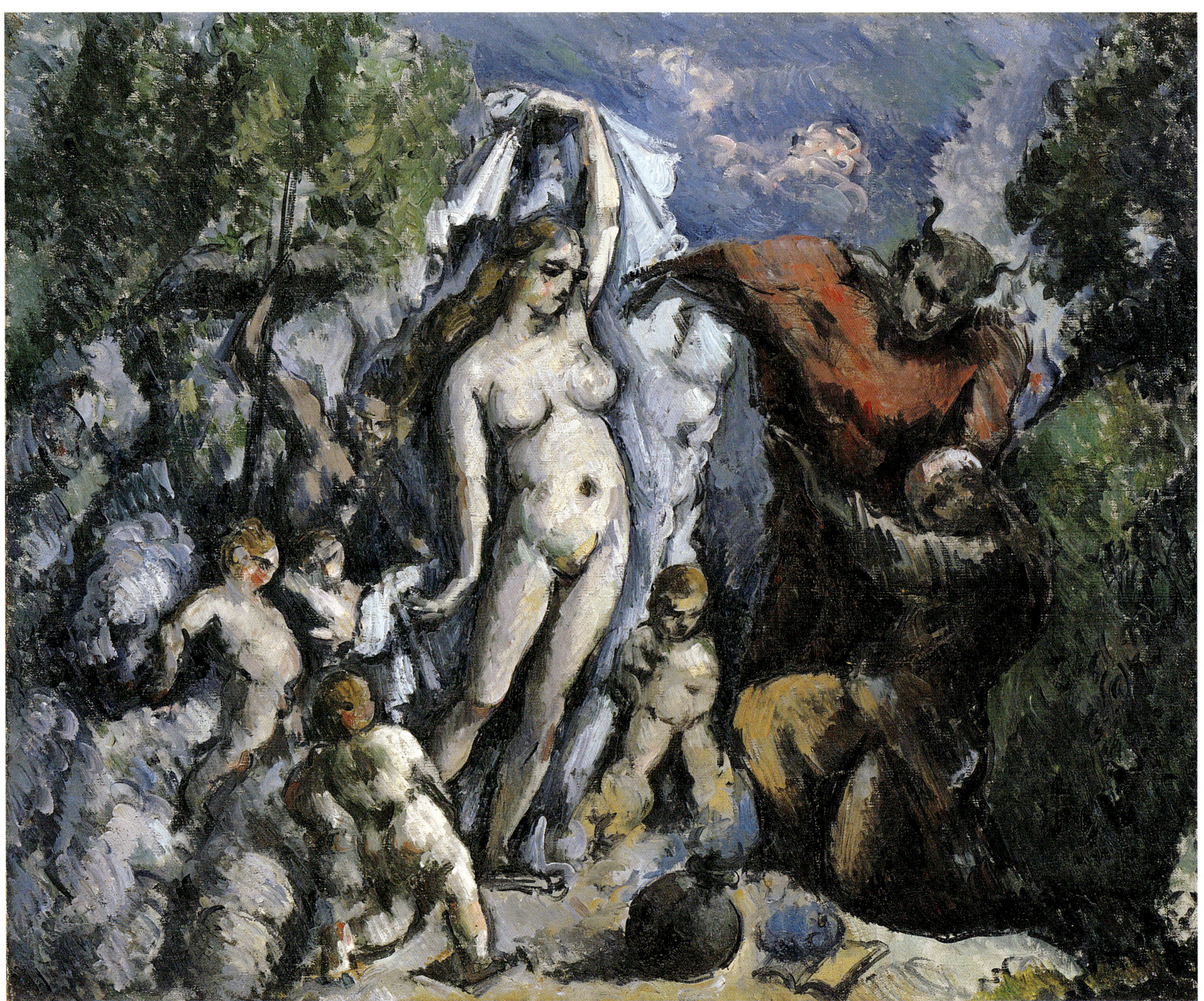

57
Eugène Carrière
Woman with Bare Breasts. Nature, undated
Oil on canvas, 61 × 49 cm
Paris, Musée d'Orsay
(cat. no. 11)

Carrière cultivated a style characterised by hint and suggestion as exemplified in this fantasy on female sexuality. A woman is shown emerging from the haze. One of her breasts and the ring on her finger act as fixed points drawing the viewer's gaze further into the picture. Here, the sensual aspects are developed through meticulous brushwork. Carrière really wanted to be a graphic artist, but a Rubens exhibition in the Louvre in 1862 is said to have persuaded him to choose painting. His predilection for shades of grey and brown and for hazy effects testify to his training in the graphic arts.

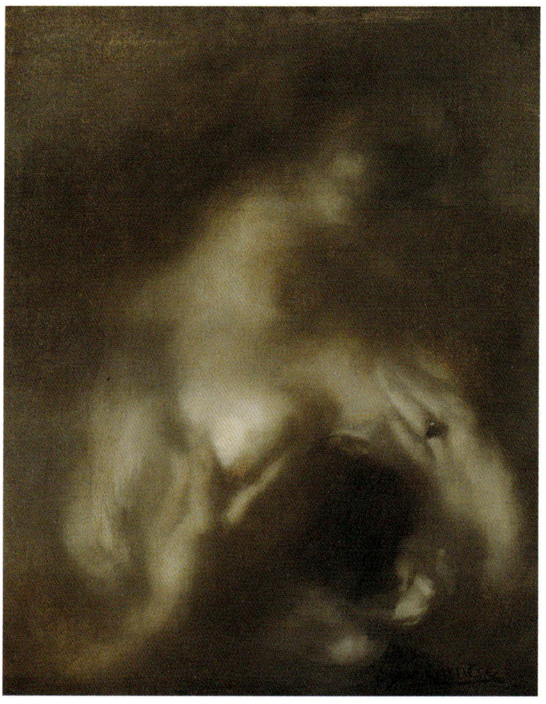

outlines of the women. But this contour line is perhaps still less ideal, still more material and "painterly" than in Manet, even though, on the other side, there is no doubt that this is an instance of inserting a "classical" contour line, i.e. a contour line which demarcates and defines differences. A rift seems therefore to be installed, almost, between the outer appearance of the line and its semiotic function, as though the function which determined the difference should be drawn out of the line's material, physical and painterly reality. It is possible to observe this problematic unfolding differently in other works by Cézanne: as contour lines, which are not the real thing since, despite being physically clear and present, they bear no relation to the painterly-defined boundaries of the figure. The contour, the boundary, thus comes to emerge as something located somewhere "between" the painted components and the more or less freely hovering, but materially well-defined line.

Interpreted in this manner the contour line emerges in this painting in such a manner that the function — the "contents", so to speak — is extracted from the physical materiality in such a way that it recalls the principle of the creation of forms in the vegetation's constructive strokes, which may be further interpreted in at least two ways. One is an attempt, through the painting's creation of forms, to depict the way in which the world comes into being through the painting, which answers perfectly Cézanne's own formulations on painting as "a harmony parallel with nature". At the same time it permits the understanding in formalist terms of what was here understood in realist or phenomenological terms. In formalist terms it can be understood as an investigation of the principles of painterly creation of forms itself, in relation to which the subject of the work is no more than a pretext.

This is not, however, the entire story: the line with its very physical presence, which is anything but neutral, cannot "retreat" behind its "syntactic" function. It is far too violent for that, so that the very violence of the line cannot but be interpreted as the trace of the process, the passion which generated it.[18] So much less, if one notices that the violent contour line is just that, a line which defines the boundaries *of the woman's body*, as if the passion is, perhaps, that very passion which condenses two desires: the desire to break down these boundaries and merge or fuse with the desired body — and at the same time the opposite desire, a desire to restore subjectivity, identity, difference.

The signs of Classicism are, as can be seen in the works, and as I hope I have been able to demonstrate here, multifarious, both as regards their external expression, the physical appearance, and as regards function. Above all I hope I have succeeded in suggesting that if one brings a different perspective to bear on tradition, and if one examines the French painting of the nineteenth century through such a lens, there is no question of the picture becoming simpler and easier to read as an overview, but, as far as I am concerned, it gets a bit more exciting.

[1] The most advanced and thought-out exposition of this traditional concept is probably to be found in the work of E.H. Gombrich — to be precise, in his book *Art and Illusion* (London, 1959), specifically the chapter, "Truth and the Stereotype".

[2] This way of formulating questions about tradition is greatly inspired by Norman Bryson (cf. his *Tradition and Desire* [Cambridge, 1984]) — and by Michael Fried's analysis of Manet's "sources" (cf. *Manet's Sources* from 1969 reprinted in *Manet's Modernism* [Chicago and London, 1996]).

[3] The question of how to define a very influential artist's own identity on one side and his influence and significance for artists inspired by him on the other is given an alternative perspective by Michael Baxendall vis-à-vis Cézanne in *Patterns of Intention* (New Haven and London: Yale University Press, 1985), especially the chapter "Intentional Visual Interest: Picasso's Portrait of Kahnweiler", pp. 41–73.

[4] Behind this reasoning lies the semiotic concept that a work has no intrinsic meaning. Instead signification is always produced through its relation to other works, with which it is associated or compared, consciously or unconsciously. As will appear it is furthermore my view, that as far as pictorial art is concerned, it is, to a high degree, tradition, i.e. the historical dimension of the picture, which constitutes the works' horizon of interpretation, as distinct from verbal languages' synchronous language system of Saussure and Hjelmslev.

[5] This is not the place to attempt an in-depth elucidation of the attendant theoretical implications of this. I shall restrict myself to stating that, consistent with what I consider to be the case with Bryson, I see the concept of tradition as it is used here as having at least three dimensions: firstly the standard notion of tradition in art history (cf. Gombrich), secondly Saussure's concept of language system or *langue*, and thirdly Freud's understanding of the super-ego.

[6] Charles Baudelaire, *Le peintre de la vie moderne / The Painter of Modern Life* (multiple editions).

[7] It may be difficult today for us to fully appreciate the status of Raphael for nineteenth-century French — and international — painting, worshipped as he was as the absolute master of painting, besides whose oeuvre all that followed was mere decline. It is thus not fortuitous that one of the first trends to seek a new foundation for painterly expression called themselves Pre-Raphaelites. Ingres himself was not the least of those who regarded Raphael as a divine ideal, to whom he remained faithful throughout.

[8] The term "condensation" comes from Freud and designates the fact that a sign, e.g. an element in a dream, can signify many different, possibly contradictory things at the same time.

[9] This thesis is put forward by Peter Galassi in his influential text "Before Photography" which was written as a catalogue text for the exhibition *Before Photography* at the Museum of Modern Art in New York in 1981.

[10] This formulation contains barely concealed, but vague references to the psychoanalyst Jacques Lacan, who, more than anyone else has analysed the role of visuality in the dialectic of desire and the constitution of the subject. See in particular Jacques Lacan, *Séminaire XI. Les quatre concepts fondamentaux de la psychanalyse* (Paris: Editions de Seuil, 1973). English translation *The Four Fundamental Concepts of Psychoanalysis*. It is a corresponding duality between loss and desire in the paintings of Gérôme and Ingres, not least in their treatment of the signs of Classicism, that I have here tried to approach with the aid of the photographic metaphor. Finally I should like, in this context, to draw attention to the way Christian Metz (inspired by Freud and Lacan) points out that a sign which is created "against" a passion, is also made "in" it, and that it therefore contains its opposite. I shall return to this in connection with an analysis of the function of the contour line in Cézanne's *Bathers*; Christian Metz, *Le signifiant imaginaire. Psychanalyse et cinéma* (Paris, 1977), pp. 96–7. English translation *The Imaginary Signifier*.

[11] Michael Fried, *Manet's Modernism* (Chicago and London, 1996), pp. 35–36.

[12] The formation of a subject as something which is constituted in an encounter with, or reflected in, the gaze of another: these formulations again refer to those of Lacan.

[13] Formulated in the categories of peircean semiotics one can say that the signs in themselves ("signs' firstness") are separated from or problematised in relation to their secondness (their relation to the designated "objects") and their thirdness (their relation to the "interpretant" — all the other signs or the totality, in relation to which the present sign acquires its meaning).

[14] "The reciprocity of coming into existence of subjects and objects, of consciousness and matter". When writing these words, I apparently contradict the central point made by Alois Riegl in *Das holländische Gruppenporträt* from 1931. Here Riegl asserts that in Baroque art, particularly in Rembrandt's art, and maybe most directly in *The Night Watch*, we encounter a perfect parity between subject and object. Prior to the Baroque the object dominated the subject (the "haptic" or the tactile over the optic) but after the Baroque it is the subject which dominates the object, the optic over the haptic. Now it is naturally difficult to bring over and discuss Riegl's Hegelian dialectic of subject and object in my more semiotic terminology. Nevertheless I intend to give Riegl his due and at the same time maintain my points. There is little doubt, namely, that what I call signification, the very coming into existence of sign and signification and which I have sought to define in my text, and whose introduction into painting as a specific method of production of meaning was accomplished most crucially by Manet and Cézanne, i.e. that instance when subject and object are produced as a difference — all this is to be found, in the work of Riegl, within what he understands as the subjective — and this to such a degree that he apprehends the almost formless pulsating energy of a Monet as something which represents a genuine abolition of "Kunstwollen" as such, i.e. of art

as such. Against this I should try to insist that Manet and Cézanne introduced into painting a new mechanism of signification, that is not without affinities to the epistemological break introduced into the humanities, by Saussure's theory of signs; cf. Jacques Derrida in *De la grammatologie/ On Grammatology* (Paris, 1967).

[15] Cf. also Heinrich Wölfflin, *Kunstgeshichte Grundbegriffe* (1915). English translation *Principles of Art History* (1950).

[16] This way of analysing signification, i.e. the processes by which meaning is created is, as I hope it can be seen, not unrelated to the already discussed Lacanian analysis of the creation of the subject as an effect of the dialectic of desire and loss. Such an assertion however is not enough to substantiate the claim that it is the basis of representation in the paintings of Manet, inasmuch as it is a premise for the analysis of all signification, and thereby it is not in itself object-sensitive. Against this it is an underlying premise for the analyses suggested here, that semiotic theory and Lacanian psychoanalysis belong to the very same concept of signification of which Manet's painting is one of the first examples in the history of art; cf. above as to the constitution of Manet's historical contribution.

[17] This analysis of mine does probably insufficient justice to two artists, Renoir and Gauguin: I am well aware of this. Both Renoir's *Boy with a Cat* and Gauguin's *Woman Sewing*, in particular, deserve greater attention than I have been able to give here.

[18] Both Merleau-Ponty and Meyer Schapiro mention that in the works of his youth from the 1860s, Cézanne develops a decidedly expressionistic style of painting, which anticipates the Expressionism of the twentieth century. See Maurice Merleau-Ponty, "Le doute de Cézanne", in *Sens et nonsens* (Paris: Les Editions Nagel, 1948); Meyer Schapiro, *Cézanne* (London: Thames and Hudson, 1988).

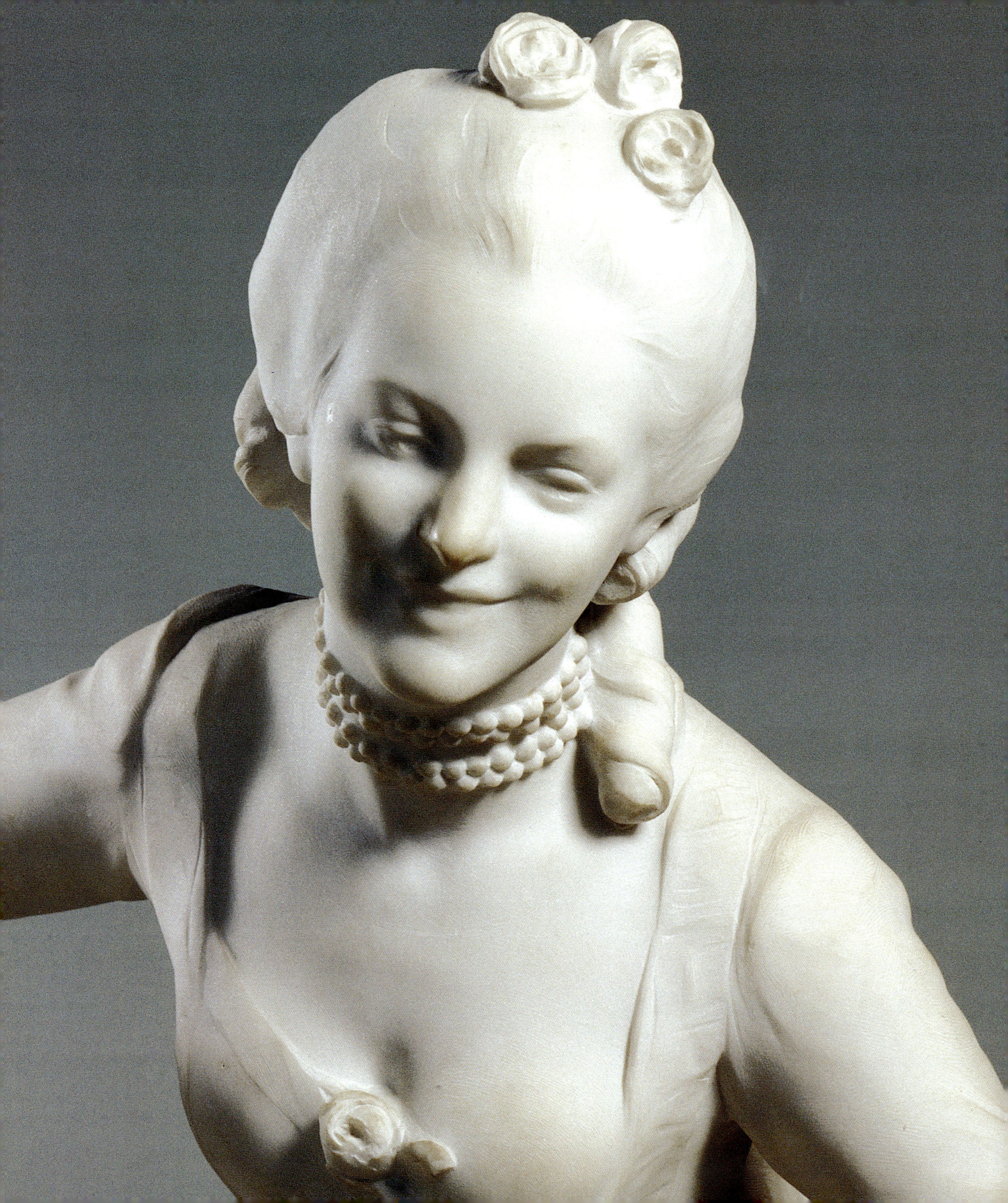

Flemming Friborg

Behind the Looking Glass. Carl Jacobsen's Ideals in Sculpture

58
Antonin Mercié
L'Opéra Comique (1897), detail
(full fig. 59)

Carl Jacobsen (1842–1914), Director of the Carlsberg Breweries in Copenhagen from 1887, is the founder of the Ny Carlsberg Glyptotek. Impressionism and "the new painting" as such made their breakthrough around the time when Jacobsen established himself as an art collector on the grand scale, but the patron held no esteem for these artistic developments. His ideals were of a different order. A view of some of his principles as a collector of sculpture might contribute to a broader understanding of the mechanisms involved, where Tradition and the Modern are concerned.

In 1863 Jules Verne wrote a little book about the Modern. The work was entitled *Paris in the 20th Century*, and true to form Verne sketched out a cocksure portrait of progress and its protagonists, culture and customs — this time the focus was not on the moon, the bowels of the earth or any such unknown region, but on the French capital itself. It proved impossible to find a publisher for the book, and it was not until the 1990s that the work was rediscovered in one of those tricks of fate so obedient to the mythical dictates of art: it reappeared in the form of a manuscript discovered in a safe. It is far from being the author's unknown masterpiece, but the unassuming novel's description of its age contains many thought-provoking moments which relate to the theme of this exhibition. Here we are in the year 1960, a hundred years after the period when Verne was actually writing. A cynical main character tips the culture the following salute, accompanied by some sound advice to his friend, the optimistic man of letters: "... if you haven't got something really staggering to report, who on earth will have the slightest interest in listening to you? Art is no longer possible if it comes about as a tour de force. In this age of ours Hugo will recite his 'Orientales' while leaping from one horse to another, while Lamartine, with drooping head, will pour out his 'Harmonies' from a flying trapeze!"

"The world of today is one great tent of clowns, where people crave entertainment in the form of every kind of monkey business. When all is said and done, you are simply fulfilling your destiny! You are a great poet! I myself have seen what you have written. You accept my judgement however, that your work does not suit the taste of the time".

"And why should that be the case?"

"Come on... Yours are the traditional subjects of poetry, and under the present dispensation that is quite unacceptable. You go into raptures over flowering meadows, verdant dells, clouds, stars, love — all in all, a whole lot of shop-soiled merchandise which nobody wants anymore".

"But what else can one write poetry about?"

"You should pay tribute to the marvels of industry!"[1]

If one removes the most extreme of Verne's cultural pessimism, one ends up with an enthusiastic description of a brave new world — a world of modernism, where the greatest interest is that in the new, and where the guiding principle behind artistic development is innovation — change at any price. What is striking is how this and the thoughts behind it closely resemble the praise offered up much later by Futurism to progress for its own sake; that supreme confidence of victory and the firm conviction of the excellence of everything leaves no room for the opposite point of view in this fiction conjured up by the writer. Verne the prophet himself, was, apparently, something of a conservative in his views on the innovative in music and painting — there was no room in his vision for Wagner's *Gesamtkunstwerk* or Realism, and this strikes a curious note, particularly when seen against the absurd notions he was ready to accept, not to mention his own foretelling of the opportunities offered by the technical-mechanical sphere. An apposite example is his comments on a contemporary painter, seen from the fictive standpoint of the narrative in 1960: "... even as early as the last century Realism overstepped the boundaries of propriety. It was said of Courbet that at one of his last exhibitions he ostentatiously turned towards the wall and executed one of the healthiest, but least elegant of life's functions. The birds of Zeuxis would have scattered in terror!"[2]

In the hands of Verne the fantasist, the words have the ring of prophecy, despite his avowed intention to shock his epoch, but also betray the era's embryonic confrontation with classical, academic virtues. Judging by his actions as a collector, Carl Jacobsen, founder of the Glyptotek, shared Verne's opinion, to a greater extent, of the avant-garde in painting which was to play such a crucial role in the development of the art of the twentieth century. Salon sculpture and the excesses of Rodin were his passion — so much so in fact that, as far as his own Parnassus was concerned they came to supplant Thorvaldsen and Danish painters of the Golden Age as well as that country's artists of the 1870s. Both the Salon and Rodin gained a massive foothold in the Glyptotek's collections, side by side with classical Greek and Roman sculpture and works of art from the key eras in the history of Egypt.

It is enlightening that even Jacobsen was prepared to cultivate a certain notion of progress albeit as he saw it. Another pioneer in another field altogether — and for many contemporaries a heretic of dimensions — once wrote these lines, describing his views on art: "I should begin by saying that I am no connoisseur of art, merely a layman. I have often noticed that it is the content of a work of art which affects me more powerfully than its qualities of form and technique, which, on the other hand, would be of first importance to the artist himself". The words are those of Sigmund Freud; they form the introduction to his short essay, "The Moses of Michelangelo", published in 1914 — the year Carl Jacobsen died. However much they might have disagreed on other issues, these two formidable figures of their age would have been in complete agreement that content was the crucial element in art; for Jacobsen it was the most important single force in any consideration of art. Freud's predilection for the narrative content in sculpture derives from his desire to find evidence of a human being's personality. Of all the arts it is sculpture which comes closest to the human form: sculpture imitates it and comprehends it so as to be able to reveal what lies within the human soul in all its aspects — it is here that personality expresses itself. For Freud the work of art is like the dream, an obscure matter which requires elucidation. The spiritual tiger-leap into the new century by psychoanalysis transformed

59
Antonin Mercié
L'Opéra Comique (1897)
Carved in marble (1900),
h. 184 cm
Copenhagen, Ny Carlsberg
Glyptotek
(cat. no. 46)

The woman appears to be an actress, bowing as she smilingly receives applause. In a piquant fashion, one of her breasts has emerged from her low-cut dress, suggesting a mood of decadent abandon or popular vulgarity which is consistent with the symbolism of the figure. *L'Opéra Comique* is, in fact, an allegory of a specific type of popular opera that arose in France around 1750. The woman is accordingly dressed in the eighteenth-century Rococo manner and is like an enlarged version of a porcelain statuette. The popular musical genre and mantelpiece decorations have thereby adopted the monumental format.

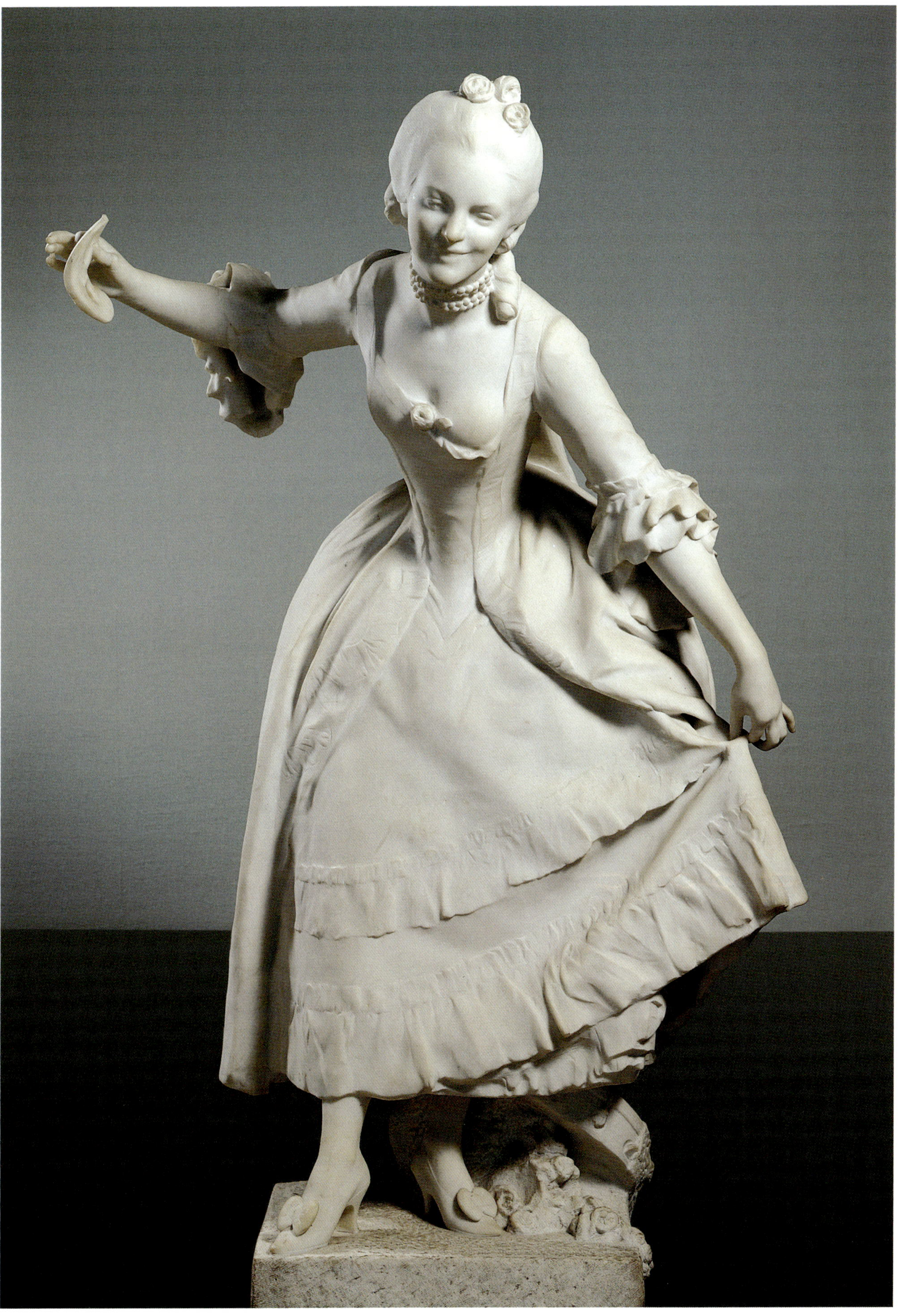

modern science into a serious rival to the definition of culture influencing such patrons of sculpture as Carl Jacobsen. Figurative art could provide illustrations in the process of psychological interpretation, which could reach deeper than had previously been possible within the compass of art alone. The work of art could be enlisted in the service of psychoanalysis as (historical) research material on a particular personality. By examining the work of art under his particular "microscope" Freud both ground it down, and, simultaneously, moved it into a construction where it was merely one of many constituents of an eventual examination of human thought processes.

Exactly how much Carl Jacobsen was acquainted with the views on art of the Viennese doctor is not known: judging by the psychological profile which gradually emerges of the industrialist,[3] it seems certain Jacobsen would have been implicitly opposed to Freud's work, since he would have seen it as an attempt to demolish that concept of human ideals by which he himself set such store.

By going beyond the old world's concept of man, psychoanalysis simultaneously realised and cancelled out the idea of exploring man through art. The new science of the psyche was an attempt to map out all the resources of the soul, but at the same time it deprived man of full mastery over these powers and the way they behaved in the conscious and unconscious. The concept of humanity was now expanding in ways in which the departing century either could not, or would not accompany it. In the first instance, the investigation of the psyche was a natural scientific development in the same fundamental spirit as that which had shaped Carl Jacobsen himself. The nineteenth century exhibited a decided tendency to the encyclopaedic. There were catalogues covering everything and now the object of scrutiny was to be the human being, who was still, despite Darwin, the master of creation. Freud's psychoanalysis can be seen as the crown of critical natural science bestowed on the achievement of Darwin; if the theory of the origin of species was correct, a science of the mind would complete the picture of homo sapiens precisely by exploring the depths of that conscious faculty which separates man both from the animals and from his forerunners on the evolutionary ladder. Whereas Darwin had advanced in his system of comparisons to the point where he could establish a theory grounded in empirical data, the psychoanalyst could interpret his material to a far greater degree of refinement. Freud regarded interpretation as a fundamental scientific condition and saw nothing amiss in its crucial role for the theory of psychoanalysis, any more than he regretted the ensuing suggestion of freedom from the rigid concept of science. He was a cool rationalist; in "Die Zukunft einer Illusion" from 1927 he posits — even if he goes about it *sotto voce*, and with a degree of circumlocution — a future where not only religion but also metaphysics of any kind, will be regarded as abuses of the reasoning faculty, a deviation from the path. This is the victory of psychoanalysis: the complete takeover by the pure reason of a positivist science.

Beyond the purely scientific sphere, the story with respect to reason and emotion was quite different. The relative freedom permitted by a system of thought based on interpretation makes it possible to reopen an irrational breach in what is, otherwise, the rational, historically-ordered world established by Darwinism. This is why, despite its difficult beginnings, the work of Freud and his successors achieved such significance in the twentieth century. Psychoanalysis's power of suggestion is evident in numerous cultural echoes, just as its vocabulary has been borrowed to connote things of which its founders could never have conceived. Merely the names bestowed on the basic elements of sexual activity have left their mark on figurative art, which is called "modern art": note the crucial anachronistic concept —

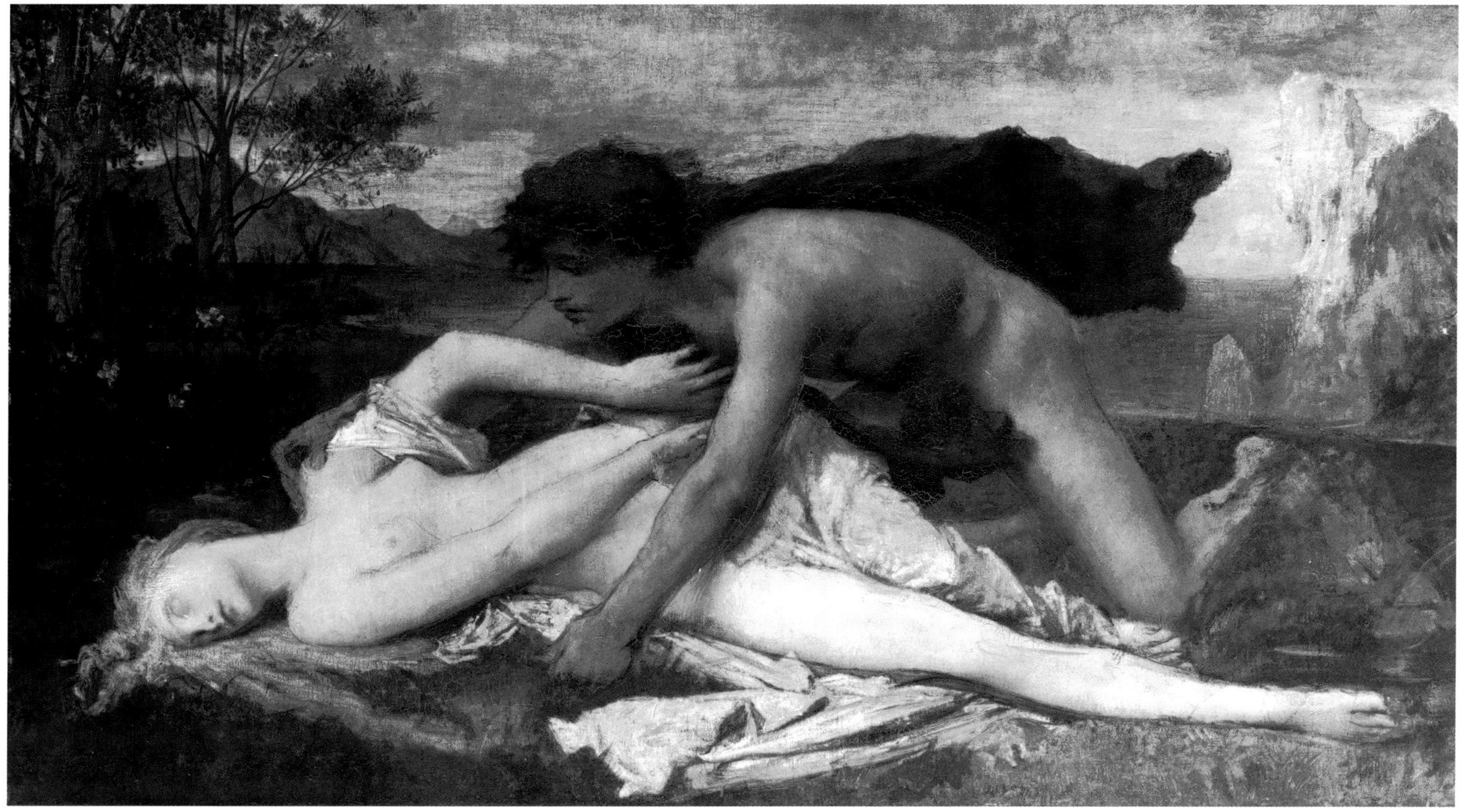

60
Jules-Elie Delaunay
The Death of the Nymph Hesperia (1859)
Oil on canvas, 76.5 × 138 cm (unfinished)
Copenhagen, Ny Carlsberg Glyptotek
(cat. no. 24)

In his *Metamorphoses*, Ovid tells the story of the nymph Hesperia, who tries to save herself from the lusts of the Prince Aisakos. During her flight she is bitten by a snake and dies. Delaunay shows the emotional moment when Aisakos, repentant but still possessed by his unfulfilled desire, embraces the nymph's lifeless body. The painting contains a host of contradictions between her white "marble" corpse and Aisakos' dark, living body. The figures are placed in an Arcadian landscape which merely functions as a backdrop. Although the painting is unfinished, it was exhibited at the Salon of 1863, where Delaunay achieved his breakthrough.

since the art of any period is modern for its age. Its own age turns the modern into a style, makes it enter a specific historical framework and permits it to embody the collective effort to reject everything that is old. The drive now is to go beneath the exterior of sculpture and painting, and their ideal forms, and reach a truer reality which does not necessarily correspond to the one outwardly presented. This expansion of the concept of man contains abstraction in embryo. Jacobsen and Freud stand on opposite sides of the line marking the beginning of the Modern. With Jacobsen an epoch comes to a close, as can clearly be seen from his cultural activities. As one of the last great collectors in the old world, Carl Jacobsen wished to be involved with art: art's power to ennoble, was, he continued to believe, its most valuable quality, as he never tired of proclaiming. Art should be able to teach us about the human being, its aspirations and its needs, since art held the mirror up to mankind. Jacobsen's belief was that this mirror gave us the opportunity to improve ourselves within a process which advanced historically. It is this ennobling principle, under the eyes of eternity, to which we should aspire.

Not Painting but Sculpture

One remains a child of one's time, even in those things one believes to be a reflection of one's innermost self, Freud philosophised: Carl Jacobsen was in no way opposed to this thesis. As far as Jacobsen was concerned, contemporary French art of the avant-garde was anathema. His priority was time-honoured: let each period or style be illustrated by its very greatest works. Thus the Italian Renaissance was exemplifed by Raphael, Rembrandt was hailed as the greatest of the seventeenth century Dutch painters; France was represented by David and later exponents of the Salon. There was a single Millet — to exemplify the didactic principle[4] — and works by the principal Danish Golden

Age painters of the school of Eckersberg. This approach was inoffensive, but there is the abiding impression that Jacobsen never developed a deep understanding of painting as an art form. Once back in the world of sculpture he felt himself on much safer ground: here there was scope for his talents, a chance to make a difference. One can clearly observe how his acquisitions policy changed over the years, and his personal taste was mixed in equal amounts with a regard for the overall composition of the collection, but the *leitmotif* was the lessons sculpture could teach about mankind.

Jacobsen wanted to present a selection of sculpture which was both of the highest levels of excellence and as representative of the various periods as possible in his Glyptotek, in the tradition of the encyclopaedists of his age.[5] The period of 1880–90 was marked by a plethora of initiatives in the Danish cultural scene and Jacobsen was involved in most of them. 1896 saw the opening of the new Statens Museum for Kunst and the incorporation into it in the same year of a Museum of Casts (previously part of the Royal Danish Academy for the Arts). Museums were being built all over Denmark and those in the provinces were now acquiring works of note. All of this was in the spirit of educating the population: nothing less than a regular cultural mobilisation was in progress.

Jacobsen's view of museums was that they should provide fertile ground among the population for the growth of an unforced experience of art. This programme should be started from scratch, and the acquisitions should range from the art of ancient Greece and Rome right up to the sculpture of the present day. Jacobsen was one of the first to accord recognition to Rodin, who was still regarded by many as avant-garde, but he purchased just as extensively among the sculptors of the French Salon who were not. He became the leading patron for the generation of Danish artists who succeeded Thorvaldsen, in all their diversity[6] — though his favourite aspect was work which could serve some concrete purpose, either in the sphere of the decorative, or the context of portraiture. One look at the contemporary scene revealed that there was more than enough to do in Denmark, where, Jacobsen opined, sculpture, was particularly deserving of support. He issued his "manifesto" as early as 1878, when, in a letter from Paris, he wrote, in some bewilderment, of his encounter with modern French sculpture at the Salon. He asserts that France is in the vanguard in this field, not least because artists dare give equal priority to undertaking the more difficult work as they do to the more accessible styles of painting.[7] Jacobsen's choice of words is significant: "For us Danes there is something strange about even the best French sculpture; and, in this matter, our national character is not entirely blameless. But the fact is that neither has the powerful influence of Thorvaldsen yet spent itself, nor has it borne the fruit one could have hoped for: to wit a vital flourishing school. It has, rather, sharpened the critical sense and made sterner demands on the creatures to which sculpture has given life than in other spheres [...] if we now have difficulties in enthusing over those many figures which we once gladly observed — yes, and still do, to an extent today — in attitudes of leaping or running, it is because our great master has taught us that statues should not hop about on one leg, but stand on two. But perhaps it is precisely this critical sense which is the reason that the great works of foreign art have only imperfectly moved us here in our native land. Indeed, it has become *de rigeur* to find nothing of value in Canova; Rauch and various Frenchmen have been tolerated, but to the point of being practically ignored. The sculpture of France is a vigorous affirmation of life: it can no longer be ignored".[8]

The difference between Danish and French, was actually between the two national characters — or "Natureller" (natural dispositions), as they were known at that

61
Jean-Baptiste Carpeaux
The Prince Imperial with His Dog Néro, 1865
Silver-plated bronze, h. 136 cm
Copenhagen, Ny Carlsberg Glyptotek

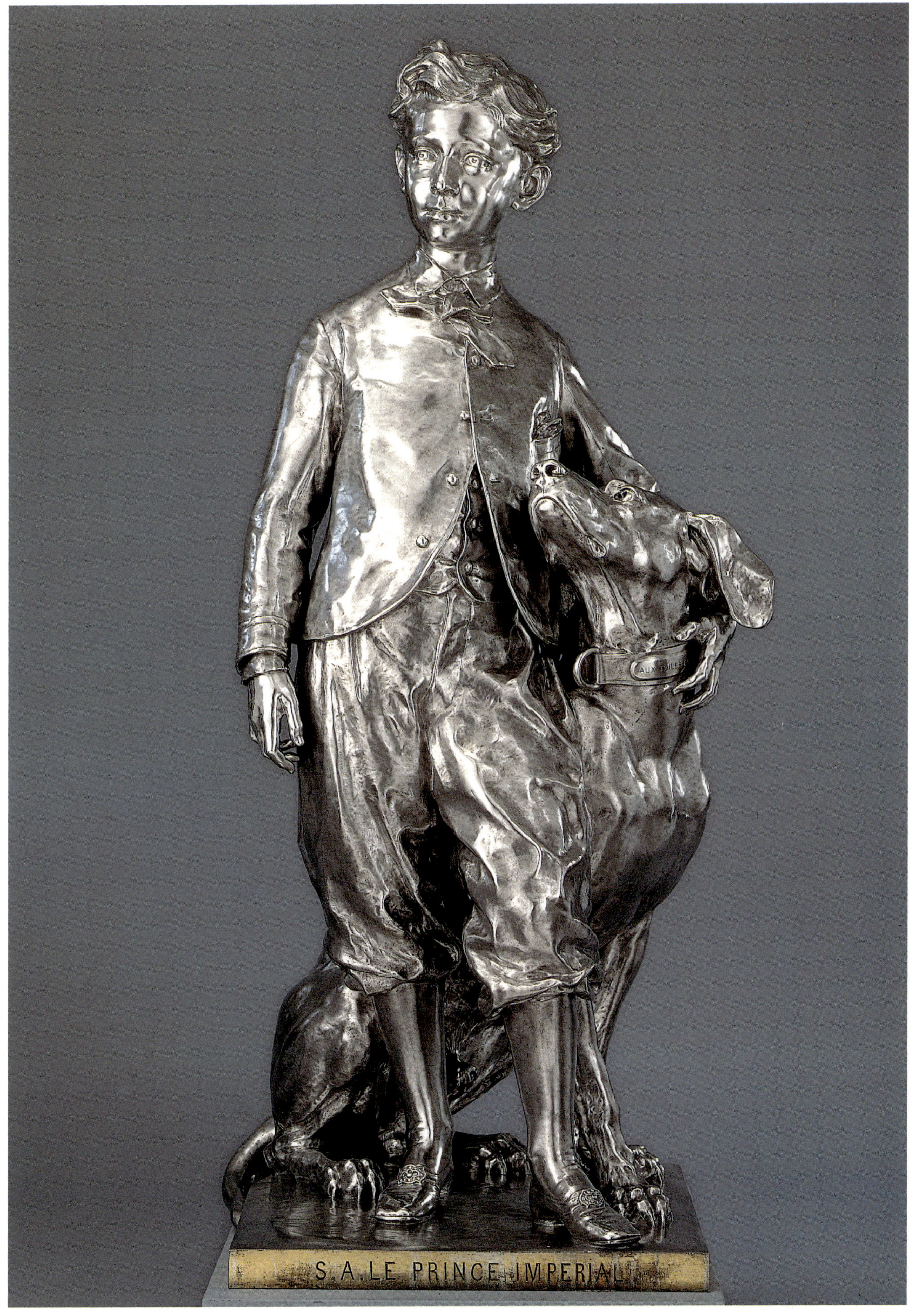

time, and was, at root, more psychological than purely aesthetic. In Jacobsen's letter there is a clear statement of the position he assumes vis-à-vis the artistic developments of the future. Full justice is accorded, as always, to Thorvaldsen, but his time is past and there is no excuse for becoming mired in tradition. There was an elegant parricide implicit in this reckoning with Thorvaldsen, Jacobsen's artistic hero, and the great cultural bastion of his childhood home. Simultaneously, however, this presages the next step in the development of Carl Jacobsen's cultural consciousness — the chauvinist is now accompanied in his progress, by the cosmopolitan. French sculpture had what Jacobsen so eagerly sought, namely the quality of permanence,[9] which was, for him, the defining feature of Classicism. But at the same time it was *modern* art, and in this respect, Denmark was lagging behind. "Save in our own land, the products of this new breed wander the world over in incarnations of bronze in every conceivable size", as "witnesses of this new age". And, it begs the question, exactly what was it Jacobsen saw in these figures? *Music* by Delaplanche (cat. no. 23, fig. 35), which he included in this category, was not an easy work to respect. Jacobsen spoke warmly about the naked limbs rendered in an outstanding (un-Danish) manner, the soulful expression, the originality of the theme, and the "Raphaelesque" spirit of the work. She was but one example, and the young *amateur* was well aware of the antipathy such "spiritual" over-indulgence would encounter in Denmark. It was, in fact, this resistance on which his status as a patron was based. Jacobsen realised disappointedly, that to install a figure of comparable theme and execution as the French *Music* in a Danish public space — such as the Royal Theatre — would be impossible. Denmark was an "inhospitable shore" — this painful expression was tantamount to an accusation of barbarism. Jacobsen's mission was already beginning to take shape in his mind. It was concerned, not with turning what was Danish into French, but with the necessity for self-development, and thus moving up a step or two on a ladder which was not merely one of aesthetic taste but also of human enlightenment. Delaplanche's figure was a modern classic — this indicated that there was such a thing as context. Sculpture should ennoble the Danish public, the artists, the cities — and posthumous reputations, that of Jacobsen himself as much as that of the entire nation. "To have been is nothing. To be is momentary, and to become is for eternity", as Jacobsen had had inscribed in Latin and capital letters in the Winter Garden of the Glyptotek.

Jacobsen wished to contribute to the emergence of a new Danish art of sculpture, which would perpetuate Thorvaldsen's memory, more than his style. The patron was aware of changes on the international scene, and it was too late to accomplish anything further with an art of sculpture which was rigidly neo-classical. This is an example of both trains of Carl Jacobsen's thought vis-à-vis the museum. Art must, on the one hand, be seen as a cavalcade of selected triumphs, with the stylistic development clearly indicated in its chronological sequence; on the other hand the future must be planned on the basis of the present. The driving force behind Jacobsen's endeavours was a concept of history which owed less to the attitude of the professional academic than to the burning enthusiasm of the amateur, and he himself emphasised that his standpoint was beyond any narrow scientific confines.[10] Science could, however, be a discipline of considerable assistance, and in this respect Jacobsen had a decided flair for finding the right colleagues.[11]

Cataloguing was an aspect of the museum world which, though devoid of any individual artistic vision, was, according to Jacobsen, perfectly valid for the coming ages. Beginning in 1879, Jacobsen purchased works by the European neo-classicists starting with Carstens, through Canova, right up

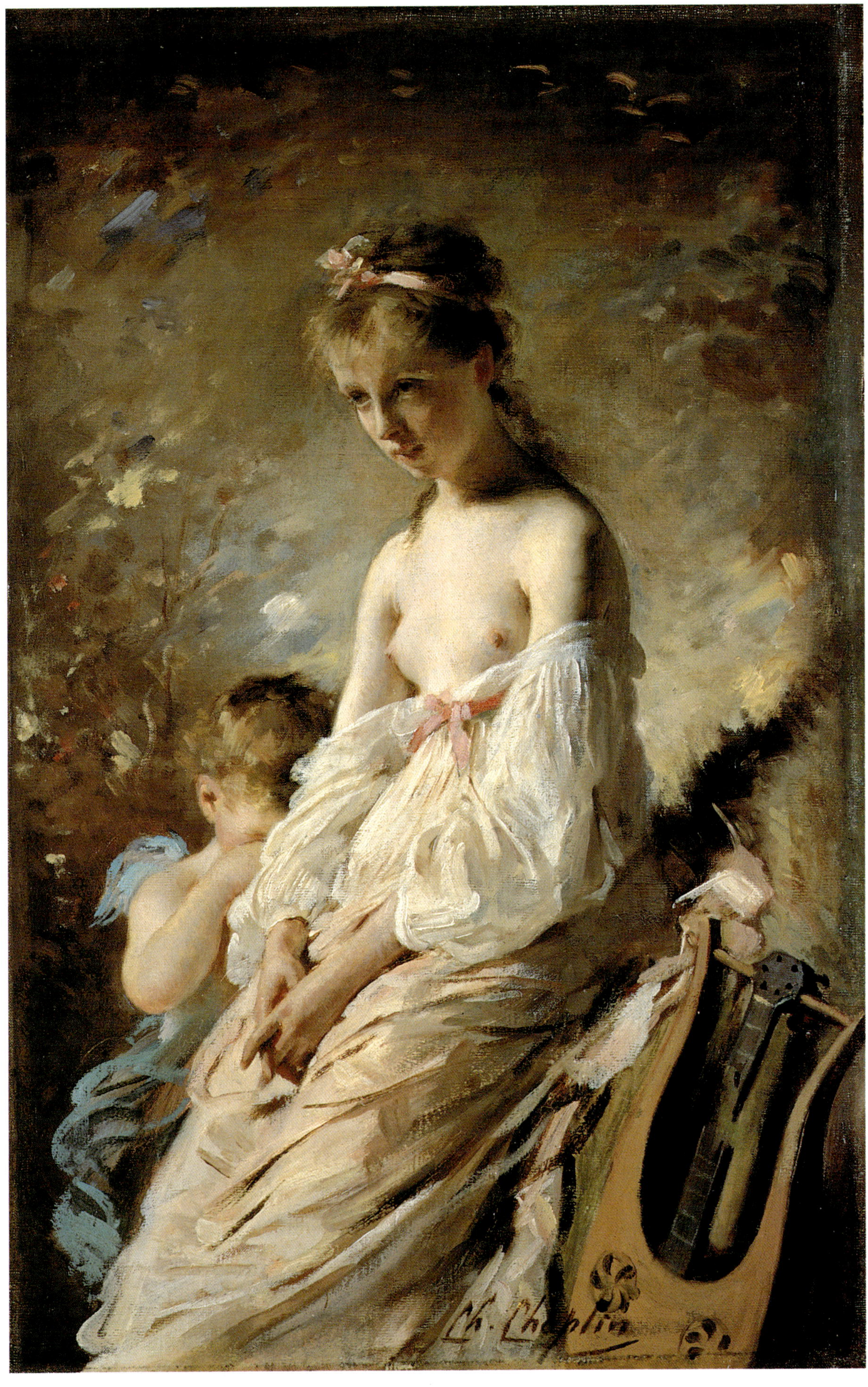

62
Charles Chaplin
The Broken Lyre (1875)
Oil on canvas, 41 × 26.5 cm
Copenhagen, Ny Carlsberg Glyptotek
(cat. no. 16)

The critics of the day lavished especial praise on Chaplin for works like this, in which he employs pastel-like shades to portray a young woman. The motif was inspired by the eighteenth-century Rococo and moves along the borderline between the mythological and the allegorical. The broken lyre symbolises the girl's lost innocence. In a realistic setting, this theme would have become an account of downfall and degradation. Here, under the cloak of idealism, it becomes a fluttering, erotic, piquant exercise more suited to being presented in the Salon. It is works of this kind that have since made the term "Salon Painting" a term of abuse.

to Rauch. The resulting catalogue of these works clearly demonstrates the evolution of style over a particular period. Having firmly established Thorvaldsen as his point of departure, Jacobsen seems to have been determined to demonstrate the international persistence with that austere neo-classicist ideal in which the Danes had such a tremendous stake. By the same token, however, many of these artists had a certain influence on the subsequent development of Danish sculpture. This was particularly the case with those of the German schools, whose reputation in Denmark at the time the collection was established, was, according to Jacobsen, quite unjustifiably poor.[12] Their incorporation provided an invaluable historical dimension: by examining German, English and Italian sculpture from the period 1800–90 it is possible to trace the points of similarity and contrast in artistic expression over the course of time as well as to take account of any specifically national characteristics. The Glyptotek's collection of modern sculpture follows on chronologically from the brilliant Age of Thorvaldsen and further enhances his reputation as the founding father of a canon, both within the frontiers of Denmark and beyond! Jacobsen wanted to illustrate and keep up with the European development from 1800, from which Danish art was now estranged, and even though he himself had lost faith in any Danish potential to perpetuate the ideal.

Art in the Service of Ethics

The Glyptotek was not the first instance of Jacobsen realising his idea of art's power to ennoble. The Albertina Trust was established in 1879, and named after Bertel (Alberto) Thorvaldsen, as an invocation of past greatness in the service of a new beginning; the object was to grace the public spaces of Copenhagen with sculpture, chosen from among, "the outstanding classic works of Past and Present which, it must be felt, have meaning for the ages to come" as it was expressed in the instrument of foundation, formulated by Jacobsen himself. He was not thinking of Danish art; and lest it be forgotten — the establishment of the Albertina Foundation was not intended to let either national or local government renege on their obligations to Danish art.[13] This provoked substantial debate among the initial members of the trust: besides Jacobsen himself these included H.N. Hansen, Mayor of Copenhagen, and the architect Meldahl, who was Director of the Kunstakademi. The personal make-up of this body was highly inflammable, and it was only a matter of time before the inevitable conflagration.

Jacobsen was a poltician in the grand manner — his lofty ideal prompted him to disdain the petty infighting such confrontations sometimes occasioned. Art was the perfect arena in which nations could compete against each other, and the major exhibitions of French and international art held in Copenhagen in 1888 and 1897 respectively were impressive assemblies of contemporary European art. The first exhibition of French art in Denmark was in 1888, and came about rather as Jacobsen's response to the great Nordic exhibition of Industry, Art and Agriculture held the same year. Jacobsen had suggested that the exhibits be displayed in combinations which encouraged the drawing of comparisons — exhibition space would be provided to house a selection of works by the leading French artists of the age — selected by Jacobsen himself, of course. When his suggestions were rebuffed, he organised his own French exhibition. This was accomplished, starting entirely from scratch and with breathtaking expedition: it was a success that demanded to be followed up. Under the self-conscious banner of "The Athens of the North", Copenhagen had, at a stroke, established itself as a cultural capital on a par with the others. Since the year was 1897 this put it in direct competition with Stockholm which had been planning a similar event for some years.[14] Something of a strategist, Ja-

63
Jean-Jacques Henner
Nymph Resting, undated
Oil on canvas, 26 × 40 cm
Copenhagen, Ny Carlsberg Glyptotek
(cat. no. 36)

The history and mythology of the ancient world were Henner's great interest. Here, in a small study, he has portrayed his favourite motif, the nymph. But the nymph is alone, present as a white figure against a dark landscape without any mythological reference. She is more than anything an erotic motif, the object of the observer's gaze as she reclines there with her sensually flowing red hair blending into the surrounding landscape. The old Italian Masters inspired Henner to use the soft outline and the powerful *clair obscur* effect in which the light figure appears against a dark background.

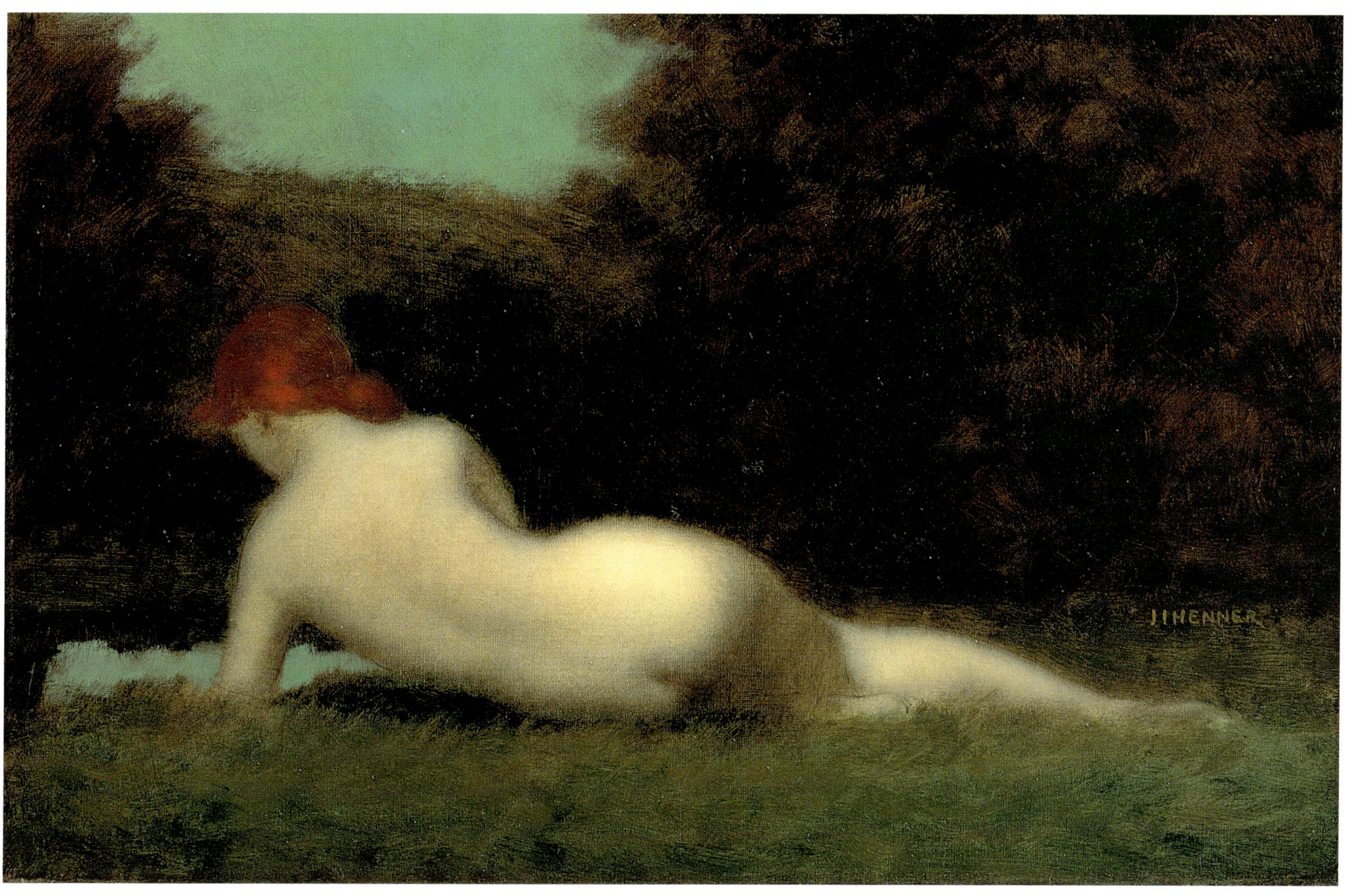

cobsen made the international exhibition part of the extension to his own newly-opened Glyptotek — quite literally in the sense that he supplemented the back of the Dahlerup Building with an extensive if temporary pavilion. Every modern work in the Glyptotek was on show when the guests packed into the extension. The gesture was also aimed at the city councillors of Copenhagen, who had been sceptical about the necessity of a planned extension to the Glyptotek, then stalled by lack of funds. Sadly, the exhibition was a massive flop, the public stayed away in droves and Jacobsen must have been cursing the Neanderthal level of the Danish art world.

Jacobsen had fully committed himself to the belief that it was possible to drag oneself out of the provincial wilderness. The only way innovation was going to gain a foothold in the national artistic arena was as inspiration from outside — and even then it would be subject to the intense scrutiny of a stern Danish cultural consciousness. But though nobody was nursing any expectations that Copenhagen would become the centre of the art world, it had not escaped notice how fast the focus had shifted from Rome to Paris. Since pace of change had rocketed, there seemed no good reason why the Danish capital should not also share in the benefits. As far back as the 1870s there had been substantial support for the promotion of the culture of Denmark/Scandinavia as opposed to that of Central and Southern Europe and in the arts there remained the dilemma of whether to be national or international. Carl Jacobsen was accused of unpatriotic cultural politics, but he was committed to a greater issue and acquisitions of works from other countries (particularly France) and exhibitions acted as a kind of spiritual first aid for Denmark. Others would have to worry about domestic support for the arts, and then only once this was forthcoming and a favourable cultural climate had been achieved. In this context the concept of "classical" was crucial: Jacobsen's definition was based purely on durability — permanence. The trustees of the Albertina Foundation manoeuvred between the patriots (Meldahl and Hansen) and Jacobsen's insistence on French contemporary art by reaching a compromise — anytime there was disagreement the purchase would be made of the cast of a sculpture from Antiquity: yet again Carl Jacobsen carried the day.[15]

It was vital for Jacobsen's plans for the Albertina that art be seen in the open air. Copenhagen was to be of glorious appearance, richly provided with works of art — this was non-negotiable. Museums *per se* already existed — but they were for the initiated, and thus for the elite. The Foundation was to contribute to democratisation, but also to the cultivation of a natural appreciation for art. This idea appears later in a slightly modified variation in Jacobsen's attitude to his collection of antiquities. Working to the same pattern as before he outlined his acquisitions policy to the archaeologist Wolfgang Helbig, who was chiefly responsible for the rapid growth in this area of the collection in the original Glyptotek. It went as follows: aim to acquire the very best, but if *the* absolute masterpiece is unavailable then accept something second-class as long as it is instructive. Copies have their own merit even if they are only plaster — as long as they are executed so that the content *and thus the value* are maintained. On 20 February, 1890, writing to Helbig about what a statue can tell us, and using as a point of departure the particular type "Pudicitia",[16] Jacobsen says, "Wenngleich doch also der Kunstwerth unseres Replik minimal ist so meine ich doch wir *müssen* das Stück erwerben. Die ungeheure Popularität der Statue wird sich auch hier wiederholen. Diejenigen die die Griechische Köpfe vorbeigehen, werden an der Pudicitia still stehen" (Irrespective of whether the artistic worth of our copy is minimal, it is something we must acquire. The enormous popularity of the statue will thus be self-proliferating: and those content to walk past the Greek portrait heads will be forced to pause before Pudicitia).[17]

The Glyptotek should never risk descending to the level of sterile academicism, but aspire to be a truly spiritual place, dedicated to the cult of art, and with an ambience all its own. Jacobsen was obsessed with the notion of attracting visitors from every class and he used his status as an amateur as a point of departure from which to acquaint himself with "the common people".

The way Denmark lagged behind was a symptom of a fundamental ethical problem: this was, at least, the view of Jacobsen, who looked up to the great civilizations of the ancient world. Despite the fact that the value of Neo-Classicism was gradually becoming purely relative, the presentation of Antiquity as an integrated ethical-political system was widespread just prior to the turn of the century, where it seethed with "classicising" concepts, not all of them of particularly sound formulation. Jacobsen was under the influence of his mentors in the archaeological field, and yet strong-willed enough to develop his own vision of the museum — one which was, in fact, more romantic than classical. The cultural figure on which he chose to model himself was, accordingly, Ludwig I of Bavaria, who was not only one of the great collectors of the first half of the nineteenth century, but also a transitional figure between the stern Neo-Classicism and the idealisation of Antiquity by an emotional Romanticism. It is, however, one thing to be able to chart cultural lines of descent, and quite another to create a collection rich in experiences for its visitors: and scientific organisation had to give way before Jacobsen's ideals. He would, after all, far prefer to see things with his own eyes than through the spectacles of scientific consciousness. Jacobsen wished to supply the nourishing fare the Danes needed — prepared (naturally) by himself. It should be appetising, so that it would be less crucial if the academics and specialists looked askance at it: there would be plenty of other things to their taste in the Glyptotek. The museum was structured in layers, which should, ideally be of finer and finer quality as they reached the top.[18] In the matter of attracting people's interest the key words were effect and variation. It was for this reason, for instance that the long sequence of Roman portrait-busts should be interspersed with other types of antiquities, such as statues and sarcophagi. "Die Glyptothek soll meine Landsleute lehren dass Sculptur etwas Schönes ist, meine Sarcophagen sprechen laut zu den Massen, während Rayets archaische Kopf nur an den wenigen eingeweihten redet!"[19] (The Glyptotek shall teach my fellow-countrymen that sculpture is beautiful, my sarcophagi forcefully appeal to the masses, while Rayet's fine head will only communicate with the initiated!).

Sarcophagi had a certain advantage in that they could be read as stories in pictures, miniature tableaux with a narrative continuity. The possibility of showing intact, completed statements had always been viewed by Jacobsen as equivalent to supplementing the delicate victuals of sophisticated culture with a healthy leven of coarse bread. It corresponds somewhat to the picture narratives provided for the illiterate in some Romanesque village churches, and the intention was no less a part of a similarly grand design. In Carl Jacobsen's book, a genuine classical work always depicted a person as he sees, or has seen himself, "naturally". This he felt was the true path to understanding the grandiose idealising depictions which sculpture vouchsafed those prepared to give the works a closer examination.

It followed that the ancient statues should be as complete as possible. In this respect Jacobsen shared the ideas of the early nineteenth century in favour of the restoration of antiquities, undertaken by professionals — i.e. the sculptors of the time. There were then no specialist conservators as we know them today — yet, so it was asked, who could better comprehend the work of a vanished artist than a fellow artist? There is a suggestion here of continuity, which put Carl Jacobsen firmly on the side of art and romanticising, rather than archaeology. Taking this line to its logical conclusion dictated that "completion" was, in fact, only paying homage to the original artist, in that one was restoring the unity of the work without which the entire concept of the sculpture could not survive intact. For the observer the isolated fragment serves no purpose, since its ruinous state reduces its narrative power. Thus it is incapable of conveying the desired, ennobling message: this is the pivotal element in this ethical-populist, and paradoxically ahistorical construct. The nascent modern revolt against the concept of the finished work, with its high-gloss finish, as opposed to its salute to an open, thoroughly sketch-like and significantly less polished work which drew its inspiration from Michelangelo, was not part of Jacobsen's brief: those works of Rodin he did acquire tended to be the most ostentatiously intact — not those of an experimental or proto-abstract character, where the sculptor made a serious break with the possibilities of his medium. Neither *Balzac* (cat. no. 54, fig. 39) nor *The Gates of Hell* were to Jacobsen's taste,[20] and he felt moved to suggest several changes he wished to be made in the execution of his own edition of *The Kiss* — changes, which, he felt, would enhance the clarity of the work.[21] At all events, on the philosophical-aesthetic level the patron demonstrated a laudable awareness of the technical considerations. Ideas relating to ethical dictates, how the love of art relates to science as a discipline,

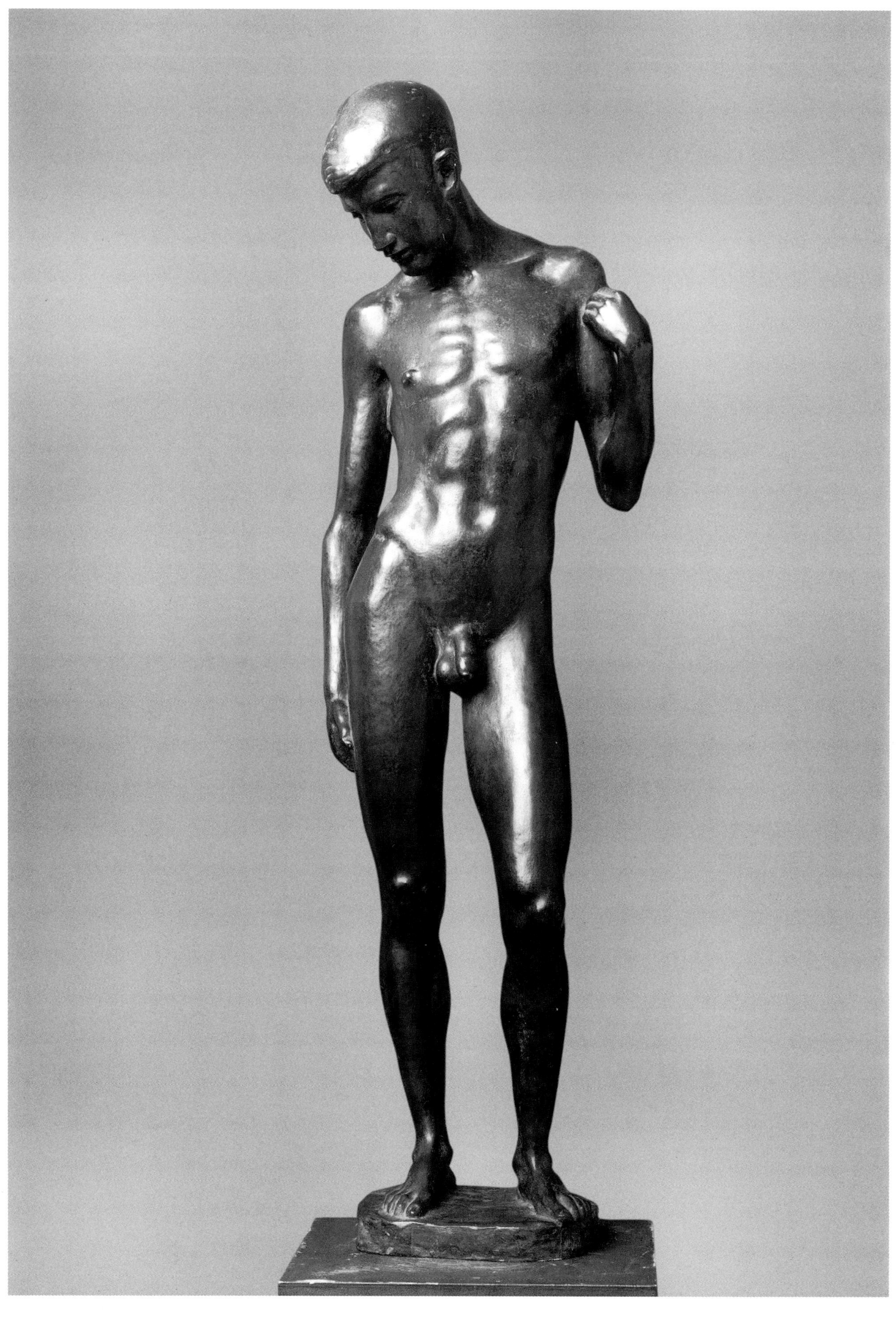

64
Aristide Maillol
The Young Cyclist, 1907
Bronze, h. 98 cm
Copenhagen, Ny Carlsberg Glyptotek
(cat. no. 39)

With *The Young Cyclist*, Maillol starts out from the classical tradition of portraying a standing nude figure. But the work has been freed from any literary or mythological context. It was given its title because Maillol's model came to the sittings on a bicycle. In the gentle lines of the slender figure, Maillol has tried to make all the shapes of the body fuse into a whole. The figure is built up on the classical notion of form, where the contours are clearly defined: the thin body, however, sharply differentiates the youth from the idealised boys' figures of Antiquity.

the internal and external organisation of sculpture, as well as meditations on the relation between the original work of art and the copy are frequent elements in the history of ideas of that period.[22] Jacobsen may have taken inspiration (not to mention ammunition) for his enterprise from one source in particular. The afore-mentioned points can all be found in a coherently reasoned cultural-historical construct in the work of his friend (also, for a brief period, a colleague in the museum world) the art historian, Julius Lange (1838–96).

An Encyclopaedist

Julius Lange was one of the age's perspicacious aesthetes and his efforts towards the examination of art history from a scientific view-point were characteristically ambitious. As the first Danish art historian to have had a university education, as well as being a prolific producer of academic papers and a stimulating lecturer, he left his mark on the cultural thinking of the time: his contribution to the history of sculpture is, in this context, of particular significance.

He expressed himself on the subject from the 1870s onwards, often from a partisan viewpoint. Lange's views on art dictated that the primary duty of figurative art is to be the bearer of narrative content. Good art refers to something other than itself, in fact it even cancels itself out so that we can better observe its object.[23] It is a given that art also possesses an aesthetic value in the eyes of a professional — it is not merely a question of the actual artistic worth. This is actually a discussion about information, where the layman should be given first consideration. And sculpture was a particularly suitable medium because of its ability to produce an immediate likeness of the human being.

In 1874 and 1876 Lange gave two lectures in the Kunstforeningen (The Art Circle) and among the topics they covered were the projected Glyptotek and sculpture in general. His fundamental thesis can be summed up thus: "And what can conceivably be more enlightening than to see the various eras' and nations' supreme depictions of the man-made light before us! Is that not something that goes beyond the narrow confines of any particular academic discipline, and can, with justice be given a name which rings loud and true for many Danes, a *Folkehøjskole*".[24]

Through sculpture Lange was engaging in what would today probably be termed "history of mentality". Man has a predilection for the self-reflective in any context, particularly in art. We are always looking for something made in our own image, even in such "abstract" things as stones, clouds or other products of nature, Lange had written.[25] He constantly employs the Danish word "selvbevidsthed" — which might be translated into English as "self-awareness". In Danish, at least, this was a peculiarly modern term, which was then coming into increasing use: it is self-awareness which separates us from animals, and in figurative art we frequently express ourselves in depictions of our bodies, souls and in idealised likenesses.

Lange's plan for the Royal Collection of Casts on the ground floor of the newly opened Statens Museum for Kunst was based on these ideas and came to fruition in the course of several years. It was supposed to be a cavalcade of the masterpieces of sculpture and illustrate the development of European sculpture from Antiquity up to Neo-Classicism, observed as two separate directions: that of the South and that of the North.[26] Their respective courses and characters, quite independent of each other could be traced by taking the route to the left or the right on coming into the museum's entrance hall. The left wing dealt with the civilizations on the Mediterranean littoral from Egypt to the Greco-Roman period, the Gothic, the Renaissance and Neo-Classicism. To the left were the cultures of the North, from the "Barbarian Peoples" right up to 1800. The great synthesis followed midway in the rearmost room of the building, where Canova, representing the South met Thorvaldsen representing the North. From the history of ideas standpoint this harmonious convergence was decidedly loaded: it was also internationalistic. The development of Nordic sculpture had "been subsumed into the currents of world development", and had acquired its "definitive character". The historicising culminates in the ideal images of Neo-Classicism. Both conflicting national boundaries and differences in style and expression of former ages were swept off the table by the meeting of the two giants of nineteenth-century sculpture at their common objective — the rebirth of Antiquity. These were hardly new ideas. As far back as 1872, Lange had pronounced the cast to be of equal value to the original — ethically, anyway; the difference between the original and a good copy lay purely in the sentimental value. Their *story* was the same; exactly the view expressed by Jacobsen to Helbig.[27] All their shared beliefs notwithstanding, Jacobsen and Lange were divided precisely over the presentation of the Royal Collection of Casts. The basic, two-track layout was not to Jacobsen's taste, and when Lange died suddenly in 1896, Jacobsen, now the Director, changed the configuration of the exhibits. He noted the change in another context: "Being Director of the Collection of Sculpture has been an arduous undertaking. To be honest, I felt obliged to dispense with Lange's entire plan for the display of the casts. This has cost me dearly, of that there is no doubt, but between you and me his project could never have been realised".[28] Jacobsen did not forget to emphasise the Greek contribution as the supreme achievement in art, which was also the ideal perspective of Winckelmann on which much Neo-Classicism was based[29] — though Jacobsen gave it a romantic packaging. Thorvaldsen or no Thorvaldsen, the historicising project and the Nordic wing as an independent chapter here had to step aside, when one's ideal was clear before one: and this is the practical difference from Lange, who was, in all other respects, a self-declared Hellenist. Lange and Jacobsen had been of one mind on the power of all art to ennoble, but on nothing else. Jacobsen had appropriated every possible device that would assist him in sharpening his romantic-idealistic points of view with Lange the historian. Lange was even harder on himself when it came to revaluing previously-held opinions. Three years after Lange's death saw the appearance his three-volume work *The Presentation by Sculpture of the Human Figure*, which covered the discipline from the earliest Greek art up to his own era. Though only the torso of an opus, it is a coherent theoretical work with a large section devoted to art history. The concluding chapter of the last volume has the superscription, "Slutning paa det Hele" ("The End of Everything") and the tone is premonitory. Lange discusses the age's emerging advocacy of the training of the body in order to strengthen the spirit, referring to so-called Vitalism's sometimes fanatical cult of the body, which thrived in Europe from around the turn of the century. These concepts were to be subsumed in ideas concerned with the superiority of certain races — a set of "theories" which were to reach a monstrous culmination in Nazi Germany.

It resembled something Greek — though in fact it was nothing of the kind. Lange comments drily that although modern art will reap the benefits of physical exercise, we will never compel "the Gods to turn up at our Olympic Games [...] We must learn to perceive that that which characterises the pinnacle of Sculpture's achievement in the depiction of the human being, will never, owing to the nature of the problem, correspond to the pinnacle in Mankind's development of a self-consciousness. It will, in contrast, indicate a very first stage, which should be put behind us, and which, in reality, is far behind us. I believe that many people in our age are capable of perceiving this and have already whispered something of this nature quietly to themselves, just as I am convinced that all truth and all carefully developed ideas of history tend in this direction. [...] the most [...] would be unwilling to make any such pronouncement about art, that great and venerable force of creation in human life, to which we owe such an infinite debt. It is just like taking the best of it away, letting it know that, however, in basic terms, it has been deposed. Yes, I genuinely believe that to be so, just as I believe, that it *did* once occupy the seat of dominion over human life. But I do *not* believe that art can ever be — nor ever has been, anything other than a form of expression, which, in itself, makes no demand on devotion or enthusiasm, beyond that it possesses content. This content — and its extent depends on the nature of the creature — is now, in the development of the race, demoted to a lower level and to a more relative significance than that it formerly possessed. One finds within no pessimistic mistrust about such development [...] Increasingly, the art of the future will be, in part, illustrations to poetry, and partly retrospective art, that which is second-hand. Chief among all those men who have brought art into this road of diminished future, is Thorvaldsen".[30]

Bringing about the rebirth of Antiquity was an impossible project. Lange writes off European art, and into the bargain goes that Dane who had, otherwise, previously contributed so much to put Denmark in the "Cultural Currents of World". Cultural pessimism set in with Lange, despite his assurance, that he was simply describing the inevitable. The malady was internal, and a result of an absence of natural content which art could hand down — a content which, according to this reasoning, was most clearly expressed in ancient Greece, whose art was allegedly uncontrived, immediate and natural. The *unnatural* triumphs as a loss of innocence, or mankind's Fall from Grace, brought about by man's own self-awareness which leads him away from his natural self. "Progress" for Lange marches in the direction of the literary take-over and the illustrative use of art, or an artistic process of endless self-reflection in place of a more natural reflection of the human being. Both the present and future have definitively set the corporeal in the driving seat.[31] Art was deposed, just as Freud would force metaphysics from its central position. The language is perfectly consistent with Lange's own choice of words. Jacobsen, however, was not such easy prey for pessimists.

A New Generation

When in the 1920s the Glyptotek was under the direction of Carl Jacobsen's son, Helge, the green light was given on contemporary French art. Already as far back as immediately after his father's death in 1914, Helge had started a comprehensive collection of Impressionists, which was bequeathed to the Glyptotek in 1927. Starting in 1922, Carl Jacobsen's collection of Renaissance and Baroque art passed to the Statens Museum for Kunst through a system of "equal exchange". This was a consequence of Helge Jacobsen's succeeding his father as Director of the Glyptotek. Many works of Neo-Classicism, beginning with the Canova casts were phased out in a major purge of the modern collection. Times were changing at Dantes Plads, there was less compulsion to feel fettered by a universalist, art-historical perspective. The modern collection was now seen to exist in its own right, on equal terms with the museum's collection of antiquities. The reorganisation was confirmed by the purchase, in 1923, of nineteen French masterpieces, by painters from Manet to Van Gogh, from the Ordrupgaard collector Wilhelm Hansen. Sic transit — the principal elements of Carl Jacobsen's acquisitions policy were banished to the vaults. His beloved Salon works were eclipsed by modernist art in the succeeding decades, and it was not until around 1980 that they were hauled out of oblivion to be re-exhibited in their old surroundings, a facet of the history of the museum collections. In contrast, Rodin, in the neighbouring room, retained his throne. Carl Jacobsen, who wanted to be modern, still had a candidate for the post.

Among the late acquisitions of the brewer for the modern collection, there is a large number of works by the Belgian sculptor Constantin Meunier (1831–1905). He occupies a special position in the Glyptotek by being represented by almost fifty works. Around 1900, Meunier was, with Rodin, one of the most significant representatives of early modern sculpture. His predominant theme was the suffering of the oppressed working class. In his work their daily labour under inhuman conditions was elevated to a level of allegorical significance, and itself became a mental image of human misery; starting from a thoroughly religious foundation and reaching towards living human beings, Meunier mixes Christian themes (*The Prodigal Son*, *Ecce Homo*) with the close observations of everyday life made by the artist himself in the Belgian mining villages, the iron foundries and among the fishermen of Ostende. The social realist side of his oeuvre is seen to greatest advantage in his grandiosely conceived *Monument du Travail*, a workers' monument for the town of Louvain, for which many of Meunier's individual works were sketches.

It may seem somewhat baffling that an industrial magnate such as Carl Jacobsen should want to see precisely this monument in Copenhagen. In many letters to Jacobsen, Meunier expresses his joy over the boldness necessary to support the idea of the work and the nobility of the whole issue. The plan was, however, never realised, though in 1908 the Glyptotek arranged a major exhibition of Meunier in Denmark, and Jacobsen managed to secure all 41 of the exhibited bronzes for his collection. These are examples of Meunier's most important works, and they demonstrate his talent for modelling the figures in a smaller format. He preferred clay and believed that it was only in the bronze casts that what had been modelled in clay was truly able to live on. Carving in marble was not his concern.

Meunier's worker realism is about salutation, not lament. His somewhat changeable status in subsequent art history is a particular result of the inevitable comparison with Rodin, whom Meunier admired. Rodin's ideals, technique and artistic vision range from naturalism to the grandiose symbol-laden allegory and his work hovers in a constant experimental game between the material, the chosen theme and time itself. With Meunier repetition is a function of an undeviating and pathos-laden message in the spirit of the age. This idealism, camouflaged as realism appealed also to the domestic literary milieu, in which worker and peasant life had only just been "discovered". The foundation was provided by people like Johannes V. Jensen, who eulogised the physically demanding but "healthy" or natural life in the country as opposed to a barren, city-dwelling intellectualism. Lesser writers followed in his wake. Thus we have J.I. Kronstrøm (1878– 1933) composing heroic poems on the themes of Meunier, based on the works in the Glyptotek. In his collection of short stories *The Martyrs* Kronstrøm takes as his point of departure the Meunier bust *The Martyr* (fig. 65) and evokes an Expressionist-Christian image of the millions of slaves throughout history. In 1917 the same writer brought out a brief biographical sketch called *The Sculptor of Labour Constantin Meunier*, in which he praises the artist's fidelity to the downtrodden.

Carl Jacobsen, who was less sentimental about such things regarded Meunier as yet another of the progressive forces in international sculpture. From Meunier there was much to learn: he was in the classical tradition in that he strove for the human ideal at the same time as concerning himself with a subject area — the breakthrough and con-

65
Constantin Meunier
The Martyr, 1887
Bronze, h. 66 cm
Copenhagen, Ny Carlsberg Glyptotek

Meunier occupies a special position in the Glyptotek by being represented by almost fifty works. Around 1900, he was, with Rodin, one of the most significant representatives of early modern sculpture. His predominant theme was the suffering of the oppressed working class. In his work their daily labour under inhuman conditions was elevated to a level of allegorical significance, and itself became a mental image of human misery; starting from a thoroughly religious foundation and reaching towards living human beings, Meunier mixes Christian themes with the close observations of everyday life. *The Martyr* is both allusive of Christ and of countless slaves through history — and thus evokes man's general condition on earth.

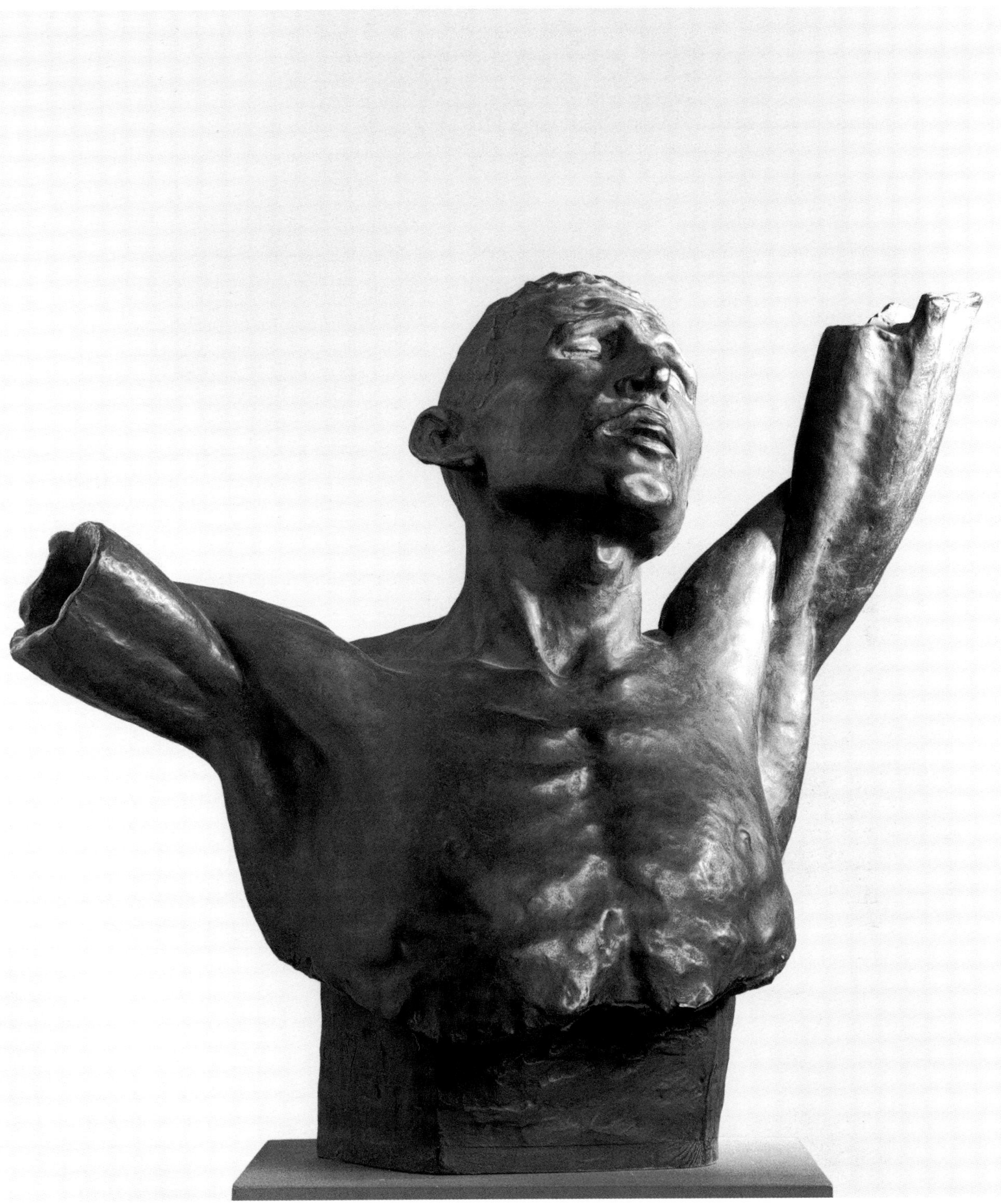

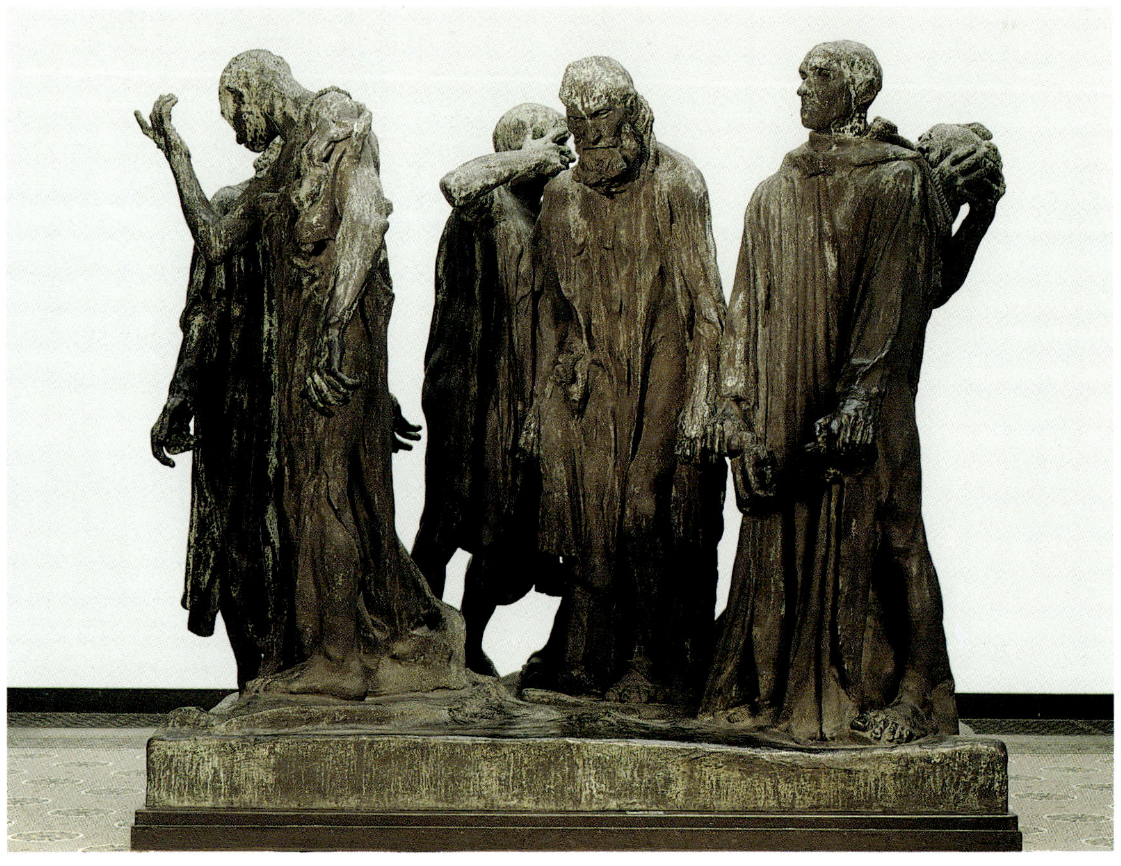

66
Auguste Rodin
The Burghers of Calais, 1884–88
Bronze, h. 213 cm
Copenhagen, Ny Carlsberg Glyptotek

"A pathological Cult of the Patina has possessed the sculptors of today, and has found a classic expression in the grisly sight which greets the poor pedestrian on the right of the new Glyptotek", wrote a Danish critic in 1904. The "grisly sight" was this version of *The Burghers of Calais*, set up by Carl Jacobsen in August 1903. Jacobsen knew Rodin personally, and acquired more than two dozen of his most well-known sculptures — captivated as he was by their edificatory themes, more than by those traits that Modernism has recognised in Rodin: the range of his ideals, technique and artistic vision, from Naturalism to grandiose allegory, and the constant experimental game between the material, the chosen theme and time itself.

solidation of industrialism, which Jacobsen had seen at first hand in his own brewery and with whose many facets he must have felt familiar. Here was an art which took up the challenge and depicted the human being at the stage it had now reached. Rodin and Meunier together formed the vanguard of a truly modern sculpture — a sculpture in tune with the issues of the age. One cannot help but be reminded of Verne's fictitious account of true poetry, quoted at the beginning of this article. Jacobsen's self-appointed role as the chief whip of Danish sculpture occasioned him a certain amount of abuse. Ove Jørgensen wrote in the Danish periodical *Tilskueren* (1904) about the "odious practice" in a review of the spring exhibition as follows: "Sculpture [in Denmark] has been at its weakest for a long time. This be the verse: Rodin and Meunier are the only salvation, the escape from 'the Classical Wilderness of Stone', also known as 'the Immortal Beauty of Antiquity'. I shall not dwell on the brazenness by which the two artists have been apotheosised into a higher unity, which is doubtless owing to the fact that they, by the grace of one man's munificent generosity, have made their triumphal entry into this city". The message was unequivocal, and later in the article there were the words, "The bronze figures on exhibition are resplendent in all the colours of the rainbow, and the visitor has ample opportunity to study the pathological Cult of the Patina, which has taken possession of the sculptors of today, and which has also found a classic expression in the grisly sight which greets the poor pedestrian on the right of the new Glyptotek".[32] The grisly sight in question was Rodin's newly-patinated *The Burghers of Calais* (fig. 66), set up by Carl Jacobsen in August 1903.

The art historian, Francis Beckett, on the other hand, showing considerable technical insight, wrote about Meunier's works in *Illustreret Tidende* (a Danish magazine) on the occasion of the opening of the exhibition in 1908. For Jacobsen it was an ideal

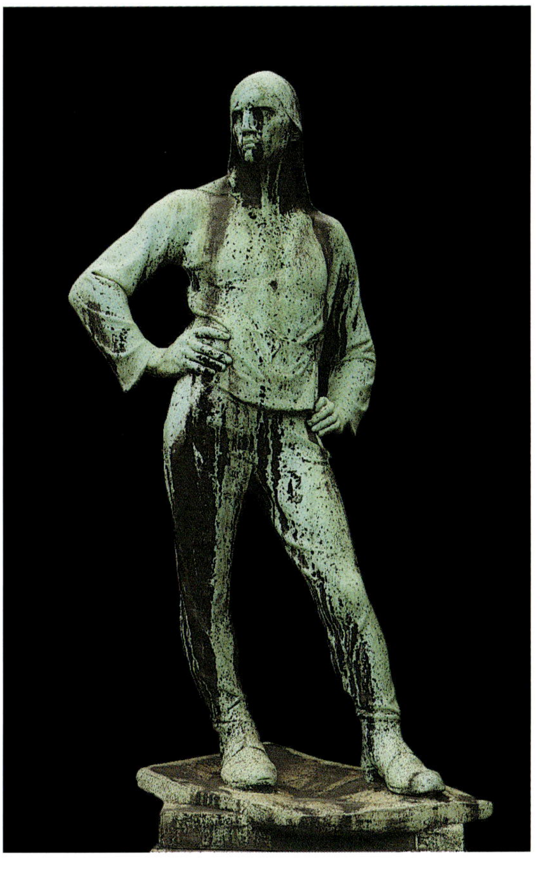

67
Constantin Meunier
The Docker, 1893 (cast 1906)
Bronze, h. 220 cm
Copenhagen, Ny Carlsberg Glyptotek

Meunier is first and foremost a storyteller in sculpture, and it is ever the theme at hand that is the case. His bronzes are not, as with Rodin, subject to experiment or reflections on the possibilities of the material, but two-dimensional, "painterly" figures in three dimensions. Meunier risked breaking his neck by making sculpture on the large-scale format which demanded the techniques of classical sculpture. Nevertheless, his full-figure sculptures are obviously based on classical traditions. *The Docker*, along with well-known works such as *The Smith*, *The Fisherman* and the gang of miners are like modern versions of the heroes of Antiquity — and therefore they are eternal — tragic yet serene.

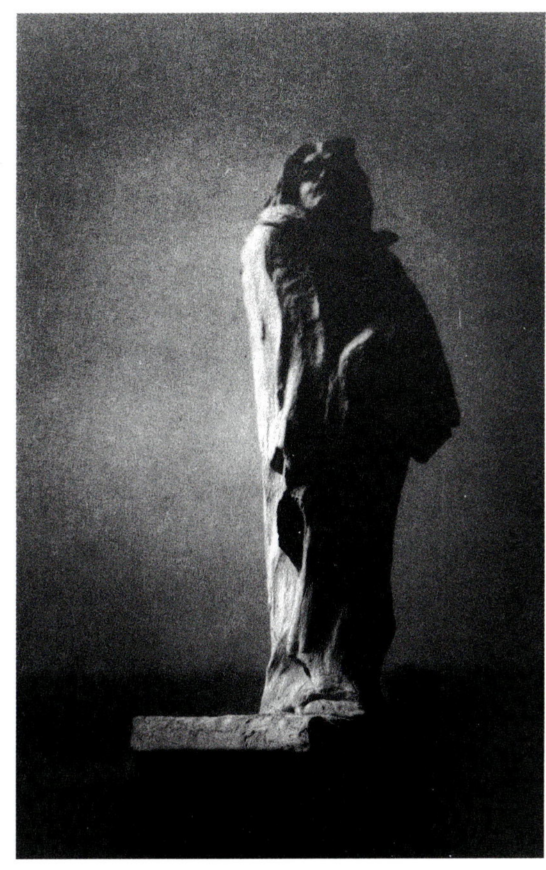

68
Edward Steichen
Balzac by Rodin, 1898
Albumen print, 19.3 × 21.2 cm
Paris, Musée Rodin

Rodin's *Balzac* was a favourite object for the photographer Steichen. Its monumental depiction of the artist as a genius, at once present in the world and removed from it, in his own higher sphere, appealed to the era — and to certain romantic notions still in favour with Modernism. The photograph makes use of a landscape setting worthy of the romantics, and sets the human-size figure off dramatically and monumentally against the evening sky. Where Rodin rendered his sitter an object in the clasp of modern sculpture and its materials — a "lump" of bronze most of all — Steichen takes the vision further; by focusing mainly on the great author's silhouette, he underlines the particular strength of Rodin's work. The sinister appearance of the cloaked figure is a closed and silent form.

opportunity to commission works. But the young art historian was not solely out to flatter. Beckett, the pupil of Lange (and a future director of the Casts Collection who sought to realise his teacher's projects)[33] was enthusiastic about the modern element in Meunier's work. Beckett focused on the vital feature: "In Danish we call Meunier a sculptor, but this term is actually misleading. He has never carved images out of stone; the fair, sentimental marble would not suit his virile, serious art. Rather it is the dark metallic ore which was called into being to support his creations. But for Meunier bronze was not a material whose beauty he emphasised by unassisted finishing touches, finely chased; for him the bronze was merely an enduring cast of his clay figures. In every one of his bronzes one can clearly detect the clay model beneath. If we are to give his profession a name which most clearly expresses his work, we should say, rather than sculptor that he was given to the shaping of plastic form".[34]

Indirectly Beckett identifies here a new predilection for the momentary visual impression behind the Belgian's artistic concept, and it is at this point that the question of the artist's modernity is concentrated. It is particularly in the smaller works that he manages to apprehend the fleeting instant, in both a painterly and sketch-like manner, catching the figure's most important features. It is most often torsos, or bodies fragmented in some other way, which would normally be found in an artist's sketch-book — "his works are sketches, and they have all the good qualities of sketches: freshness, fieriness, warmth, vividness. But Meunier's art never reaches beyond the sketch", wrote Beckett, and thus he characterises Meunier firmly as the man of the modern age. But there was an underlying injunction to Meunier, no matter how indirect: he should never seek to overstep his own boundaries by aspiring to the monumental. Meunier *the Painter*, through stubborn persistence risked breaking his neck by making sculpture on the large-scale format which demanded the techniques of classical sculpture. Nevertheless, his full-figure sculptures are based on classical traditions. *The Smith* and *The Fisherman*, *The Docker* (fig. 67) and the gang of miners are like modern versions of the heroes of Antiquity — and therefore they are eternal — tragic yet serene.

Meunier had no interest in the complexities of form of classical sculpture, nor its peculiar way of posing problems; his overriding concern was to express an idea rather than to proceed soberly in the manner of the classically-trained technician he was not. Meunier was a *storyteller*, and that accorded well with Jacobsen's ideals. The most modern element in Meunier's art is his apparent "conceptualism". The ends have justified the means and his division of form into segments bears witness to an impatience with the inert material out of which his subjects were to emerge. The hollow busts of workers, where the bronze is like a thin, undulating cape, create the impression that they are thus because a back part or any *de facto* mass at all was unnecessary for the presentation of the theme: from painter to sculptor and back again.

In his purchase of works by Meunier, Carl Jacobsen was in no sense making a break with his fundamental views on sculpture — what was the basic issue was the content, apprehended in the surface of fine bronze. That the large figures by the Belgian resembled classical sculpture only increased Jacobsen's enthusiasm for Meunier. He had in no way been infected by Beckett's cautious scepticism regarding the modelling. Such sculpture was obliged to thrive side by side with the classical works in the rooms of the Glyptotek. Jacobsen was branded by the nineteenth century, a mark which made him single-handedly see nurturing ideals precisely where nascent Modernism saw an independent and abstract form — unfolded against a background of the human body as mass, contour and volume, more than merely containing a soul. The self-reflective art of the twentieth century rapidly distanced itself from the human ideal and the neatly rounded-off form which Jacobsen loved and defined as the classic, "natural" content of sculpture. Though the honour was posthumous, Lange had been proved right.

By uniting the ancient and modern collections of the Glyptotek, Hack Kampmann's building brought about the realisation of Jacobsen's dream for the museum. The Kampmann Building was opened on Seven Sleepers Day, 27 June , 1906. Despite the hectic nature of the final phase of building, Jacobsen clung stubbornly to this date. His motive is readily understandable; the day takes its name from a legend from the seventh century about seven Christian men who were walled up alive in a cave during the persecution under the Emperor Decius. They fell asleep and did not awake until 200 years later, in 447, by which time the Empire, now ruled by Theodosius II, had become Christian. It seems all too likely that Carl Jacobsen had sought a parallel: he, too, would remain at his post in the museum until the world was ready and an art with the complete human being at its centre was ready to flourish freely and naturally — again? But this never came about, and Jacobsen's ideals were not again to proliferate — for now, time and tide were against him.

[1] Jules Verne, *Paris in the 20th Century* (1863), p. 64 ff.

[2] *Ibid.*, p. 125.

[3] K. Glamann, *Beer and Marble. Carl Jacobsen at Ny Carlsberg* (Copenhagen, 1995).

[4] *Death and the Woodcutter*, after the fable of La Fontaine — a moral fable in which Jacobsen detected a kindred spirit.

[5] Carl and Ottilia's deed of gift of 1888, the foundation of the Ny Carlsberg Glyptotek. Reproduced *verbatim*, in full in e.g. Carl Jacobsen, *Ny Carlsberg Glyptoteks Tilblivelse* ([The Genesis of the Ny Carlsberg Glyptotek], Copenhagen, 1906).

[6] E. Bencard and F. Friborg, *Danish Sculpture around 1900* (Copenhagen: Ny Carlsberg Glyptotek, 1995).

[7] Jacobsen was later to take the offensive by combining plaster casts with paintings in the new Statens Museum for Kunst, because painting could function as a lever to (aid in) the experience of sculpture; CJ Oct. 1902, see M.-L. Berner, "Den kongelige Afstøbningssamlings his-

torie", in *Kunst og Museum* (special issue, 15 Annum, no. 1, 1980), p. 35.

[8] Carl Jacobsen, "La Musique", in the Danish magazine *Ude og Hjemme* (no. 65/1, 1878), p. 142 ff.

[9] *Ibid.*: "Works of art which reach beyond Time and give voice to the spiritual strength of their creators".

[10] Jacobsen, 1906, on his "feu sacré" and the love of art as a driving force.

[11] Glamann, 1995, p. 304 ff.

[12] Jacobsen, 1906.

[13] Carl Jacobsen, letter to member of the Albertina Foundation, mayor of Copenhagen, H.N. Hansen, 15 October, 1879, Ministry of the Interior KKJ, no. 28 38/46.

[14] Various newspaper articles of the period.

[15] T. Holck Colding, "Carl Jacobsen og legatet Albertina", in *Albertina. Et legats historie gennem 100 år 1879–1979. Af Dyveke Helsted, Torben Holck Colding og Torben Melander* (Copenhagen, 1979), p. 17. The Classical as a compromise — and the one from which Jacobsen derived most benefit. He had already put five casts from ancient sculpture on his list at the foundation of the trust.

[16] Correspondence quoted from Mette Moltesen, *Brewer Carl Jacobsen's Thoughts on Ancient Sculpture*, in *Acta Hyperborea II* (Copenhagen, 1990), p. 260.

[17] *Ibid.*

[18] *Ibid.*, pp. 255–57. For a long time Jacobsen was not overly fond of such works as *The Running Niobid* (NCG IN 520, ca. 440–30 B.C.) as it struck him as "not up to the standards of the Glyptotek". Later he completely revised his views, as he became ennobled by art...

[19] Letter to Helbig, 16 September, 1887, quot. after Moltesen, 1990, p. 254.

[20] A.-B. Fonsmark, *Rodin. La collection du Brasseur Carl Jacobsen à la Glyptothèque — et oeuvres apparantées* (Copenhagen, 1986), p. 39.

[21] *Ibid.*, p. 46.

[22] See Berner, 1980.

[23] *Om Kunstværdi. To Foredrag* ([The Value of Art: Two Lectures], May 1874 and February 1876, collected and published, Copenhagen, 1876), p. 5.

[24] J. Lange, *Om Vore Skulptur- og Malerisamlinger* ([Concerning our Collections of Sculpture and Painting], Copenhagen, 1893), p. 39. *Folkehøjskole*: a term coined by the Danish theologian N.F.S. Grundtvig (1783–1872), literally a "School for the People", a term indicating a sort of school in which every Dane, irrespective of background, could follow courses and engage in talks with his fellow men. This system prevails even today and is widely sought, by Danes of all age groups. For Grundtvig, however, it also represented a state of mind, a special edificatory notion of being Danish.

[25] And, significantly enough, only in a European perspective. Lange wrote about the difference in the stages of development between the different parts of the world: "Karl Madsen talks so beautifully of the admiration of the Japanese for 'that, which according to the Bible was created before the evening of the sixth day', but this very artistic admiration for and preference of Nature above Man is what makes [Japanese art and culture] un-European. Europe is Europe, exactly because Man is a European discovery and its true favourite". Lange, *Japan-Europa* (1886), quot. from *Samlede Skrifter* (Collected Works, III), pp. 190–91. There was, however, a place for non-European cultures in the Casts Collection in the Entrance Hall as an early history insert before the actual tour.

[26] Lange, 1893, p. 22.

[27] Julius Lange, *Kunstmuseet og Afstøbningssamlingen* [The Art and the Collection of Casts], speech to the Academy at the annual dinner, 31 March, 1872, in Lange, *Billedkunst. Skildringer og Studier fra Hjemmet og Udlandet* ([The Figurative Arts. Presentations and Studies at Home and Abroad], Copenhagen, 1884), p. 537 ff.

[28] Carl Jacobsen, in *Politiken*, 31 August, 1897; a sharp commentary on Professor Vilhelm Klein's unqualified handling and interpretation of Jacobsen's International Exhibition of the same year.

[29] Berner, 1980, p. 37.

[30] J. Lange, *Menneskefiguren i Kunstens Historie. Fra den græske Kunsts Blomstringstid indtil vort Aarhundrede* ([The Human Figure in the Figurative Arts from the Flowering of Greek Art to Our Own Century], Copenhagen, 1899), pp. 510–11.

[31] *Ibid.*, p. 509.

[32] Ove Jørgensen, *Foraarsudstillingerne* ([The Spring Exhibitions], Tilskueren, 1904), p. 447.

[33] Berner, 1980, p. 42.

[34] F. Beckett, "Constantin Meunier", in *Illustreret Tidende* (no. 7, 1908), p. 80 ff.

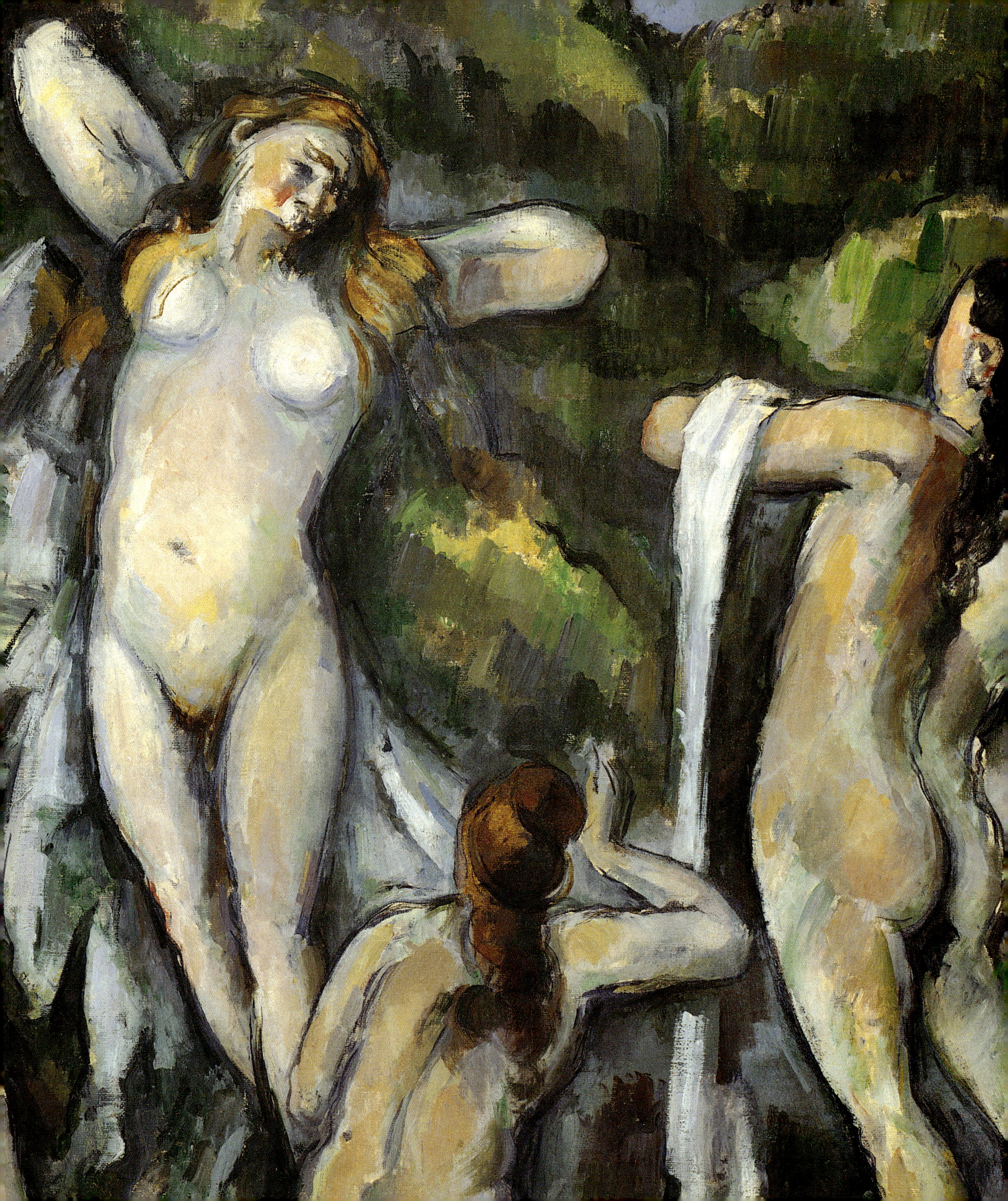

Artists' Biographies

69
Paul Cézanne
The Bathers, ca. 1888–90, detail
(full fig. 75)

Eugène-Louis Aizelin
(1821–1902)
Trained at Ecole des Beaux-Arts and making his debut at the Salon in 1852, Aizelin's work was first and foremost to provide sculpture for the ornamentation of public buildings in the new Paris. Examples of his work include large commissions for Garnier's Opera House — as was the case with Carpeaux — and responsibility for the decoration of the main façade of the church of Saint-Roch. Aizelin's sculpture, which exhibits virtuosity throughout, appealed by virtue of its extremely refined handling of material and trompe l'oeil effects. Many of his subjects were taken from the Bible or literature of the previous century. Especially Goethe fascinated many artists of the age (Tissot, cat. no. 59, fig. 19). His novel *The Apprenticeship of Wilhelm Meister*, dating from 1794–96 was the point of departure for Aizelin's *Mignon* (cat. no. 1, fig. 8) which he exhibited at the Salon of 1881.

Louis-Ernest Barrias (1841–1905)
Though originally trained as a painter, Barrias became one of the most highly-esteemed sculptors of his time. He was a pupil of the academic sculptor J. Cavelier, and commenced studies at the Ecole des Beaux-Arts in Paris under François Jouffroy in 1858. Barrias came second in the Prix de Rome competition of 1861, made his debut at the Salon of the same year, and won the Grand Prix de Rome outright in 1865. During the 1880s he executed a series of large allegorical sculptural works for the public space: one of these was a monument to the defence of Paris. He had won the commission in a competition in which one of his rivals had been Rodin. Barrias had a predilection for female allegorical figures, one of which is *Nature Revealing Herself to Science* (cat. no. 2, fig. 41), whose sensual qualities are typical of Salon sculpture. In 1894 Barrias succeeded Cavelier as Professor at the Ecole des Beaux-Arts and was described by a critic as truer to the teaching of the Academy than any of his colleagues. Nevertheless some of his later works seem to have been inspired by Rodin, whose *The Age of Bronze* (cat. no. 51, fig. 34) he admired. At the Salon of 1872 Barrias won a Medal of the First Class for his work *The Oath of Spartacus*, which was interpreted in the light of the French defeat in the Franco-Prussian War, as was the case with numerous other sculptural works at the same Salon. Critics tended to regard Barrias' works as "genuine French sculpture".

Jules Bastien-Lepage (1848–84)
Bastien-Lepage was trained at the Ecole des Beaux-Arts, joined the studio of the academic painter, A. Cabanel, in 1868, and made his debut at the Salon in 1870. Bastien-Lepage was inspired by such masters of previous ages as Watteau, Holbein and Ribera, but developed a predilection for subjects of a social realist nature. One example of this is *The Beggar* (cat. no. 3, fig. 21), which illustrates how he combined an academic training with an interest in both Courbet-inspired Realism and photographic detail with a technique influenced by Impressionism. With this special "Salon Realism", where everyday life is depicted in large format, Bastien-Lepage adopted the new tendencies in painting without making any critical break with tradition. This may be the reason why he continued to enjoy the Salon's recognition as one of the greatest painters of his age and be of considerable significance to numerous artists both in and outside France.

Camille Bellanger (1853–1923)
Bellanger was trained at the Ecole des Beaux-Arts by the most successful academic painters of the time, A. Cabanel and A.-W. Bouguereau. Tending to paint historical and genre subjects, he won second prize in the Prix de Rome Competition of 1875. He achieved recognition and success with works such as *Abel* (cat. no. 4, fig. 33) which was exhibited at the Salon of the same year. The painting is a typical academic work reflecting how both religious and historical narrative were used as the point of departure for depictions of the human body. The work is also evidence that not only the female, but also the male figure was presented as a sensual object in Salon painting.

Emile Bernard (1868–1941)
Bernard commenced his artistic training at the atelier of the historical painter Cormon, where his fellow students were Louis Anquetin and Toulouse-Lautrec. Two years later, however, Bernard was dismissed for investigating the colour theories of the Impressionists and Post-Impressionists: he believed that it would be

70
Emile Bernard
Nymphs, After Bathing, 1908
Oil on canvas, 121 × 151 cm
Paris, Musée d'Orsay
(cat. no. 5)

With these three nudes, Bernard has revised the traditional monumental figure composition. He has simplified the women's bodies and emphasised the two-dimensionality of the shapes so that the figures are endowed with rhythmic weight instead of plastic fullness. They are dispersed decoratively across the painting, providing a balance to the surrounding Arcadian landscape. The whole work is clearly influenced by Bernard's earlier experiments with cloisonnism in which dark outlines surround surfaces of light, even colour.

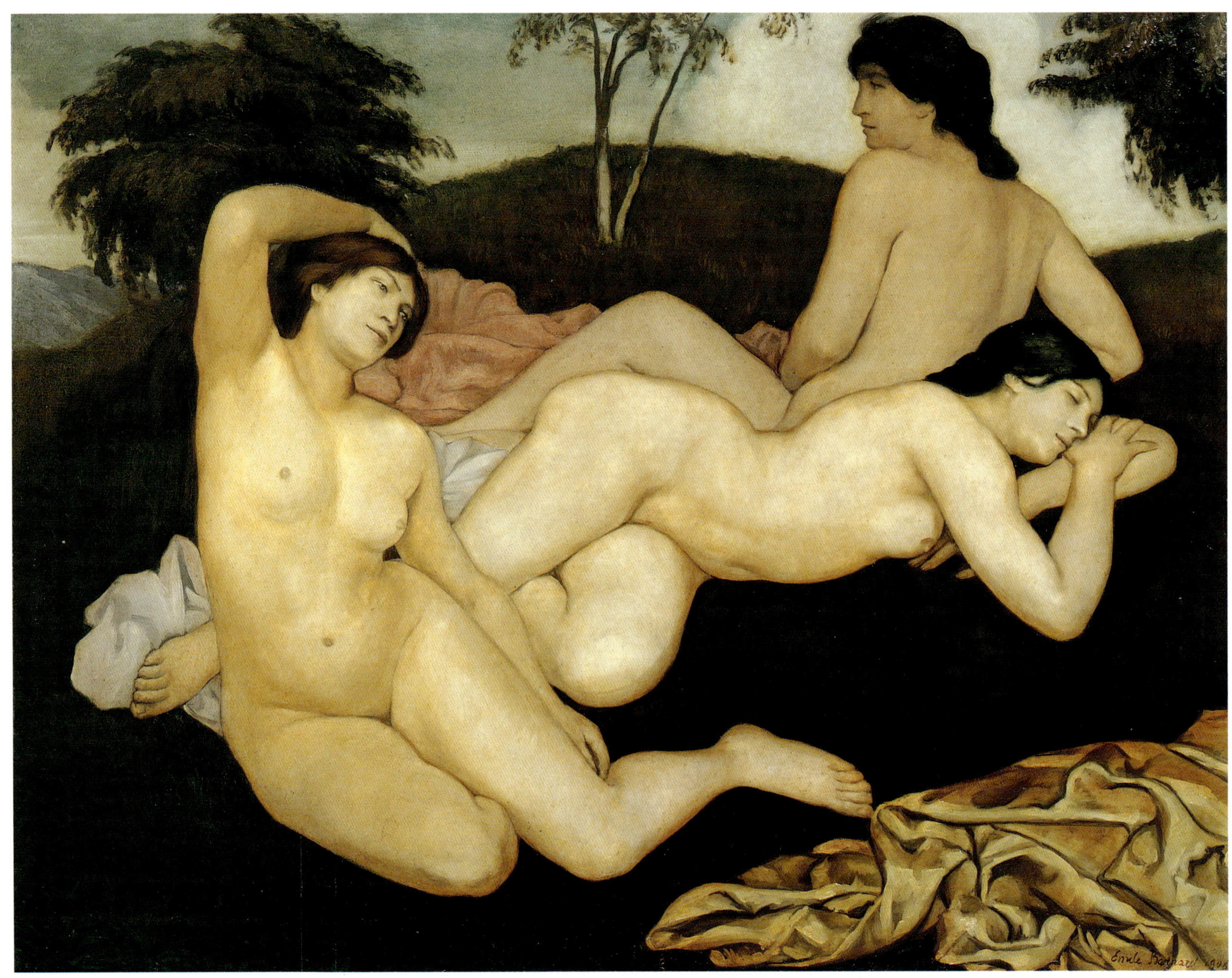

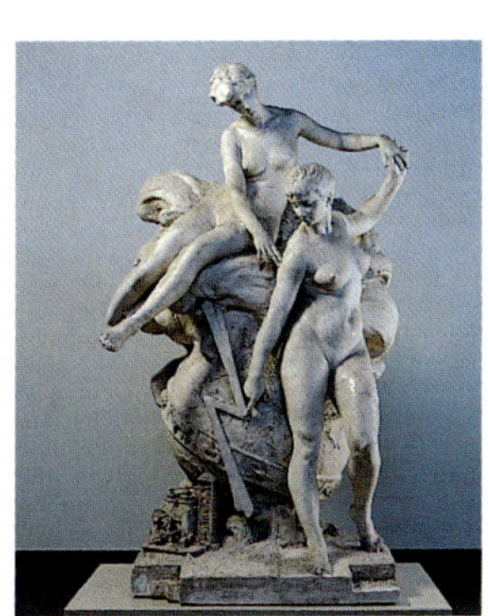

71
Louis-Ernest Barrias
Electricity (1889)
Plaster, h. 222 cm
Copenhagen, Ny Carlsberg Glyptotek

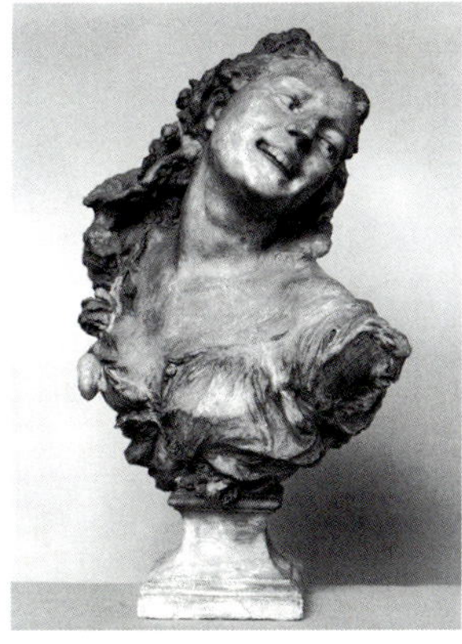

72
Jean-Baptiste Carpeaux
Bacchante with Roses, ca. 1872
Patinated plaster, h. 63 cm
Copenhagen, Ny Carlsberg Glyptotek

possible to express oneself more dynamically by simplifying both form and colour. Working together with Anquetin he developed the cloisonné style, which is characterised by dark outlines enclosing surfaces of light, uniform colour as in stained glass. In the summer of 1888 Bernard joined Gauguin in Pont-Aven, and has since claimed the credit for having introduced Gauguin to Synthetism. After protracted periods in both Italy and Egypt, Bernard abandoned the simple, decorative painting for more realistic depiction. A stay in Venice in 1903 prompted him to change his direction yet again and reintroduce the traditional, monumental figure-compositions in modern painting, an example of this being *Nymphs, After Bathing* (cat. no. 5, fig. 70). Bernard was an early catalyst in the modern movement: among his activities was the organisation of the first retrospective exhibition in France of paintings by his friend Van Gogh. In 1905 Bernard established the art magazine *La Rénovation esthétique*, which contributed to the redefinition of the Symbolist doctrines prevalent during his youth.

Léon Bonnat (1833–1922)
Bonnat commenced his academic training in Madrid. Among his later places of study was the atelier of Léon Cogniet at the Ecole des Beaux-Arts in Paris. In Rome he undertook an exhaustive study of the masters of the High Renaissance: this was consistent with his activities in Madrid where he had made a point of copying the works of Velázquez at the Prado. The inspiration thus gained comes through in Bonnat's portraits, one being the *Self-portrait* (cat. no. 6, fig. 16). Bonnat became the most celebrated portraitist of the Third Republic and achieved international recognition for the way he managed to depict his subjects in a style both realistic and flattering, something which particularly appealed to the new bourgeoisie. With his many pupils Bonnat encouraged the study of a realism which was in accordance with contemporary academic norms, thus avoiding the political implications in notions of realism such as that of Courbet. Bonnat later taught at the Ecole des Beaux-Arts, becoming its Director in 1905, and was to maintain his close affiliation with the circle of academic painters despite his friendship with such artists of the avant-garde as Degas and Manet. Towards the end of his life, however, Bonnat adopted techniques from the now established Impressionism and Post-Impressionism, tendencies against which he had fought all of his life. Bonnat's oeuvre is thus suffused with considerable variations in style and adaptability, which made him popular in his own time, but less highly-regarded by posterity.

Adolphe-William Bouguereau
(1825–1905)
Bouguereau began his study under F.E. Picot at the Ecole des Beaux-Arts in 1846, making his debut at the Salon in 1849. In 1850 he won the Prix de Rome, spending his next few years in that city. Following his homecoming, Bouguereau enjoyed enormous success and became a loyal pillar of the academic edifice: his stylistic development followed a set pattern and he preferred mythological, religious or genre subjects, such as *Girl with Grapes* (cat. no. 7, fig. 9). Bouguereau ignored the rising demand for pictures reflecting modern life, but managed even so to maintain his enormous popularity with the public and some critics. Others derided his work as the very incarnation of "slick" academic painting: it is said that when Renoir first took to wearing glasses to correct his short sight he threw them aside saying, "My God! They make me see just like Bouguereau". Bouguereau was staunchly opposed to all the new developments in painting and his position on the Parnassus of tradition incensed Cézanne to angry abstention from "Monsieur Bouguereau's Salon". During his lifetime Bouguereau received every artistic and social recognition imaginable, and he was made Professor at the Ecole des Beaux-Arts in 1888. The Impressionist circle coined the expression "bouguereauté" to be applied to any work of art which was unduly polished and academic in its execution.

Emile-Auguste Carolus-Duran
(1838–1917)
Carolus-Duran was a sought-after portrait painter in his time. He received his academic training from F. Souchon, a former pupil of David, and also attended the alternative art school, the Académie Suisse. While at the Louvre, making copies of the old masters, he met Fantin-Latour and Manet as well as Courbet, who was to prove an important source of inspiration. Carolus-Duran made his debut at the Salon in 1859 and the following year received the Wicar Prize which made possible a stay in Rome (1862–66). From 1866–68 Carolus-Duran was in Spain, where he encountered the work of the Spanish masters, who were to be of crucial significance for his painting. The influence of Velázquez, for instance, is clear in the *Portrait of a Little Girl in Spanish Costume* (cat. no. 8, fig. 18). As a portraitist Carolus-Duran understood how to adapt his style to his subject. He thus frequently depicted his artistic colleagues in a series of realistic works, but opted for a more elegant approach when painting the women of the haute bourgeoisie — and it was these works which brought him recognition. Carolus-Duran occupied a central place in the contemporary French artistic scene, being one of the co-founders of the Société des Beaux-Arts, of which he became president in 1898. In 1905 he was made Director of the French Academy in Rome.

Jean-Baptiste Carpeaux
(1827–75)
Carpeaux started at the Ecole des Beaux-Arts in 1844 and two years later joined the atelier of F. Rude. In 1854, on his second attempt, he won the Prix de Rome: during his succeeding stay in the city he became deeply fascinated by the work of Michelangelo. In this way Carpeaux was to prove the real impetus behind the preoccupation with the Renaissance and the cult of Michelangelo which took hold of French art around 1850 and inspired sculptors such as Dubois and Mercié.
Carpeaux became the Second Empire sculptor par excellence, and his work has become synonymous with the artistic outlook of the entire period. His artistic spectrum ranges from Rococo to Realism and gives sculptural form to an equal extent to decoration, virtuosity and volume — features which made him the most popular portrait sculptor of his time. He also challenged "good taste" with such works as his masterpiece, *Dance*, which caused a scandal with its wanton nude figures, by many considered inappropriate for the decoration of the façade on the opera house designed by his friend Garnier. Carpeaux's range is apparent in *Negress* (cat. no. 10, fig. 42): here the theme of slavery is transformed into a sensual-erotic interplay between the rope and a human

73
Eugène Carrière
Place Clichy, Night
(1899–1900)
Oil on canvas, 33 × 41 cm
Paris, Musée d'Orsay
(cat. no. 12)

Carrière made his Salon debut in 1876, two years after the First Impressionist Exhibition. He would really have liked to be a graphic artist, but an exhibition of Rubens in the Louvre in 1862 is said to have persuaded him to choose painting. Carrière became known for his misty pictures which consist almost exclusively of finely matched shades of brown and grey, with a few "Impressionist" strokes of paint in intense colours to produce a contrasting effect. The picture of night on the Place Clichy in Paris is a study of darkness and haze. Houses and streets are almost erased, on the verge of being invisible. This suggestive art made Carrière much loved by the Symbolists, who also cultivated the ambiguous and the nebulous.

body in a delicate performance, which at the same time reflects on the role of the fragmentary in sculpture.

Eugène Carrière (1849–1906)
Carrière began his career as a lithographer, but decided to become a painter after seeing Rubens' works at the Louvre in 1868. He entered the Ecole des Beaux-Arts in 1870 and was trained in the academic style by A. Cabanel, making his inconspicuous debut at the Salon in 1876. Having achieved no success as a painter, he was obliged to support himself otherwise for a number of years: this included work as a graphic artist. In the period 1880–85 he worked in the Sèvres porcelain factories, where he met Rodin, who was to become a close friend. Despite his admiration for the older masters, Carrière was, in his early works, most inspired by his contemporary colleague, J.-J. Henner. Increasingly he concentrated on grey-brown nuances, with only a hint of any other colours and, from the mid-1880s, his works were characterised by a Leonardo-inspired sfumato, out of which the figures seem to emerge. Carrière was of great significance for the Symbolist movement, and numbered among his friends, besides Rodin, the poets Verlaine and Mallarmé, and the art critic Edmond de Goncourt. In 1884 Carrière finally achieved success at the Salon, and thereby occupies a position between it and the avant-garde.

Paul Cézanne (1839–1906)
In 1861 Cézanne became a pupil at the alternative art school, the Académie Suisse, and in the following years he submitted his work to the Salon, though without success. He was never to be admitted to the Ecole des Beaux-Arts, but nevertheless Cézanne continued to seek the approval of the artistic establishment, despite a tendency to associate more with kindred spirits in Monet's circle: he also contributed to the First and Third Impressionist Exhibitions. Pissarro became of crucial significance for his work, but in Cézanne's painting it is the substantiality of things which is dominant, and his pictures are devoid of the atmospheric play of light so characteristic of the Impressionists. An admiration for Delacroix and Courbet pervades Cézanne's work, whose analytical relation to subject and reality came to exert an influence on the pioneers of Cubism, immediately after his own death. Cézanne stands as one of the most enigmatic figures in modern painting, one reason being his complex relationship to tradition. He was eager to "renew" painting, but he wished earnestly, as he himself put it, to "make something enduring out of Impressionism; like the art in the great museums". His ambitions are encapsulated in the following, famous quotation, where, in admiration of the greatest French landscape painter of the seventeenth century, Nicolas Poussin, he declared his desire was to "remake Nature in the likeness of Poussin's painting".

Charles Chaplin (1825–91)
From 1840 Chaplin was a pupil at the Ecole des Beaux-Arts in Paris and was, like J.-J. Henner, attached to the atelier of M. Drolling. He made his debut at the Salon of 1845 and his earliest works reveal his interest in realistic painting. After 1851 he abandoned that in favour of a style altogether more graceful and decorative which was inspired by artists such as J.-B. Greuze and J.-S. Chardin. This change of manner secured him popularity as a portrait and decorative painter, one of his assignments being the ornamentation

74
Paul Cézanne
Achille Emperaire, ca. 1868
Oil on canvas, 200 × 120 cm
Paris, Musée d'Orsay

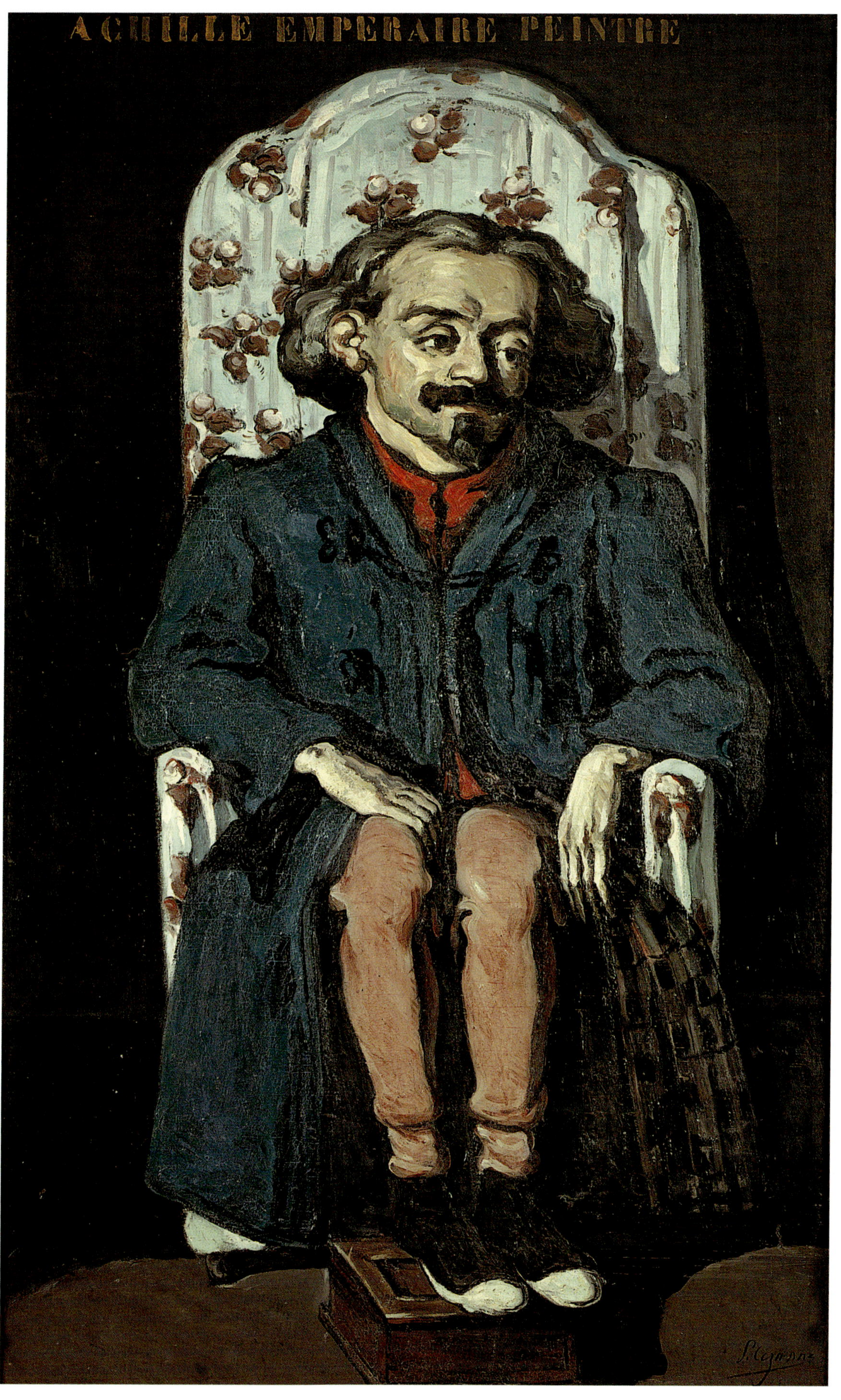

75
Paul Cézanne
The Bathers, ca. 1888–90
Oil on canvas, 73 × 92 cm
Copenhagen, Ny Carlsberg Glyptotek
(cat. no. 15)

Cézanne's work was, in his own words, an attempt to "make something enduring out of Impressionism; like the art in the great museums". His endeavours were, however, misunderstood by the critics of the day while the coming generation of painters were quick to acknowledge his importance. One example of this process is the way this painting was adopted very shortly after being exhibited: Picasso "borrowed" the central female figure, using the same pose in his famous *Les Demoiselles d'Avignon* from 1907. Cézanne had thus become *the tradition*, a guideline and inspiration for modern painting. The critics, however, were not to catch up until some ten years after Cézanne's death when they had become familiar with the idiom of Cubism. Cézanne remains one of the crucial figures of twentieth-century art.

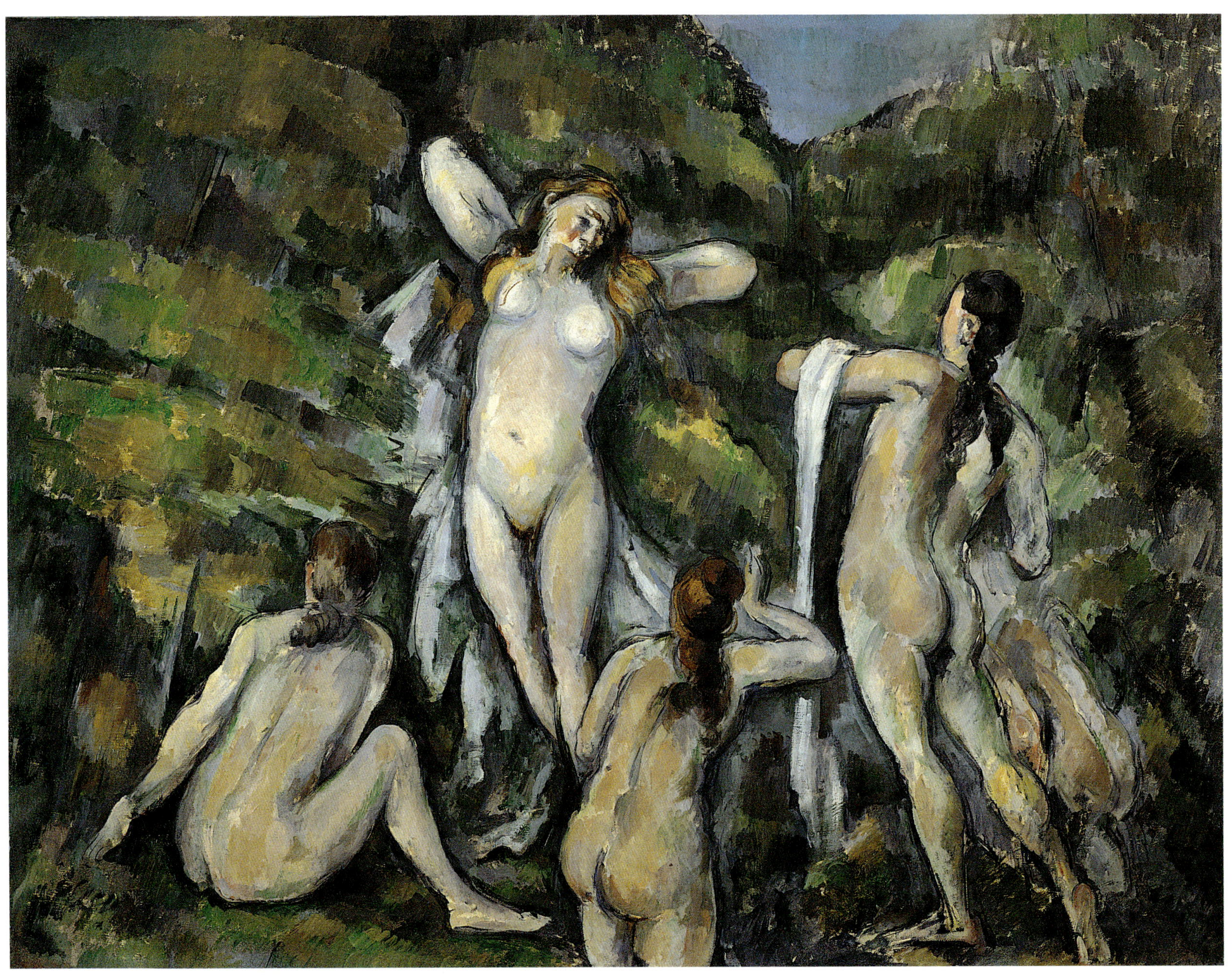

of the Elysée Palace in Paris. The Rococo influence is characteristic in Chaplin's depictions of half-undressed women posed in an atmosphere of eroticism (*The Broken Lyre*, cat. no. 16, fig. 62). Such works also appealed to the popular taste during the Third Republic and served to consolidate his success. Chaplin's painting is thus an example of how many Salon painters utilised stylistic features from various periods of art history, whenever it suited their own purposes.

Charles Cordier (1827–1905)
Cordier was trained at the Petite Ecole in Paris and made his debut at the Salon of 1848 with an orientalist plaster bust, Saïd Abdallah of the Darfour Tribe, of which he received a commission for a bronze from the French government. For fifteen years, beginning in 1851, Cordier occupied the post of ethnographic sculptor for the Natural History Museum in Paris, where he was able to use his art in the service of science. The job took him on a series of journeys to Algeria, Greece and Egypt, where, through his encounters with the local population, he built up a repertoire of "ethnic types". These works gave Cordier the opportunity to combine his academic training with a passion for "oriental" subjects and exotic, coloured materials. One example is the *Jewess from Algiers* (cat. no. 17, fig. 10), from around 1862, which, with its sensuous, coloured materials appealed to the Parisian upper class. It was to be Cordier's greatest success and an important work in the nineteenth-century's rediscovery of polychrome sculpture. Like many of his colleagues, Cordier worked with architects in the construction of new public buildings in Paris, two of these being the Louvre and the Paris Opéra.

Gustave Courbet (1819–77)
From his youth, Courbet was driven by a deep commitment to Socialism, which left its mark on the critical attitude he assumed towards the academic art world. In Paris he preferred to follow training at private academies. He painted from life as well as copying the old masters in the Louvre, while his earliest works were inspired by the literary Romanticism of such authors as Victor Hugo, George Sand and Goethe. His first major success came with a self-portrait, accepted by the Salon of 1844, and it was precisely this genre which became a constant theme in his oeuvre. An example of this is his famous work, *The Wounded Man* (cat. no. 19, fig. 14) from 1854–55, where he depicts himself as a suffering "romantic" type. During the following years the Salon jury refused most of the works Courbet submitted, but in 1851 he achieved his eventual breakthrough with three works which rejected, once and for all, the idealism of the Academy, and thus sparked the debate on Realism. In 1855 another of Courbet's works was refused by the Salon, after which he demonstrated his dissatisfaction by opening a pavilion housing a special exhibition of his own work under the title of *Le Réalisme*. By the close of the Second Empire, Courbet was no longer regarded as an enfant terrible, but acknowledged for his contributions to Realism. Through his stubborn resistance to the official art of the Academy, Courbet opened the door for Impressionism.

Thomas Couture (1815–79)
Couture was a promising pupil at the Ecole des Beaux-Arts, and at an early stage of his training was tipped to win the Prix de Rome. However, this never happened, and in disappointment Couture turned his back on the Ecole des Beaux-Arts and went his own way, though without rejecting the academic tradition outright. He sought to revitalise Salon painting by having traditional, literary subjects arrayed in vibrant colours and a painterly texture which recall Delacroix, and thus to bring about a compromise between the old and the new schools. In his attempt to assume the legacy of Gros and David, he embarked on his monumental work, *The Decadence of the Romans* (a preparatory oil shown here, cat. no. 21, fig. 50) which became the main attraction at the Salon of 1847. Here he presents an orgy, in which the debauched revellers appear in stark contrast to the illustrious Roman statues behind them. The work was interpreted by some critics as a scandalous satire on the July Monarchy and a foretelling of the fall of the regime. The same year Couture opened an atelier in Paris to provide an alternative to the Academy. Here he encouraged his students, one of whom was Manet, to retain the pure colours and the fresh brushstrokes of the sketch in the finished work. It was through such instruction that Couture became significant for the new trends in painting.

Edgar Degas (1834–1917)
In 1855 Degas entered the Ecole des Beaux-Arts, where he studied under Lamothe, a former pupil of Ingres. Degas made a thorough study of the great masters throughout the history of art, and embarked on a career as a painter of portraits and historical scenes. In 1861 he met Manet, who introduced him to the circle of painters who were later to be known as the Impressionists. Although it looked in the 1860s as though Degas' career would follow the academic pattern, he was, within a few years, to be himself one of the leading exponents of the new painting, as well as being one of the principal organisers behind the Impressionist exhibitions. His depictions of modern life, the daring compositions and the unusual viewpoints were partly the result of his interest in photography and Japanese woodcuts. In the course of the 1880s Degas began to sculpt figures in wax as a way of analysing the motifs of movement which he used in his painting. Only one was ever intended for public view, namely *Dancer with Ballet Skirt, Fourteen Years Old* (cat. no. 22, fig. 36), shown at the 6th Impressionist exhibition in 1881. The work caused a scandal, partly on account of its "realistic" effects, which struck most people as radically ugly.

Eugène Delaplanche (1836–91)
Delaplanche received the traditional academic education at the Ecole des Beaux-Arts. He had already exhibited twice at the Salon, when he won the Prix de Rome in 1864 and set off to learn about the Italian sculptural tradition. His *Eve After the Fall* was modelled during this time, and became one of the best-known contemporary depictions of Eve. It demonstrates the influence exerted by Michelangelo. At the Salon of 1870 the work was a great success, although some harboured misgivings that Eve's mature, sensual body and the expressiveness of the whole work were of a boldness which was scarcely decent. It was just such sensual representation of the more or less nude female body for which Delaplanche became famous. His most celebrated work was the allegorical sculpture *Music* (cat. no. 23, fig. 35), which delighted the public and the critics at the Salon of 1878, and became the first French sculpture to be pur-

chased by Carl Jacobsen. Delaplanche's enthusiasm for the Italian sculptural tradition affiliates him with that group of sculptors who were referred to as The Florentines, namely Falguière, Mercié and Dubois.

Jules-Elie Delaunay (1812–91)
Delaunay commenced his studies at the Ecole des Beaux-Arts in 1848. Having acquired complete mastery of the entire Neo-Classical repertoire of motifs, he made his debut at the Salon of 1853. A characteristic example of Delaunay's favourite world of themes is *The Death of the Nymph Hesperia* (cat. no. 24, fig. 60) which, accompanied by two other works, became the toast of the Salon of 1863, and was to constitute, in fact, his breakthrough. In 1865 he won the Prix de Rome, where he went to spend the next few years. While in Rome he became friend with Dubois and Henner and it was during this time that he executed the sketch for his principal work *The Plague in Rome* (cat. no. 25, fig. 5), which demonstrates in exemplary fashion his iconographic and stylistic attitudes. The scene combines his favourite themes — the Christian and the Classical — in one dramatic narrative, which hails Christianity's healing power over heathen belief. From 1870 Delaunay concentrated increasingly on portraits and religious ornamentation assignments in churches. In 1879 he became a member of the Académie des Beaux-Arts, and in 1889 he was made head of one of the ateliers at the Ecole des Beaux-Arts in Paris.

Paul Dubois (1829–1905)
In 1856 Dubois commenced his training as a sculptor at the studio of Toussaint and made his debut at the Salon of 1857. The following year he entered the Ecole des Beaux-Arts. During a lengthy stay in Italy he encountered the sculpture of the Renaissance master Donatello, which was of crucial importance to his own work. Together with Falguière and Mercié, Dubois became an exponent of the Neo-Florentine style, which came into fashion in the 1860s and thus bestowed on these artists the appellation The Florentines. The inspiration of Donatello is particularly clear in *Florentine Singer from the Fifteenth Century* (cat. no. 27, fig. 32) from 1865, which is very close to the Renaissance sculptor's famous *David* (1440–42). Dubois' representation of the boy's slender figure became an enormous success, winning him a Gold Medal at the Salon of 1865 and prompting the critic Paul Mantz to hail Dubois as "one of the hopes of modern sculpture". In 1873 Dubois was made Curator of the Luxembourg Museum in Paris, an office he held until he succeeded Guillaume as Director of the Ecole des Beaux-Arts.

Raymond Duchamp-Villon (1876–1918)
Duchamp-Villon's original field of study was medicine, but during a protracted illness he learned to sculpt in clay. In 1898 he abandoned medicine in favour of sculpture, in which he never received any formal training. Duchamp-Villon was particularly preoccupied with figures of humans and animals and exhibited regularly at the Salon. One debt evinced by his early works is to the expressive realism of Rodin, but from 1907 onwards he attempted, like so many of his contemporaries, to distance himself from the older master by simplifying his figures. His aim was to combine the sculptural ideals of Antiquity with a new, dynamic and geometric concept of form. At the same time, he became interested in the opportunities offered to sculpture by Cubism, then in its breakthrough. His attempts to freeze the dynamic development of forms in time and space are rooted both in the essays of Futurism to depict movement and in Cubism's desire to represent more than one side of the subject simultaneously. He wrote: "the machine has dominion over us, and we cannot understand life without it". Duchamp-Villon became a respected member of the Parisian avant-garde, one of whose endeavours was their exhibition of 1912 under the name Séction d'Or. Together with his brothers Jacques Villon and Marcel Duchamp he played a central role in the development of the aesthetics of Modernism.

Henri Fantin-Latour (1836–1904)
Fantin-Latour was trained at the Petite Ecole (1850–56) and in 1854 entered the Ecole des Beaux-Arts, which he left after less than a year. Like many of his colleagues he acquired a thorough knowledge of the tradition by copying the old masters at the Louvre. Even at this early stage, Fantin-Latour's painting was proceeding in two distinct directions simultaneously: one comprised pictures based on the imaginary and one on realism. The realistic side was reinforced when, in 1859, Fantin-Latour met Courbet and, for a subsequent period, became a pupil at his atelier. Thereafter he regarded himself as a Realist, though he continued to draw systematically on the painting of the past, just like most of his ambitious colleagues, including Manet. Fantin-Latour also established a friendship with the circle of painters since known as the Impressionists. He shared their taste for modern life, not least their contempt for anecdotal themes, but despite his interest in the effects of light, painting in the open air had no appeal for him. He declined to exhibit at the First Impressionist Exhibition of 1874, instead he exhibited regularly, and with some success, at the Salon. In the group portrait, *Homage to Eugène Delacroix*, from 1864, Fantin-Latour combined his artistic affiliation with both the avant-garde and the tradition by painting a group including Manet, the poet Baudelaire and himself in front of a portrait of the late, romantic painter Delacroix. Fantin-Latour gave expression to the romantic side of his interests in a series of pictures which drew their inspiration from contemporary German music (Schumann, Brahms and Wagner). He also painted mythological scenes featuring such figures as Danaë, Aurora and the nymphs. It was his later, poetic compositions, such as *Night* (cat. no. 29, fig. 77) which brought him most renown.

Paul Gauguin (1848–1903)
Gauguin started out as a stockbroker and never received any formal artistic training. It was his encounter with the landscape paintings of Corot around 1873, which proved the motivation for Gauguin's own artistic career. During the 1870s he became acquainted with the Impressionists, forming a close relationship with Pissarro, who, in a sense, became his teacher. Gauguin made his debut at the Salon of 1876 and from 1879 to 1886 he was a contributor to the Impressionist Exhibitions, where, at least initially, he was frequently the target of hostile criticism. But in 1881 his *Woman Sewing* (cat. no. 30, fig. 12) met with a favourable reaction — acclaim about which he was non-committal, as he felt he was being misunderstood. Gauguin's artistic career was already parting company with Impressionism as early as the 1880s, and the encounter with Emile Bernard was critical for Gau-

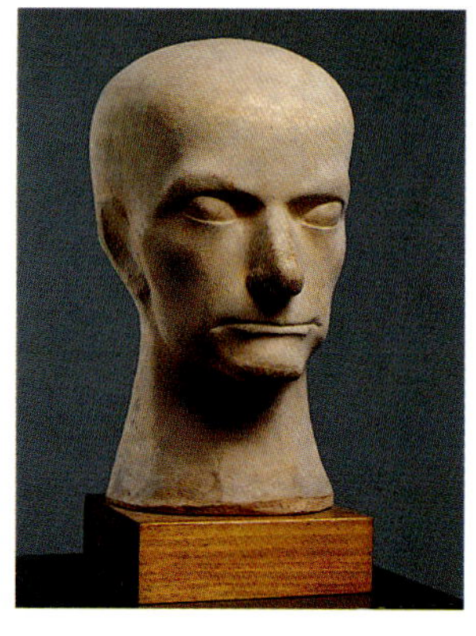

76
Raymond Duchamp-Villon
Charles Baudelaire, 1911
Terracotta, h. 42.5 cm
Copenhagen, Ny Carlsberg Glyptotek
(cat. no. 28)

It was the poet Baudelaire in his famous 1863 essay, "The Painter of Modern Life" who encouraged the artists of the day to portray their times as they really were. He thereby acquired considerable significance for artists like Manet. Duchamp-Villon's portrait of the poet expresses a modern concept of form, but also stands indebted to ancient sculpture. Although a few of Baudelaire's facial features are recognisable, the portrait makes little attempt to achieve the illusion of the soft surface of the skin. Duchamp-Villon has instead built up the face of clear surfaces and by dint of this simplification created a compact whole that acquires a certain Cubist quality.

77
Henri Fantin-Latour
Night (1897)
Oil on canvas, 61 × 75 cm
Paris, Musée d'Orsay
(cat. no. 29)

As the allegory for Night, the woman has become a romantic dream figure under Fantin-Latour's brush. Like many contemporary artists, Fantin-Latour was deeply interested in the painting of earlier eras, and with its gentle, slurred strokes this picture forms an example of the way in which the eighteenth-century Rococo was adopted to the taste of the day. At the start of his career Fantin-Latour considered himself a realist and was a friend of Manet. In late works like this, however, he concentrated on a more subjective vision, moved by longing and escapism. In German music of the period, he discovered precisely that dreamy, idealistic quality which for him was absent from modern life.

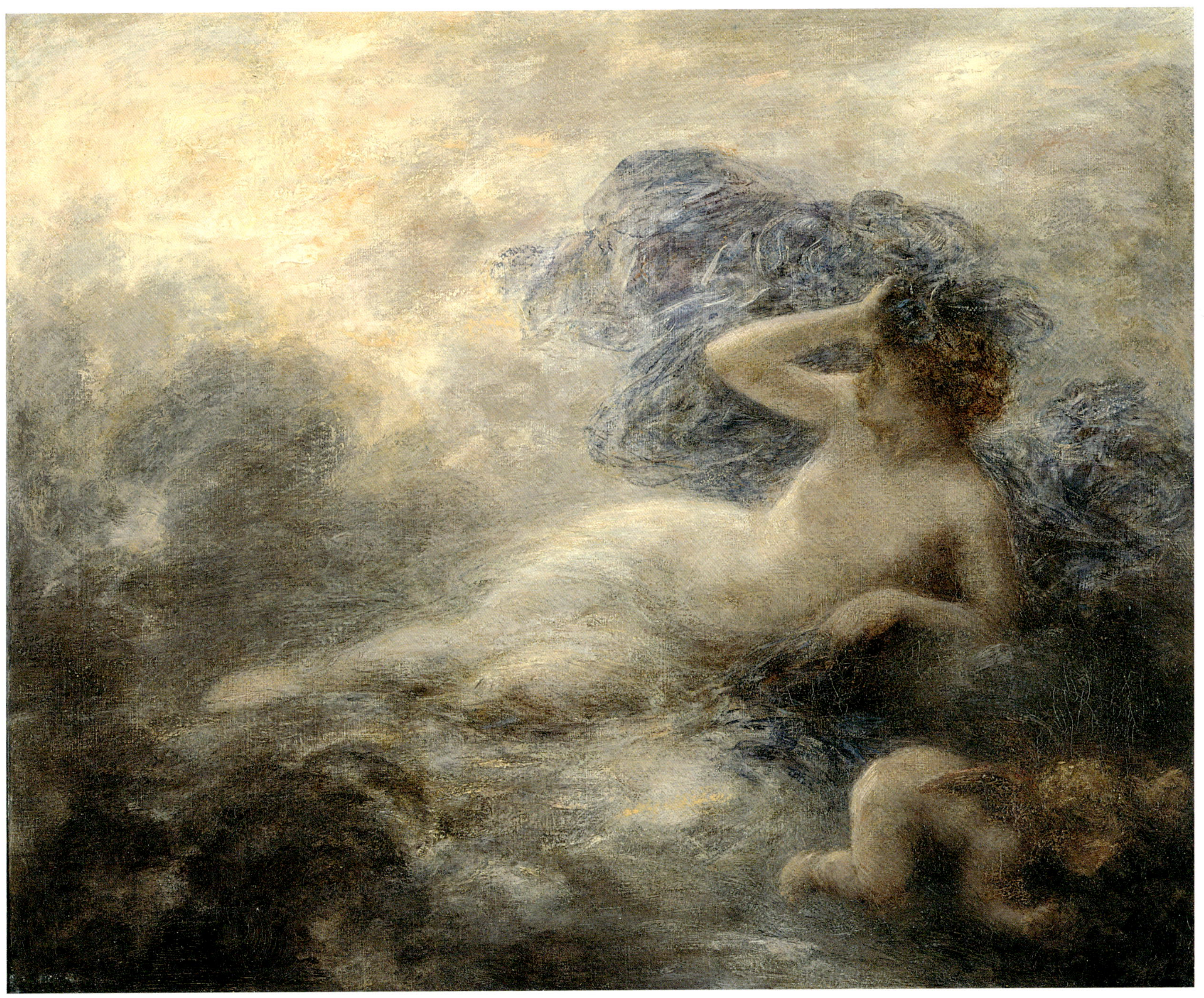

guin's development of a representation of form, based on outline or contour, just as, in 1886, he was affected by his acquaintance with Van Gogh. After a brief stay in Denmark, Gauguin abandoned his Danish wife in Copenhagen in the summer of 1885, devoting himself henceforth entirely to painting, sculpture and pottery. He developed his own distinctive form of expression with heavy symbolic overtones, culminating in the famous Tahiti pictures from the last years of his life (1890–1903).

Jean-Léon Gérôme (1824–1904)
The painter and sculptor Gérôme was trained in the academic style as a pupil of Delaroche and Gleyre. In 1847 he made his debut at the Salon with the painting, *The Cock-Fight* (cat. no. 32, fig. 46), a typical example of his use of anecdotal and classicising themes, built up in harmonic composition, the lines being of great precision as in the Neo-Classical school of Ingres. This work established Gérôme as one of the most successful painters of the academic tradition and prompted one critic to call him "an eye astonishingly open to beauty". His extensive travels in Egypt and the Middle East exposed him to colourful scenery which made him a representative of Orientalism. In the late 1870s he started to turn out three-dimensional versions of the figures in his paintings. One example of this is the sculpture *The Gladiators* (cat. no. 33, fig. 7), which won him a medal at the World Exhibition of 1878. Gérôme enjoyed great popularity and had a crucial influence as the disseminator of the academic tradition through his teaching at the Ecole des Beaux-Arts: it was from this bastion that he staunchly resisted every new development in art, especially Impressionism.

Henri Gervex (1852–1929)
Gervex' early teachers included Stevens, and later, at the Ecole des Beaux-Arts, both Cabanel and Bastien-Lepage. In 1874 he made his debut at the Salon and his early works are ample testimony both as regards style and subject to these teachers' considerable influence. However, after a few years, the actual style of Gervex's painting and his choice of subjects from the modern world around him reflected an increasingly Impressionist disposition. He attracted considerable attention in 1878, when his painting *Rolla* was removed from the Salon Exhibition, on the grounds that it was too controversial, despite it having been passed by the jury. The subject is taken from a poem by Alfred de Musset, which describes a young man of the upper classes who commits suicide having squandered the family fortune, most recently during a visit to a prostitute. The picture was subsequently exhibited in the gallery of the art dealer Bague, where it became the runaway success which established Gervex' reputation. For the World Exhibition of 1889 he worked together with Stevens to produce *Panorama of the Century*. This work assembles the famous politicians, artists and writers who illustrate the history of France since the Revolution, and it became the main attraction at the Exhibition. In 1890, like so many of the leading artists of the time, Gervex broke away from the official Salon to become a founding-member of the Société Nationale des Beaux-Arts, under whose auspices he exhibited regularly until 1922. Gervex' popularity in his own time and his subsequent neglect have at root the same cause, i.e. his ability to keep pace with the change in taste without really grasping the essence of the new painting.

Constantin Guys (1805–92)
Guys belongs to the first generation of illustrators who were employed by France's new illustrated magazines. After some years as a correspondent for these publications, he settled in Paris at the end of the 1850s. Here he depicted with wit and vitality Parisian daily life — women in crinolines, horse-drawn carriages in the Bois de Boulogne, social life and carnival scenes in sketches which are characterised by simple energetic brushstrokes covered with a thin wash. The works were extremely popular and Guys enjoyed great regard among such influential critics as Baudelaire, who immortalised him with the epithet "the painter of modern life" in his famous essay of the same name. Artists such as Delacroix and Manet, who himself owned much of Guys' work, admired the skill with which he could endow his subject with a sense of the momentary, in a direct and merciless fashion. His characteristic style is exemplified in *A Courtesan* (cat. no. 35, fig. 47), which shows a representative of the decadent side of the modern life.

Jean-Jacques Henner (1829–1905)
Henner entered the Ecole des Beaux-Arts in 1846, to be taught, like Chaplin, by Drolling, himself a pupil of David. In 1858 he won the Prix de Rome and spent the next five years at the French Academy in Rome. Here he became fascinated by the surrounding landscape, and drew inspiration from such older Italian masters as Caravaggio and Titian. Thus Henner's painting is distinguished by a powerful chiaroscuro effect, where light figures emerge from a dark background, and outlines are softened by the use of sfumato, inspired by Correggio. In 1864 Henner returned to Paris and exhibited with great success at the Salon until 1903. He became particularly famous for his idyllic depictions of nymphs in dark landscapes where the white female figures, with their tresses of brick-red hair underline the paintings' sensual quality (cat. nos. 36 and 37, fig. 63). In these works Henner strikes a symbolist note, later taken up by artists such as Gustave Moreau.

Aristide Maillol (1861–1944)
Maillol's initial career was that of a painter and tapestry designer and in 1885 he was accepted by the Ecole des Beaux-Arts on his second application. Here he was a pupil of Cabanel and Gérôme, but he rapidly developed a critical attitude to the academic work method, which he found uninspired and irrelevant. Maillol was more interested in the new trends in painting and in his early works he demonstrates the powerful influence of Puvis de Chavannes, Gauguin and the Nabis group, of which he became a member in 1894. Maillol shared the interest of the group in art and design, and began to work with tapestry, but gradually shifted genre to sculpture. He had a vision of sculpture as the medium of eternity, and desired, through a harmonious abstraction to purge sculptural expression of literary associations and replace these with a simple, universal language of forms. The result was a monumental sculpture which was compared by the critics with famous works of Antiquity, and caused them to hail Maillol as a "Classical artist" of the same stamp as Cézanne. It is in its way a paradox that Maillol's references to the tradition of sculpture were not read as reactionary, but, instead, made him one of the principal exponents of modern sculpture.

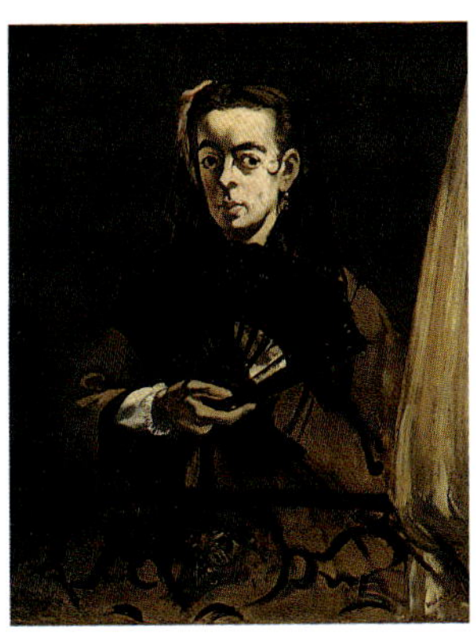

78
Edouard Manet
A Lady at Her Window
or *Angélina*, 1865
Oil on canvas, 92 × 73 cm
Paris, Musée d'Orsay
(cat. no. 41)

Angélina has stepped out of the darkness of her room and is exposed in the harsh light on the balcony. She has drawn the curtain aside and taken the fan from her face. With his brutal brushstrokes and bare, monochrome areas, Manet has turned the picture into a merciless, "decadent" presentation of a woman who is no beauty in theconventional sense, yet is putting herself on display. Manet's aim was not to flatter his model, rather he has taken pains to bring out her true features, while at the same time giving her a theatrical air by presenting her in Spanish costume. The Baroque-inspired pattern created by the ironwork of the balcony underlines the decorative effect.

Edouard Manet (1832–83)
From 1850 to 1856 Manet attended the painting school of the academic artist Couture, where he was made aware of the academic tradition and was encouraged to retain the pure colours and the lively brushstrokes of the sketch in the finished work. Manet undertook many journeys to the great museums of Europe, where he learned from the great masters of the past, especially Titian and Velázquez, who would be of crucial significance for his work. Manet evolved a complex relationship with tradition, in that he attempted to bring the eternal, Classical aspects of art together with the contemporary in his painting. He shared the viewpoint of his friend, the poet Baudelaire, on modern life, and was influenced by the realism of Courbet. These different influences combine in *The Absinthe Drinker* (cat. no. 40, fig. 49) which was rejected by the Salon of 1859 — evidence of the incomprehension which greeted much of the new painting on its appearance. In 1861, however, the Salon accepted two pictures by Manet which received a positive reaction for their combination of a truly contemporary realism with an influence from the past Spanish masters, but the following years saw scandal follow scandal. Thus it was that Manet was accused of vulgarising tradition when, at the Salon of 1865, he showed *Olympia* (fig. 55), painted in 1863, a gloss on Titian's famous *Venus of Urbino*, who in Manet's painting appears in the guise of a modern courtesan. Manet became one of the most important figures in the background to Impressionism, but despite his role of mentor to the younger artists, he deliberately absented himself from their exhibitions. Instead he sought with dogged persistence to have his painting accepted in the academic circles: in this he finally succeeded, shortly before his death.

Laurent-Honoré Marqueste
(1848–1920)
Marqueste attended the Ecole des Beaux-Arts where his teachers included the highly esteemed, academic sculptor Falguière. Marqueste won the Prix de Rome in 1871, made his debut at the Salon in 1874 and exhibited regularly throughout his career. He chose to abide by the strictures of the Academy and thus preferred mythological themes and cultivated a virtuosity in the execution of detail while avoiding compromise with the clean, overall lines of the sculpture. Typical of Marqueste was his emphasising of the delicate and sensual aspects of the works. This was not confined to the smooth surface of the marble: a subject such as *Galathea* (cat. no. 43, fig. 37) invites the spectator's gaze to wander all over the woman's body. With his references to tradition, the elegance of the Renaissance and the dynamic spiral compositions of the Baroque, Marqueste was a typical Salon sculptor. He received numerous prizes and medals for his work.

Henri Matisse (1869–1954)
Matisse was originally a lawyer by profession, having no serious interest in art until he was 31. In 1892 he abandoned his legal career and moved to Paris, where he studied for a while with Bouguereau. When Matisse failed the entrance examination for the Ecole des Beaux-Arts, he became instead a pupil of the Symbolist, Gustave Moreau: during this period he also copied the old masters at the Louvre. In 1896 he made his debut at the Salon, achieving success with works, which, at that stage, were influenced by the old Dutch masters. By the following year Matisse had altered his style: it was now inspired by Impressionism, and therefore aroused the displeasure of the conservative critics. In 1899 he registered at the school of painting run by Carrière, where his output included a series of life studies inspired by Cézanne. It was after this that Matisse developed his characteristic, brightly-coloured painting, under the influence of Gauguin and Van Gogh. He also ventured into sculpture, in which he investigates the interrelations of form, space and ornamentation (*Decorative Figure*, cat. no. 44, fig. 44).

Antonin Mercié (1845–1916)
Like Marqueste, Mercié studied under Falguière at the Ecole des Beaux-Arts. In 1868 he won the Prix de Rome and spent the next few years at the French Academy in Rome. It was here that he modelled the work which was his first and greatest triumph, the Neo-Florentine bronze statue *David*, which earned him a Gold Medal. He achieved further success with the bronze group *Gloria Victis* (cat. no. 45, fig. 30) in which he managed to combine the measured elegance of Renaissance sculpture with a Baroque dynamic. The work was exhibited at the Salon of 1874, purchased by the French state, and cast in numerous examples to be set up all over France as monuments to those who fell in the Franco-Prussian War of 1870–71. The work thus acquired tremendous symbolic value for the resurgence of French national feeling in the wake of the defeat. Mercié's later works were of an academic, but less virtuoso character, and the prolific sculptor enjoyed particular success with tomb monuments. Many of his works were produced in reduced format, in bronze and unglazed porcelain, finding a wide market. Mercié received numerous awards, was Professor at the Ecole des Beaux-Arts from 1900, and from 1913 president of the Société des Artistes Français.

Claude Monet (1840–1926)
Monet received tuition from the marine painter, Eugène Boudin in his hometown of Le Havre, before moving to Paris in 1859. Here, however, he did not seek admission to the Ecole des Beaux-Arts, as he considered the training too conservative; instead, from 1860 onwards, he attended the unofficial art school, the Académie Suisse, and from 1862 he received tuition at the school of the academic painter Gleyre. It was here that he met Renoir, with whom he painted in the open air, directly from the subject, inspired by the Barbizon painters, such as Rousseau and Corot. He was also influenced by the Realism of Courbet, which at that time represented the avant-garde in French art. Monet made his debut at the Salon of 1865, and achieved a degree of popularity; during the following years, however, many of his works were rejected. In his early painting he attempted to capture the changing interplay of light and colour, sometimes approaching this by painting the same subject repeatedly. It was, in fact, Monet's painting *Impression: Soleil levant* (Impression: sunrise) from 1872 which prompted the critics to belittle the new trend in painting with the term "Impressionist". Monet became one of the leading figures in the new painting, as he retained that apprehension of the appearance of nature which was the whole basis of Impressionism. Cézanne characterised him thus: "He is only an eye, but my God what an eye!" In the course of the 1890s Monet's increasing success made it possible for him, around 1900, to settle at Giverny outside Paris, where the garden became a centre for the

last twenty years of his painting. So, the lily pond there became one of Impressionism's most famous subjects.

Pablo Picasso (1881–1973)
Pablo Ruiz Blasco was only 11 years old when he entered art school. Three years later he was accepted at the Academy of Art in Barcelona, and in 1897 this exceptional student transferred to the Academy of Art in Madrid. In the capital he made detailed studies of the great masters at the Prado: Velázquez, Titian, Van Dyck, Rubens and El Greco. Finding the teaching at the Academy uninspiring, however, he left Madrid only a year later and returned to Barcelona, where he became one of the driving forces in the city's avant-garde circles. Seeking fresh inspiration, he travelled to Paris to explore the art milieu, and it was during a couple of longer visits to the city in 1900 and 1901 that he began to sign his works with his mother's maiden name, Picasso. During this period he drew inspiration from Toulouse-Lautrec and the Post-Impressionists, both as regards subject and style. This development is exemplified in *Spanish Lady in Crinoline* (fig. 26), where the brushwork approaches the Pointillist. In other works from 1901, Picasso experimented with such approaches as the cloisonnism of Emile Bernard, though his pictures from later that year seem to be inspired by the expressive style of El Greco. It was by this route that Picasso embarked on his Blue Period, which lasted from 1901 to 1904, by which time he had taken up permanent residence in Paris. The succeeding years were to witness the Rose Period, in the course of which it is possible to note the increasing influence of Cézanne. An example of this is Picasso's appropriation of the pose of the woman in *The Bathers* (cat. no. 15, fig. 75) for the central figure in his own key work *Les Demoiselles d'Avignon* from 1907 (MOMA, New York). Subsequently, in the years 1908–14, Picasso, in the company of Georges Braque, launched Cubism, and expanded his activities to include pottery and sculpture. Thus Picasso worked his way through the various avant-garde developments of the preceding century, gradually attaining complete control of the artistic repertoire. Later in his career, he was to wrestle with tradition in a series of paraphrases of masterpieces from previous eras. Picasso's oeuvre has since assumed the character of a long triumphal procession, and his enormous output stands as a monument to the important currents marking Modernism.

Pierre-Auguste Renoir (1841–1919)
As a young man, Renoir worked as a porcelain-painter at the Sèvres factories, but in 1862 he became a pupil of Gleyre, who also taught Monet and Sisley. Rococo painting from the eighteenth century was an important source of inspiration for Renoir who took enthusiastically to carefree subjects, just as he had a preference for a palette dominated by light, fresh colours. Quite early in his career he began painting in the open air, directly from the subject. Thus around 1869 Renoir and Monet went together to the popular restaurant on the Seine, "La Grenouillère", and painted a series of pictures which are characteristic examples of early Impressionism (see cat. no. 49, fig. 53). In addition to these depictions of modern life in and around Paris, Renoir worked with larger, more traditionally-structured atelier compositions. *Boy with a Cat* (cat. no. 50, fig. 54) may be one of these Salon-intended works, but Renoir never exhibited it. From the 1880s onwards, he concentrated on large-scale compositions featuring either mythological episodes or unpretentious everyday scenes, often of bathing or washing. It is Renoir's late works which draw most consciously on tradition, his sources ranging from Rubens, to Boucher and to Ingres. Picasso and Matisse were both admirers of Renoir on account of these works, which managed to be faithful to tradition and yet modern at the same time.

Auguste Rodin (1840–1917)
Posterity regards Rodin as the greatest sculptor of his time, as well as the man who made this medium truly modern. However, before he achieved that status, Rodin had to struggle frequently with the art establishment of his day. He entered the Petite Ecole at the age of 15, applied three times (all unsuccessfully) for entrance to the Ecole des Beaux-Arts, and never won the Prix de Rome. Instead he had private tuition and supported himself by working as an assistant for various decorative sculptors, and at the Sèvres porcelain factories. Quite early on, Rodin's work exhibited the influence of Michelangelo, which increased following a stay in Rome. The Renaissance master's famous work, *The Dying Slave* inspired Rodin's own *The Age of Bronze* (cat. no. 51, fig. 34), which attracted considerable attention at the Salon of 1877 on account of its realism. In later works it was to be Michelangelo's characteristic *non-finito* treatment of the stone in particular — whereby certain parts of the work were polished smooth, while others were left roughly-hewn — which was the particular source of inspiration. As Rodin himself put it, "It was Michelangelo who freed me from the academic". From 1880, Rodin worked on the monumental bronze doors *The Gates of Hell*, which occupied him for the rest of his life. The doors themselves were never finally realised in his lifetime, but served as the point of departure for a long series of independent works (cat. nos. 52 and 53, figs. 40 and 38). During the 1890s Rodin achieved increasing international renown.

Alfred Sisley (1839–99)
In 1862 Sisley joined Gleyre's atelier, where he became friends with Monet and Renoir. These friendships proved of far greater significance to Sisley's development than any academic training he received. Throughout this period Sisley, like other young painters, submitted works to the annual Salon exhibition. His work was favourably received by the jury in 1866, 1868 and 1870, but rejected in 1867 and 1869. Sisley developed his characteristic style in the early 1870s, influenced both by the light brushwork of Corot, and by other Impressionists, particularly Monet. Sisley participated in four of the eight Impressionist exhibitions. At the first one in 1874 he exhibited *The Flood* (cat. no. 55, fig. 6) which received a positive reception, and was highlighted as one of the exhibition's most outstanding landscapes. Works such as this gained Sisley the appellation, "the lyricist" and caused him to be regarded as one of the most gifted representatives of the "classic" Impressionist outdoor painting. Although posterity has permitted Sisley to be overshadowed by his Impressionist colleagues, his significance for the new painting was acknowledged by friends and writers on art of his own time. Matisse once asked Pissarro who was a typical Impressionist, and received the answer, "That's Sisley".

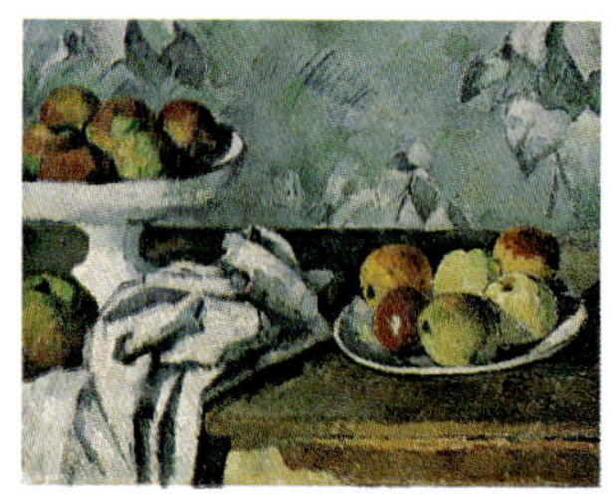

79
Paul Cézanne
Still Life with Apples in a Bowl, ca.1879–82
Oil on canvas, 43 × 54 cm
Copenhagen, Ny Carlsberg Glyptotek
(cat. no. 14)

Cézanne painted a number of pictures with the same basic elements as here: a broad wooden shelf containing fruit against a background of bluish grey wallpaper with flowered motifs. The edges of the shelf divide the picture into two horizontal sections that underline the two-dimensional surface of the painting. But the horizontal lines are broken by the round shapes which thus create the feeling of depth in the picture. In this way Cézanne has created a composition which combines the classical genre of "still life" with a modern decorative pattern.
The picture was part of his continuing efforts to delve into the secret nature of things and to make even everyday articles into objects for the analytical eye of visual art.

80
Alfred Stevens
The Hunters of Vincennes
or *What People call Vagrancy*,
ca. 1855
Oil on canvas, 130 × 165 cm
Paris, Musée d'Orsay
(cat. no. 56)

Portrayals of everyday life appear now and again in Stevens' work, but rarely in such monumental form as here. Poor people put out on the street are here shown in large format: the relief-like composition forms a scene in which the figures move like characters in a drama acted before those contemplating the painting. Here are the soldiers and the poor family, as well as the more affluent woman holding out her hand to give alms to the poor.
In this way, the work is about charity, but it is more sentimental than political in its portrayal of social injustice. The uniforms are reproduced with photographic realism, while the walls and the snow are portrayed in a more relaxed manner in the nature of sketches.

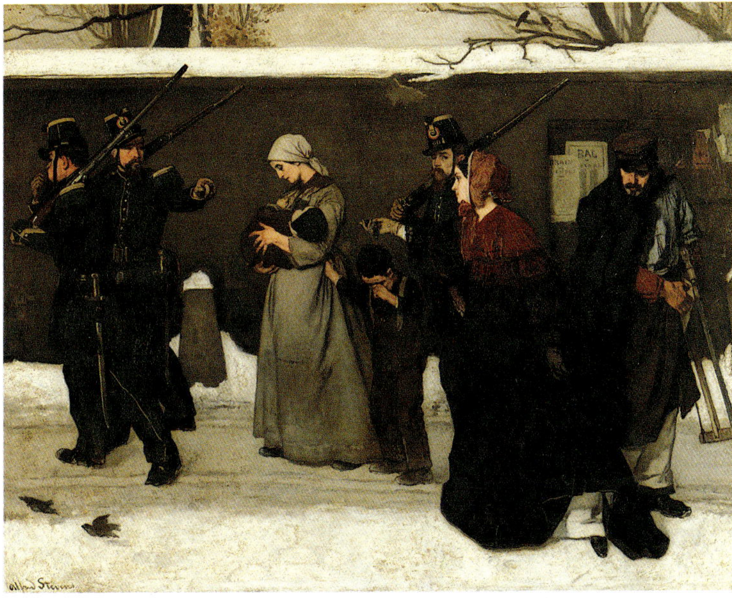

Alfred Stevens (1823–1906)
Stevens was born in Brussels and received his artistic training at the city's Art Academy, where his teacher Naves introduced him to the school of J.-L. David. In 1844 Stevens went to Paris where he was initially a pupil of the academic painter Roqueplan, before entering the Ecole des Beaux-Arts to be taught by the Neo-Classicist Ingres. Stevens made his debut at the Salon of 1853, and his early works such as *The Hunters of Vincennes* (cat. no. 56, fig. 80) bear witness to his profound debt to the repertoire of themes of his friend Courbet. After 1855, however, Stevens abandoned the historical and social subjects in order to concentrate on the depiction of contemporary women of the Parisian middle class. He shared the Impressionists' interest in Japonism as is apparent from the work *The Blue Dress* (cat. no. 58, fig. 25), and was friends with Manet and Berthe Morisot. Stevens' association with the Impressionists did not leave any traceable influence on his technique, despite the fact that during the 1870s it became less academic and more influenced by the effects of photography. Moreover he declined to contribute to the First Impressionist Exhibition in 1874. Together with his former pupil, Gervex, he executed the work *Panorama of the Century*, an illustration of the century's history since the French Revolution, which was to be the main attraction at the World Exhibition of 1889.

Jacques-Joseph Tissot (1836–1902)
Tissot, one of whose teachers was Flandrin (himself a pupil of Ingres) made his debut at the Salon of 1859, where he exhibited with success until he moved in 1871 to London, on account of the Franco-Prussian War. During the period 1872–81 he exhibited regularly at the Royal Academy in London, where he had made his debut in 1864. In his early works Tissot was, like many of his contemporaries, fascinated by Goethe's *Faust*, and painted a series of pictures inspired by it. Several of these, one of which was *The Meeting of Faust and Marguerite* (cat. no. 59, fig. 19) were exhibited at the Salon of 1861. During the 1860s he devoted himself increasingly to the painting of contemporary subjects, and thought of himself as a modern painter. Throughout his career, however, he remained faithful to the traditional, craftsman-like perfectionist mode of painting, not permitting himself to be influenced by the Impressionist technique, despite being a close friend of Degas and acquainted with the other Impressionists. In 1882 Tissot returned to Paris and painted a series of pictures of modern Parisians. His works are thus a demonstration of how the academic tradition could be influenced by avant-garde tendencies. Towards the end of his career Tissot became increasingly religious and executed two major series of paintings on Christian themes.

Vincent van Gogh (1853–90)
The son of a Dutch clergyman, Vincent van Gogh was influenced by religious ideas from an early age. Passionately concerned with alleviating the sufferings of mankind, his initial vocation led him to train for the priesthood, but around 1880 he became convinced that his true calling was that of an artist. In 1886, following an academic training as a painter in Antwerp, Van Gogh moved to Paris where he received further tuition in the atelier of the Salon painter, Fernand Cormon. It was, however, his encounter with the work of such artists as Degas, Pissarro and Gauguin which was to prove of crucial significance. Van Gogh parlayed his powerful social commitment into depictions of the Belgian miners and peasants. His inspiration was partly drawn from the works of the caricaturist Daumier and the social realism of Millet. The latter was to have a profound influence on him: thus in *The Sheep-Shearers* (fig. 27) Van Gogh has transferred the motif from one of Millet's graphic works to canvas, even preserving the original format. Influenced by both Impressionism and Japanese woodcuts, Van Gogh's paintings underwent a certain change in the late 1880s, despite his inability to share the Impressionists' enthusiastic view of modern life. He was drawn rather to the negative and melancholy aspects of existence in the modern metropolis, besides being, in any case, more interested in the symbolic and expressive values of colours. At the end of the 1880s Van Gogh decided to move away from the city and in 1888 he attempted to create an artists' colony in Arles, where he was joined by Gauguin. Through this encounter Van Gogh found reinforcement for his conviction that by emphasis, simplification and torsion it was possible to achieve a more distinctive and relevant emotional expression than that of the Impressionists: "Instead of accurately reproducing what I can see with my own eyes, I use colours more arbitrarily in an attempt to express my self more powerfully". Van Gogh's capacity for bringing the sensation of nature together with intense intellectual and emotional activity in painting places him in the forefront of the precursors of Expressionism.

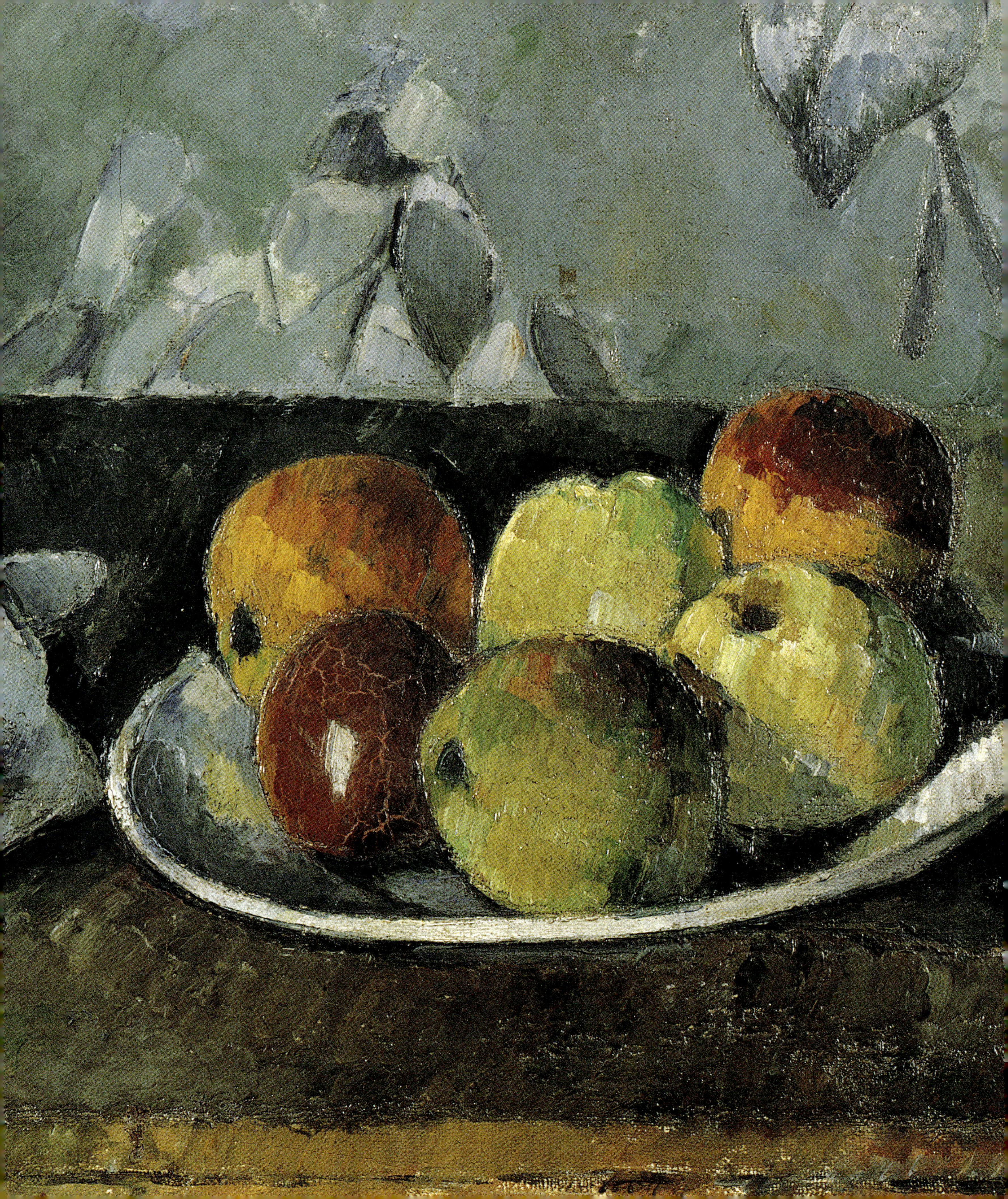

List of Works

81
Paul Cézanne
Still Life with Apples in a Bowl, ca.1879–82, detail
(full fig. 79)

1
Eugène-Louis Aizelin
Mignon, 1881
Marble, h. 137 cm
Copenhagen, Ny Carlsberg Glyptotek
(fig. 8)

2
Louis-Ernest Barrias
Nature Revealing Herself to Science (1893)
Carved in marble (1895–97), h. 253 cm
Valby, Carlsberg Museum
(fig. 41)

3
Jules Bastien-Lepage
The Beggar, 1880
Oil on canvas, 193.5 × 180.5 cm
Copenhagen, Ny Carlsberg Glyptotek
(fig. 21)

4
Camille Bellanger
Abel, 1874–75
Oil on canvas, 110 × 216 cm
Paris, Musée d'Orsay
(fig. 33)

5
Emile Bernard
Nymphs, After Bathing, 1908
Oil on canvas, 121 × 151 cm
Paris, Musée d'Orsay
(fig. 70)

6
Léon Bonnat
Self-portrait, 1855
Oil on canvas, 46 × 37.5 cm
Paris, Musée d'Orsay
(fig. 16)

7
Adolphe-William Bouguereau
Girl with Grapes, 1874
Oil on canvas, 140 × 62 cm
Copenhagen, Ny Carlsberg Glyptotek
(fig. 9)

8
Emile-Auguste Carolus-Duran
Portrait of a Little Girl in Spanish Costume, 1870
Oil on canvas, 41 × 39 cm
Copenhagen, Ny Carlsberg Glyptotek
(fig. 18)

9
Emile-Auguste Carolus-Duran
Edouard Manet, 1880
Oil on canvas, 65 × 54 cm
Paris, Musée d'Orsay
(fig. 17)

10
Jean-Baptiste Carpeaux
Negress (1868)
Carved in marble (1869), h. 67 cm
Copenhagen, Ny Carlsberg Glyptotek
(fig. 42)

11
Eugène Carrière
Woman with Bare Breasts. Nature, undated
Oil on canvas, 61 × 49 cm
Paris, Musée d'Orsay
(fig. 57)

12
Eugène Carrière
Place Clichy, Night (1899-1900)
Oil on canvas, 33 × 41 cm
Paris, Musée d'Orsay
(fig. 73)

13
Paul Cézanne
The Temptation of St. Anthony, ca. 1875
Oil on canvas, 47 × 56 cm
Paris, Musée d'Orsay
(fig. 56)

14
Paul Cézanne
Still Life with Apples in a Bowl, ca. 1879–82
Oil on canvas, 43 × 54 cm
Copenhagen, Ny Carlsberg Glyptotek
(fig. 79)

15
Paul Cézanne
The Bathers, ca. 1888–90
Oil on canvas, 73 × 92 cm
Copenhagen, Ny Carlsberg Glyptotek
(fig. 75)

16
Charles Chaplin
The Broken Lyre (1875)
Oil on canvas, 41 × 26.5 cm
Copenhagen, Ny Carlsberg Glyptotek
(fig. 62)

17
Charles Cordier
Jewess from Algiers, ca. 1862
Onyx, partially gilt, bronze, silvered bronze, enamel, semi-precious stones, h. 92.8 cm
Amsterdam, Van Gogh Museum
(fig. 10)

18
Gustave Courbet
Self-portrait, ca. 1850–53
Oil on canvas, 71.5 × 59 cm
Copenhagen, Ny Carlsberg Glyptotek
(fig. 15)

19
Gustave Courbet
The Wounded Man, 1854–55
Oil on canvas, 81.5 × 97.5 cm
Paris, Musée d'Orsay
(fig. 14)

20
Gustave Courbet
Three English Girls at a Window, 1865
Oil on canvas, 92.5 × 72.5 cm
Copenhagen, Ny Carlsberg Glyptotek
(fig. 13)

21
Thomas Couture
The Decadence of the Romans (sketch), 1847
Oil on canvas, 52 × 84 cm
Paris, Musée d'Orsay
(fig. 50)

22
Edgar Degas
Dancer with Ballet Skirt, Fourteen Years Old (1879–81)
Bronze, tulle and silk, h. 99 cm
Copenhagen, Ny Carlsberg Glyptotek
(fig. 36)

23
Eugène Delaplanche
Music, 1877
Carved in marble (1878), h. 172 cm
Copenhagen, Ny Carlsberg Glyptotek
(fig. 35)

24
Jules-Elie Delaunay
The Death of the Nymph Hesperia (1859)
Oil on canvas, 76.5 × 138 cm (unfinished)
Copenhagen, Ny Carlsberg Glyptotek
(fig. 60)

25
Jules-Elie Delaunay
The Plague in Rome, 1869
Oil on canvas, 131 × 176.5 cm
Paris, Musée d'Orsay
(fig. 5)

26
Paul Dubois
Narcissus Contemplating His Reflection in the Spring (1863)
Carved in marble (1899), h. 185 cm
Copenhagen, Ny Carlsberg Glyptotek
(fig. 31)

27
Paul Dubois
Florentine Singer from the Fifteenth Century, 1865
Cast in bronze (1897), h. 155 cm
Copenhagen, Ny Carlsberg Glyptotek
(fig. 32)

28
Raymond Duchamp-Villon
Charles Baudelaire, 1911
Terracotta, h. 42.5 cm
Copenhagen, Ny Carlsberg Glyptotek
(fig. 76)

29
Henri Fantin-Latour
Night (1897)
Oil on canvas, 61 × 75 cm
Paris, Musée d'Orsay
(fig. 77)

30
Paul Gauguin
Woman Sewing, 1880
Oil on canvas, 114.5 × 79.5 cm
Copenhagen, Ny Carlsberg Glyptotek
(fig. 12)

31
Paul Gauguin
Chanteuse, 1880
Mahogany, plaster, paint and gilt, Ø 53 cm
Copenhagen, Ny Carlsberg Glyptotek
(fig. 11)

32
Jean-Léon Gérôme
The Cock-Fight, 1846
Oil on canvas, 143 × 204 cm
Paris, Musée d'Orsay
(fig. 46)

33
Jean-Léon Gérôme
The Gladiators (1878)
Bronze, h. 50 cm
Copenhagen, Ny Carlsberg Glyptotek
(fig. 7)

34
Henri Gervex
Madame Valtesse de la Bigne, 1889
Oil on canvas, 200 × 122 cm
Paris, Musée d'Orsay
(fig. 23)

35
Constantin Guys
A Courtesan, 1850s
Watercolour, Indian ink and white body colour on paper, 17 × 15 cm
Copenhagen, Ny Carlsberg Glyptotek
(fig. 47)

36 and 37
Jean-Jacques Henner
Nymph Resting, undated
Oil on canvas, 26 × 40 cm each
Copenhagen, Ny Carlsberg Glyptotek
(fig. 63 [cat. no. 36])

38
Aristide Maillol
Desire, 1904
Terracotta, 115 × 106 cm
Copenhagen, Ny Carlsberg Glyptotek
(fig. 28)

39
Aristide Maillol
The Young Cyclist, 1907
Bronze, h. 98 cm
Copenhagen, Ny Carlsberg Glyptotek
(fig. 64)

40
Edouard Manet
The Absinthe Drinker, 1859
Oil on canvas, 180.5 × 105.6 cm
Copenhagen, Ny Carlsberg Glyptotek
(fig. 49)

41
Edouard Manet
A Lady at Her Window
or *Angélina*, 1865
Oil on canvas, 92 × 73 cm
Paris, Musée d'Orsay
(fig. 78)

42
Edouard Manet
The Execution of Emperor Maximilian (sketch), 1867
Oil on canvas, 48 × 58 cm
Copenhagen, Ny Carlsberg Glyptotek
(fig. 51)

43
Laurent-Honoré Marqueste
Galathea, 1884
Carved in marble (1904), h. 180 cm
Valby, Carlsberg Museum
(fig. 37)

44
Henri Matisse
Decorative Figure (1908)
Bronze, h. 73 cm
Copenhagen, Ny Carlsberg Glyptotek
(fig. 44)

45
Antonin Mercié
Gloria Victis, 1874
Cast in bronze (1905), h. 309 cm
Copenhagen, Ny Carlsberg Glyptotek
(fig. 30)

46
Antonin Mercié
L'Opéra Comique (1897)
Carved in marble (1900), h. 184 cm
Copenhagen, Ny Carlsberg Glyptotek
(fig. 59)

47
Claude Monet
Windmill and Boats near Zaandam, Holland (1871)
Oil on canvas, 48 × 73.5 cm
Copenhagen, Ny Carlsberg Glyptotek
(fig. 24)

48
Claude Monet
"Les Pyramides" at Port-Coton, Belle-Île-en-Mer, 1886
Oil on canvas, 59.5 × 73 cm
Copenhagen, Ny Carlsberg Glyptotek
(fig. 52)

49
Pierre-Auguste Renoir
La Grenouillère, 1868
Oil on canvas, 66 × 81 cm
Stockholm, Nationalmuseum
(fig. 53)

50
Pierre-Auguste Renoir
Boy with a Cat, 1868–69
Oil on canvas, 124 × 67 cm
Paris, Musée d'Orsay
(fig. 54)

51
Auguste Rodin
The Age of Bronze (1875–76)
Cast in bronze (1901), h. 180.5 cm
Copenhagen, Ny Carlsberg Glyptotek
(fig. 34)

52
Auguste Rodin
The Shade (1880)
Cast in bronze (1902), h. 192 cm
Copenhagen, Ny Carlsberg Glyptotek
(fig. 40)

53
Auguste Rodin
Pygmalion and Galathea (1889)
Carved in marble (1907–10), h. 76.9 cm
Copenhagen, Ny Carlsberg Glyptotek
(fig. 38)

54
Auguste Rodin
Balzac, 1891–92
Bronze, h. 106 cm
Zurich, Kunsthaus
(fig. 39)

55
Alfred Sisley
The Flood, 1872
Oil on canvas, 45 × 60 cm
Copenhagen, Ny Carlsberg Glyptotek
(fig. 6)

56
Alfred Stevens
The Hunters of Vincennes
or *What People call Vagrancy*, ca. 1855
Oil on canvas, 130 × 165 cm
Paris, Musée d'Orsay
(fig. 80)

57
Alfred Stevens
The Joys of Family Life, ca. 1900
Oil on canvas, 65.5 × 51.5 cm
Paris, Musée d'Orsay
(fig. 22)

58
Alfred Stevens
The Blue Dress, undated
Oil on panel, 31.9 × 26 cm
Massachusetts, Sterling and Francine Clark Art Institute
(fig. 25)

59
Jacques-Joseph Tissot
The Meeting of Faust and Marguerite, 1860
Oil on canvas, 78 × 117 cm
Paris, Musée d'Orsay
(fig. 19)

60
Jacques-Joseph Tissot
Chrysanthemums, ca. 1874–75
Oil on canvas, 118.4 × 76.4 cm
Massachusetts, Sterling and Francine Clark Art Institute
(fig. 20)

Index

Page numbers in italics make reference to illustrations and captions